D1498662

A Matter of Panache

A career in public education.
A traumatic brain injury.
A memoir of surviving both.

Debra Sanders

Outskirts Press, Inc.
Denver, Colorado

The opinions expressed in this manuscript are solely the opinions of the author and do not represent the opinions or thoughts of the publisher. The author has represented and warranted full ownership and/or legal right to publish all the materials in this book.

The names and identifying information of all schoolchildren have been changed in order to protect their identities. All other names are real, unless otherwise noted. The events, conversations, and reflections revealed in this book were reconstructed through the use of letters, emails, notes, and journal entries that document the events that are portrayed. The author acknowledges that people cited in this book may have differing recollections and interpretations of the events portrayed in this book.

A Matter of Panache:
A career in public education. A traumatic brain injury. A memoir of surviving both.
All Rights Reserved.
Copyright © 2008 Debra Sanders
V4.0

Front Cover design by John Drew (www.johndrew.com) and Nate Myers
Back Cover Design by Nate Myers

"Ms. Debra" by Sara, age 8

This book may not be reproduced, transmitted, or stored in whole or in part by any means, including graphic, electronic, or mechanical without the express written consent of the publisher except in the case of brief quotations embodied in critical articles and reviews.

Outskirts Press, Inc.
http://www.outskirtspress.com

ISBN: 978-978-1-4327-2816-8

Library of Congress Control Number: 2008932259

Outskirts Press and the "OP" logo are trademarks belonging to Outskirts Press, Inc.

PRINTED IN THE UNITED STATES OF AMERICA

This book is dedicated:

To children with special needs and their parents, with the hope that you will trust your voices and keep trusting them, until they are heard above the din.

To our returning soldiers and their families and to every person and family touched by a traumatic brain injury. Never underestimate the range of its impact, and remember: one day at a time. It really does keep getting better.

To *Mary Rubadeau, Carl Knudsen, Jim Foster, and Donna Peterson*—four educational administrators who continue to model the passion, ethics, creativity, and stamina that set the bar for all that I value and respect in public education.

To *Jeanne Sorenson, Paul Sorenson, Monique McDermott, Val Roberts, Mo Sanders,* and *Barbara Silversmith*—each of whom stands out far above the crowd by exemplifying what school leadership, vision, and ethical practices in public education are all about.

To *Tom Prentice*, *ToniJo Dahlman,* and *Dave Thomas*—who put me on the right road and taught me how to stay there.

And, last but certainly not least, this is dedicated to *Katie, Kyle,* and *Ryan*, in memory of your mother and my friend, and to their dad, *Buck* (Earl), who was the most devoted, loving, and nurturing husband a person could ever hope their sister-of-the-heart to find.

Author's Note:

Panache is not something a person needs in order to be successful in life.
Unless, of course, it is something one has had all their life and then loses.
In that case, having panache could be an important matter.

A very important matter, indeed.

Ahh..What playgrounds exist! Here I
am on top of an iceberg somewhere
in southeast Alaska, 1985

Table of Contents

Prologue

Pa·nache: noun
Definition: spirit, brio, charisma, dash, flair, flamboyance, flourish, style, swagger, verve, vigor, élan

Panache. Now that is a word my mother would have enjoyed people using to describe *her*. It conveys such vitality; such spunk and vigor. I first remember hearing this word when I was about four years old, which is when the movie *Auntie Mame* was released and my mother took to singing and dancing her way around the living room. My mother thought Auntie Mame had *panache,* and clearly my mother thought this was a good thing to have.

At four, I thought panache had something to do with singing and dancing well, and it was clear to me that my mother could do neither (truth is, my mother couldn't even carry a tune much less sing a song). I am pretty sure I conveyed my observations loud and clear, despite the fact that doing so might not have been in my own best interests. At that young age, I had not yet discovered that some insights are best kept to oneself; and of course, I had not yet divined that I had inherited my mother's lack of musical and rhythmic genius. Once I came to recognize my own flaws and failings, it didn't take long for me to understand that a person needs to be allowed to make up with enthusiasm what they lack in talent and grace. This, I think, was one of my life's first great lessons.

After my childhood introduction, I doubt I thought about the word panache again until quite recently. It's not a word commonly used today. It certainly isn't a quality I recall ever thinking about *needing*. I had grown up aware that I was an enthusiastic, intense person and that my intensity could be pretty contagious when channeled in positive directions, but the notion of having or not having panache had never entered into my consciousness.

By the time I was an adult I had funneled all my passions and enthusiasms into working with children in public education. I felt fortunate to find myself continuously surrounded by people who not only embraced my intensity, but were able to help me manage it. By the time I had spent eighteen years in Alaska, working in some of the most challenging educational environments imaginable, I had become quite adept at handling my own passions and enthusiasm. I knew which impressions to keep to myself and which to share, and I knew how to communicate my insights in a way that embraced people rather than offended them. I enjoyed working with even the most resistant of educators. I had, over the years, learned how to infuse both administrators and teachers with a kind of confidence, knowledge and excitement such that they were far more likely to step out of their comfort zones and consider alternative ways of disciplining, teaching, and supporting students.

This all changed on April 7, 2003—the day I rolled my truck driving to work and found myself diagnosed with a head injury. At the time, I was aware that something was not right in my head, but I was not aware of the multitude of ways that "not being right in my head" had impacted me (and all those around me). I had walked away from the accident with my passions intact, but suddenly instead of inspiring and leading others, I found myself alienating them. Instead of galvanizing others, my intensity and advocacy for children and for educational change began to polarize them.

I felt like Alice after she fell down the rabbit hole. It seemed as if one minute I was driving to work on a familiar road and the next I was hurtling through a foreign landscape on a road that kept taking me deeper and deeper into a disordered, bewildering, and very frightening world. If the journey of a thousand miles begins with a single step, I'd say mine started not just with a step, but with a plummeting nose-dive down a hole where nothing was as it seemed; and where the most familiar and routine of people, places, and events took on qualities that rendered everything and everyone—myself included—entirely unpredictable.

Especially myself.

At one point Alice said, *"...When I get home, I shall write a book about this place...if I ever do get home."* I could relate to Alice's fear about not finding her way back home, because it was a very long time before I found myself back on any sort of familiar road. I have to say that I never did quite make it home again; although, I think I can say that I have found my way to a place where I have learned to *feel* at home. Interestingly, unlike Alice, it never occurred to me that I might write a book about the journey.

Apparently it was never my destiny to be an Auntie Mame. It seems instead it was to journey into a world of mad hatters and queens, where time stood still and ran backward; and where I had to keep changing into a different person in order to feel oriented in the world again. Once there, it seemed time to share the story of the children who inspired my passions, as well as that of the head injury that rendered passion without panache my own personal recipe for disaster.

Having never written a book before, I must say that I found the task a bit daunting. It helped to keep in mind the King's advice to Alice: *"Begin at the beginning and go on until you come to the end...then stop."*

Given that advice, it seemed the best place to begin would be the remote corners of Alaska, for that is where I began my life as a "village-hopping, tundra-trekking school psychologist." Only by being exposed to the children, administrators, philosophy, and experiences that nurtured and honed my intensity and passion for approaching old problems in new ways, can a person truly appreciate the significance of what occurred twenty-two years after I first began my adventure in education.

So, now as they say, *north to Alaska.*

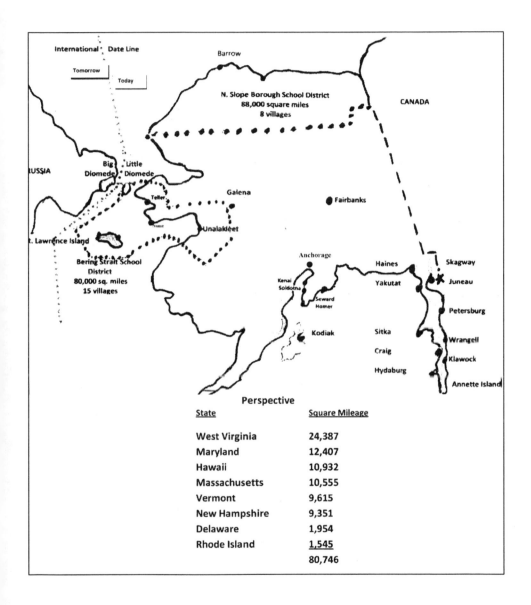

International Date Line

Tomorrow

Today

Barrow

N. Slope Borough School District
88,000 square miles
8 villages

CANADA

RUSSIA

Big Little
Diomede Diomede

Teller

Nome

Galena

Fairbanks

Unalakleet

t. Lawrence Island

Bering Strait School
District
80,000 sq. miles
15 villages

Anchorage

Kenai
Soldotna

Seward
Homer

Kodiak

Haines

Yakutat

Sitka

Craig

Hydaburg

Skagway

Juneau

Petersburg

Wrangell

Klawock

Annette Island

Perspective

State	Square Mileage
West Virginia	24,387
Maryland	12,407
Hawaii	10,932
Massachusetts	10,555
Vermont	9,615
New Hampshire	9,351
Delaware	1,954
Rhode Island	<u>1,545</u>
	80,746

PART I:

In the Beginning
Outside the Box

*The adventures first...explanations
take such a dreadfully long time.*

The Gryphon to Alice

All in a Day's Work
April 1986, Brevig, Alaska

Open up. Come on...come ON! I silently cursed at the window while madly attempting to free it of a six-month buildup of snow and ice. The sounds of slurred speech and boozy laughter combined with the *thwack* of a splintering door jamb to give me a pretty good indication that an attempt was being made to break into the principal's office on the other side of the wall from where I was standing.

Standing, I might add, at 3:00 in the morning dressed in nothing but a white silk nightshirt and unlaced hiking boots.

It was April 1986, and I was in a school in Brevig Mission, Alaska—a small village of about two hundred people tucked away in a region known as the Norton Sound. Like many of the remote villages in this northwestern part of the state, the predominant residents were Inupiat and Yupik Eskimos. Brevig was a quiet village where many of the people maintained the subsistence lifestyle that allowed them to sustain themselves on the moose, fish, reindeer, and whale that they hunted. They lived in simple plank homes that had been built largely with money received from the U.S. government, and generally speaking, there was little need for an exchange of cash dollars to take place between the villagers. There were no banks in Brevig Mission, Alaska just as there were no stoplights, intersections, department stores, movie theatres, shopping malls, Dairy Queens, bars, or liquor stores.

Brevig—like many villages in Alaska—was "dry." This meant that according to the law, it was illegal to consume, buy, or bring alcohol into the village. This didn't mean, however, that no one in the village ever drank. It was not an unknown phenomenon to find that a middle-of-the-night plane with a cargo full of bootleg whiskey had landed and delivered copious amounts of alcohol for the residents to share. I had discovered a few months earlier that the quiet and friendly people I encountered on a daily basis seemed to make a Jekyll and Hyde-like transformation once a liter of Jack Daniels or a few six-packs of beer hit the bloodstream, and the transformation was one that suggested I might not be as welcome when alcohol was involved. Many of the Eskimo people, from whom I was learning so much, did not seem to like white people when they were drinking. At least that was my impression. And I am most definitely a white person.

As the only educational psychologist for the fifteen schools that made up the Bering Strait School District (BSSD), it was standard practice for me to spend my nights away from home as I traveled between villages. Most of the time, I slept in the schools since they were usually the newest and most modern building around. This was certainly true in Brevig, where the school was the only building in the village with running water. In spite of the fact that the showers turned my hair various unflattering shades of orange, I, like everyone else, really appreciated this modern convenience, and I didn't mind at all that I was relegated to sleeping on school floors in exchange for an orange tinged shower.

There are only 1,800 students in the BSSD; however, they are spread out over *80,000* square miles—an area roughly the size of New England, West Virginia and Hawaii, combined. Each week, backpack and sleeping bag in tow, I would travel from my home village of Unalakleet (yoon-a-la-kleet) to a school in some other part of this vast geographic region. My days were spent with the children and teachers; my nights were spent on the floors; and despite the sixty- and seventy-hour workweeks, I loved the adventure I was living as a village-hopping, tundra-trekking school psychologist.

I had spent a lot of nights alone in the various schools over the course of this school year, but never before had I experienced any feelings of fear. Admittedly, my self-protective instincts had become aroused upon occasion—like when I found myself alone in a house with a highly intoxicated woman who was waving a loaded shotgun and ranting about something I never did quite figure out. I'd never seen someone so drunk they actually foamed at the mouth; and when she smashed the gun into the window and started waving around both the bullet-loaded shotgun and a large, jagged piece of glass, admittedly I began to feel a bit...twitchy. But I hadn't been afraid. For one thing it had been broad daylight, and I had been dressed. It's remarkable how much more frightening things seem when one is in a dark room in the middle of the night scantily attired.

In Brevig, I always chose to sleep in the school's library. Partially this was because it was the only carpeted room in the school, but mostly it was because I am partial to books. I continually held out the hope that if I spent enough nights on library floors, by osmosis I might be able to fill my brain with every classic and current book I no longer had time to read. Glamorous as my job was (and it did, after all, allow me to dress in outfits that ensured it never mattered if I gained ten or, for that matter, a hundred pounds), it just didn't leave me with a lot of free time.

There was a sudden moment of quiet on the other side of the wall. Holding my breath and trying to assess if the intruders were leaving or making their way into this room, it did cross my mind to wonder what exactly I would do were I to be discovered in my little silk nightshirt. The oddest things go through a person's mind when they are jolted into a middle-of-the-night panic, and there I was with little beads of sweat running down the back of my neck and thoughts of the irony that this was the first night in eight months I had not gone to sleep in ratty old sweats.

And I'd been having such a good time.

This was my last night "on the road" before I would be picked up by my favorite bush pilot and flown back to my apartment in Unalakleet. All week I had been sleeping and working in the school in the nearby village of Teller when a call came in asking if I could make it over to Brevig for a day or two. Transportation into, out of, and between villages in wintertime is via snow machine, plane, or dog team—and despite people's conception of Alaska's wealth, there sure wasn't a private plane on standby in the school's backyard waiting to accommodate my every need. Generally someone would have transported me the ten miles between Teller and Brevig on the back of their snow machine (which is exciting in its own right), but the custodian and I had become buddies over the week, and he offered to shuttle me in a sled pulled by several of his hardworking huskies.

There are some advantages to being in the school at all hours of the day and night, and one of them is getting to know the other people who hang out there when everyone else is gone.

"I'm going to go to work by dog team!"

How cool is that?!

The immediate sound of splintering wood did a good job of reminding me that despite surprise dog sled rides, there might be one or two *slight* downsides to my current job—the most immediate being that I needed to get far away from those on the other side of the wall. This meant working my way into a room adjoining the library, which was not as simple as it might sound since that room's door sported a large pane of glass directly facing the individuals seemingly intent on making a piñata out of the principal's doorway. Unfortunately it was my only option out of the library. Knowing there were casement windows with small hand cranks on the other windows, I was optimistic that, unlike the frozen double hung windows in here, those would open. Being spotted was a risk I was willing to take because, clothes or no clothes, if those cranks turned; for sure I was going to engage in my first experience in arctic window jumping.

I was well aware as I inched my way in the dark that grace and stealth were two words that had never been uttered within proximity of my name. Echoes of my parents, teasing that I was the only person they knew who could stand in the middle of an empty room and trip, were not doing a lot to boost my confidence; so when I did make it into the other room without alerting anyone to my presence, my first instinct was to form a triumphant fist and shout *"Oh yeah*!" I figured maybe I better try the window before celebrating my newfound grace, however, which was a good thing because the first window crank I tried was frozen just as solidly shut as the windows in the library. I could hear the ongoing commotion—now less than fifty feet from where I was standing—and as my breathing accelerated, it began to resonate like a tsunami rushing through my ears. I'm pretty sure it was about then that my anxiety level started to catapult off the charts.

The second window crank I tried felt like it might give and I began to rotate it with a sort of manic determination. Actually, manic determination might be a slight understatement because just as the window opened, the little handle flew off its socket and, sounding like thunder in a tunnel, bounced its way off the ledge and began rolling across the linoleum. In two seconds flat—and with all the finesse of a penguin on dry land—I was out that window. I landed (indelicately, chest first and with a resounding thud) in a deep snowbank. Scrambling as fast as I had landed, I took off running toward a row of trailers that housed the teachers. I imagine, with my hair flying and my unlaced boots flapping, I looked like a crazed apparition in the night.

Make that boot. My *one* unlaced boot was flapping. Apparently I had left one behind in the snowdrift.

It's amazing the distance that can be covered in icy temperatures when adrenaline is blue-streaking through a body, and the one thing I knew for sure at that moment was that I wasn't about to turn around and go back for a boot. I wasn't even about to turn around and see if I was being chased.

"Cindy! Harry! Open up! Open up!" I was simultaneously shouting and banging on the door with equal frenzy when suddenly Harry and his wife Cindy were both standing there staring at me as if I were a half-naked lunatic from some other planet.

"What the...?" Harry started.

"There's guys, drunk guys, breaking into the school," I said as Cindy pulled me inside and went to get a blanket. "Scared the frickin' *pee* out of me," I added, taking a deep breath.

"How'd you get out of the building?" Cindy asked. She had this look on her face that seemed to be a cross between extreme amusement and serious concern.

"Jumped! Jumped out the window. In fact, out **your** window—the window in your classroom."

"Nice going, Sherlock," Harry said, punctuating his words with short applause. "Maybe next time you should try wearing some arctic gear before jumping out windows in sub-zero temperatures." Looking down toward my feet he tacked on, "Shoes might help, too."

"Very funny, Harry." My heart was still beating about ninety miles an hour. "All my clothes were in my backpack in the bathroom—which I couldn't get to from the library." I was suddenly aware of just how cold I was. "I think I lost my boot in the snowbank."

"Oh, don't get me wrong. It's just that it's not often we get to see our psychologist looking so...casual," he said with a laugh.

Smacking Harry and telling me to ignore him, Cindy headed off to the kitchen to make hot chocolate while I filled Harry in on the rest of the details.

After listening, and in a tone considerably less jovial, he said, "Okay, I'll call Dave and we'll head over there. All the money from tonight's basketball game is sitting on the desk in the office. I locked it up in there before coming home." As an afterthought he added, "Just figures this would happen the one week I have to stand in as an acting principal."

Harry is a big man. Really big. He must be six foot four at least, and Dave—while not quite as tall and broad as Harry—is no horse jockey. Harry, grabbing his shotgun and telling Dave to grab his, suggested that I wait with Cindy in the trailer. I may not always be the sharpest knife in the drawer, but when I have the option of drinking hot chocolate and thawing out versus going back into a school to square off with highly intoxicated, crowbar-wielding prowlers, I don't have to be directed to the kitchen.

It wasn't until after Harry left that I began to wonder what he and Dave would do once they got inside the school. Although at times there might be someone appointed as an officer in the village, it's inconsistent and they are usually related to at least half the population—which makes upholding law and order a bit of a problem. The nearest state troopers are a hundred airplane miles away in Nome, and while the school came equipped with a shower, to my knowledge it did not come with a twenty-four-hour holding tank.

As Harry explained it later, he and Dave met at the front door and, shotguns in hand, entered the building. They no sooner got inside than an unknown number of darkly clothed individuals hightailed it out the back door. Knowing Harry and Dave, they probably would have held chase had they not immediately seen a cardboard box filled with what apparently was intended to be the big haul. Looking through it, Harry noticed a pack of frozen hamburgers taken from the school's kitchen, along with some ivory pieces and the school's Polaroid camera. Suddenly he started laughing, and said, "Dave! Come here. Take a look at this."

Dave reached for the stack of Polaroid photos in Harry's outstretched hand. Among them were pictures of three young Eskimo men capturing one another on film as they foraged in the kitchen, looked through drawers in classrooms, and put a crowbar into the frame of the office door.

"Perfect. Just perfect! I'll call the troopers, and *they* can go round them up." In his best Paul Harvey imitation, Dave laughed, adding, "And now...for the *rest* of the story!"

Harry called and told us to come on over to the school, and the four of us spent the next couple of hours creating our own ruckus as we cracked jokes and relived the entire experience while waiting for the troopers to fly in. By seven in the morning—just as we were getting ready to open the school doors for the day—the troopers had arrived. They quickly went about tracking down the individuals who had so generously given their identities away in photographs; and in a way that surely only happens to petty criminals in Alaska, the intrepid intruders were handcuffed and treated to a private flight to Nome.

I knew that by the time Tweeto—my favorite bush pilot—picked me up for my own private plane ride, I'd be able to entertain him with stories the whole way back to Unalakleet. What a week! I had completed twelve evaluations (a record I would thankfully never break over the next twenty years); I'd commuted between schools with the help of a semi-toothless custodian and his beautiful dogs; I'd experienced a middle-of-the-night adventure in terror inspired by criminals who joyfully recorded themselves in action; and I was about to hitch a ride home in a two-seater airplane that was piloted by a cute guy who just happened to have all of his own teeth.

I had a great job!

There is a hotline that runs between the villages that rest along the Bering Sea, and it was quickly communicated that a crazy "Gussak"—*white woman*— had jumped out the window barefoot and captured drunken men who were breaking into the school. For a short period of time, at least in that small part of the world, I had my fifteen minutes of fame. As I traveled from village to village over the next two months, people would say in their heavily accented English, "Hey! You! You that *Gussak* that jump barefoot in the snow and got those guys caught! Tell us. Tell us the story!"

In the world of Yupik Eskimos, to tell the story is to create history and entertainment both, and everyone wanted the story. I was branded a hero, and my name was even in the *Nome Nugget*, Alaska's oldest newspaper.

Me? I always thought Harry and Dave were the heroes. I still do.

This event occurred during the 1985-86 school year, and it set the tone for my next seventeen years of work and adventure in a place where you are hired—and rewarded—for your ability to be creative, flexible, and to think outside the proverbial box.

Way outside.

Glamour Girl
year
after year.
Season
after
season
I am under
there
(somewhere)

Go North Young Woman

It is always a curiosity to people how those of us not born in Alaska wind up living there. For many, it's the culmination of a lifetime dream of living on the Last Frontier that pushes them north. Others seem to venture there with the idea of making big money fishing off the crab and salmon boats in the summer and then find that they are in no hurry to leave. Others are simply curious adventurers who make their way to Alaska and discover that, for a while anyway, their traveling feet are stilled.

I, however, wound up there on a lark.

Well, not a lark exactly, but certainly not through any long thought-out plan resulting from years of wishing, dreaming, and strategizing. Quite frankly, the thought of moving to Alaska had never even occurred to me. As it happened, I was on my way to the jungles of Mexico when, just before I hit the California-Mexico border, the chairperson of my graduate program managed to get a message to me:

Before you reach the border, call me. There is a PAID internship available in the fall in Juneau, Alaska. Lots of limited English speakers there, too…you interested?

At the time I had just completed the coursework to obtain my graduate degree as an educational psychologist specializing with bilingual/bicultural children. I had already conducted much of my research in Mexico during the previous two years, and I had taken courses at Autónoma University in Guadalajara the previous summer while living with a local family. My plan had been to spend one more summer in remote villages in Mexico gathering final data, and then move from my home in Idaho to San Francisco, where I had been accepted into an internship program. While the internship was a position that offered a bit of prestige, it did not offer a paycheck. The year was 1984 and paid internships were practically nonexistent. This was my second round of graduate school—having completed my master's degree seven years earlier—and to be stopped at the border with a dangling carrot in the form of green cash was indeed tempting. At twenty-nine I was getting tired of making educational loan payments.

But…*Alaska?*

Although I was looking forward to my upcoming internship, I had absolutely no desire to live in a big city; and so, sitting in the library in a California border town, I started reading about Alaska. I was astonished to find myself reading about a place right here in America where there are villages without roads, and where houses are built on pilings above the permafrost. A place where people eat whale blubber (*surely* that couldn't be true!), and moose wander onto golf courses and into people's backyards. I read that Alaska is a place where it's nighttime twenty-four hours a day and daytime for twenty-four hours through the night; and where both salmon and cabbages can and do weigh more than sixty pounds. True, I also read about mosquitoes as big as hedgehogs, and bears over nine feet tall, but truth be told, I was probably less intimidated by that information than I was by the thought of living in the midst of clogged highways and concrete backyards.

Never mind that I had just invested a few years and more than a few dollars trying to become fluent in a language I probably would have no need for in Alaska. Never mind that the vision of my future involved immersing myself in a culture that I had been studying since I was fourteen years old—which is when I was afforded the unique opportunity to spend six weeks in rural parts of the Mexican countryside teaching English to little girls. Within just a few hours of reading about the remote villages of Alaska, I found myself easily seduced from the plans I had been so confident in making, and I placed an excited call to the chair of my department. After gathering all the necessary information from him, I managed to secure a phone interview with the people from the Juneau School District; and the rest, as they say, is history. I was offered the internship position, and with barely a second thought at the turn my life was taking, I resumed my trek into Mexico to finish my summer's work. Then, swapping sandals for boots and pesos for dollars, I pointed my car due north and headed toward the Land of the Midnight Sun.

Although I only intended to stay for nine months, I remained for nearly twenty years.

* * * * *

Alaska has a way of burrowing into a person's soul and tethering them there forever. Certainly it does not do this to everyone, but for me, the magic began the moment I stepped off the ferry and onto Juneau's shores. There was a nearly detectable shift somewhere inside of me as I looked up at resplendent, towering mountains framing the town, and as I listened to the comical, rhythmic barking of the harbor seals against the noise of everyday, downtown traffic. It was early August and the sky was profoundly blue. The hillsides and mountains were rich with multiple shades of green and splashes of the yellows, reds, and whites suggestive of wildflowers still in abundance. The ocean water, calm in the Juneau Harbor, sparkled and glimmered under a surprisingly hot and bright sun. It left me not just breathless, but in some way profoundly altered.

Soon after arriving, and long before I caught my breath, I learned that over the course of the school year, I would be working in six different schools. Over the next nine months I would discover that within each building I would be serenaded by some combination or variation of the sights and sounds of my first Alaskan day. And right alongside the geographic Alaskan wonders, I would learn of the sights, sounds, and movement that choreograph life behind the eyes of every child.

Never once would I not thrill to the experience of it all.

During that internship year in Juneau's public schools, I would learn about so many things I had not even known were a part of the world I lived in. I would be introduced to the ever-changing, always fascinating world of tidal pools; to the joy of picking and eating fiddlehead ferns; to the rank stench of skunk cabbage and the spongy fragility of muskeg meadows. It was during this year that I first saw, touched, and walked on a glacier; and when I first marveled in the revelation that places exist *right here in America* where only thirteen miles separate a downtown area of less than one square mile from a massive ice field nearly three times that size. A place where one hundred and thirty miles of hiking trails surround a city whose main road system stretches only forty-five miles, end to end.

It has been one of the great fortunes of my life that I ended up as an intern, not in San Francisco, but in a school district that offered me this spectacular introduction to a world where such geographic juxtapositions exist. A district that, in addition to providing me with this incredible exposure to nature, provided me with mentors who would introduce, instruct, and model the absolute sanctity of maintaining both professional ethics and a commitment to doing the research and legwork necessary to provide exemplary services to children and their teachers. My supervisors held me to a standard of excellence that was at times daunting; and yet it was in being held to this standard that I learned how to effectively write (and rewrite) the reports that are a critical component of every school psychologist's job. By being held to such a rigid standard of excellence, I learned how to persevere in finding answers to seemingly unanswerable questions when it came to understanding how, why, and what children need in order to be successful. And by having the role of a school psychologist effectively modeled for me, I learned how to put theory into practice. By never accepting placid rhetoric and by demanding that no recommendation be written into a report or spoken in a meeting if it is not practical, doable, and understandable, my supervisors ensured that during my internship year (similar to a teacher's student teaching year) I learned to be as effective as I was efficient. As analytic as I was empathetic.

And not to be ignored among my many learning experiences is the fact that I learned how to carry on in a place where it can rain as many as two hundred and sixty days a year. Among everything else, I most definitely got a taste of living life in a rainforest that year. By the end of my internship I sincerely contemplated telling my supervisors that having webbed feet should be a prerequisite to the next intern hired for the job. Little had I known on that first day when I arrived to all that glorious sunshine that I would experience thirty, forty, even fifty days running when the sun never shone and the rain never ceased. It's probably a good thing that the job description did not include the information that people from Juneau move to Seattle to experience better weather.

Eight months into my internship, an opportunity unfolded that offered me a glimpse of life in some of the most remote villages in the state. It came to me by way of a remarkable woman named Mary Rubadeau, and, by the time it was over, I knew that it would take something of immense dimension to ever edge me out of Alaska. If my initial step onto Juneau's shores initiated the tethering process that would keep me within the state, by the end of my first trip with Mary Rubadeau, the process had begun that would keep the state within me— whether I resided there or not.

Mary, as the director of special education for the Bering Strait School District (BSSD), had been in desperate need of someone to immediately travel to eight of the district's fifteen remote village schools. For some reason, the regular psychologists who served the district were not available, and Mary needed someone with an abundance of energy, a sense of adventure, and sufficient skills to administer necessary tests to students in special education (students who were predominantly Eskimo and not always English proficient). Mary called the Juneau School District looking for someone able to fly in very small planes and willing to engage in what she referred to as a *blitz* trip, meaning a harried, rushed adventure that would probably require working a minimum of fifteen-hour days and sleeping on school floors. Was there anyone available who could possibly come to the BSSD for eight days? I'm quite sure that my supervisors never discussed the option among themselves; rather they scattered in search of the frizzy-haired intern who they all knew was ripe for the opportunity.

Sleep on floors? Fly in bush planes? Meet Eskimo families? In truth, I probably would have paid the Bering Strait School District, the Juneau School District, and all my graduate advisors for the experience, had it been required. I was hooked two seconds after finding out that one of the BSSD villages was actually located so far north and to the west that the International Date Line had been bent in order to assure that all of Alaska remained in the same day.

So far west the International Date Line had to be **bent?** *You have got to be kidding me.*

I jumped at the chance to experience a blitz trip.

Well, I didn't actually jump, as I had a cast on my foot extending almost to my knee (compliments of a weekend racquetball tournament), but I *would* have jumped even if my whole body had been in a cast!

And so, this is how in the spring of 1985, I found myself flying from Juneau to Anchorage, changing planes, and then flying another four hundred miles into an Eskimo village that, by September of 1986, I would be calling home.

Landing in Unalakleet launched the beginning of the week I would come to think of as the most pivotal experience of my lifetime, and indeed, it was a blitz trip. A trip during which I probably tested more Native American children in a week than most school psychologists have the opportunity to evaluate in a decade and where I was introduced to a world where people wore kuspuks[1] over blue jeans and used jigging sticks[2] dipped in icy holes to catch smelt,

---

[1] kuspuk: Usually a calico sort of top or parka worn by women. It has a roomy hood, large front pocket, a ruffled bottom, and lots of trim.
[2] jigging stick: A wooden stick with a line and hook that is dropped into fishing holes and wiggled up and down.

tomcod, and trout that they would eat alongside loaves of Wonder bread and boxes of pilot bread. A blitz learning experience of working in a place where an ancestral language without tenses merged with modern English to manifest itself in children, who said things like, "I present you," to tell me that they were going to give me a present or, "I jokes," when they wanted me to know they were teasing about something. It was a week in which I noticed, but did not listen to, eyebrows nearly imperceptively raised in answer to my questions.

Listening to eyebrows speak took me nearly a year to figure out. A year of continuously repeating simple questions *(Did you have a good lunch?)* and of giving people of a different culture the extra time I thought perhaps they needed, or desired, before responding (as all my higher level textbooks and instructors had reminded me to do). After nearly a year of asking, waiting, and then asking the same question again in a different way *(Was your lunch good?)*, I finally figured out that when you ask an Eskimo child a question, a slight arc of the eyebrows, without any change whatsoever to facial expression, means "yes."

For quite some time the inhabitants of this world treated me very kindly, if a bit distantly. I am quite sure they assumed I was retarded and must be respected, though perhaps not embraced. Maybe this was a test of all Anglo outsiders...seeing how long it took them to figure out the eyebrow thing. In my case, it took a long time, and I can only give praise to the entire region of villagers who took it upon themselves to patiently educate this nascent woman from the Outside. Eventually I was embraced; although I am not sure I ever convinced anyone I was not retarded.

Despite my rather stiff-legged and clumsy entrances and exits from the small planes, and my presentation as a somewhat dimwitted but friendly *Gussak*, the trip was a resounding success by everyone's standards. A month later, upon completing my internship with the Juneau School District, I was offered a job in Juneau with an agency that provided itinerant services to small and remote districts throughout the state, and would therefore get to spend all my time going to such remote places.

As it turned out, one of the agency's contracts was with the BSSD, and when Mary heard I had been hired, she requested me as the psychologist assigned to her district. I couldn't have been more thrilled, and I spent my first year as a "real" school psychologist serving not only the fifteen schools of the Bering Strait School District, but fifteen other schools, each a part of school districts located somewhere between the most northern tip of the state and the most southern. Come Monday morning, I would hop on a plane (actually, I would hop on a series of planes) and spend a day or two in Barrow—the administrative center of the North Slope School District—before being flown around for a week to ten days, dividing my time between that district's seven other villages. Then, wrapping up my work (for that trip, anyway), I would hop on another series of planes in order to land in Unalakleet and do the same between some combination of their fifteen village schools. A weekend in Juneau (if I could squeeze it in) would separate visits to my northern schools from visits to my southern ones.

Although I wasn't speaking Spanish, my experience of having worked with bicultural and bilingual populations—along with the time I had spent in small and poverty-stricken villages in Mexico—was of great benefit as I listened, observed, and interacted with not just the Yupik and Inupiat Eskimos of the north, but also with the various Indian and Russian Orthodox populations found in southeastern and central Alaska. As I was addressing issues of abuse, neglect, alcoholism, limited English proficiency, and clashing cultures and values, each place presented me with enormous challenges and opportunities to grow, both professionally and personally. It seemed like there was an unlimited number of creative and excited teachers willing to try anything I might develop that would help children learn better and be more emotionally stable. It was the greatest first-year learning experience one could possibly have, as there simply were no boxes to contain me. There was no one saying, "We can't do that," or "That can't possibly be developed." Services were so limited and the needs were so great that as long as I was willing to put in the time, dig deep, research endlessly, and develop programs and plans in an attempt to improve things—there were always, always teachers and administrators excited to try them out.

I was ecstatic. I absorbed everything I could about native cultures, language patterns, and the many similarities and differences between those raised in the remote villages of Alaska and those of us raised in the more mainstream parts of America.

I couldn't have dreamed a better job for myself.

Blueberry the Clown and Fishhooks

The juxtaposition of Native and westernized Anglo cultures is observed throughout all villages in Alaska, but perhaps nowhere was it more visible to me than on the island of Little Diomede, the most remote of the BSSD villages. Located just one mile from the International Date Line and two miles from the Russian village of Big Diomede, Little Diomede is the most extreme northwesterly possession of the United States. It seemed less like a village to me than a motley assemblage of thirty or forty precariously perched wooden homes on a pile of rocks that was continually exposed to a biting wind and a seemingly ever-present fog that merged with choppy waters to beat against a rugged shoreline. It was hard for me to believe that a hundred and fifty people had ever chosen this rock as the setting for their permanent home.

There wasn't a flat spot on the island, and for this reason I could only travel there by helicopter in the fall or by ski plane in the winter. The discovery that small planes in Alaska have skis instead of wheels just tickled my Midwest-reared, suburban-raised funny bone. The fact that such planes could only land in Diomede after the Bering Sea had frozen sufficiently for villagers to venture outside and carve a small runway on the snowy, icy sea was fodder for many a journal entry. And when I wasn't recording thoughts about the terrain and the transportation modes, I was writing about the children.

The children of Little Diomede seemed like wild little Angora goats to me—scurrying up and down steep trails, lost within the folds of their bulky, fur-lined parkas. More than once I wondered if all the children were bowlegged from having grown up without a flat surface to negotiate. I don't know if they were or were not, but I do know that those kids surely must have had calves and thighs of steel, the way they scampered up, down, and around the rocky island.

In the mid-1980s there was only one phone for the island. It was a radio phone that sometimes worked and mostly didn't due to the formidable weather conditions that continually plague the islanders. It was not unusual to arrive in Diomede only to find myself socked in for an extra day (or more) because some act of Mother Nature prevented any planes or helicopters from landing on or leaving the island. I learned early on to have a few extra sets of socks and underwear in my backpack as I traveled through the region.

My mother would have been proud.

Once when I was in Diomede, a young boy ended up with a fishhook in his eye, but due to fog, he could not be flown to the nearest hospital in Nome for three days. The village health aide had to keep him sitting upright until he could get off the island and receive medical intervention.

During another of my unplanned extended trips, I found myself staring out the second-floor window of the school, mesmerized by the silence I felt as I viewed what seemed like an endless stretch of gray. In the distance I noticed a bowed figure walking across the ice—a wooden bar with a swinging bucket on each end, stretched across the back of his (or her) shoulders. It could have easily been a scene from a thousand years ago. I wondered where this person was going, as, at the time, no one from either country was allowed to cross the International Date Line.

From Little Diomede we could see the small shacks on the island of Big Diomede, where Russian soldiers sat 24/7, training their binoculars and guns on anyone who might be thinking of crossing over. I was always curious how people knew exactly where this imaginary line was, but somehow everyone knew and no one violated the boundary. So, where was a person carrying buckets going to go? And for what possible reason were they walking alone on the frozen sea, in the direction of a forbidden country?

Later I was to learn that the person had been walking to an opening in the ice in order to dispose of trash. And while that initially shocked my recycling-oriented self (even in the mid-eighties), it did not take me long to understand that the reality of life on Diomede included the necessity of melting ice and snow for water during the winter months and dumping the contents of your honey buckets (a euphemism for toilet) into a spot where the frozen sea sported an opening—as well as accepting that medical care was not always available in a timely fashion.

The residents of Diomede were, and are, a rugged and hearty bunch, to say the least. Not necessarily eco friendly, but certainly hearty and rugged.

The interlacing of cultures I observed in Diomede fascinated me. On one hand, residents walked a mile across the ice to dump garbage; on the other, the small wooden homes clumped side by side on this rocky island were increasingly equipped with satellite dishes that brought everyone into the world of television twenty-four hours a day. Beneath traditional parkas made of caribou skin and lined with fur, children and elders wore modern baseball caps with popular team names blazoned across the front. And despite not having running water or flush toilets, the girls, just like girls everywhere, pored over makeup tips found in outdated issues of *Seventeen* magazine.

In the early and mid-1980s, walrus skin boats (called Umiaks) still functioned as a practical mode of transportation when the water was free of ice. Food was buried beneath the permafrost, and ivory carving, whaling, and harvesting crab defined the lifestyle. And yet, the kids in Diomede—just like all kids in those years—were walking around practicing break dancing, rooting for the Chicago Bears, and bleaching pieces of their hair platinum. (Unfortunately, they were also sniffing gasoline in order to get high, thus providing me with my first experiences in assessing for brain impairment.)

It was a fascinating collision of cultures—as well as a potentially cataclysmic one—as seems to be true in most situations where old-world traditions seek their place among modern technologies. Or perhaps more accurately, modern technologies seek their place among old-world traditions.

It wasn't until 1982—just a couple of years before my first trip there—that mail was delivered to Little Diomede on a regular basis. Prior to that time, people received mail sporadically, as it could only be delivered by Umiak, a once-yearly barge, or the occasional cargo plane that, since no landing was possible if the Bering Sea was not frozen, would circle the island and toss sacks of mail down to the villagers. I suppose in those days people weren't ordering eggs or china from the Sam's Club catalog.

I didn't know about such important things as mail delivery when I made my first trip to Diomede. Mail was something that had been delivered daily all of my life, and the notion that its arrival would create excitement had never crossed my mind. On my introductory visit, I was both mesmerized and terrified by what seemed like a whole village suddenly materializing beneath the hovering craft that contained me, the pilot, and my ever-present backpack. A hovering craft that was attempting to make—or so it seemed to me—a precarious vertical landing on a conspicuously small, flat square of cement.

Oh, my gosh! I thought to myself, looking out the window and feeling like an immediate celebrity. *All these people here just to greet me. Wow.*

I figured there weren't many visitors to Diomede, and a helicopter bringing in someone new must be a pretty big deal. While this was true to some degree, I quickly learned that the helicopters and planes delivering me were also delivering the mail. I was rapidly humbled and brought back to reality regarding my celebrity status. Tempting though it was, I could not delude myself for long into believing that all the waving, cheering, and frenetic energy was aimed in my direction. Which was probably a good thing, as it's always good to keep one's perspective in check.

I do have to say, however, that I actually did generate a fair amount of excitement and activity that *was* all my own, and which had nothing at all to do with the postal deliveries. Beginning with my first trip there, and continuing each time I returned, from the moment I emerged from the aircraft a flurry of strange questions would be discharged in my direction. It was almost a surreal experience to step from behind the large bubbled window of the helicopter into the sounds of thickly accented English spoken simultaneously to a legion of hands reaching out to touch my hair.

"Who you be?" I would hear, usually from a child of about eight or nine.

"Are you *Blueberry the Clown*?" some other child would shout—huge chocolate eyes wide and excitement barely contained beneath a bulky parka.

I came to discover that *Blueberry*, aka the visiting nurse, made a yearly appearance (the nurse more often, but Blueberry only once a year), and the native children had as much trouble telling Anglo women apart (even when in our view we bore no resemblance to one another) as we had telling them apart. At the time, those of us who traveled there thought it so strange that the children mixed us up, just as I am sure they found it strange that we did the same. It wasn't until much later that I understood the brain enough to have an explanation for this odd phenomenon.

"Can I touch yer her?" a heavily accented and bold voice would inevitably ask as the shy others stared at the ridiculous mass of curls tumbling from my head and reaching somewhere near my shoulders. My hair was in such stark contrast to their thick, straight, and very dark manes; and I was to discover that reactions ranged from simple, silent stares of awe as children tried to figure out, *How you do that?* to the near hysterical giggles that sometimes stopped adolescent girls in their tracks.

I loved being in Little Diomede, and if the bowlegged, round-cheeked, dark-eyed children were not enough to thrill me, Little Diomede was the only place in the world that I had ever been where I could walk out and straddle an imaginary line, and realize that one half of my body was standing in today (on one continent), and the other half was touching tomorrow (on a different continent).

Talk about weird juxtapositions.

•Flying into Diomede
•Two little girls, w/Big Diomede in the background
•Diomede Houses

High Bars and Boxed Wine

Diomede was not by any means the only fascinating place I landed. After two or three weeks of northeast and northwest village hopping, I would head back to Juneau, where I would unload my backpack, do laundry, and repack so that, come Monday morning, I would be ready to leave again. Having traveled north, it would be time to head to the Tlingit, Haida, and Tsimshian Indian villages scattered throughout the Alaskan panhandle. Float or other small airplanes (usually four-seater mail planes) would glide over the Alaskan Marine Highway, offering me breathtaking views of the glacier-cut fjords and the islands blanketed by dense rainforests. The one to three hundred inches of rain experienced in those parts of southeastern Alaska created more shades of green than I could find names to describe. It would be so vastly different from the miles (and miles) of frozen tundra, meandering rivers, and snow-covered rolling hills I had just experienced in the interior and northern areas that it was hard for me to believe all these places belonged to the same state.

Despite the many cultural and topographical differences between my northern and southeastern schools, there were several similarities. Villagers in both parts of the state struggled with the complex dynamics that were rooted in balancing traditional ways with twentieth-century ways. The villagers of both areas were sending their children to schools that required mastery of a curriculum born of alien concepts and values, taught in a language that frequently was not spoken other than within the walls of the school building. And the breadth and depth of problems in both areas presented an educational psychologist with more challenges and work than could be accomplished in a lifetime.

There was another similarity, one that had a lifelong impact on me both professionally and personally. In each village school, whether it was predominantly made up of Yupik, Inupiat, Athabascan, Tsimshian, Metlakatlan, or Anglo students, there was the opportunity to develop creative and innovative interventions for struggling students. Certainly there were teachers and administrators living and working in these villages because they were unable to "fit" anywhere else or because a higher rate of pay drove them north of their roots. But by far what I encountered most often were creative, skilled, intelligent, and extremely well-traveled educators who had landed in these diverse and remote villages because somehow they were drawn to them. People who were excited to try new ideas, willing to learn new programs, and who thought that having a psychologist around with an endless supply of ideas and energy was just about the greatest thing since the advent of the weekly mail delivery.

Looking back, the classroom-based programs and interventions we developed for children were really quite remarkable. It's hard to fathom that I found the energy to keep the physical and cognitive pace up week after week, year after year. The only explanation I have ever come up with is that when there are no limits placed upon what one is able to try, instead of energy being siphoned away by frustration and the kind of negativity that often comes with working within bureaucracies, each person is fed, nurtured, and enhanced by the collective energy of people working together. When I finally did leave Alaska to work elsewhere, this would be what I would miss the most.

But in 1985, I couldn't have been happier. I was thirty years old, with thirty schools, and I was seeing parts of Alaska not many have the good fortune to experience. I loved each place I found myself in. BSSD was my favorite place to work, and Mary Rubadeau was by far the administrator I had grown to like and respect the most.

By the end of my first year, Mary convinced me to leave Juneau and the statewide consulting agency and move north to Unalakleet, in order to work for her full-time.

It was, without question, the smartest career decision I ever made.

* * * * *

Thirty-four years old at the time we met, Mary didn't fit the stereotypic picture some might have of what a high-powered educator in the rugged and remote regions of Alaska might look or be like. Tall, slender, and blessed with the kind of sturdy beauty that lasts a lifetime, Mary had been an award-winning equestrian throughout her college career in a prominent eastern school. She had sailed much of the western hemisphere with her husband, and had traveled a good part of the world with a pack on her back.

Mary could have (had she wanted) become a successful administrator in an insulated, wealthy prep school rather than in this remote village of some seven hundred Eskimos that sat between the Unalakleet River and the Bering Sea, four hundred air miles from the nearest city of any size. What made Mary so fascinating was that she was there by choice—not for the money, and not because she didn't fit anywhere else—but because she loved what she did and thrived on surrounding herself with others who shared both an awe and a respect for other cultures and other ways of doing things.

Mary was calm, organized, and quick to smile. She modeled an impeccably ethical approach to providing educational services to children with special needs, and she displayed an uncanny vision of what services could and should look like in public education. Mary encouraged—demanded—that those who work for her think broadly, challenge the status quo, and ask questions in order to move beyond doing work at just a legally required, acceptable level. *Acceptable* would never have been good enough for Mary because it was not good enough for kids—not if we wanted them to truly succeed.

With Mary we all worked with a sort of crazed mania, but when Saturday night rolled around, you could count on the Rubadeaus to make sure there was a beach bonfire going with plenty of good food, good music, boxed wine, cheap beer, and endless amounts of laughter. We worked hard and we played hard. And we had fun doing both.

Mary set the bar for everyone I would work for in the future, and she nurtured my skills and talents in a way that allowed me to set the bar for myself. Between the two of us, my bars became solidly established, and they were very, very high. It wasn't until much later that I would realize just how high they were.

In 1988, Mary left the BSSD and, taking me with her, moved to the larger Kenai Peninsula Borough School District located in central Alaska. I was to spend another six remarkable years under her direction, and would have worked for her forever had she not chosen to accept a much-coveted superintendent position in Juneau. By then, moving back to Juneau was no longer an option for me. Although I continued working for the Kenai School District for a year, I then branched out on my own and created a private consulting business that, in addition to my job teaching classes at the local branch of the University of Alaska, provided me with a wonderful professional career as well as a balanced personal life.

It was in my capacity as a private consultant that I discovered Galena, and like many of the villages I had encountered throughout my years in the state, Galena—with its myriad of complexities, culture, and challenges—fascinated me. I loved being able to fly there for a week or two, immerse myself in the work, and then return to my (by then more settled) life in Kenai.

It was a lovely blend of two very different lifestyles.

Galena
1998

"...Here, you can have this." I was speaking to a teacher sitting near the front of the room as I waved a hundred-dollar bill in front of her. "Read that paragraph, and this crisp new Ben Franklin is yours!" I was conducting a workshop for teachers in Galena, and I was using a simulation activity I had learned from a man by the name of Richard Lavoie (my absolute guru/hero when it comes to training parents and teachers about kids with learning disabilities). In this case, the teachers were experiencing what it's like to have a learning disability prevent them from reading the passage correctly. And they were experiencing the frustration of being treated as if laziness and a lack of motivation were the only reasons they were not being successful.

"Come on," I said. "This is easy stuff. You're just not trying, guys. All you have to do is read a couple of lines!" I placed the bill on the teacher's table as if to prove that if she really wanted to, she could read the unreadable passage in front of her.

Looking around, I was just starting to offer the hundred-dollar bill to anyone in the group who would read what was written on the paper in front of them when suddenly the sound of thundering jet engines drowned out my words.

Holy God! I thought to myself, utterly paralyzed by fear. *We're being attacked!* As the roaring sound intensified, an adrenaline rush replaced fear, and in sheer panic mode, oblivious to anything or anyone else around me, I looked for the nearest table to dive under. I could feel my heart pounding as the thought ran through my head that the Galena Air Force Base, on inactive status since 1993, would surely come alive if the threat of attack was not just imminent, but in progress. It was 1998 and long before September 11, but the sound of those engines inspired terror just the same.

Laughter, at first scattered and delicate, became increasingly louder as one by one the teachers allowed suppressed chuckling to overtake any sense of social propriety and erupt into full-blown, from-the-belly laughter. As their collective release penetrated my panicked state, I looked around at this group of teachers who had become my professional friends over the years I had been flying in and working as a consultant, and I wondered what on *earth* had just occurred.

"Oh, my gosh, Debra. I wish I had a picture of your face. You should have seen yourself. That was just priceless!" one my teacher-friends said, laughing without one bit of shame.

"Oh, wow...obviously no one let you know..." another, slightly more compassionate teacher said, busting up mightily, nevertheless.

"*What?*" I asked, looking around. "What is going on? What *was* that?" My heart was beating about eighty times its normal rate, and I still had that *whooshing* feeling in my ears that comes with a massive adrenaline rush.

"It's the F-15s," said Bruce, one of the elementary teachers. "They do this once or twice a year. It's just a training exercise to make sure everything is still working." He paused before cracking up, adding, "I take it no one remembered to tell you this was set up for this morning."

"Oh, my gosh," I said. "Oh-my-gosh. I thought we were being invaded."

I sat down, more than slightly embarrassed at my less than valorous reaction, and let my heart rate slow while everyone else pulled themselves together for entirely different reasons.

Galena is a small village located on the north bank of the Yukon River— about one hundred and twenty-five miles south of the Arctic Circle and two hundred seventy miles west of Fairbanks. With six hundred and fifty residents, it's the largest of the villages that make up the Yukon-Koyukuk region of Alaska, and it's the hub for the government and transportation services in this western interior region.

Galena is a unique village, even in a state full of unique villages. There are several things that contribute to this, but most people credit two historic events. The first is that in the 1940s, the United States established an Air Force base there. Prior to that time, Galena was very isolated, with almost no contact with the world beyond those people who lived along the Yukon River. Establishment of a military presence in Galena not only brought tremendous economic growth, but also a permanent runway that accommodated jet service. Both the economic growth and the jet service connected Galena to the world in a way virtually unknown prior to that time.

It also contributed to a new generation of mixed heritage children calling Galena their birthplace—and where an Alaskan is born and buried is not an insignificant detail to those who live in the various villages.

The second, and perhaps in some ways the more influential of the events to shape Galena's culture, happened in 1971 when the mighty Yukon threw a not-so-little tantrum.

The Yukon River has long been a powerful friend to the Alaskan people who live along its banks. Springtime thaw of the river, following eight or nine months of freeze, is cause for all kinds of celebrations, marking as it does the end of a long and harsh winter. Flooding during this time is no surprise to native Alaskans, and establishment of any village along the river has always included preparation for such an event: food caches are stored out of danger's way, and homes and other buildings are erected beyond what would be considered flood zones.

No amount of foresight, however, could have prepared the little village of Galena for what happened in May 1971, when the Yukon River brandished its authority in a calamitous and unprecedented way. The thawing river ice jammed just below the village. With a force and brutality never before witnessed, once the jam broke, massive, thundering blocks of ice swept through the village, along with thirteen-foot waves of water that destroyed everything in their path. Although the Air Force base sat dry behind a 136-foot dike that excluded the village, nothing else remained of what had been home to three hundred Athabascan Indians.

It was the rebuilding of the village—not the flood—that so shaped the culture and essence of what Galena was to become.

Two brothers, Jimmy and Sidney Huntington, and a man by the name of John Sackett spearheaded the reconstruction of Galena. Sidney opted to remain in the original site and concentrate on the rehabilitation of the area now referred to as Old Town. Jimmy was not a supporter of land ownership (residents in Old Town could buy and sell the land outright according to the Alaska Native Claims Settlement Act). He worked with a group of individuals interested in leasing land. They established homes in the area now known as New Town, which is located on Alexander Lake, two miles from the original village.

By the end of 1972, just one year after the devastating flood, there were four hundred Athabascan people living in Galena—one hundred more than before the flood—along with the five hundred members of the United States Air Force who were stationed there.

Jimmy is no longer alive; however, Sidney—now well over ninety years old—continues as an active leader and highly respected elder in Galena. While there is a dichotomy between the more traditional Old Town and its subsistence lifestyle, and New Town, where more modern homes and offices reside, the two "towns" are not segregated from one another and both equally contribute to making Galena what it is today.

I have sat by the banks of the Yukon, and I have listened to the sounds of the ice breaking. Some years it has been thunderous, with muffled booms and groans that are punctuated by a hundred varieties of snapping, crunching, and cracking sounds that must be a mere fraction of what villagers heard in the spring of 1971. In my mind I can almost imagine the ear-splitting roar of exploding water and massive blocks of ice as they crashed through the village, but I cannot even begin to imagine the terror it must have brought or the despair that it left behind. That this village recovered to become what it is today is testimony to a few remarkable men and the hundreds of men and women who banded together to do what Native Alaskans have always done, and that is to survive.

It is one of the things so bewitching to me about Alaska: this ability of its people to survive.

Cowboy Panache and Frostbite

Corporal Farley S. Seward stood straight and tall, wearing a beige fur cap and black goggles. His black hair and beard, in stark contrast to the white coat, gloves, pants, and boots that have become associated with his name, contribute to the look of a man who is both rugged and dashing. Corporal Seward is a well-educated soldier, having graduated from transportation school in Fort Eustis, Virginia (home to the U.S. Army Transportation Corp) and the U.S. Army Armor School in Fort Knox, Kentucky. He's a qualified expert with the M-16, M1911A1 automatic pistol, and the M-60mmMG; and according to his official biography, he excels working in an environment that is unforgiving. This soldier has to be tough and he has to be cool; and by everyone's description, he is both of these.

And he comes with his own Snow Cat!

Corporal Farley S. Seward, better known by his G.I. Joe name, *Frostbite*, is a hero to many. But despite his popularity, not many know that Frostbite's real name is Farley or that he went to transportation school. What even fewer people know is that, according to his official biography, Hasbro's Frostbite was born in *Galena!*

It is understandable that people associated with Galena are proud of the individuals who brought their resourcefulness and grit to the rebuilding of the village after the 1971 flood. And with no disrespect meant to the significance of this in Galena's history, I think it is only fair to point out that while Sidney and Jimmy Huntington, along with John Sackett, are men rightfully credited with many of Galena's successes, none of them were born there. Of them all, only Frostbite was born in Galena, and I think this is a claim to fame worthy of note.

That said, for me there is one other character, though a nonfictional one, who has found a way to put Galena on the map, at least as it relates to education. This man's name is Carl Knudsen, and while not everyone supports the educational Goliath that Galena has become as a result of this man's influence, there is something very impressive about a remote village of native Alaskans—who for decades failed in the public school milieu—to have emerged as a model of academic success and stellar academic programs.

Carl Knudsen is the man responsible for many of my experiences in Galena over the seven-year period from 1995-2002, and he is responsible for profoundly influencing my beliefs, views, and philosophies regarding what can be accomplished in public education if one is willing to stretch and think outside that time-honored square box.

I first met Carl in 1995, and before I could even glance at the face of the man standing in front of me with an outstretched hand, I couldn't help but notice his substantial girth. Girth punctuated in the middle by a large silver and turquoise Montana belt buckle. The belt buckle and the scent of his liberally worn cologne are two of three characteristics that stand out to me about my first meeting with Carl.

Looking to be in his mid- to late-fifties, on the day we met, Carl was wearing jeans and a sport coat. While this is not, in and of itself, unusual business attire in Alaska, Carl Knudsen was also wearing cowboy boots. And I do mean gen-u-ine, Abilene-brown, goat-with-snip-toe cowboy boots.

Those boots are the third characteristic forever etched in the memory of my introduction to this man who came to profoundly impact my life.

It was my first year working as a consultant to Galena, and it was Carl's first year working as the superintendent, having just arrived in Alaska from Montana. As I took his hand and returned his firm handshake, I wondered if he had any idea that it dropped to sixty degrees below zero in the wintertime in Galena. And as I walked away and headed toward the classrooms, I remember thinking that over the past eleven years I had encountered plenty of odd-duck school administrators, but I didn't think I had ever met one quite so...*vivid*...before.

This one, I thought, *this Carl Knudsen, he's different to be sure.*

A real live Montana cowboy.

In truth, I am not someone who often passes judgment after an initial impression, as I honestly believe it isn't quite fair to form opinions based on a brief first encounter. Still, at the time, I couldn't help but wonder if I would actually be able to work for someone who wore cowboy boots and turquoise jewelry—and whose cologne was applied with sufficient intensity to clog my sinuses.

As it turned out, this Montana cowboy ended up providing me some of my life's most important lessons, not the least being to honor the old adage about not judging a book by its cover. After my first year of working on a consultant basis for him, Carl, just as Mary had done, offered me the opportunity to work for him full-time. Although I deeply loved what I was doing, making the choice to work only for him was, without a doubt, the *second* smartest career decision I have ever made.

During my years of working for Carl, I was able to refine and expand my skills in a way most professionals only dream about; and I was to learn that there is no vision too big, no dream too vast, and no place too small or remote to turn those visions and dreams into a reality.

Without a doubt, Carl Knudsen displayed a sense of panache. *Cowboy panache,* to be sure—but panache, nevertheless.

My mother would have enjoyed Carl.

The Low Price of High-Priced Tickets
Fall 1999

"Debra. We're going to need you to come on in to Galena. We have major issues right now." It was my boss, Jim Foster, calling me on the cell phone from Galena as I headed to the district's Anchorage office.

"How come? What's up, Jim?" I asked as I attempted to negotiate the road construction, which seemingly popped out of nowhere.

"Had a break-in last night at the school. Twenty-two thousand dollars worth of damage to computers and to the building. We know the three kids who did it, and we're going to need you to help us get a manifestation determination meeting in place and figure out a plan for these boys."

As Jim was telling me this, I could feel my foot pressing down on the accelerator as my anxiety level crept upward. *Twenty-two thousand dollars in damages! Was I going to have to get the preliminary work done for three manifestations?* I knew that if all three boys received special education services, that's how many preliminary reports I would have to complete in the next week.

A manifestation determination is a federally mandated requirement when a student in special education is at risk for expulsion due to a drug or weapons violation; or for having committed a violent crime on school grounds. It's a good law, but one that requires that a great deal of preliminary work be completed in order to carry out the determination in a fair and just manner.

I was grateful that the administrators I had worked for over the last fifteen years had all been creative and committed educators who kept legal and ethical matters in mind when it came to issues involving children in special education. Though I had never experienced it, I had heard plenty of stories regarding administrators who did not honor the intent of the various laws and who violated important student rights in their need or desire to move quickly through the various required procedures. And while I really was happy that I did not work for this type of administrator, at that particular moment— swamped with work and driving amidst the work zones and detours in the city of Anchorage—all I could think was: *Where am I going to find time to pull all those preliminary reports together?*

"Okay, Jim," I said, trying not to sound whiny. "Let me wrap things up here, and I'll be in on the first morning flight."

It was the 1999-2000 school year, and I was working full-time for the Galena School District, with half my time spent outside the village in programs operated around the state, and half my time spent living in the village, working in its two schools. After spending two weeks in Galena, my plan had been to spend a couple of days working in Anchorage and then fly to Juneau to consult with the staff involved with one of Galena's distance programs.

Guess that plan is going to change in a hurry, I thought, wondering how often I would be able to continue getting away with stealing time from one site in order to give it to another. Although people were really forgiving of my sometimes erratic and less-than-dependable schedule, I always worried that the time would come when someone would get really frustrated and start complaining. And while I wouldn't have blamed them a bit, there was only one of me, and I couldn't always be where I was needed as quickly as one would hope. The pace and schedule demanded by this job was something I both loved and lamented.

As I preoccupied myself with thoughts of organizing (reorganizing), packing (repacking), making reservations, and wrapping up the work I had been in the middle of, I was distracted by bright colors flashing in my rearview mirror. *What the...?* I thought as I adjusted my mirror to deflect the lights.

The flashing colors belonged to the Anchorage Police, who were pulling me over for violating the speed limit in a work zone.

Awww, dang it! I thought. *I bet there's a double fine for this one.*

Indeed, I was cited for speeding in a work zone, and after the officer handed me what turned out to be a *$130* ticket, I decided that perhaps this would be a good time just to go back to the apartment the district kept for those of us who traveled all the time and pack my clothes. Driving toward the apartment, I tried mentally calculating how to most efficiently get everything done in order to leave for Galena the next morning, a feat that was going to require another really long workday for me if I wanted to keep everyone happy. I had just parked the car in the driveway and was starting to open the door, when my then-young puppy, Teek, bounded across the seat in the excited way he had when interested in meeting someone new. To my absolute astonishment, there was a policeman standing there, his car parked directly behind mine—running and with lights flashing.

"Hello, ma'am. Didn't you see me behind you?" he asked.

"*Whoa!* Wow. No, actually...no. I mean, *gosh,* how long were you there?" I was really flustered. He had taken me by such surprise, and I am quite sure I stuttered as I looked around to see if the neighbors were watching me get arrested in the middle of the day, for who knew what.

"May I see your license and registration please?" I handed these to him, wondering if my ticket from fifteen minutes earlier would show up in his little car computer. "Are you aware that the speed zone in this neighborhood is twenty-five, and that I followed you all the way in at thirty-five the whole time?"

"Um, no sir. I mean, yes, I am aware that the speed limit is twenty-five...but not that I was going over it. I'm really sorry... *Wow!* I didn't even see you behind me." I was babbling. Never a good thing for me to do and almost always what I revert to when nervous. "Are you going to give me a ticket?" I didn't mean to sound pathetic, but I *was* hoping he would take pity upon me and my eight-week-old puppy, and maybe let us off with a warning.

He didn't have to answer as he tore the perforated sheet off his pad and handed it to me.

"Cute dog," he commented. "Slow down, Ms. Sanders. And...stay alert, please."

I humbly accepted my second ticket of the day and went inside to pack.

Jeez, I thought. *Talk about spacing out.* While I frequently could find myself highly absorbed in a task that was of significant interest, it was rare for me to be completely oblivious to my surroundings. Especially when behind the wheel of a car.

As I walked inside to pack for both Teek and myself (Teek always traveled with me on my trips), I wondered if my administrators might consider this a work-related expense. It was, after all, due to my phone conversation with Jim that I had just sustained a few hundred dollars worth of tickets.

On the other hand, maybe it would be best not to bring up the fact that one of their employees was dumb enough to get two citations before nine o'clock in the morning.

On the Map

"Hey, good morning, Debra! Are you heading back to Galena already?" It was my favorite of the ticket agents who worked at the Frontier Flying Service desk. The same one who had checked me *into* the Anchorage airport just two days earlier when I had returned from Galena.

"Oh, yeah. I'd probably think life was boring if I slept in the same bed three nights in a row!" It was impossible not to stifle a yawn as I said this. "Actually," I said, only half laughing, "it might be kind of nice to sleep in the same place for a few consecutive days." *Or weeks,* I thought, but did not say. "Is it on time, or do I get to snooze on the chairs before we leave?"

It was six o'clock in the morning, and while Frontier's flights were often on time, it was not unusual to be delayed for hours by ice, wind, or some other creative expression of Mother Nature's occasionally volatile temperament.

"We've got you going in the 1900 Beechcraft, and it's on time, far as I know."

"Too bad," I groaned. "I really was hoping for extra sleep time!" Not that I wouldn't sleep like a baby for the entire hour that it took to go the five hundred and fifty miles that separated Anchorage from Galena. I was like an infant in one of those Snuglis when I got on a plane. All those years of flying when I was exhausted had created an automatic stimulus-response: I got on the plane; I sat down; I entered deep sleep. I rarely saw the end of the runway. I was famous for my airplane power naps.

* * * * *

I had spent the previous evening, after talking to Jim at length about the situation, contemplating options that might be doable with the boys who had broken into the school. There would be a meeting with all the members of each boy's team (made up of his parents, the principal, special education teacher, and at least one of his regular education teachers, among other professionals that might be involved in the student's program). I knew that not one of us held the belief that expulsion would be in any of the boys' best interest, but I also knew we all believed it critical that the boys be held legally accountable for their actions and make full restitution. And perhaps most importantly, we all believed that kids in trouble needed to have an opportunity to learn and gain necessary skills to make wiser decisions in the future. Expulsion rarely, if ever, accomplishes these things.

These were not going to be easy plans to develop. The good news was that I wasn't developing them alone. I had the administrators and the school board behind me philosophically, and the principal and teachers involved were all creative individuals who had no qualms about imposing severe consequences when necessary, but who did not happen to think suspension or expulsion were the only available options. It would take us all some time; it would take energy maybe not all of us were feeling we had at the moment, but we would all rally somehow and figure it out. This wasn't our first experience with such challenges, and I was quite sure it would not be our last.

That's part of what made my job so much fun.

At the time of this incident, I had been working for Carl for almost five years and Jim Foster for nearly four. I felt about them much as I had about Mary Rubadeau—no matter how much I gave, no matter how many hours I worked, I never felt as if I was being overworked or undervalued. I got back from these administrators as much as I put in. Between all of us, we made sure the kids in the district received services in a way they were entitled to by law and deserving of for no other reason than they were children and we were public school educators. Given my administrators' own commitment to this, there was little I would not do that either Carl or Jim asked of me.

I did not always feel this way about Carl—in fact, when I first met him, I actually kind of dismissed him as a weird, pipe-dreaming sort of cowboy. Kind of scary to think my impression could be so far off base (after all, given my profession, I think I'm supposed to be more insightful than that. Or, at least, never admit that I'm not!).

I remember the first meaningful conversation I had with Carl following the day I had paid such attention to his boots (really, I coveted those boots, but I probably wouldn't have admitted that at the time). It must have been close to the end of the first semester—near the Christmas break—and during the second of five one-week trips I would be making there over the course of the school year.

"I've started to implement this great idea. It's fantastic. We're gonna set up satellite offices in Anchorage, Kenai, Fairbanks, Wasilla, and Juneau. We'll staff 'em with certified teachers, give every family a computer, and run a distance delivery home-school program. I think we can get seven hundred students if we approach it right."

How do you teach if you're living hundreds of miles from your students? I wondered. *How do you run and* _fund_ *a school program like that?*

As these questions popped into my mind, Carl was excitedly going on about his idea. I didn't know him very well at this point, and his ideas were so far beyond the scope of anything I had encountered in public education that I pretty much decided the man was crazed. I paid little attention to what Carl Knudsen was up to outside the little village school of Galena that year.

One year later, not seven hundred, but almost *four thousand* students were enrolled in Carl's home-school program from all parts of the state. They were served through five satellite offices and staffed by certified teachers. Just as he had envisioned. Known as the IDEA program (Interior Distance Education of Alaska), this was to become a protocol for many of the online home-school programs that later followed—both in Alaska and in the continental United States.

It was in 1996 that Carl recruited Jim Foster, a longtime friend and professional colleague who had spent thirty years creating programs and developing innovative projects in Montana. Jim was hired to be the director of special education and, whether by title or just design, the assistant superintendent. From that point on it would be Jim more than Carl that I had the most daily interaction with, but my relationship with Carl always remained a connected one. Like Carl, Jim wore cowboy boots, big buckles, and the proverbial ten-gallon hat—but I had already learned not to judge these men by their bowlegged walk or choice of footwear.

By 1997, Carl had formed a partnership between the Galena School District and the United States Air Force; and utilizing the by-then vacant buildings and barracks (since the base was on inactive status), the district created a residential high school program. It was a program available to students from all over the state, and it offered some of the most sound, innovative, and demanding academic and vocational programs I had (or have) ever worked for.

Within the same time frame the residential program was being developed, Carl formed additional partnerships between the Galena School District and the Department of Defense schools. He expanded the original IDEA home-school program, which initially only served families living in Alaska. By 2000, it was a home-school program serving families stationed in Korea, Japan, Guam, Australia, and Hawaii; and it was continuing to branch into other countries. Teachers were hired and trained to perform in the same capacity as those who worked in the satellite offices set up around the state of Alaska, except the international home-school teachers traveled overseas once or twice a year to meet with their assigned families face to face. Business was conducted using computers, phones, distance delivery methods, and some remarkably creative techniques developed by the various people Carl and Jim had recruited from every corner of the country.

Once thing about Carl Knudsen—he was intent on hiring the best and the brightest. I never saw him in action at a career fair, but I am quite sure he showcased his *panache* in such a way as to excite passionate educators and stimulate their brilliance. I imagine many a fine candidate found himself or herself sitting at home following their interview, anxiously waiting to hear if *Mr. Knudsen* was going to offer them a job in this strange, faraway, and utterly remarkable school district. Those who were hired nearly always proved themselves up to every expectation Carl established.

As Carl's programs grew, so did I. I was thriving. I was working, learning, and living at a pace that kept me stimulated and excited all the time. As had always been true working for Mary, mediocrity was a word that never passed Carl's or Jim's lips. They had ventured to a small, remote village in Alaska where the winters lasted from October to April; where temperatures reached sixty degrees below zero; where the student population was nearly 100% native Alaskans who had historically failed in the westernized public education school system; and they put it on the map. Not just the Alaskan map—they were putting Galena on the *world* map.

To Carl's credit, even though I so shallowly dismissed him early in our acquaintance, he was gracious enough to take me along on the ride, and for that I am forever grateful.

These two men—Carl Knudsen and Jim Foster—showed me that no place is too remote or too small to house big dreams. I knew at the time that I was privy to something remarkable, but it would not be until I left Alaska and worked elsewhere that I would come to know just how exceptional my experiences in public education had been.

I was teaching, providing therapy, writing, learning, and using every ounce of my intellectual and creative energies to help create and implement programs that were good for kids. And my role models were my administrators.

At the time I had no idea just how very unusual this was. Or, how difficult life would become when I was to combine a head injury with a bar that stood so far above the norm that no one could possibly touch it.

Not even me.

My traumatic brain injury would leave me so baffled and filled with self-doubt that I would have no way to gauge if the chaos I found myself immersed in was due to me or to the fact that I had been exposed to a world that simply did not exist where I ended up landing.

But I am getting ahead of myself. Before I managed to mangle my brain, I moved to live and work in Galena full-time.

Pink Hearts and the Little Princess
December 2001, Galena, Alaska

By the end of the 2000-2001 school year, I had submitted a proposal to Carl and Jim that would enable me to live and work in Galena full-time. The proposal was based on a five-year plan that would involve developing collaborative programs with teachers in addition to providing intensive intervention to children on a daily basis. Their approval was another example of their willingness to do what it takes to keep the needs of the kids as the top priority.

I'm sure it was challenging to find it in the budget to pay me to work full-time in Galena, which, of course, then necessitated hiring a second psychologist who could assume the responsibilities of serving the home-school program. But the troubles and issues that Galena kids brought to school were significant. It was hoped that by expanding the early intervention programs we had been developing over the previous six years, we could have a notable effect not just on students' academics, but also on their ability to become productive and positive community members. Although Carl had a full-time counselor placed in both the city school and the residential school, by hiring me full-time we hoped that with our combined energies and talents we could establish programs that would not otherwise exist.

On paper I imagine it was hard to justify a full-time psychologist for two hundred and fifty students; in reality, the administrators obviously recognized that this is what it would take to effect significant and long-term change.

I do not know where Carl and Jim found the money to fund this position, but they did; and in the summer of 2001, I moved to Galena.

* * * * *

I was standing in the hallway in front of my office—a room that had quickly become a hangout favorite since I had started working full-time at the beginning of this school year. Kids were coming in from recess, and suddenly I heard a familiar voice calling my name.

"Hi, Ms. Debra," said my friend, Tanya Korta, as she approached me, holding the hand of one of her kindergarten students. "Angela[3] needs to see you," she said, handing off a dark-skinned, pretty little girl whose almond-shaped, coffee-colored eyes seemed to strongly convey her current

---

[3] The names and identifying information of all school children have been changed in order to protect their identities.

sentiments: *Bite me.* "Angela was running around the playground kissing boys," Tanya continued, nonplussed. "I told her she needed to stop, and when she didn't, I put her in time-out for five minutes and told her we needed to talk with Ms. Debra."

Angela was wearing a sweet pink T-shirt with hearts and the words *Little Princess* scrolled in flowery letters on the front. Despite the T-shirt, I surmised that this was probably not one of Angela's better "little princess" days.

"Sounds like Angela and I have some work to do," I stated as her hand was transferred to mine. "Tell you what, Ange. You go on into my room and decide who'll join us today, and I'll come in right after I talk with Mrs. Korta for a minute."

Angela, letting go of my hand, let herself into my room—a room set up with my many helpers. Two nearly child-size dolls, Molly and Wally, sat at a round table in the center of the room. I long ago forgot which child named them. Some of my puppets and dolls get new names with every child who uses them, but some, like these two, have the same name with everybody. In this case, Molly and Wally had been in some classrooms with me, and their names had stuck.

The room was a comforting place for kids, teachers, and administrators alike. Though it was small, it had its own personality—always smelling of vanilla, and with the sounds of tranquil music (or rock 'n' roll, depending on the time of day) bringing people in when the door was open. There was no stigma to spending time in this room; the kids adored it. One of the third grade students had made a caricature cardboard doll of me with long and wild curly hair shooting out from all directions. The doll was on the outside of the door with a sign that read: *Ms. Debra's P.S. room.* The P.S. stood for problem solving, and it had become somewhat of a badge of honor among the elementary students when they could enter with a problem and leave having come up with their own solutions to try.

I so loved being in the school. It was the first time in my career I was not dividing my time between distant schools, and I loved the intensity and creativity I could bring to the job by being there every day. I worked just as hard and just as many hours as I always had, but there was something uniquely gratifying about putting all that time into one place that I had not previously experienced.

In the back corner of the room, in an unruly pile, lay a family of dolls—including some with anatomically correct parts and removable clothing. Situated around the room were the farm animals, teddy bears, baby dolls, and miscellaneous puppets and stuffed animals that seemed to come in so handy when a child needed someone to talk to who could be trusted. Or needed someone trusted to talk for them.

And in a tall cabinet by the door, there were seven shelves of the tools so valuable to every therapist working with young children: baby bottles, toy handcuffs, swords, trucks, cars, houses, fairy godmothers, ogres, toy guns, clay, paint, crayons, and dozens of other items that allow children to tell their stories in the way most familiar: through a world of play.

Carl and Jim, along with the elementary principal, Chris Reitan, made sure that I had the budget needed to be well equipped to do my job.

Angela knew each item in my room. She had been coming in every day for months, and through our work together, she was moving from being an angry, mean, aggressive child who had been a threat to other children, to one who was learning the skills necessary to successfully participate in a classroom both socially and academically. Academics challenged Angela, and she had already been retained in kindergarten once. At times, her acting-out behavior was clearly an attempt to avoid tasks that were difficult for her to understand or master, but at other times, Angela's acting-out behaviors were unrelated to academic demands; rather, they were related to social ones.

Angela had a history of displaying a variety of inappropriate behaviors, which ranged from sexual acting out (such as taking off her clothes or trying to touch other children in the genital area), to physical acts that showed a remarkable capacity to inflict harm or pain on a peer.

Earlier in the school year, Angela was observed to callously push a little girl down the icy metal stairs that lead to the school; and when confronted, she looked the teacher directly in the eye and, with no obvious signs of lying or remorse, denied that she had anything to do with what happened. Working with Angela reminded me of an old movie called *The Bad Seed,* starring Patty McCormack. McCormack played a little girl who looked like an angel and yet was fully capable of carrying out murderous plans for those who crossed her. The difference was that in the movie the little girl was portrayed as having been *born* a bad seed with nothing that could be done to change her, while it was our belief that given intensive and consistent intervention, Angela could indeed learn to manage her emotions in ways that did not cause harm or pain to others.

We'd made enormous progress. Tanya, Angela's very gifted and dedicated teacher, and I worked as a team. We had become a well-oiled machine whose parts relied on each other to keep things working smoothly, and although there were times we weren't sure we were making progress, we were finally seeing that the hours and hours of time invested were clearly paying off. Angela had not displayed an aggressive or violent act in nearly two months. She was beginning to internalize and demonstrate the skills every child needs in order to be successful in a classroom; and her sexualized acting-out behavior had substantially diminished.

It was not a good sign that Angela had been trying to kiss boys on the playground.

Walking into my little room, I saw that Angela was sitting at the round table with Wally and Molly, and that she had pulled over my desk chair—the one on wheels. I wondered if she was going to be "Ms. Debra" today. "Being Ms. Debra" was one of the many scenarios Angela frequently acted out in my room—scenarios that helped her learn the social skills she was so desperately lacking, and that gave her the opportunity to express the anger and rage she so deeply experienced. There had been times that Angela would instruct, "You be Angela," while she would take the role of the mother. In those scenarios she most often handcuffed me to a chair or table leg and then acted out a variety of situations in which a mother was helpless to save the child, and equally helpless to save herself. I had been shot, stabbed, run over, and killed-by-incineration in a building engulfed by flames. So far, in Angela's role-plays, the mother had never been able to rescue her child.

Recently Angela had begun to use Wally and Molly to act out specific sexual acts. I kept detailed notes of every session and, in fact, videotaped most of Angela's sessions as I was pretty sure the time would come when they would wind up in a courtroom. To date, however, nothing Angela had acted out had been substantial enough to warrant social services taking her out of the home. They needed something more specific than her acting out sex scenes with the dolls, hurting other children, associating love with pain, and/or trying to touch other children's genitals. Social service workers in bush Alaska are spread very thin, and the process of getting assistance could be maddening as there was not a full-time caseworker living in the village. Caseworkers in the area traveled up and down the Yukon and functioned under a triage model at all times. Galena has actually always been the healthiest of the villages within the region (a region that has five times the national suicide rate and ten times the national fetal alcoholism rate), and often the social worker is out of the village more than in.

It isn't a matter of competence; it's a matter of funding. There simply are not enough caseworkers to manage the myriad of social problems that exist in this little slice of America.

Getting a caseworker to evaluate a child, much less remove them from their home, requires pretty hard-core data rather than the "reasonable cause to suspect" reports that are required of all teachers and school personnel across the country. Although I had made many phone calls regarding this little girl, no caseworker had—to that date anyway—further investigated the situation.

I was so grateful that I had a principal supportive of what I was doing, and with whom I could continually talk over the situation. Chris was the one who arranged for me to have the video equipment so that I was able to keep tapes of my sessions with Angela.

And indeed, the time did come when the tapes were subpoenaed into a court of law.

* * * * *

Sitting down at the little table, I greeted Wally and Molly pleasantly. The "four" of us made small talk for a couple of minutes (with Angela answering for Molly and me answering for Wally) before I said, "Angela, we need to talk about kissing."

"I don't want to."

"I know you don't, but we need to...because kissing just got you into trouble on the playground. Tell me why *you* think kissing got you into trouble."

"Because it's bad," she stated, figuring this was the right answer and looking down at the table.

"Well, no, Angela—kissing is not bad. Sometimes you kiss your mom, right? Right here, I bet." I pointed to my cheek, and she looked at me with her eyes wide.

"Do you think it's bad to kiss your mom?" I asked innocently, as if honestly confused by the matter.

Angela shook her head no, her eyes never leaving mine.

"Well...I think you're right...it's not bad to kiss your mom on the cheek. How about Gramma—do you ever kiss Gramma on the cheek?"

She nodded yes...her eyes still glued to my face, clearly wondering where this was going.

"And that's not bad, either," I stated gently. "We kiss all kinds of people that we care about." I turned to look at the Molly doll. "Right, Molly?" Molly nodded in agreement, and for the hundredth time I felt grateful for the construction of this doll-puppet, which allowed me to control her head and body so easily.

"What got you into trouble, Angela, is that you are a little kid, and little kids are too young to be chasing and kissing each other—especially when they have been told to stop."

"Can I go now?"

"Nope."

"How come?" she asked, the hint of a petulant whine starting.

"'Cause we still have some kissing-talk to do...so I can help you. You've already let me know that you know lots about kissing. Remember when Wally put his tongue in Molly's mouth? That let me know you know some stuff about kissing, right?"

"Uh-huh." Angela's eyes were back on my face, staring at me, looking into me as if she looked hard enough she could pull out the words she needed to tell me the rest of her story. But those words had to come from Angela, not me. And at some level she knew this. Even at the tender age of seven.

"You know, Angela...I think you've been letting me know lots of things. You help *me* understand what you know, and then that lets me help *you*. And that's what people do who care about each other, right?" With her eyes riveted to mine and her head nodding, I continued, "Yeah, we help each other figure things out. Remember what you showed me with the dolls—with their private parts? That was kind of like you telling me a story about what you know, right?" This referred to a recent session where Angela had acted out genital contact between the Wally and Molly dolls, as well as with the anatomically correct family dolls.

Again, Angela nodded yes. I looked thoughtful, my chin in my hand and a slightly confused expression on my face. I looked over at Molly, then at Angela, and then back at Molly.

"Molly...I have a question for you. Why do you think Angela hasn't told me how she learns this stuff? Do you think it's maybe because she doesn't want to get someone in trouble?"

Molly shrugged.

"Or maybe because it feels good and she's afraid I might stop it?"

Molly looked at me, then at Angela, and back at me, shrugging again.

"Do you think Angela is afraid she would be hurt if she told?" I asked Molly, looking at her intensely.

At this point, Angela abruptly rolled the chair backward across the room as far as she could go, and with it backed up against the cabinet, she answered for Molly in a very soft voice.

"Afraid of getting hurt."

"Oh, my..." I nodded, as if suddenly experiencing an epiphany. "Is Molly right, Angela? Have you been worrying about being *hurt* if you told me things?"

Big eyes with rare tears beginning to form warned me to tread softly and carefully. It is important not to put forth any words or suggestive information that might contaminate a disclosure, and I could feel that Angela was getting very, very close to using not Molly, but her own ability to communicate to tell me something important. I knew this was a very vulnerable and very fragile child at this moment.

"Can you tell me who you're afraid will hurt you?" I asked her gently.

"My dad," she said. It came out in a feathery sort of whisper.

"You're afraid if you tell about kissing and the stuff you showed me with the dolls, that your dad will hurt you?"

One tear rolled down Angela's cheek as she nodded yes. I had never seen her cry before.

"Oh, Angela...you are such a brave girl for telling me this. It must be so *hard* to be so afraid and worried all the time." I continued to comfort and praise Angela as I explained that I would be talking to my friend (social services), and that they might want to talk with her, too. It was important to assure Angela that we would make sure she was safe, and that she would not be hurt for telling me such important information.

I asked Angela if she would like to stay a little longer or go back to her classroom. "Can I put your earrings in?" she asked hesitantly. Almost shyly.

Not long ago I had removed my earrings and placed them on my desk. In our session later that day, Angela, spotting them, asked if she could put them back in my ears. Months earlier, I would not have considered allowing her an opportunity to be that close to me physically. There was no doubt that Angela, holding an earring near my face, would have felt compelled to turn it into a miniature stabbing weapon. It seemed that for Angela, the more she cared about someone and wanted them to care about her, the more she struck out, making sure to inflict pain.

But we had been working on the concept of gentle touch for quite some time, and little by little Angela had demonstrated an increasing repertoire of tender and softhearted behaviors. Angela, it seemed, was beginning to understand that love did not have to hurt.

So on this day, trusting my instinct more than for any other reason, I agreed to let Angela put my earrings back in my ears.

The look on her face when I told her she had been so gentle I had not even felt them slip through the holes was touching enough to melt the heart of a diehard cynic.

The next day, Angela came to my room and asked to try again. She had brought a newly made friend with her—something in and of itself worth celebrating—but it was the manner in which she instructed this little girl that so captivated my heart.

"Watch," Angela had said, adopting the tone of one who takes their responsibility for teaching very seriously. "It's important to always, always be *gentle*." As she carefully slipped the earrings through the holes in my ears, Angela explained patiently, "When people like each other, they be nice and don't hurt them. You can't be mean or people won't like you." When the little girl asked if she could try putting my earrings in, too, Angela answered, sighing patiently, "No, not yet. You have to practice more first."

If personal pride could inflate a seven-year-old, Angela would have resembled a mighty puffer fish at that moment.

It was, in psychobabble speak, a milestone moment.

My immediate concern, however, was that Angela could well be experiencing the intensely conflicting feelings that are frequently common to children who finally verbalize unspeakable secrets. And while milestones do occur, so does regression.

"Will you use very gentle touch, Angela?" I asked her quietly.

"I will," she said earnestly. "I will be very, very gentle."

And so, I took out my earrings and handed them to her. With the care and concentration of a surgeon operating on a baby, Angela put the earrings back through the holes in my ears.

"That, Miss Angela, was your most gentle touch ever," I said and, giving her a big hug, asked if she was ready now to go back to class.

"Yep," she said, smiling.

Angela had been in my room for nearly two hours, yet despite the intensity and enormity of what had transpired, she radiated a happiness I had not before observed in her. Slipping her hand into mine, Angela and I walked together down the hall toward the kindergarten.

A few feet before we reached the room, I felt a little tug on my hand, and Angela motioned to me with her finger. As I got down on my knee, Angela brushed the hair away from my face, and holding my chin, she turned my head so she could whisper into my ear.

"I love you," she said, barely loud enough for me to hear.

Stunned, I was on my knee looking at her when Tanya came into the hallway to ask if Angela would be rejoining them. Still feeling that place in my heart so touched by the surprise and the genuineness of Angela's words, I sent her scampering into the classroom and quietly told Tanya not to send her home when the bell rang.

Heading back toward my office, I felt both relieved and heartsick to place the call to social services. Even though I know play therapy is a viable, legitimate, and powerful tool, some part of me always hopes that maybe a child's story is made up—a make-believe version created from exposure to television or movies. Experience usually tells me when this is the case and when it is not, but either way, as an educational psychologist, it is not within the realm of my job to pursue disclosure at this point. That job is within the domain of the social services worker and the police. It is my job to work with the child in school if there is negative impact and fallout from their experiences or from the disclosure itself.

Much later that night, long after the social services people had come and gone; after the female police officer had interviewed Angela; and long after Tanya and I processed the whole day with one another, I lay in my bed and silently thanked Carl and Jim for the way they approached education. There is no doubt in my mind that, were it not for their insight and willingness to bring me to this village full-time, this little girl would have remained in an abusive setting for much longer.

Possibly for years.

Puppets, Paint, and Bad, Bad Feelings

January 2002, Galena, Alaska

"Happy New Year!"

It was Denise, my friend of thirty years, and her three children on the phone.

"Well, hey! Happy 2002 to you, too!" I said. "What are you guys up to?"

"Not much. We're all just hanging out today, and thought we'd call."

The next few minutes were spent catching up with the eleven-year-old twins, Katie and Kyle, and fourteen-year-old Ryan. Listening to each one's rendition of their Christmas haul and various school adventures and woes made me laugh, and always filled me with a special kind of happiness. Ryan had spent three weeks with me the previous summer—a trip I offered to each of my godchildren when they turned fourteen—and to my surprise and great happiness, Denise had met us for the last five days, and we all celebrated together. The twins were just counting down the time until their fourteenth birthday when they, too, could each choose a trip with "Aunt Debra."

After a few minutes, I said to them, "Okay, guys. I want to talk to your mom now." After a few more rounds of, "Oh, one more thing" and "Wait, Aunt Debra! I just need to tell you..." the kids were all off the phone, and there was the telephone quiet that exists between two not so rambunctious adults.

"And you?" I asked. "How's Buck? How are you? How's school?" Denise taught at a school for gifted elementary kids, and "teacher talk" was always a favorite between us.

"Good. School is good." There was the briefest of pauses before she added matter-of-factly, "Actually, I had a colon biopsy come back positive. I'm going to have some surgery in a few days." She said this with a casualness that I knew belied the seriousness of what she was disclosing.

"What are you telling me here, Denise?" I asked, with a sickening thud settling in my stomach. Denise had surmounted a frightening bout of cervical cancer in 1997 and had been cancer free and healthy since then.

"I have cancer."

I *hated* it when she was so nonchalant about dramatic things.

Of course, maybe I just wanted some old-fashioned hysteria to represent what my insides were experiencing with the sound of those three words.

"It's going to be fine," she assured me. "They can get it all by taking out my intestines. I won't even need chemo." This was staggering to me. She was telling me that she would wear a colostomy bag for life as if reporting on the pollen count in Des Moines.

"So, okay, when do you want me there?"

"I don't. You have to work." She was using that tone that indicated no discussion allowed. "We'll be fine. Buck will take some time off of work—we'll be okay." Buck (real name Earl) was Denise's husband of twenty-five years.

Denise was a woman of gifted intellect who could be a great deal of fun, as well as rather formidable at times. She was dynamic, self-assured, bossy, and very, very stubborn. And she was more than a little familiar with my experiences, first of my mother's cancer and subsequent death, and much more recently, my father's. She knew the *C word* had the potential to evoke monster-sized reactions in me, and she wanted to keep things calm...even-keeled...*not* dramatic.

I understood this. A thirty-year friendship gives one plenty of time to learn how someone handles big and little crises, but for once I barreled over Denise's veneer of control and apparent imperturbability. By the time the conversation was over, we had agreed that I would talk to Carl, Chris, and Jim, and request a leave in order to be in Colorado when she came home from surgery.

* * * * *

While Denise underwent colostomy surgery, I was trying to organize things at school so that I could be gone for several weeks. My three administrators, always supportive, had unquestioningly granted my leave, but there was much to be done to make sure things continued to run smoothly in my absence. The kids were in the habit of checking in with me every day, often many times a day; and by this time, I had co-teaching lesson plans going on in several classrooms.

Leaving for a month would be difficult. I felt so strongly committed to Galena, and I had tremendous loyalty toward Carl and Jim, but this did not involve a conflict of priorities for me. Denise, Buck, and the kids were not just friends—they were my family. Self-selected perhaps, but family nonetheless.

A knock at the door interrupted my thoughts. Opening it, I saw Charlie, another of the kindergarteners that I worked with intensely, both in the classroom and in the therapy room. It was not his scheduled time.

"Mrs. Korta told me to come here," he said, brown eyes drooping and his usual dimples barely evident in a face that looked more than a little sad.

"Well, Charlie," I said, getting down on my knee in my eye to eye position, "what did Mrs. Korta want you to come in here and do?"

Shrugging, Charlie walked into my room.

"Tough day?" I asked as I watched him wandering around the room, gathering up a variety of painting supplies. This alone answered my question. Charlie wanted to interact with the paints only when things were very bad or he was very, very angry.

Recently Charlie had been moved to a foster home, and while this had helped stabilize his behavior a great deal, like many children in abusive homes, he wanted to be with his parents. Prior to the foster home, he had been living with his father—his mother having abandoned them both in order to pursue her drug habit full-time. But Charlie's dad was a drinker, and his alcoholic binges resulted in neglect and abuses that made it impossible for this little five-year-old to successfully function in or out of school. We could always tell when Charlie's dad was on a bender—his classroom etiquette reverted to a combination of foul words and quick fists. Charlie knew more words for male genitalia than I did, and he chose to use them in some startling (and remarkably creative) combinations.

The earnestness with which Charlie was gathering up the needed supplies spoke volumes. I helped him spread out the plastic cloth that was critically needed when he engaged in painting. It was as if all the chaos in this little boy's life and heart went into what could only be seen through someone else's eyes as a catastrophic mess. Fortunately, we didn't have visitors during these sessions.

Charlie began by dumping half of the pint-sized bottle of red acrylic paint in the center of the tarp, followed by the same using the black paint. Then the blue, more red, and more black followed. In went a handful of play dough, which he ground down into the wet paint, creating a mound that looked like a child's post-Halloween gastric overload reaction. More black paint on top of that, and then in went the Kleenex, the lids, and the empty paint containers— all thrown in as if the frustrations of the world were being collected and dumped into a contained hazard zone. Except for the sound of his breathing, there was silence in our little room.

Suddenly, Charlie stopped his cathartic dumping and walked over to the puppets, telling them that he was really, really mad at his dad; and telling them that his dad *never* visits. Because it was a Monday and visitation would have occurred on Sunday, I was guessing that Charlie's dad had not shown up. Again.

Puppet Bob, who knows *everything* and is a favorite of all kindergarteners, went on my hand in a hurry. Bob is a multicolored, long-haired, and wild-looking monkey, with wire-rim glasses perched on his nose and long arms that wrap around the waist of the person doing the speaking for him.

"Well, I bet your dad loves you even if he doesn't visit," Bob said encouragingly.

"Uh uh," Charlie said emphatically.

"Well...mayyyyybe..." Bob used a tone Charlie was familiar with and which usually caused him to listen intently, "...mayyybe Charlie's dad doesn't visit because he worries about not being a good daddy, and he is working on how to be a better one." There had been some talk in the village that Charlie's dad might enter a rehabilitation program.

"Uh uh. He doesn't visit because he doesn't *want* to," Charlie said with the wisdom and insight of a little boy whose heart had been crushed far too many times. He went over and put the large toucan puppet on his hand, squaring off and facing Bob.

"Well, what do *you* think?" Bob asked Toucan. "Do *you* think Charlie's dad just doesn't know how to be a good dad right now?"

"No!" Toucan shouted with clarity. "HE KNOWS HOW."

"Hmmmm...well," Bob said thoughtfully, "then I am not sure WHY Charlie's dad doesn't visit, but I know Charlie feels really, really bad inside about this. *Man*...it's a crummy feeling when dads don't visit." Bob paused before continuing. "One thing I know for sure, though—Charlie's dad and mom both love him very much...even though they don't act like it a lot of the time. Should we tell Charlie that?" Bob directed the last part to Toucan.

"I heard you guys," Charlie said pragmatically, looking at Bob. "You don't have to tell me." Gathering the puppets and putting them back in their usual spots on the shelf, Charlie went back to the floor and added more paint to the four-by-three-foot conglomeration that was oozing emotional angst.

Miraculously Bob popped back up on my hand after a few minutes and in his monkey sort of way said, "Know what *I* think? I think this floor is just like Charlie's insides! Just a big bunch of baaaad and messy feelings!"

Charlie looked at Bob—this crazy orange and pink monkey. I nodded in agreement. Turning to Charlie and handing him a stack of recycled paper scraps, I said, "Here, Charlie, you take this pile of paper and rip 'em up! Just rip 'em up and throw them into the pile. Every one of those pieces is a bad, bad feeling that you are just going to throw away!"

With each piece thrown, Charlie shouted: "THAT IS A BAD FEELING" and "THIS IS A BAD, BAD, BAD FEELING!" The amount of paper he used was somewhat staggering.

When I thought Charlie had sufficiently gotten out his rage and his hurt, we said a little mantra indicating that the bad feelings were all out and he didn't have to hold them inside anymore...so now there was room inside for gentle and happier feelings.

Then we rolled up all the bad feelings into a huge ball and ceremoniously dumped them into the garbage can.

"Whew!" Charlie said, breaking into a smile and revealing deep dimples on each side of his face. "I was in here a long time today!"

Charlie had spent ninety minutes in my room, and while he was certainly ready to return to his classroom, no longer a risk for hurting others or acting out in a loud and disruptive manner, I couldn't help but wonder what would transpire during the month I would be gone.

Sisters of the Heart
March 2002

Looking out the window of the airplane, it was hard to believe I was making a second trip out of Alaska in less than three months. I had spent a month with Denise following her surgery, and while flying home, it seemed clear to me that my time in Alaska was nearing its end. I never thought I would leave this state that I loved so much, but here I was, flying to Salt Lake City in the middle of March, having taken another week off work. Joyce, my friend of more than twenty years, was going to meet me at the airport. I had an interview with the San Juan School District in Blanding, Utah, the day after tomorrow.

Blanding. What a name for a town. I mean, towns' names reflect their character. Evergreen, Colorado. Blue Lake, California. Cottonwood, Idaho. Mountain View, Hawaii. Sunsweet, Georgia.

Blanding, Utah?

I did not think the name itself was a terribly encouraging endorsement of the area.

When I returned to Galena from Colorado at the end of January, I conducted an online search for available jobs within a day's drive of Colorado Springs—somewhere that was not all concrete and exhaust fumes, but would still allow me to be close to Denise and her family. My first search brought me to the San Juan School District, a rural district unfurled over an eight thousand square mile area, and made up of thirteen schools—many that reside on or near Navajo Nation land. In many ways, this area struck me as similar to Alaska, with its abundance of open space, ready access to outdoor adventuring, and influence of Native Americans. I knew if I was ever going to leave Alaska, it would be to a place like this.

I did hope Blanding's name represented something other than its dominant characteristic.

I stared mindlessly out the airplane window and into the empty space. Space that was quickly filled with images and emotions spanning eighteen years of living in a wild and fascinating place.

What was it about this woman that would—that could—make me contemplate uprooting my life...have me flying to the middle of some desert to check out living in a town of 2,000 staunch Mormons when I am happily living in a state and enmeshed in a life that brings me tremendous joy?

This question swirled in my head even as a certainty that it was time to leave was settling in my heart.

Denise was a woman with a titanic presence—that was for sure. She had this air about her, this bossiness that I both loved and hated. I loved her take-charge, I-am-in-control confidence, and I envied her apparent comfort with herself no matter what stage of life (or weight) she found herself.

Yet, there were limits on what Denise and I would discuss with one another. We never discussed politics, and most of the time I tried to avoid discussing religion, although Denise made equal effort for us to have these discussions. Once we were both married, we rarely—if ever—discussed sex (although when we were in college that was a subject tackled with great gusto). What kept Denise and me tethered seemed to be some sort of internal checks and balance system that our friendship brought to each of us. We seemed to borrow one another's traits at times, or at least gain some sort of vicarious comfort from their existence in the other's life. While I valued—and frequently envied—Denise's make-lemonade-out-of-lemons (and smile while you do it) approach to life, and her apparent management of a family and a career without any sort of ongoing drama, Denise envied my willingness and my ability to wear my heart on my sleeve and my thoughts tattooed across my forehead. Denise loved the fact that I didn't have to vie for control—that somehow I got around the need to always appear stoic and in charge—yet still came across as a strong and competent woman.

I think Denise and I had always wanted to become a little bit more of what the other one was—to share our traits and lend more balance to our own lives. Denise was a very pragmatic balance to my sometimes self-flagellating Sarah Bernhardt; and I was the wandering explorer to the stay-put mother and married woman that she had become.

Perhaps all of this had something to do with what was leading me away from Alaska after all this time—wanting more balance as I settled into some modicum of middle age. Wanting to be less dynamic on some levels, more on others. Wanting less drama. Less stress. Less constant change.

And then, too, there was the fact that, no longer married and with several very stressful personal years (and more than one marriage) behind me, I was not interested in watching people struggle with cancer from a distance. I had done that. Denise had watched me do that with both my parents, and she knew the toll it had taken. She would never be comfortable with the idea that I would disrupt my life to participate in life's trials with her; and frankly, I wasn't sure I had it in me to go through that a third time.

When I was in my mid-twenties and living in Idaho, my mother succumbed to cancer after a battle that left her—at the age of fifty—weak and uninterested in taking on any more challenges. She had battled the disease since my early college days, and she was rightfully weary. Toward the end of her life, I was flying back and forth between Idaho and Ohio every month—a challenging experience for a twenty-five-year-old trying to stay on top of things at work, remain in a troubled marriage, and let go of a dying mother. Neither my mother nor my marriage survived.

My father, much more recently, had engaged in his own battle with cancer. During the last three years of his life, more times than I cared to remember, I had flown back and forth between Alaska and Colorado, where he moved after my mother died. Coping with the chaos that accompanied my attempts to keep my personal life, yet another struggling marriage, and my teaching and consulting life in any kind of order while flying back and forth was unimaginably taxing. It was an inordinately stressful time, and one that I didn't want to repeat.

Toward the end of my father's siege, I took Teek, who was then about eight months old, and we drove down from Alaska to live with my father in the twelve-by-fourteen-foot hospice room that was his home for the remaining four months of his life. Instead of struggling with the competing forces of two separate lives, I declared a physical and emotional priority: my dad and his journey. Everything except what was transpiring in the room where I, Teek, and my dad lived, laughed, and cried was put into a way-station to be dealt with later.

My father was a fascinating man in many, many ways and a frustrating one in more ways than that. With his round belly, white hair, and, at times, snowy white beard, he looked like a Semitic Santa Claus. For as long as I could remember, my father had smiling, loving eyes that crinkled in their corners. I loved my father's eyes, and to this day I am a sucker for a man with crinkles in the corners of his eyes.

My father was at once both a simple, gentle man, and a man who far too often was a challenging force to contend with for those who loved him. Although he possessed remarkable innate intelligence, along with a degree from the prestigious University of Oxford, England, a lifetime of insecurities, personal frustrations, and professional failures had saddled my dad with enough baggage to weigh down whatever sleigh might be sent for his last ride.

It was during the last four months of my father's life—a time when no one pushed him to live up to anything or to be anything other than a dying person—that he seemed to reconcile things within himself and live in the present in a way I had rarely known him to do. With no one expecting him to get dressed, to get better, or to be anything other than what he was at that moment, for the first time in my life, I saw my father blossom.

The opportunity to have experienced this was an extraordinary gift, and the lessons absorbed during those summer months were both profound and peripheral. None, however, was as powerful as what I learned about the importance of accompanying someone you love, as far as they will allow, on that parting of the ways voyage.

I didn't know what road this newest bout of cancer was going to put Denise on, but I knew that if I wanted to be the sister-of-the-heart we had always claimed ourselves to be, then I needed to be closer than the four thousand miles that currently separated us.

Sisters of the heart. That's what we called ourselves. Toni Morrison got it right when she referred to sisters as being someone very much ourselves, and very much not ourselves—a special kind of double. In ways, this so perfectly described our connection. Certainly what existed was unique in order to have kept Denise and I tethered for thirty years, because there was no question but that we were, and always had been, one unlikely duo.

* * * * *

Fall Semester 1973, Bowling Green, Ohio

"You look like a star child."

I stared at the blond girl with the indigo-colored eyes who was standing inches in front of me. I didn't think this was what the instructor had in mind when he set up this little icebreaker game. It sure wasn't what I had in mind, anyway. I was thinking more along the lines of, "Hi, my name is…"

"Well," she said, apparently noting my lack of response, or more likely, my perplexed expression, "the professor said when the lights go on we're supposed to say the first thing that pops into our mind. So! There you have it: you look like a star child." Smiling with enthusiasm, she said all this as if in command of tremendous insight into such profound things as star children.

"What's a star child?" I asked.

"I don't know." She shrugged. "But you definitely look like one."

I was contemplating the possibility that I had developed some sort of weird ball of plasma emanating from my head, when she added, "My name is Denise. I'm a sophomore."

Denise Kruse from Parma, Ohio. It was 1973. And except for both of us having been raised in Ohio and being sophomores in college, we were just about as different as two people could be.

Soft and silky, long blond hair tumbled toward Denise's shoulders in a way that I would have sold my favorite uncle for if I thought that somehow I could impersonate it. I, on the other hand, was saddled with an unruly mop of waves and curls that only posed for hair and defied even my best Dippity-do and extra-large juice can attempts to get it to smooth out and behave. In those days of post-lacquered beehives and pre-Farrah Fawcett curls and bounce, hair like mine was a humiliation. Hair like Denise's was to be coveted.

When I first met her, Denise was enrolled in R.O.T.C. and confidently headed toward a career in the Air Force. She was a staunch Republican who had been raised in a conservative and strict Catholic home. I was a tree-hugging Democrat who wore black anti-war armbands in high school (never mind that I didn't really understand much about Vietnam); and I had been raised by liberal parents who considered their religion in terms of cultural issues as compared to issues of God, Satan, and matters of redemption.

She was an extrovert who could—and would—talk to anyone and everyone.

I lived alone in an off-campus house and wrote bad poetry and worse songs. I was an introvert in an extroverted kind of way, while Denise was an extrovert in every sort of way.

One thing Denise and I did have in common was having grown up with brothers and never getting that experience of having other girls in the house besides our mothers. Suddenly, we were privy to that magical camaraderie we had both observed in friends who had sisters, to that special kind of double. It was like being gifted an insta-sister.

We became inseparable.

Shortly after we met in class that night, we found a funky old house near campus and moved in—spending our remaining college years together. I graduated before Denise, as I had put myself on an academic fast track by taking a ridiculous number of classes each quarter. When I graduated, I moved to Colorado—having discovered by that time that living in the West was a far better match for my spirit than I had ever found in the Midwest.

Denise graduated the following year and was sent by Uncle Sam to continue her education as one of the first two women in the Air Force to become trained as a top secret missile control officer. To our absolute delight, she was stationed at NORAD Mountain in Colorado, and our unlikely, but heartfelt connection continued.

A decade later found Denise still in Colorado, and while she was no longer an active member of the Air Force, and no longer Catholic, she still had her long, silky hair. She had replaced the Pope with Rush Limbaugh and Ted Haggart's New Life Pentecostal Church, and while she was immersing herself in the world of believers who spoke in tongues, I submerged myself in the lives of Eskimos who lived in remote villages scattered along the Bering Sea. Certainly, the Eskimos I was living among spoke a language vastly different from anything I had previously known; however, Denise's Pentecostal experiences and my foray into the Yupik world shared little in common.

Still, our unlikely pairing continued, and twenty more years of frequent phone conversations and yearly visits kept us tethered. Nearly three decades after our first meeting, Denise and I still shared an inexplicable bond.

Despite this, it was surprising to people I knew that I would even contemplate leaving Alaska to move closer to her as she battled this illness. In many ways it was surprising to me as well, although a Baggie in my freezer with her name and phone number helped explain my willingness to move four thousand miles away from a life I loved.

We had been talking on the phone one Sunday afternoon in the year 2000, not long after my father died. I had experienced two miscarriages over the last twelve months, and at the time, I was in the process of a divorce and living alone.

In a self-pitying moment of despair, I said, "You know what, Denise? I'm going to end up with tags on my toes one day."

"Tags on your toes?" she repeated, not quite sure how this related to whatever we had been saying.

"Yeah. You know...like, if I die, I probably won't even be discovered for a week or something. No one will even know I'm dead until the neighbors call in about the smell, and then the police will break in and find Teek lying over my dead body and no other apparently concerned family members around... So they'll just tag my toes and dump me, unclaimed, into some pauper's grave," I finished up dramatically.

"Oh, go get a freezer Baggie, a Magic Marker, a pen, and some paper," Denise said, laughing.

"What?" This seemed cruelly unrelated to the heartbreaking angst I had just exposed.

"Just do it! Go get a Baggie, marker, pen, and paper, and come back to the phone. And make sure it's a freezer Baggie," she added.

Never one to ignore her commands, I retrieved the items, saying, "Okay, Ms. Teacher. I have them. What do I do now?"

"You have to write in marker on the outside of the Baggie in really big, bold letters: IN THE EVENT OF MY DEATH, PLEASE OPEN THIS AND FOLLOW THE INSTRUCTIONS INSIDE!"

"Why?" I asked. "I mean, why would I put that in my freezer, along with outdated leftovers and smelly ice?"

"Because the church ladies always clean out freezers first, and they'll find it. And inside the Baggie you need to put my name and phone number with clear instructions to call me immediately."

"I don't know any church ladies, Denise. I don't go to church." I figured there would be no way church ladies would ever hear of my demise, much less the need for a clean-up operation.

"It doesn't matter," she said pragmatically. "They always find their way into dead people's homes where there isn't any family to clean out the house and take care of things. And they *always* clean out the freezer first. Trust me. They do."

Denise was a very devout, churchgoing woman—certainly she knew more about such things than I did.

"So, what else do I put in the Baggie?"

"Well, you have to make sure to say what should happen to Teek. And put in any important papers that might be needed, like a copy of your will. Then," she continued, "as soon as we get off the phone, you need to sit down and email me or send me instructions about what you want done with your email account, what friends you want me to contact, where your important papers are—stuff like that. I'll make sure that all of your wishes are honored—you know, like if you want to be buried, cremated, scattered in the mountains...all of it." Denise paused before adding, "And, Debra...if you want to be buried, you can always go where I'm going." I knew she'd added this because of a discussion we'd had a week or two earlier about the fact that I really wasn't close enough with my biological family to have been included in their end-of-life plans.

I felt like I lost my orphan status that day, and as much as we laughed about that conversation later, every now and then she would check with me—always asking me quite seriously if the Baggie was still in my freezer.

And I always—with a palpable sort of loving and devoted feeling in my heart—assured Denise that, indeed, the frozen Baggie with her name and phone number was still there, sitting comfortably on top of the 1986 leftover spaghetti.

So, maybe leaving Alaska had something to do with wanting to feel as if I was heading into that middle-aged vortex with some sort of intact family unit in place. While my family unit might indeed be an appointed one, what better reason could there be for making a life-impacting change than a sister of the heart—one who would make sure you have a Baggie in your freezer so that your toes never get tagged.

Whatever the pull, it was clear I was acting on it because within less than forty-eight hours I would be interviewing for a job that, if offered, I was pretty sure I would accept.

Of course...it never occurred to either one of us that I might not be the one to die first.

A young Denise in her Air Force days, late 70s

Power Suits and Bungee Cords
March 2002

Joyce met me at the plane, and I smiled as I saw this woman who, though so different from Denise, had so similarly impacted my life. Where an invisible filament that kept us tethered attached Denise and me, Joyce and I were bound by a thick bungee developed throughout years of thinking alike, feeling alike, and taking turns holding each other up during our real and imagined crises. Over the years, Joyce and I had explored a continent's worth of new emotional territory in our lives; and our cord had been strengthened by the many times we had found ourselves struggling both philosophically and emotionally as we pushed and questioned ourselves relentlessly.

Although very different from one another, each of these women played an enormous role in my life, and I loved them both with my complete and total heart.

"Heyyyyyy-heyyyyyyy," laughed Joyce as she hugged me. "Welcome to Salt Lake City and the land of the *Big M* problem." After a brief pause she added, "You sure you know what you're doing?"

"Do I *ever* know what I am doing?" I shrugged, only half-joking. "I figure I'll interview for this job and see what Blanding's like, and then decide." As an afterthought I added, "I mean, if I do move there, well, you guys have survived all this time as non-Mormons in the province of the LDS[4] majority, right?"

"It hasn't been easy."

Joyce and her husband and children had moved to Utah twelve years earlier, and I spent a portion of every summer with them. I was well aware of the struggles they—and Joyce in particular—had experienced trying to fit within a Mormon community. And I certainly knew how hard it had been on the kids to be in schools where they were a small minority of individuals who did not attend church—the LDS church in particular. The fact that every public high school in Utah is connected to an LDS seminary provoked many conversations in their home over the years.

"Yeah, I know, it's weird that I'm interviewing for this job...and yet, I don't know...it just feels like I need to check it out. I mean, just to live in the same state with you again would be worth it." Joyce and I had lived in the upper and lower parts of a house in Idaho when we were both young and married. I thought about that for a minute before tacking on, "Well...maybe worth it."

Laughing and grabbing my luggage as we headed toward the car, Joyce asked, "So, do you know what you're going to wear?"

---

[4] The Church of Jesus Christ of Latter-Day Saints.

"Oh, yeah!" I smiled. "I get to wear my five-hundred-dollar *power* suit."

"Your *what*?" Joyce asked. While five hundred dollars might not be much for many women to pay for a business suit, Joyce and I were notorious for buying a significant portion of our wardrobes at thrift stores. Five hundred dollars was something one put toward a mortgage payment, not an item of clothing.

"I never told you the story of my suit?"

As Joyce shook her head, I said, "Oh, Joyce, let me tell you—*this* is a story. Suffice it to say, I never *intended* to buy a five-hundred-dollar suit!"

"Well, what happened?"

"It's too long to get into, but I'll tell you this much... Do you remember the crazy mother I would tell you about on the phone? The one who wanted me to take a paragraph out of the psychological report I had written on her daughter?"

"Sort of," Joyce responded with a sheepish kind of honesty. We often forgot things that we had confided to one another and lamented over. It was one of the nicest parts of our friendship that we never held it against each other that we might not have been listening with full and rapt attention.

"Well, this mother—this crazy, crazy mother—wanted me to delete a paragraph from my psych write-up on her daughter. That might not be a big deal most of time, but in this case it was, because taking out the paragraph really altered some important information—information that another school would need to know in order to help her.

"Anyway, long story short, the mom complained, and when Jim and Carl stated that I was the professional and they would stand behind my decision, she took it to the next level—to something similar to a due process hearing level."

"You are *kidding* me," Joyce said. Although she had chosen to be a stay-at-home mom, Joyce had once been a teacher and was very familiar with the implications of a parent pushing a district toward any sort of legal action.

"No. No, I'm not. It was a nightmare. Anyway, by the time it was all over, the district had spent *eighteen thousand dollars*. If you don't consider the money aspect of it, we did win. I mean, the ruling upheld that the paragraph needed to stay in the report."

"When did all this *happen*?"

"Oh, it's been awhile now—but it dragged on for some time. The thing about it that's so amazing is how supportive Jim and Carl were, Joyce. I mean, I took an *ethical* stand, and it cost them a *lot* of money. They very easily could have just told me to back down and take the damn paragraph out of the report. But they didn't. Jim told me he trusted my professionalism and agreed with me that to alter the report in the way the parent wanted would change the perception of this girl's needs. He said he wouldn't be held hostage to parents threatening suit, and would stand behind whatever decision I made."

"You are so good in your job," Joyce said, with a real earnestness that I always appreciated.

"No. No, I'm not, Joyce. I'm just really passionate about it. And bull-headed."

"You're good at it, too."

"Yeah, well, it's a lot easier to be good at it working for people like Jim and Carl. I don't know what I would have done if they had demanded that I take the paragraph out of the report. I don't think ethically I could have done that."

We had reached the house by this time, and Joyce parked the car. Just as she started to open the door, she turned to me and said, "So...what does all that have to do with the five-hundred-dollar suit, anyway?"

"Oh, jeez." I laughed. "Well, Jim and the attorney had spent four hours with me in Anchorage the Sunday before the hearing—prepping me and making sure I wouldn't fold or lose my temper or something. Before that, I hadn't even thought about what to wear. The attorney had asked, and I just said, 'Oh, something, you know, something that's okay.' But after four hours of mock badgering, when I left I thought, *Hoh boy. I need something new to wear. Something that I feel really, really confident in.* So, I went to Nordstrom, which was around the corner. It was twenty minutes before closing on a Sunday night, and the hearing was at eight o'clock the next morning. I grabbed a bunch of suits that looked like they would fit and raced into the dressing room to try them on. I found a simple pantsuit that was perfect, except the pants were too long, and the saleswoman told me her friend upstairs in alterations could fix that in five minutes. So, I looked at the price tag and saw it was two hundred and fifty dollars. I nearly died, but it was six o'clock and they were closing, so I said I would take it."

"I thought you said it was five hundred."

"Yeah, well, when the clerk rang it up, I discovered that the two-hundred-and-fifty-dollar tag was the price for just the pants, which were already in the process of being altered. I was too embarrassed to tell her I couldn't possibly pay that much for an outfit."

"Oh, my God," Joyce said, with full understanding of the significance of my having spent five hundred dollars on something I would probably never wear again.

"Yeah. So. *That's* what I'm wearing to the interview."

"Can't wait to see it."

"I don't even *like* it that much." I laughed as we went inside. "It's not even that cute. And it cost almost as much as the rent for my Galena cabin."

* * * * *

I'd never really interviewed for a job before. Not in the way most people have, anyway. I'd been remarkably fortunate in that for the last eighteen years I had simply been recruited—or taken along, as when Mary Rubadeau took me with her from the Bering Strait School District to the Kenai District. Prior to that, it seemed like somehow I managed to be in the right place at the right time for interesting, challenging jobs to drop in my lap. It's as if I have always had a guardian angel watching over me, whose sole responsibility has been to ensure that I felt like I was residing in some kind of professional heaven.

But now I was going to have to face walking into an *interview* situation—

one of those real live grown-up kinds of things where I am outnumbered at a big table, and people ask me questions that they (whether they admit it or not) definitely have a mind-set about how they want answered.

I was pretty sure that saying what people wanted to hear for the sake of approval was not a strong suit of mine.

What if I totally blew this interview? My real fear was that I had been in bush Alaska so long that I would come across as backwards and out of touch with the rest of the world; that—despite the fact that I was a voracious consumer of the current research, and took ongoing classes all the time to upgrade my skills—somehow I was still far, far behind the rest of the world in public education.

Time was going to show me just how little I knew about current practices in public education outside of Alaska, and would, in fact, confirm that Carl and Mary had set me on a path far, far ahead of the mainstream in terms of experiences and practice. At the time of the interview, however, that particular scenario never entered my mind, and I could only worry that a committee of people was going to feed me questions and find me sorely lacking.

And that made me feel very nervous.

At the time, I decided I was just going to have to settle for the fact that I was as prepared and able as I was capable of being. I loved what I did. I did it well. And I had been publically awarded for my commitment and hard work. I had never been in any kind of trouble, and administrators had always sought me out for counsel and seemed pleased by my involvement with their schools. *These things and a power suit*, I told myself, *will just have to provide me with the confidence I need when I arrive in that interview room.*

Or at least make me look good while I fake it.

Joyce and I drove from Salt Lake City to Blanding, a six-hour drive that took us through the mountains and the canyon lands. I was sold long before we ever pulled into Blanding.

While certainly not a town that wows you with its beauty upon first glance, Blanding does offer a fascinating multicultural history that includes a rich legacy left by the Anasazi Indians: an uncountable number of ruins that suggest their occupation in the area dates back as early as 600 AD. Navajo, Ute, and European influence are also evident in and around the town, which was settled by the Mormons in the late 1890s when Albert and Walter Lyman explored the area after receiving a revelation that one day an LDS temple would tower among the sagebrush and wheat fields.

The Temple did get built, although not until a hundred years later, and in nearby Monticello, not Blanding.

Reading the travel brochures and taking little side trips as Joyce and I made our way from Salt Lake City had me nearly jumping out of my skin at the discovery of so many national parks and opportunities to ski, raft, kayak, and hike within close proximity of Blanding. Not that anything could ever replace Alaska, but there was no denying that this little town of about three thousand provided the door to a climate, road system, and veritable playground of activities that had simply not been available to me there.

Joyce and I drove into Blanding to scout out where my interview was going to be held the next morning. After that we figured we would be free to play for the rest of the day, and it was clear that we had numerous recreational opportunities to choose from.

Blanding, like all Utah towns, is laid out in a square grid, with the streets identified both by number and direction (such as 200 north, 400 west; or 325 south, 100 east), and finding our destination proved remarkably easy. The school district's administration building turned out to be located at the T of the road we drove into town on, and we didn't even have to look for it. It just appeared in front of us, before we even had to stop and ask for directions.

I took that as a good sign. I am a very directionally-challenged individual.

"Joyce, this is incredible. Look at our little map here—we can go right up this road and in less than one mile be in the mountains. I had no idea Blanding was at an elevation of six thousand feet." I was pointing to the mountain in front of us, and the map on the seat between us.

"Look at this," Joyce said as her finger began to trace a route from Blanding to Hovenweep—a place that, according to our brochures, is *"noted for its solitude and undeveloped, natural character—a group of six well-preserved village ruins over a twenty-mile radius of mesa tops and canyons, that dates back as many as ten thousand years."*

"We could go this way and be in Hovenweep in about half an hour, and if we want, we could just loop around and end up in Cortez for dinner," Joyce continued, nearly as excited as I was.

"Oh, my gosh, Joyce—I want to go to Mesa Verde! Look at this, it's right outside of Cortez. Remember we went there with the boys when they were little?" I was referring to a wonderful road trip Joyce and her two sons and I had taken many years earlier.

As an afterthought, I asked, "Joyce, wait, how can Mesa Verde be this close to Blanding? I'm confused." It suddenly seemed as if I had lost my bearings entirely, combining new with the familiar, but with no real point of reference to orient me.

Joyce laughed, saying, "That's why I'm driving. Just tell me where you want to go, and we'll go there. Wherever you want."

"Okay, let's go to Hovenweep. I really want to see those Puebloan ruins." We were still parked in front of the administration building, and with this, Joyce started the car and glanced at the map.

"No. No, wait! Wait, I want to go here. Look, look at this: *Newspaper Rock*. It says it's a petroglyph panel etched into sandstone, and it looks like a newspaper. I want to go there! I bet we can climb the rock and read two thousand years worth of Anasazi news!" I was beginning to sound giddy.

"Okay," Joyce said agreeably as she put the car in drive.

I could feel my heart rate upping as I continued to look at the little tourist brochure that had Blanding in the middle of a big circle, and a multitude of tourist locations circling around it.

"No, no. Hold on a sec... Newspaper Rock is to the northwest...maybe we could go in that direction AFTER the interview... Today I think you're right, we should go east. We could go southeast to Hovenweep and then keep heading east and hit Cortez," I stated, still pointing on the map.

Joyce looked at me.

"Yeah. Do that. That's good. I can settle down, I swear. We'll go to Hovenweep."

"You're sure?"

"Sure. Yep. Very sure. I swear."

Joyce was smiling.

"I can't help it," I said. "I mean, there's only the twelve-mile road to the *dump* in Galena. I'm getting a little overstimulated, I think." I was laughing, but in a hyperactive sort of way, as if I'd been left alone in a candy shop for four or five hours. *"Joyce!"* I said quite suddenly, as a major lightbulb went off in my head.

"What?" she said, reflexively slamming on the brakes.

"You think there might be a *Wal-Mart* in Cortez? Holy smokes. What if I could drive to a Wal-Mart in, like, less than two hours?! I'll bet there's thrift stores there, too. I mean it says here, it's a town of eight thousand people!" To me that sounded *huge*.

"Deb-ra!"

"Okay, sorry. I'm just so excited. It's just a little Outside-Of-Alaska-Overstimulation Syndrome," I added. "It's a well-known, but temporary psychiatric state that occurs in longtime residents," I explained in my best psychologist voice.

"Well, you about gave me a heart attack. I thought there was a deer or something in the road." Joyce said this with something like irritation in her voice, but I could tell, really, she was amused. At least I hoped she was amused. She was still smiling, anyway.

"Deer!" I said. "Joyce, there probably *are* deer all around here. Oh, my gosh. I could live in a town that is *spitting* distance from the canyon lands, has roads to bike on everywhere, is within driving distance to a Wal-Mart—well *maybe* on that one—and where probably there's more wildlife than people."

Joyce kept her eye on the road, rather than pointing out the obvious, which was that I had perhaps been leading a very sheltered life.

"I'll get this all out of my system today," I assured her. "Tomorrow I will enter that room in my five-hundred-dollar power suit just as calm and controlled as the Dalai Lama."

"Well, for your sake, I hope so," Joyce said, looking at me with that crooked half smile of hers.

"It's a good thing you're the one with me," I said. "I would hate to expose this side of myself to just anyone."

The Interview

I could not get over how warm the morning felt. Joyce and I had risen early to take a walk before my interview. In Galena, in mid-March, temperatures were still hovering in the mid-twenties during the day and at or below zero at night. What had felt like temperate spring days just forty-eight hours earlier, suddenly seemed less like something to brag about as Joyce and I walked in the early morning hour dressed in jeans and T-shirts. I always came to Utah to visit Joyce in the summers, but it had been a very long time since I had experienced springtime outside of Alaska. Seeing this much green in March, well, it just had an electrifying effect upon me.

Walking into the interview, I was greeted enthusiastically by Tony Done, the director of special education. He introduced the other two committee members: both women—one a special education teacher, the other Tony's assistant. Both seemed to be personable and nice. I was still very nervous—a feeling that intensified when they sat me at the head of a long conference table.

I am a percher. I mean, my most comfortable and relaxed position is to squat on a chair my feet on the seat, my arms over my bent knees, and my butt about four inches off the seat. Jim Foster used to tease me about never sitting down like a normal person.

But here I was sitting at the head of the table in a power suit with both feet flat on the floor, and it was making my armpits begin to sweat.

"Welcome to Blanding," Tony began with a smile. I noticed that the portfolio I had sent through the mail was sitting on the table. "How was your flight and drive in?"

"Oh, good. It was all great. It's *beautiful* around here." Silently I reminded myself not to give in to my nervous tendencies toward babbling. I was hoping I didn't have anything like rice cakes sprinkled on my jacket. I am notorious for my rice cake eating habits, and like with Hansel and Gretel, the crumbs can often be used to track me down. I had been too nervous to want much breakfast, and I had eaten some rice cakes on the drive over.

Tony went on to explain the process of the interview, which would involve each of them asking me a set of questions and giving me time to respond. At the end, there would be time allowed for any questions I wanted to ask of them.

Each question they posed increased my enthusiasm and excitement. These people were talking *my language*! They were asking me about working with disturbed children; about my experience with assessment tools for culturally and linguistically diverse populations; about my background and experience with Native Americans. Each question they presented led me to forget about being interviewed, and allowed me to get going on my favorite subjects: kids, education, strategies, therapy, and intervention.

I was having fun, and even my armpits had started calming down.

Toward the end of the interview, Tony asked if I had any questions. Not being a person of tremendous subtlety, I said, "Well, the only thing I really was wondering about was the Mormon piece. I mean, I'm not LDS, and I wondered if you felt this would be a problem for families or teachers here."

There was a moment of silence in the room, and I thought that perhaps I had just committed a major faux pas. The three interviewers exchanged darting glances, and then Tony offered, "No, I don't think that will be a problem at all. There are people here who aren't LDS."

"Oh, okay. I just...you know...thought I should bring that out into the open. The fact that I'm not Mormon, I mean."

Tony half hid his smile and assured me that it would be just fine.

He began to tell me things about the area—how rural it was, and some of the challenges the district had in serving the diverse and vastly spread out schools. It had been ten years since a full-time psychologist had served the district, and the needs were great. He mentioned the difficulties they had in recruiting competent teachers and support personnel, explaining that highly qualified people were far more enticed by the cities and mainstream interests offered in the northern end of the state.

I assured Tony that the rural location of the San Juan School District did not deter me one bit. In fact, I preferred it.

"I don't think there's anything you can tell me that's going to scare me off," I said. "I mean, you can *drive* to a Wal-Mart from here!" Indeed, Joyce and I had discovered one in Cortez the day before. The two women glanced at each other as I continued, "I understand remote districts and their needs, and I'm not just saying that to get the job. I mean, San Juan is spread out—I can see that—but you are spread out over eight thousand square miles, and some of my districts have been spread out over *eighty thousand* square miles. Where I live now, if I want to go to a Wal-Mart, I have to *fly* there." I thought about this for a second. "Jeez," I practically crowed, "you guys have a *movie theater* in this town."

"Well, it's heated by coal," Tony threw in, as if to temper my expectations.

"It's a movie theater!" I reiterated with excitement.

A get-your-popcorn-and-candy, sit-down movie theater!

By the time I left the interview that morning, there was a comfortable and relaxed feeling among us.

By the time I flew home, I had a job offer in hand.

Broken Thumbs and Cracked Hearts

Returning to Galena, I immediately went to my office to catch up on mail and memos, and to see what notes had been left regarding the things that transpired during my weeklong absence.

As I opened a letter, my stomach turned over with a resounding thud as I realized I was looking at my contract for the 2002-2003 school year—accompanied by the usual instructions to sign it by the last day of the month. Contracts always come out in March in Galena.

How am I going to tell Jim and Carl that I'm leaving? The very thought of having to explain that I would be leaving, after all their effort and commitment to bring me into the village full-time, left me feeling sick with guilt.

Jim was a bit more gracious with the news than Carl, actually. Although Carl did not outwardly display any kind of anger or resentment, an interesting thing transpired a few weeks later.

Carl and I had established a verbal agreement regarding my salary. We had created a one-hundred-and-fifty-day contract, rather than the standard one-hundred-ninety-day contract. The understanding was that if it was clear in April that what was in place needed me to be there for the remaining six weeks, Carl would hire me at that time through a different budget, and pay me the same daily rate as he had when they independently contracted with me for services. This worked well for both the district and me, and I had no problem whatsoever with the arrangement.

To my surprise, however, when mid-April rolled around and it was time to extend the contract, Carl did not do so—feeling, I suppose, that there was little point since I would not be carrying services into the next year. Carl Knudsen did not become a visionary by being a bleeding heart. He is a businessperson, and while he will more than go to bat for his employees in order to make sure they have what they need to do an exemplary job in their position, he was not about to do so for someone giving him nothing in return. To pay thousands of dollars to extend my contract to the end of the school year made no fiscal sense when no long-term benefit to the district would be received.

It should not have been the crushing blow to me that it was when the contract was not renewed. It had just never occurred to me that I would not finish out the school year.

I was not the only one reeling from the surprise. Teachers who had no idea my contract was not set up to take me through the end of the year were understandably shocked upon finding out that my contract was going to expire in two weeks and that I would no longer be working in their classrooms or with the students. It placed all of us in a very awkward position. I certainly was not going to undermine Carl or his decisions in any way. On the other hand, teachers needed to know that I was not *choosing* to leave them without continued support services, six weeks before the school year ended.

It was a very difficult time.

I contemplated staying in the village and volunteering my time until the end of the school year, and this seemed like a possible option until I considered the fact that I would not be under contract and would, therefore, be personally liable for malpractice. I certainly was not doing anything that would result in someone suing me, but I worked with a very high-risk population of children, many of whom came from unstable and volatile homes. It would be foolish to disregard the possibility that it could occur. Such unfortunate things happen to good people all the time.

Ethically, the situation presented a huge dilemma for me. I have always prided myself on practicing in the most ethical and responsible manner possible—putting the children first, and following the established guidelines of the National Association of School Psychologists (NASP). Was it ethical to leave six weeks before the year was over? On the other hand, would it be ethical to volunteer and continue my work when I was not under a school contract?

The angst and stress of being uncertain how to handle this was fairly intense, but in the end, I felt that, as the superintendent, Carl had made his decision, and I needed to honor that. Rallying support in the hope that the superintendent would change his mind would most likely end up serving no one well.

And so, I began to pack boxes and inform both teachers and children that I would soon be leaving.

* * * * *

"Hey, Jeff, can I borrow your truck?" I asked the sixth grade teacher. "I need to take about twenty boxes to the post office to be mailed." With the river still frozen and no barges running, the only way I could move my belongings, my books, and professional items was through the U.S. Postal Service.

"Sure. The keys are in it," Jeff said with a smile.

A tall, slender man, Jeff was an experienced teacher, although this had been his first year of teaching in Galena. He had come to Galena from another village, and all year it had been a pleasure to collaborate with him. Jeff had one girl in particular in his classroom who I worked with a great deal, and we had developed lesson plans and treatment plans together all year. I think we were both disappointed not to have the last six weeks to wrap up our cooperative plan and see this girl through her sixth grade graduation.

Early in the school year, I had discovered just how effective a teacher Jeff was as I observed his handling of the September 11th tragedy. A television had been set up in the library—an open area one enters immediately upon coming into the front doors of the school. Jeff and I were standing there, watching in horror as the World Trade Center towers crumbled to the earth as if made of sand. The reality of the number of people inside those walls was seeping into our souls with a grief and a terror neither one of us had ever experienced, when one of his students walked in, looked at the television, and said, "This is so cool, man! Look at those towers crash down!"

Horrified, I would not have faulted Jeff one bit had he jumped all over this student for his insensitivity and callousness. But even in the midst of his own state of shock and despair, Jeff recognized the teachable moment in this—knew without having to think about it that to the children in this village, there *was no* reality to what they were seeing on television. None of these children had been to New York—few had been outside of the village, much less outside of Alaska. But they all had seen movies, televisions, and video games in which burning, crashing, and explosions were the norm. If we wanted them to understand the events that were unfolding, we were going to have to teach them.

And teach them he did. That entire week and long after, Jeff's curriculum focused on the World Trade Center, on politics, on terrorism, and on the personal loss that occurred to everyone who knew someone in that building. Hands-on projects took the place of silent reading time, and letters thanking the firefighters of New York were mailed before the week's end. Never was there a more compassionate group of sixth graders than what emerged from his classroom that year.

Indeed, he would be another one of the teachers who I would dearly miss collaborating with—it was an equal exchange of learning that we gained from one another.

Thanking Jeff for the use of his truck, I was heading out the door when I heard him shout, "Watch out for the steering wheel. It's loose!"

Vehicles in Galena don't have to meet any emission or safety standards, and it's not unusual for a car to be running without a functional transmission (its driver just stops and puts more fluid in every few miles) or with, say, a door duct-taped to stay on.

A loose steering wheel didn't seem to be too major of a problem.

* * * * *

"Ohhhhhh...shitshitshitshitshit," I found myself saying as I hit a patch of ice and the truck started to zigzag on the road. Trying to steady the wheel, it suddenly occurred to me what Jeff meant when he said the steering wheel was loose. Unfortunately, this did not become clear to me until after my thumb was enmeshed in the wheel's uncontrolled and wildly spinning rotation.

"Yowwwww. Wow. That hurt!" I looked around and noticed I was off the road and in a shallow ditch. *Good thing that was my last run to the post office today*, I thought as I started the truck and headed toward Jeff's cabin.

Returning Jeff's keys, I told him about my little escapade on ice and showed him my thumb, which by that time was rather large and turning a few shades of blue.

"You better have that X-rayed, Debra. That looks bad."

"What can they do with a broken thumb? I'll just put a splint on it. You got any splint materials?" I asked, knowing he was the cross-country ski coach.

"I don't," Jeff apologized. "But I'll look around for something."

"Eh, don't worry," I said cheerfully. "I'll use a pencil or something."

For the next seven days, I struggled through school with a throbbing thumb twice its normal size and displaying colors that could stand in for a diversity poster. The only positive aspect of it was little Angela's reaction.

"Oooohhhhhhh," she would coo. "Ms. Debra has *such* a painful thumb." She would gently pat my hand, careful not to touch the thumb, and with every ounce of gentleness she had learned over the year, protect my thumb from being bumped, banged, or touched.

"I'll walk beside you, Ms. Debra," she would offer sweetly. "That way no one will bump your thumb."

Well, at least we have a real-life scenario where Angela can practice her newly learned skills, I thought with my usual optimism.

Still, optimism was not quite enough to make it bearable as I madly typed out page after page after page of summaries on children. Making sure that whoever followed me in this position had thorough summaries of every child and each intervention implemented was critically important to me—I certainly could not expect a new person to go through the thick files kept on every child when they first began the new job.

However, on this day, by nine o'clock in the morning—having been at the keyboard for several hours—I gave in and went next door to the health clinic for an X-ray.

"Well, you're in luck, Debra," said one of the people working at the desk. "We have an orthopedic nurse practitioner here this week. She specializes in this and she's filling in."

Great, I thought as the specialist stuck my thumb under the X-ray machine. Not that I didn't trust the usual health aides—they were all very good and competent people—I just felt better knowing the person who was going to read the X-ray did it for a living.

"You," she said, pointing her finger at me, "are on the next plane to Fairbanks."

Looking at her in surprise, I could barely spout a quick, "What for?" before she said, "You're lucky you came in today, Debra. You've broken your thumb and torn the ulnar collateral ligament. I can get you into the orthopedic surgeon that I work for—which is great, because otherwise you wouldn't get in for a month."

"What does that mean?" I asked. "I mean, what's torn?" I didn't really know what she was talking about.

"The ligament that connects the bones at the base of your thumb is torn. If you wait more than about nine days following the injury when you have an acute tear like this, the chances of it ever properly healing are dramatically reduced."

"Jeez. No wonder it hurts so much. Good thing I came in today, huh?" I smiled, thinking how lucky I was that only eight days had passed since my little encounter with the rogue steering wheel. "What do they do for it?"

"Well, it will be up to the doctor," she said. "Either he will cast it or he will take you into surgery if he feels he has to suture the ligament back to the bone."

I really did not like the sound of that last option.

In keeping with the workings of a small environment where people are looking out for one another, I had a seat on the next flight to Fairbanks and was driven directly to the orthopedic surgeon's office in a taxi that was waiting for me when I landed—thoughtfully arranged by the Frontier Flying Service people.

"Moving is certainly going to take some adjustment," I thought. I was pretty sure things didn't happen like this outside of a village.

The orthopedic doctor recommended surgery, saying that the ligament was "cleanly and completely torn from the bone."

"It is possible," he said, "that it could heal itself if I put a hard cast on it for six to eight weeks, but that is a fifty-fifty bet, while surgery almost assuredly could repair it completely."

I opted for the cast and returned to Galena first thing the next morning.

I had work to do.

* * * * *

Case notes: 5-03-2002

Angela and I had our closing session today. I presented her with her favorite magic wand as a parting gift for when she needs reminding about gentle touch and not stealing. We shared it with Ms. Hansen, her special education teacher, and showed Ms. Hansen how to use it, so now Ms. Hansen can keep it in school and help Angela if she needs it.

Angela then chose the toys that she wanted me to send over to Anne, the mental health worker who will take over her case. Angela chose the hat and glasses she uses to be "Ms. Debra," the baby with the pacifier, and the mother, father, and baby Barneys. She wanted the baby bottles she has been using all year to go with me so I would remember her.

Angela had been patting my arm throughout the day, saying, "Poor Ms. Debra. Does your thumb hurt?" and I would assure her it was protected by the cast now, and was much better because of her tender care over the last two weeks. At one point in our session, as we were painting our last picture together, Angela picked up my hand and, kissing it, said, "Poor, poor Ms. Debra."

Addendum: 5-3-2002

After school, Angela, most likely intentionally, missed the school bus. I was in a meeting with teachers and she kept coming into the room. I had to set clear boundaries of the type not needed in quite some time, in order to have her be respectful and not interrupt us.

When the meeting was over, I went into the hallway where she was sitting and waiting for me, and I offered to walk her down to the room where there would likely be a ride home waiting for her.

As we walked down the hallway, Angela grabbed my cast hand.

"Does it hurt?" she asked, looking at my thumb.

Getting down on my knee, just as I had done so many times before, I looked at her and gently said, "Yes, Angela...but it's protected by the cast, and it's much better because of all your caring touches over the last two weeks."

Angela—her expression cold and removed—gripped my fingers firmly and with a quick twisting motion, jammed them back as far as they would bend.

"Does that hurt?" she asked again, eyes open wide and innocent.

"Yes, Angela. That hurt."

Milestones occur, I thought to myself sadly. But so does regression.

Writing the last of my notes, I stated:

Angela's longstanding and poor defensive systems still lie just beneath the surface of her new, healthier behaviors. In a threatening or stressful setting, she is most likely to regress and display the behaviors of the pre-gentle Angela she has learned to be, until she has a much greater length of time to practice her new repertoire of skills, and make them permanent.

I could only hope that somehow not all that Angela had accomplished this year would be lost because I was choosing to leave too soon.

I am achingly sad to be leaving too soon, I acknowledged to myself.

The trouble with choices is that there is always a consequence to having not chosen the alternative route.

PART II:

The Injury

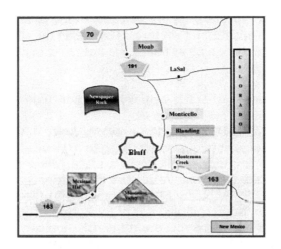

"I'm very brave generally," he went on in a low voice,
"only today I happen to have a headache."

Humpty Dumpty to Alice

What a Way to Start the Week
April 7, 2003, Blanding, Utah

"Why, you (*yewwwww*) lazy palooka. Git up! Git up, you sleepy head. Git up!"

I groaned as I listened to this poor imitation of John Wayne broadcast itself, chiding me to get up at the ridiculous hour of 4:15 a.m. I contemplated pressing the snooze button and stealing a few more precious minutes of sleep, but I knew that it was actually less painful just to get up. I *torment* myself with an alarm clock that repeats a variety of castigations in ten bad accents and imitations every five minutes. If I got up and bypassed the snooze alarm, I could avoid listening to the three amigos telling me not to lay my head back down on that pillow.

Peeelow.

I hate to get up, so there is actually a reason behind the madness of hanging on to the clock.

Having just moved to Blanding the previous June, this was my first April outside of Alaska in almost twenty years. Despite my love affair with that state, I was feeling pretty smitten with living in a place where trees bloomed and birds arrived long before the summer solstice celebration.

This was a particularly balmy Monday morning in the desert and canyon lands of southeastern Utah, and the buds of the cottonwoods and willows were near bursting. The fragrance of the tamarisk, juniper, and piñon pines combined to make me feel that lighthearted giddiness I associated with the springtimes of my pre-Alaska life. I realized I was waiting to hear the various chirps and calls of the sparrows, chickadees, finches, and juncos that I knew would merge to sound like a regular telegraph operation right outside my bedroom window, when it suddenly occurred to me that not even the birds were up yet.

I was amazed that I expected *myself* to actually get up and function at this ungodly hour. My biological clock, long calibrated to provide my deepest sleep between the hours of 4:00 and 10:00 a.m., precludes my ever scheduling early morning meetings that require me to drive any distance. It's too dangerous: my body and mind desperately want to sleep at that time, and my thought processes are never as clear and sharp as later in the day.

But on this Monday morning, I had broken my cardinal rule and agreed to attend a 7 a.m. meeting at Mexican Hat Elementary, a school nearly sixty miles from my home and main office in Blanding.

Located just outside the northern boundary of the Navajo Nation, the town of Mexican Hat is named for an unusual rock formation about sixty feet in diameter that looks strikingly like a sombrero. The town itself is a haphazard gathering of wood houses and trailers scattered along the serpentine San Juan River, and on its own it's a barren, unremarkable community—but it has been rendered spectacular by the wavy geometric colors in the rock strata that surround it. The striking gray and red rock patterns dramatically and subtly change depending on the sunlight, time of day, and cloud coverage, and once exposed to its stark beauty, it is clear why the Navajo developed the trademark patterns seen so often in their weavings.

The little school of Mexican Hat, populated with two hundred dark-haired, dark-eyed, and red-cheeked children, boasts a staff of genuinely committed educators. A blend of Anglo and Navajo teachers were always there to make me smile as I arrived to hear their welcoming greeting of *"Ya 'at 'teeh*, Ms. Debra."

"Ya 'at 'teeh." I would smile back before feigning hurt when they snickered at my obviously butchered enunciation. *"Bellagana,"* they would say, shaking their heads in mock disgust. *White woman.*

It was ritual. It was said with affection and I loved it.

There was a day, not too long ago, when I had been watching Eleanor, a short Navajo woman with a round face and gray-streaked hair, as she worked with a sixth grade boy named Willy Tsotsie. Willy, at twelve, did not have much intelligible speech, but he had a smile that could light up a dark night on the Yukon. As I was getting ready to leave for the day, Eleanor said to me, *"Hagoóónee*, Ms. Debra. Hey, Willy! Tell Ms. Debra *Hagoóónee*—good-bye."

"Hagoóónee, Mit Debba," Willy said, flashing me that megawatt, winsome smile of his.

Grinning, I repeated the Navajo good-bye back to Willy, and as I put on my coat, I noticed him staring at me. Willy didn't say a word; rather, he turned and looked at Eleanor and then, turning back to me, burst into laughter.

Eleanor, always ready to give me a lesson in Navajo pronunciation, firmly corrected me: "No. *Hagooóónee.*"

"Hagooonee," I said, smiling, thinking I was saying it better.

"No. Listen: *Hagooónee.*"

My eyebrows arched in a question mark as I said once again (though no longer very confidently), *"Hagooonee."*

Eleanor, peering at me intensely, was wagging her head back and forth. She reminded me of that woman on the old *Northern Exposure* program—the receptionist who always kept the doctor from humiliating himself too badly by maintaining a tight grip on his Anglo ways.

The Navajo language is incredibly difficult to master. It may only contain four vowels, but it seems to me like they are used about fifty times in every word. This mass of vowel pronunciation is further made difficult by the fact that it is a tonal language that uses high tones, rising tones, low tones, and falling tones. So *ee'* said in a rising tone leads to a different word than if said with a falling tone. It's an Athabascan language, and having lived in an Athabascan village in Alaska, I was already aware that for all practical purposes when it came to tonal languages, I was as deaf as if I had been born without ears.

"Try again," Eleanor instructed with mock sternness.

I tried again. This time I responded even more carefully, quite sure to repeat exactly what I thought I heard. A little puddle of drool was beginning to form at the corner of Willy's lips as he continued laughing.

"Don't you make fun of me," I teased, which, of course, set him off on another unbridled binge of his special brand of hiccupped guffawing.

By this time, even Eleanor could not keep a straight face, and smiling, I looked at her and said, "I'll be back Thursday. Give me another lesson?"

"Of course. *Hagooónee*, Ms. Debra. *Ahe'ee* (thank you)," she added, looking amused.

I waved and in perfect sign language said, "You're welcome, Ms. Eleanor."

Fortunately for me, sign language does not contain rising and falling tones.

It was this sort of professional camaraderie that wouldn't let me say *no* when teachers—in response to my request to meet about a very troubled boy I was working with—convinced me that the only time they could *possibly* meet was early in the morning...and wouldn't I, *please, just this once,* meet before school instead of after.

So here I was, on a Monday morning, fumbling around and trying to get dressed in order to be out the door by 4:45.

Before heading south, I stopped at my Blanding office and completed the usual organizational tasks required at the beginning of each week. Obsessed with not being late to this meeting, it made me happy to see I was ready to leave Blanding at 5:45.

Exactly on schedule.

Reaching into my desk to grab the keys to my district car, I was surprised to find them missing. In no mood and with no time to figure out where I might have placed them, and with little thought to possible ramifications of taking my own vehicle, I quickly hopped into my Ford Ranger and headed south.

The pull of sleep began its seductive bidding less than three blocks from my office.

Opening the windows, I turned on the radio. I listened to the disheartening news of the war in Iraq. I railed against what I thought were poor governmental policies. I sang as loud and as off-key as always. These strategies, a cup of coffee, and two No-Doz got me as far as White Mesa, the Ute Indian Reservation 10.4 miles away.

Leaving the boundary of the tribal land is the last thing I remember of the drive to Mexican Hat, until the splintering sound of the *Welcome to Bluff* sign jolted me awake.

* * * * *

Bluff, Utah, rests twelve miles south of White Mesa, on the south side of a canyon. To an unaware traveler, the richness of this town might be missed as they pass through on their way to one of the eight nearby national parks. From the highway, it's easy to observe only a scattered collection of houses surrounded by sagebrush, rabbit brush, and intermittent patches of juniper trees that produce small bold pockets of green in what at first appears to be an otherwise bland landscape. But Bluff is a town made famous by the writers, artists, photographers, river runners, and the canyoneer-maniacs who have ventured there in retreat, only to find themselves compelled to share its beauty with others. Three-hundred-foot sandstone cliffs and the meandering San Juan River frame this small community and dramatic red rock formations—sculpted over time into innumerable alcoves, canyons, and cliffs—provide both physical and spiritual shelter to residents and visitors alike.

Bluff is a spectacularly beautiful town.

Plowing through the *Welcome* sign without any sense of what had happened—what *was* happening—I could only reflexively attempt to get either back on or off the road. Not knowing where I was currently maneuvering and locked into my fifty-five-mile-per-hour speed, apparently I just kept turning the wheel—sending myself careening and somersaulting across the highway.

Like a tumbleweed in a windstorm.

For a fraction of a moment, silence dominated everything. It was the kind of silence that follows the sudden still of a terrific din, such as when an earthquake rattles every item in a home and then without warning stops as instantly as it began. I'm familiar with this silence—this split-second eternity when an earthquake ceases—and it's what I think of when I remember my truck keeling over in what seemed like slow motion.

There was one instant void of sound, one moment before the disquieting awareness of trauma began to creep into my consciousness. A moment that ended when a leaking sound exploded me into action as the possibility of a ruptured gas tank blasted through my mind.

Making a frenzied attempt to get out, I discovered my driver's door crushed and solidly wedged shut. Panic plowed through all other emotions as I lay trapped in a sideways-down truck, with a gas tank surely seconds away from explosion. The doors, unavailable as exits, left me with no alternative for escape other than fiercely pounding the shattered but intact windshield with the two-inch heels of my boots.

Despite my vigorous pounding, not a shard of glass fell my way.

Although it turned out the draining liquid was coming from my punctured water bottle, at the time I was quite sure I was within seconds of incineration. A feeling of terror like I had never before experienced catapulted me into a state of sheer panic as I continued pounding against the unyielding glass.

"Hey...you all right in there? *Hello?* Are you okay? I have an ax in my pickup. Hang on—I'll be right back." A deep voice sent an immediate sense of relief washing over me. Someone found me! Someone knew I was trapped and would get me out.

With my legs still resting on the windshield and my skirt halfway wrapped around my waist, I remember thinking how fortunate it was that I had dressed nicely that morning, and as suddenly as panic had overtaken me, I found myself inexplicably calm.

"Debra, are you all right in there? Can you hear me, Debra?" A different voice this time—a voice that knew my name.

The fact that someone apparently knew it was *me* trapped in the sideways-down truck added to the surreal quality of the moment. Of course, given that I drove a gold Ford Ranger with Alaskan license plates and a bike always secured on the tailgate, it didn't take the proverbial rocket scientist to figure out that I was the one downside-up, twenty-four miles from home on Route 191-South. At the time, however, it seemed astonishing to me that not only had I been found, but I had been identified by name.

I rolled my eyes, feeling a rueful grimace take over as I contemplated my embarrassment at being caught in such an ungainly posture, in such a very public location.

This was *not* how I intended to start my week.

No Bumps, No Breaks, No Bruises

The second voice belonged to my friend Patrick, one of Bluff's lead EMTs and another San Juan School District employee. An early riser, Patrick was on his way north to Blanding when he spotted my truck. He alerted the rest of the EMTs, who would arrive shortly thereafter, and in the meantime, he was trying to ascertain if I was conscious, hurt, dead, or somewhere in between.

"Hey, Patrick. Hi! I'm fine. I just can't get out."

"I've got the ax," said the unknown Samaritan. "Cover your face and head. I am going to bust you out. Do you have something to cover your face?"

There was a shattering of glass, but I don't remember it. I don't remember climbing out of the truck. I only remember being on the side of the road and seeing my files of confidential papers drift slowly up and down the highway's edge. As I started gathering papers, someone—a woman—was telling me she would do it for me, that I needed to sit down. I had been in an accident.

"Oh, no, I'm fine. I'm fine. These papers are confidential. I have to get them. I really have to get them. They're confidential."

"I think you need to sit down," she said gently. "You're shaking. You've been in an accident. Let me get your papers for you." The woman offering to gather papers was one of the many paramedics who had arrived at the accident scene.

Not that I was aware that there were paramedics at the scene. I wasn't.

Nor did I have any percipience that an ambulance had arrived along with the state troopers and the many people who had stopped to see if I was all right. I had no cognizance of any of them, other than the kind Samaritan and Patrick.

As I would discover later, losing the ability to be aware of anything except that which is directly in front of me would be one of the more permanent and frustrating manifestations of the accident.

At the time, however, I saw only floating papers, and, frantic about retrieving them, I was not about to sit down or let anyone else try to catch them as they aimlessly hovered along the highway's edge. I saw nothing irrational or unusual in the fact that I was insisting on walking the highway in search of scattered documents.

It was months before I would wonder how those papers had become scattered in the first place. In my mind, I had been trapped in the truck with the windows closed and a shattered but intact windshield. How could notebooks and files have been scattered along the highway?

Once that question surfaced, I similarly wondered how it was possible that the watch had blown off my wrist and landed on the highway. Or, how my wallet had ended up some two hundred yards beyond where the truck came to its apparently abrupt halt. I was certain I had done nothing other than swerve and tip over.

At the time, however, I had no questions and saw only papers—and I knew only that I wanted them back.

As to whether or not I ever retrieved them, I have no idea.

* * * * *

"Tony, I'm fine," I insisted. "I need to get to that meeting at Mexican Hat. Can you take me there?" I was sitting in the ambulance with my boss, who had been on his way to the office in Blanding when he saw my upside-down truck surrounded by paramedics.

"You aren't going to the meeting, Debra. You're going to the hospital. You just rolled your truck—you need to be checked out."

"I rolled my truck? No, I didn't," I said. *"Did I?"*

Tony nodded. "Twice, we think."

I thought about that for a minute. "Tony, I didn't roll the truck—it just tipped over. I'm fine. I need to get to that meeting. Someone needs to take me to that meeting. It's the meeting I set up on Petey Begay." Petey was one of the more complex children I worked with, and Tony was well aware of how hard it is to bring all the relevant players together at one time in order to keep a program like his coordinated and running smoothly.

"You'll reschedule it. You're going to the hospital, Debra."

"That's silly, Tony. Look at me, I'm just fine. I have to get to the school or I'll be late."

In *my* mind, I was not just being responsible, I was being very logical.

I really enjoyed having Tony as a boss. He wasn't one to disclose much personal information, but during my interview almost exactly one year earlier, I had learned that he was thirty-seven years old and had grown up in a prominent Mormon family in Salt Lake City. Apparently, somewhere along the line, Tony must have somewhat reinvented himself, evolving from a dutiful Mormon boy headed toward his mission into a man with long hair, an earring, and a remarkable knowledge of Native American culture and its traditions. By the time I met him, Tony no longer sported the long hair, but the earring remained, along with his Harley, an incredible music collection, and a love of good beer, tequila, and gathering of friends.

This may explain that hidden half smile he had afforded me at the interview, when he indicated there were people around who would be "just fine" with the fact that I did not belong to the Mormon Church.

In many ways, it amazed me that Tony had ever been hired as the director of special education in the rural and very conservative San Juan School District. I can only assume that his genuine connection to the Navajo people, and his in-depth knowledge of special education and its laws, overrode what surely must have been judged as pure Jack-Mormon behavior[5].

Over the months I had lived in Blanding, Tony and I had become friends in a comfortable sort of way, although we did not often socialize outside the school setting.

A look of obvious concern clouding his eyes, Tony tried once again to be clear about what I needed to do.

"Debra. Listen to me. You need to go to the hospital and get checked out. You're not going to the meeting. Okay?"

Less than two years earlier, a good friend of Tony's was going to graduate school while interning for him in order to become certified and licensed as an educational psychologist. In a work-related accident, she and another teacher had been tragically killed, and without being told, I knew this had been devastating to Tony on both a personal and professional level. The position I now held was the position she had been in training to assume.

As I looked at the worry etched in Tony's face, it occurred to me that the sight of my mangled and overturned truck must have brought very painful memories to the surface. The least I could do was stop arguing and go get checked out so as not to cause him any more angst than I had already done.

"Okay. I'll go. But call Mexican Hat for me and tell them why I'm not there, okay? So they know I have a good excuse and that you're making me not go."

* * * * *

I've no more recollection of everyone leaving the ambulance than I have of them arriving. As in a scene-jumping dream, as quickly as Tony and the others appeared, they were gone—and I was lying on a cot, with a kindly medic sitting next to me, soothing me with his caring voice.

"You're doing great," he said. "It'll take us about forty-five minutes to get to Monticello, so just relax if you can."

"Oh, I'm fine," I assured him. "This is so silly. I feel ridiculous going to the hospital in an ambulance." Pausing I added, "The only weird thing is my head. It feels like there's a tight rubber band wrapped around it."

"A tightness?"

"Yeah. Like a too-tight ponytail or something. It's odd."

I don't recall anything else about the ride to the hospital in Monticello. Just that too-tight feeling.

Like my head had been stuck inside a vise.

---

[5] Jack Mormon is a term that generally refers to someone deemed by Latter-Day Saints (Mormons) to be an inactive or lapsed member of the LDS Church, and who, despite maintaining positive feelings toward the Church, does not attend services and may not abide by the prohibition against tobacco and alcohol.

Keyless Gates

Sheltered by the Abajo (Blue) Mountains on the west, and the San Juan Mountains to the east, it is rumored that at one time in the 1800s, Monticello harbored so many fugitives that it was known as the Outlaw Trail. It's hard to say if this is just folklore or not, but it's easy enough to imagine bandits, cowboys, and American Indians finding enough places to hide in the mountains and canyons surrounding the town to think it *could* be true.

Twenty-five miles north of Blanding, and with a slightly smaller population of about two thousand residents, Monticello is the county seat for its fourteen thousand citizens. Although the Lymans received their revelation in Blanding in the late 1800s, fulfillment was not to occur until 1998, which is when the Mormon Temple was built and dedicated in Monticello. And while there are numerous wards throughout the region, Monticello houses the only Temple for the area's thirteen thousand members.

Monticello also houses the county's only hospital.

Shortly after arriving at the hospital, a state trooper met me in the X-ray room in order to take my statements. Confidently, I assured him that I was unscathed and functioning perfectly well. No, I hadn't rolled the truck or lost consciousness, I told him. I described for him where the accident occurred on the north side of the canyon, and in answer to his question, I explained that no, I hadn't made it to Bluff.

"Well, actually," he said, "you did make it to Bluff."

I looked at him in surprise.

"Yeah, you rolled your truck on the south side of the canyon, not the north. You were just on the outskirts of Bluff."

"*Really?* Wow." I was sure I hadn't gone through the canyon, despite recalling the splintering of the *Welcome to Bluff* sign. I obviously was not making any sort of logical connection between these two facts.

"Oh, well." I smiled, still somewhat perplexed after hearing that I had actually been on the other side of the canyon. "I'm just glad no one was hurt, and that I'm coming out of this without so much as a bruise."

Actually, once the technicians began taking their requisite scans and X-rays, I did discover that the bottoms of my feet were slightly bruised, as was my hip bone, where I must have seriously challenged the seat belt's ability to keep me confined.

Still, aside from these inconsequential owies, and the oddly constricted feeling around my head, I was pronounced fine and released to go home.

My truck, forty-five miles away, had been declared totaled and was in the process of being hauled away from the accident site along with my now defunct bike.

I was sitting quietly in the hospital visitors' lounge. I had no way to get home, and I couldn't imagine what I should do at that point.

I apparently looked as confused as I felt.

"Can I help you, honey?" I glanced up at the woman behind the receptionist counter, thinking how kind it was of her to call me honey, even though we must have been approximately the same age.

"Oh...no, I'm okay, thanks," I said. I thought about this for a second and added, "Well...actually, I was in an accident this morning, and I...I don't have a ride home."

"Are you from here?"

"No, Blanding."

"Well, is there someone you could call to pick you up? A husband, a friend?"

"Oh, no, they're all working." It never occurred to me that this might be a legitimate reason to call someone and ask if they could help me out.

Actually, it never occurred to me to make a call at all.

I fretted over this dilemma while the receptionist stared at me. Most likely she was contemplating the oddity of my not having family to call on for help. The large and extended Mormon families that heavily populate Monticello and Blanding make it very unusual for a person to be without someone nearby to pitch in and help out in a crisis.

Or, maybe she just wondered why a fairly well-dressed and professional-looking woman was acting like a lobotomy patient from the state hospital.

"Excuse me...maybe, well, actually, maybe I could call someone I work with. May I use your phone?"

"You bet, honey. Just dial nine first."

I placed a call to my office in Blanding and spoke with my coworker and friend, Alta Begay. Alta indicated that she (and pretty much everyone else) had already heard about the accident, and she would be happy to pick me up.

Within less than two hours, Alta had me back at home, and I was sending out emails telling everyone about my morning—describing how lucky I was that absolutely nothing was wrong.

Then I crawled into bed and promptly fell asleep.

* * * * *

I woke up Wednesday. At least that's what I remember doing. Apparently, between Monday afternoon and Wednesday morning my mental Palm Pilot experienced an electrical outage. As far as I could tell, I had slept the better part of nearly forty hours.

Walking into work early that morning, my head felt like it was stuffed with a mountain of cotton batting. *Gosh, did I even feed my dogs? Oh, I must have. How odd it is that it is Wednesday. Did I eat? This is so weird; I can't believe it's Wednesday. Jeez, I feel like a Martian's taken over my brain.*

The thoughts bobbled around like anchorless buoys in high seas.

Oh, well. I shrugged. *This will clear up once I've been awake a little longer.*

Sitting at my desk with a child's testing protocol in front of me, I attempted to complete the mindless task of scoring it. It was a simple task: add up a small column of one- and two-digit numbers and put the sum in the little square box at the bottom. It's a menial, tedious task that I had been routinely doing for the better part of the last twenty years.

I added.

I added again.

I couldn't seem to make my mind work. I tried again. I used my fingers. I still could not get past a couple of numbers. I could not add the column.

My friend Sandra, a teacher in the next room and a lead paramedic for the county, came in to check on me. She took one look at my face and with concern written all over hers, asked: "What's wrong? You're really pale. Are you all right?"

I stared at her, an uncomprehending look in my eye and a tight knot in my stomach. "Sandra...something is very, very wrong. I can't add. I can't think. Something in my head is very, very wrong."

Immediately plopping me into her ever-present paramedic car, Sandra drove me the twenty-five miles back to the hospital. I have no idea what she did about her students that morning; I only know that she kept me from panicking during a time when fear was beginning to suffocate the very breath from my lungs.

How could I not add simple numbers? What was wrong with my head?

* * * * *

I was kept in the hospital under twenty-four-hour observation, with the nurses waking me up every hour to ask me orientation questions. Despite the fact that I had no memory of being awakened a single time, and that I was shocked to find out it was suddenly Thursday, the nurses told me I was doing fine and would be able to go home.

"Well, so, how'd I do?" I asked the nurse, who was starting to give me home-care instructions.

"You did fine, honey (maybe everyone called me honey at the hospital). You did great on everything except knowing the day. You just kept telling us it was Monday."

"I did? I kept telling you it was Monday? That's weird," I said.

"Yep, every hour. But not to worry," she reassured me. "You have a mild concussion. You just need a little time. You'll be fine."

Unlike my first experience at the hospital three days prior, no one was about to leave me to my own devices or abilities to plan ahead. My friends, Jimmy and Ila, came to pick me up, making sure I had the paperwork and information I needed before leaving the hospital.

Ila and Jimmy, then in their early to mid-sixties, had been a couple since they were young teenagers in high school. The consummate Mutt and Jeff duo, with Ila standing all of five feet tall on her tiptoes and wearing outfits that boasted of nice material and sophisticated design, and Jimmy towering over her with his six-foot-plus frame outfitted in jeans and boots, they shared the same generous nature and concern for others' well-being. They were both *born* to grandparenting, and neither one was any happier than when their granddaughter, Victoria, came to visit from out of state. True, I wasn't young enough to be their granddaughter (or daughter for that matter), but I think in the absence of Victoria, they took quite naturally to the roles of being a fairy godmother and godfather to me. And I was quite happy and relieved to nestle into their care.

As we arrived at my house, still convinced that this would pass in a day or two, I assured Jimmy and Ila I didn't need a thing and would be just fine home alone with my dogs. I don't think they believed that, but I am quite sure I stated this adamantly and with conviction. Given that I am a grown woman, I don't suppose they felt comfortable trying to force me to go sleep at their house; and I suspect that while they *were* worried about me, they didn't really want my two eighty-pound, four-legged children to enjoy the kind of free roam in their house that they clearly had in mine.

Jimmy and Ila, making sure I had what I needed to feel safe and comfortable, left that afternoon, but for the next twelve months continued diligently in their caretaking of me.

That day—when Ila and Jimmy said their good-byes—we were all completely unaware of the road I had embarked upon. While they were more aware than I was that I certainly was not "fine," none of us had any idea just how many dramatic changes were in store for us.

At the time, I simply crawled into bed thinking how odd my head felt: as if there were a locked gate in front of my brain and I had no key. *Without a key*, I thought, *my brain and thinking processes are totally inaccessible.*

Drifting off to sleep and believing that behind the gate lay my only access to clarity, I tried to figure out where to find the key.

But before I had any ideas at all, I was deep into another thirty-six-hour nap.

The image of a keyless gate haunted me for many, many months.

* * * * *

Days and nights blended in a drugged-like state of altered consciousness. Each day during my awake-times, I discovered more and more oddities: I couldn't brush my teeth and think about breakfast; I couldn't do any two things at one time. Headaches had started to plague me; my tongue felt thick and too big for my mouth; I couldn't seem to distinguish smells and tastes; and I was dizzy and nauseated when I was up, so when I did eat—which wasn't much—I would do it lying down on my bed.

I was sleeping eighteen to twenty hours a day, and yet I would never wake up feeling rested. Instead, I would putter around in a haze until the overpowering need to sleep would overtake me again. It was two and a half years before a sleep study—with its graphs of waves and spikes indicating that I never enter Stage Four of sleep—suggested that my sleep center had been damaged in the accident. Stage Four is the time in the sleep cycle when the brain not only helps repair the wear and tear on the body, but when the consolidation of spatial and procedural memory takes place. The fact that I *never* enter this sleep cycle helps explain why I continue to need medication to remain awake, rarely recognize visual landmarks and faces, and generally walk around in a subpar state of alertness.

But I didn't know any of that at the time. All I knew is that the nurses told me I had a mild concussion, and that I just needed a little time before I would be fine.

With that information and no visible signs attesting to post accident trauma, I berated and chastised myself with increasing intensity.

This is ridiculous. *I should be back to myself and functioning normally.*

It is just a mild concussion; why do I feel like I'm getting worse *instead of better?*

Am I imagining *these things? Am I a hypochondriac? I should be able to think clearly by now.*

It was embarrassing how much I was sleeping, and I felt deeply ashamed for not bucking up and getting back to work. Each day I made a renewed commitment to it being my last day at home: *Tomorrow. Tomorrow, I'll get up and go to work.*

Each day I failed to live up to my resolve.

It is remarkable to me that no one at the hospital forewarned me that symptoms such as disorganization, memory impairment, foggy thinking, and distorted perceptions might possibly emerge over a period of weeks—or even months. Nor did they let me know that if I did experience these symptoms, I should seek further medical treatment. I have since learned that every year 1.1 million people with traumatic brain injuries are treated and released from hospital emergency rooms, and I can only hope that information about possible aftereffects is conveyed more often than it is not. Certainly, had I been told that these symptoms might emerge, I would have been far less frightened and confused—far less hard on myself, believing that I simply was not rising to the occasion and moving forward.

No one mentioned these things to me, however, and even though as a psychologist I had worked with children recovering from traumatic brain injuries from the likes of accidental gunshot wounds, I had no clue about "mild concussions." No clue that the term itself, *mild concussion*, is really a misnomer. Certainly, there was nothing mild-feeling in the discovery that I could not rely on my own memory and perceptions of a conversation, much less a day's events. There was nothing mild-feeling in the discovery that life had begun to resemble a series of disconnected snapshots, providing vague memories out of context from which I was supposed to navigate.

But the term *mild concussion* is a medical term, not a psychological one. Still, had anyone at the hospital prepared me for even *some* of the effects that were to surface, things could have been much easier to manage emotionally, even if they were not easier to manage in a practical sense.

It wasn't until many months later, when I was finally referred to a neurologist in Durango, Colorado, that I first became aware that what I was experiencing was well within the realm of "normal."

"Close your eyes for a minute," Dr. Willner instructed. "Okay, keeping them closed, tell me what you are smelling." She waved a vial of something under my nose.

"Oh...um...wait! I know that smell. I know I know that smell. Hold on..."

"That's okay, try this one," she said as she quickly waved another vial past my nostrils.

"Oh, rats...wait...wow, I know I know this smell...give me a minute." It was such an odd sensation—as if my brain were separated, with one part recognizing the smell, but being unable to access the part of my brain that would let me identify it. It wasn't a matter of recalling the right word—it was that I wasn't able to identify the smell even though it was so familiar to me.

"Orange!" I popped out, happy it had finally occurred to me.

"Close," said Dr. Willner. "You're in the right ball park of citrus. Actually it's lemon."

"Lemon?" I said. "*Really?* Not orange?" I was sure I had figured it out correctly.

"Nope," Dr. Willner stated cheerfully, moving right along to vial number three.

Dr. Willner spent more than an hour with me in that first visit, and at the end, when she said I was a textbook case and that all my symptoms were quite real, I threw my arms around her, giving her a tearful bear hug.

I suppose as a neurologist specializing in head injuries, Dr. Willner was used to surprising emotional outbursts from her patients, even if I was not used to expressing them. But to me, Dr. Willner was not just a neurologist. She was a savior. A saint.

Everything I was experiencing was real!

* * * * *

About three or four weeks after the accident, I insisted on attending a meeting with Sandra and the father of a teenager I had evaluated the first week in April—just a few days before the accident. It was important to me to be able to explain to this boy and his parents what was causing his learning challenges and assure them that there were strategies to put into place that would help. I felt it was my responsibility to attend this meeting, and I was quite certain that I should be able to do so without difficulty.

Sandra had been teaching special education for more than thirty years. Small in stature, she had a pleasantly round figure and long, sandy blond hair that probably hadn't strayed in style in about as many years as she had been teaching. With her compassionate blue eyes and a demeanor that lent itself to being called "mom" by just about everyone, Sandra was one of the first teachers I met when the school year began. Over the previous eight months, we had developed genuine respect and affection for one another, and she had been a wonderful support to me as I made the transition from living and working in Alaska to living and working in this small Mormon community.

Sandra's dress code for school was a loose-fitting blouse and a pair of jeans, and she was rarely seen with a pair of shoes on inside a school building. I know she kept them there, but Sandra was a woman of comfort—relaxed and calming and always putting others at ease. Shoes were not comfortable for Sandra, and *rules be darned,* she didn't wear them.

I knew if I were to present myself as a complete dullard or somehow otherwise embarrass myself at the meeting, Sandra would be able to rescue the situation.

"This is our psychologist, Debra Sanders," Sandra said as she introduced me. "She's the one who did the testing on Justin."

For a few minutes, I think I did quite well—explaining what kind of tests I had used, and in a very down to earth way helping this concerned parent understand the results of the testing. I have to say, I was feeling quite pleased with myself—if perhaps a bit dizzy and out of sorts. *See, I'm just fine,* I thought. *I can do this just* fine*!*

Thinking I had better quit while I was ahead, I stood up, shook hands, and said my good-byes. Turning to head for the door, dizziness overtook me, and I leaned against the wall for support. And then, in my best Scarlett O'Hara imitation, I slumped to the floor.

I am not sure exactly what Sandra did, but I am quite sure that she found a way to explain that I really was quite a competent school psychologist, and no one should let today's meeting undermine their confidence in the test results or recommendations.

"Cognitive overload," the people at the hospital called it.

"Not to worry. It will disappear soon."

Not soon enough, I muttered as I retreated to my sleep mode.

Not soon enough.

* * * * *

In the early months following the accident, people stopped by to visit, and I tried describing the frustrating realization that memories were not being created. That I simply did not recollect the previous visit, the conversation, the book I tried to read.

"Oh, shoot, we all forget things," people would comfort, but I wanted to rail against them as they told me of their memory challenges. This wasn't like them at all. This wasn't a small glitch in word finding, a temporary loss of recollection regarding what I ate for dinner last night, or an incidence of getting to a store and not remembering what I wanted to buy. This was a dark hole I was living in. A foggy, vapid, and suffocating hole that I was utterly petrified would encase me forever.

I desperately wanted people to understand my panic and confusion, yet I found myself continually trying to hide how muddled and turbid my thoughts actually were. It was humiliating to feel so opaque in my thinking. It was mortifying to think people would notice I had become stupid, like Charlie in *Flowers for Algernon*; and yet, it was terrifying to be alone with my awareness.

Spelling
April, May 2003

A small part of my job was to conduct file reviews of children who had been in special education for at least three years. I really wanted to keep working and finish out the school year, and *surely* I could at least do the file reviews, I assured Tony and Ila. As Tony's assistant director, Ila was actually my direct supervisor, but we were a small and informal department, and I tended to interact with both of them pretty equally.

Tony and Ila were the consummate cheerleaders as I continually over-estimated what I actually was capable of doing. As I tried (and tried again) to return to work, Tony displayed a tender sort of worry and fretting, while Ila gave me practical advice and encouraged me not to push too hard.

Reviewing files turned out to be more complicated than I possibly could have imagined. For one thing, light was a problem—it offended both my eyes and my head. Tony agreed to my working at home, and I managed the light issue by putting blankets over the windows. This allowed me to read with only the direct beam from a small lamp. Worse than light was noise—*any* noise. Every little noise seemed so *intrusive*. It was a good three or four months before I could even turn the stereo on to its lowest volume and listen to instrumental music, and I could only do that if there was no other sound in the room. Four years after the accident, I still could not manage the sound of a radio or TV in the background if I tried to carry on a conversation with someone. And I continue to be bothered by things like the sound of a bathroom fan if I am trying to think about things while drying off from a shower.

In order to do any work at all in those first months following the accident, there could be no sound around me, but by working at home, that was easy enough to manage. My dogs were quiet and content to lie at my feet or in bed with me, and the rural nature of my living location meant there was little outside noise such as traffic, sirens, or other city type distractions. Light and sound were manageable, given a few accommodations.

What was much more difficult to manage was the *time* it took to conduct each simple review. Tony and Ila praised me for every little task completed, but I was spending hours working in the darkened room in order to write a simple paragraph summary of the information. Often I would have to read and re-read files, sleep for several hours, and then read the same information over again in order to do the summary. I would make notes and email them to Tony and Ila; and although I knew things were taking far longer than usual, I believed that the final product was of the same quality I always produced.

One day, about six weeks after the accident, Tony and Ila came over to drop off some files and see how I was feeling. In response to my frustration over how confused and overwhelmed I still felt, Tony encouraged me, saying that he thought my brain was healing. In an attempt to reassure me, he told me that he could judge my progress by the quality of my spelling, and that it was improving.

Stunned, I adamantly denied that my spelling had been impacted at all.

"Oh, Debra! Your spelling's been *terrible* since the accident. But I can tell how you are doing by your emails, and you're doing better." Tony smiled with the ease and innocence of someone teasing a friend, having no idea he was delivering shocking news.

"No way, Tony. One thing I've always been is a good speller!"

"Yeah, well, Debra," Tony grinned in the disarming way he does when affectionately insulting someone he is comfortable with, "I have to tell you, your spelling's not so good anymore!"

I looked over at Ila imploringly, but she only nodded her head in concurrence, attempting to soften the blow by affirming, "But it really is much better, Debra. Really it is."

After they left, I immediately went and looked back at my emails from the previous month.

I was appalled to discover that indeed, I had become a terrible speller.

* * * * *

In between reading and re-reading, I would sleep for eighteen hours out of the day, and try to figure out how to rid myself of the fog that made me feel like I was standing in a deep hole and talking through a tube. How much I slept wasn't optional. I started every day with a cup of pennies, and everything had a cost, whether it was enjoyable, routine, or difficult. Brushing my teeth cost a penny. Laughing with a friend cost a penny. Reading a file cost a bunch of pennies. *Ka-CHING.* The cup would be empty and there was no reserve. When the cup was empty I had to go to sleep, and often that sleep would be interrupted by intense, blinding headaches that would leave me rocking in my bed, trying to make the pain go away by pressing in tightly on both sides of my temples. These taut, crushing headaches left me nauseated and scared.

I quickly learned that no matter how rattled and frightened I was by the intensity of the headaches, I could not permit myself the luxury of tears. The cost of crying was far too high, as it brutally intensified the headaches.

Tears, most definitely, cost way too many pennies.

Bill Cosby, Working in the Dark, and Urdu
June 2003

"Dad. Dad. *DAD!* I have to talk with you."

"*Daaa-ad.* Olivia is getting into my stuff!"

"Clare?! Clare! Did you tell Denise she can go out tonight?"

"Yes, dear, I did."

"Theo, son—I love you and I brought you into this world, but don't forget that I can just as easily take you out."

These were the lines of dialogue that, beginning about three or four months after the accident, became a daily source of comfort to me. *The Cosby Show.* Broadcast on the Nick at Night channel, I would be so happy if I was awake during its viewing time. It was very odd—I have never been an avid TV watcher—never liked having the background noise of a television in the way that so many people seem to enjoy. Suddenly I was a Cosby addict. I lived for and loved *The Cosby Show.* It became my anchor, and I laughed with their family—and was comforted by their family—as if they were my own. I still find this remarkable. Today the only television I own is a thirteen-inch antique tucked away in a closet, but at the time, during that spring and summer of 2003, Cosby was my lifeline.

Watching that show was like having a soft, downy quilt that I could wrap around myself, lose myself in, look forward to every single day.

Twice a day, in fact. I was so happy that *The Cosby Show* re-runs came on at least twice a day, although It's interesting to note that I haven't watched it since that period of time (I am, however, and have always been, a huge fan of Bill Cosby).

Several years after the accident, I became curious about the show's allure during that time period of my life, and after downloading several episodes online, it was interesting to analyze the elements of the program that I think made it so engaging and manageable for me.

In addition to it being a very funny and very well-written show, Bill Cosby tends to speak slowly—sometimes very slowly—for maximum comedic effect. There is a great deal that is communicated between family members without words ever being used, and in the spring and summer of 2003, conversation was difficult for me to follow. It seemed like everyone was talking too loud and too fast, and that left me uncomfortable and confused. But *The Cosby Show*, relying on facial expression as much as words, was a place I could go and be with people—without having to deal with the overload I was experiencing when people stopped by to visit. The episodes, minus the commercials I always muted, contained only about ten or twelve minutes of actual dialogue—just the right amount of time for me to feel a part of something, to laugh and to smile, and then to turn off so I could once again retreat into my silence.

* * * * *

Spring gave way to summer, and my days continued to consist of doing a little bit of work for Tony (never mind that school was out and the file information was long since needed), a daily walk around the neighborhood, and hours of sitting quietly with my friend Denney.

Denney was a soft-spoken man who, through his job with the San Juan County Mental Health Center, worked as a therapist part-time at Mexican Hat Elementary. His position had begun late in the year, and we didn't know each other well, but we were both there on Mondays, and we had grown comfortable around one another.

When he first began showing up at school, Denney was pretty hard to miss. This proverbial tall, dark, and handsome man, with his deeply chiseled face and mesmerizing blue eyes, would ease around a corner wearing a crisp white shirt and blue jeans, grabbing the attention of every female in sight between the ages of ten and fifty. Denney looked like the Marlboro Man that graced the billboards when I was a teenage girl. The one who sent our hormone-induced, fourteen-year-old imaginations into overdrive. Except his teeth were whiter, and his smile was more arresting than Mr. Marlboro's.

And besides all that, Denney was three-dimensional and could talk.

I decided it was my task to make sure that Denney and my friend Sharon, who also worked part-time at Mexican Hat, had plenty of opportunities to be together. I liked them both a lot and thought they would make a lovely couple. I never let it thwart my matchmaking endeavors that they seemed to have no romantic interest whatsoever in each other.

Sharon and I enjoyed spending time together outside of school. Although I was nearly fifteen years older than Sharon, we were very compatible in terms of activities such as hiking and cross-country skiing; and we shared similar career and leisure-time interests such as traveling, camping, and developing creative interventions for troubled kids. One evening when we were bored with little else to do, we laughingly perused the personal ads on the Internet (just in case Denney wasn't her knight in shining armor).

Perusing the personals was not something Sharon would be prone to doing on her own. She was a practical, earthy sort of woman who had never let a drop of makeup mar her beautiful face. Intense hazel eyes, long, wavy dark hair, and flowing, gypsy-like skirts gave her the look of an earlier generation of flower children. She was remarkably unfettered by the small vanities that plague most of us, and when I goaded Sharon into letting me write a profile for her to post on Match.com, she agreed, but never bothered to read it.

In her bio, I indicated that Sharon spoke fluent Urdu (I was curious if anyone ever *really* read all the way through these things). She was contacted by a man named Dan, and because he seemed interesting and fun, she agreed to meet him for dinner.

On their first date, Sharon was completely befuddled when Dan asked if she knew Urdu from having lived in Pakistan. Sharon, who had never heard of Urdu and had no idea it was a language, much less one she was supposed to be fluent in, found this to be a very odd question. But Dan (who obviously *did* read bios all the way through) had been smitten by Sharon's profile and picture, so he had taken the time to do a little research (since he, like all of us, had no clue about Urdu). Apparently Dan was trying hard to smoothly work his newfound knowledge into the conversation, and early in their date casually slipped in, "So...did you live in Pakistan in order to learn Urdu?"

"Huh?" Sharon replied.

"I mean, were you in Peace Corps or something?"

"Peace Corps? No, what makes you think I was in Peace Corps? I was in Vista."

"Oh. Well, I just thought you might have been in Peace Corps, and lived in Pakistan."

"But I didn't live in Pakistan," Sharon repeated, thinking what a strange conversation this was turning out to be.

"Then where did you learn Urdu?"

"Urdu?"

"*Urdu*," Dan said, a slight hint of testiness creeping into his voice. "You know—the language of Pakistan. I thought you speak it fluently."

"I don't even speak *English* fluently!" Sharon laughed, still having no idea what this man was talking about.

"But your bio said you speak Urdu."

With sudden clarity, Sharon laughed: "My *bio?* Oh! I didn't write that! My friend did. What else did it say I could do?"

Despite this awkward beginning, my matchmaking attempts were later applauded when theirs turned into a genuine romance, and Dan and Sharon ended up happily married and living—not in Pakistan—but in New Mexico.

Meanwhile, while Sharon and Dan were discussing the strangeness of any language with a name like Urdu, Denney and I continued to interact at school, and occasionally he would accompany me on hikes with my dogs.

Denney was one of the people on the road that Monday morning—one of the ones who stopped and pulled over to stare with horror at my mangled truck and the surrounding medics. Later, telling me how it impacted him thinking I was dead, he confessed to all *kinds* of closeted feelings I had no clue he had kept tucked away.

Wow.

Nothing like thinking someone is *dead* to overcome romantic shyness in a person.

Denney lived only a few blocks from me, and following his heartfelt disclosure, he became an even greater lifeline for me than *Cosby*. Every day he would come over to check on me, sitting for hours—and in his soft-spoken, soothing way, assure me that I would be okay. Conversations with me must have been maddening for Denney, yet he never let on that he was frustrated— or worried.

"Denney, I can't think. Everything is so foggy in my head."

"It's okay, Debra. It's okay. It'll get better. This won't last forever."

"But what if it does?"

"It won't, Debra. It's a concussion." Silence would rest between us for a minute, and then I would ask, "But, Denney, what if it doesn't go away? What if it never gets better and I'm like this forever?"

"Well," he would soothe in that quiescent way of his, "then you will learn to deal with it."

I would look at Denney, needing to rely on his judgment—wanting to believe that he had the answers I wanted to hear, and, for a moment, I would be still. Then panic would macerate that one borrowed instant of solace, and I would ask, "But, Denney, what if I *don't*? What if I *never* learn to deal with it?"

I imagine he sighed, but if he did, he never let me hear it.

Later, I discovered that what Denney did do was order books on head injuries so he could understand what was happening to me. It is very touching to think about him reading and marking passages as he struggled to understand what was taking place in my mind.

One afternoon, in early June, about eight weeks after the accident, Denney and I were taking one of our daily neighborhood walks when a man driving a vanload full of kids pulled over to the curb in front of us. Not recognizing him, I assumed he was a friend of Denney's, and a flood of confusion curled over me when he began talking—not to Denney, but to me. This person obviously knew me, and yet I didn't recognize him at all. I mean, his face looked familiar, but in an unfamiliar way. It was more than just not being able to place him or recall his name. It was as if he resembled someone I knew a very, very long time ago, but I couldn't quite remember who it was he reminded me of. It was the first of many disquieting encounters where familiar faces and landmarks appeared unknown to me—and oddly, *un*familiar faces appeared familiar.

"*Jamais vu,*" the neurologist later told me. "It's the opposite of déjà vu. Instead of feeling familiar, things seem totally unfamiliar. Has to do with too little connection between long-term memory and perceptions from the present."

So, what?—now I'm supposed to walk around like the welcome wagon lady, smiling and saying hello to everyone, just to cover my bases?

I knew it was going to be hard when I returned to work—this aspect alone was going to make things incredibly challenging.

It's a good thing I have the whole summer to heal.

* * * * *

When I finally did return to school, not after the summer, but nine months later in January 2004, a new first grade teacher at Mexican Hat Elementary was struggling with a very tough class of kids. She had begun her teaching career in September, and Denney had periodically told me "Christena stories" throughout the fall—partially as a way of making me feel like I was still in the "school loop," and partially because he was at a total loss for ideas on how to help her. Denney was not an educator, he was a therapist, and he had no idea how to provide assistance in such areas as classroom management or curriculum. And as I was to discover, this was most definitely one of those mixtures of children that required a teacher to know and use *every* tool in her toolbox. Unfortunately for Christena, no first-year teacher's toolbox is very full.

When first introduced, Christena smiled a shy smile and held out her hand to me. She struck me as a pretty girl, perhaps in her early twenties. There was something very sweet-looking about Christena that made her likable from the beginning. Perhaps it was the way she said, "I've heard a lot about you...from *everyone*...and I hope you can help me because I really, *really* need help." It's hard not to immediately like someone so thoroughly open about their plight.

And what a plight it was. Although not a large class, the makeup of the class was challenging. Several children displayed obvious behavior issues, perhaps due to hyperactivity or a lack of discipline and structure in the home, not having had a tightly managed classroom for the first half of their school year, or some combination of all of these. Several of the children were struggling with language issues—not because they were bilingual, but rather because they were coming from homes where neither Navajo *nor* English were spoken fluently. When children do not have a well-developed first language, inevitably reading and all language-based tasks of school come with enormous difficulty.

There were a few children already identified as having special needs such as learning disabilities; and then it was evident that a few of the children were struggling with some genuine emotional challenges. It was no wonder this brand-new teacher was at a loss as to how to approach such a complex mix of children with so many varying needs!

Christena and I worked together for the remainder of the school year, and when the year ended and the principal convinced her to loop up with this group of children and teach second grade in the fall 2004, I assured her I would still be around to offer whatever assistance I could.

It was only a couple of weeks into the new school year (August 2004) when Christena caught me in the hallway and said, "Oh, I *really* need you to come in and take a look at one of my new students."

"Oh, yeah?" I said. "New to the school?"

"No, I think he was here last year. But new to me. And a real challenge," she added.

"But you are the *master*, Ms. Anderson!" I laughed. "Surely at this point, no child can challenge your fine management skills!"

Christena shot me one of those looks that was somewhat hard to read on her genial face. Coming from someone else it might have contained the *F* word, but coming from Christena, I sensed it was more of a *Just you wait and see, Debra...then you will* know *what I am talking about* kind of look.

I assured her I would play with my schedule and find a time when I could sneak in and unobtrusively observe.

"What's his name?" I asked, before walking away.

"Ernie," Christena said. "You'll know who I mean once you're in there."

Not long after the lunch recess, I was able to go into Christena's classroom.

"MISS DEBRA!"

I had forgotten how like Norm in *Cheers* these kids always made me feel, every time I walked into the room.

So much for being unobtrusive.

I will have to be very careful in here, I thought. *I am as safe and familiar to these kids as their favorite auntie.*

To me, however, every face looked new.

One boy in the room didn't acknowledge me. He looked at me, sliding his eyes sideways and tilting his head, as if to figure out just who this popular and well-liked grown-up might be. He was a large child, weighing nearly a hundred and twenty pounds, and he was taller than the rest of the second graders around him. Like the others in his class, he was a Navajo child with brown hair and coffee-colored eyes, and he had the lighter, caramel-colored skin of many of the children.

Before I could say a word, he pulled his knit T-shirt up over his head and jiggled his stomach furiously. "Boy, I sure am *FAT!*" he said, his voice only slightly muffled by the shirt covering his face.

Down came the shirt, and with an odd-looking but wide smile, he looked me square in the eye and from across the room boomed, "*I sure am funny, huh?!*"

What I wanted to do was turn to Christena and say, "All righty, then. I see what you were meaning to convey earlier in the hallway." Instead I walked toward him, saying, "You must be Ernie."

"HEY! How'd you know my name?"

My. Does this child always boom *like this?* I wondered.

My ability to sense anything peripherally had been seemingly lost after the accident. I simply was unable to sense anyone or anything except that which was directly in front of me, so I had absolutely no idea what all the other children were doing during this exhibition. This was one of the most frustrating losses to me—not to have that peripheral perception anymore, although in this situation, I certainly didn't have to look around to guess that all eyes were on us.

It was read-aloud time, and as Christena moved to the front of the room, she gave the signal for the children to join her. They had been performing this routine every day at the same time since school had started, and it was obvious they knew what was expected of them, and they did it.

Well, most of them did it.

As I moved off to a corner, trying to position myself so that Ernie would not be able to make any eye contact with me or think that I, in any way, was watching him, the rest of the children sat on the floor in a semicircle facing Christena.

She began: "Today, I am going to read you a story called *Henry and Mudge*, by Cynthia Ryland and Sucie Stevenson."

"AWWWWWNNNNN" came a loud, yawn-like sound from the far left corner, almost but not quite out of my line of vision.

"...Henry and Mudge, a boy and his dog..."

"ERRRRRP."

"...are meant to be together..."

"I BURPED!"

I could see a little girl nudge Ernie, *"SHHHHHHHHHH,"* she said fiercely.

"...When they meet, Henry is seven and Mudge is..."

"AHHHH-IIIEEEEEEEEEEE!"

I couldn't help it. I had to look, despite knowing it would only reinforce this display of remarkable attention-getting behaviors. Glancing over, I saw Ernie with his finger shoved deep inside his nose, contorting his face. Christena's eyebrows were almost imperceptively raised, and I could see just the whisper of a smile at the corner of her lips, happy I was getting the royal show.

"...Mudge is seven weeks old," she continued with little pause.

All the children were looking at me to see what I was going to do. They had spent enough time with me the previous year to know this would never be acceptable behavior, and I *did* want to put a stop to it—on the other hand, my purpose for the moment was not to intervene; it was purely observational. I decided to hold off for a minute to see if, without attention given to him, Ernie would stop his series of acting-out behaviors.

"...Mudge is not yet huge..." Christena went on.

A commotion began, with Ernie mimicking the story as Christena read. As his well-insulated physique began rolling across the floor and around the backside of the circle, he managed to punctuate his words with intermittent noises that were sounding an awful lot like flatulence.

"*Ewwww,*" some of the other children started to moan. "*Ewwwwwww.* He farted again," they said, scrambling away.

"Okkkkayyyyy, Ms. Anderson," I said, looking at her with a cross between horror and merriment twitching in my eyes, "I believe things might quiet down in here if I were to leave for a bit."

I looked at Ernie, and in my sternest voice said, "And you, my new young friend, get to go with me." This might have been reinforcing bad behavior since all the children loved it when they could go to my funky office, located in the trailer behind the school, but I most definitely needed to remove him from the room.

Before Ernie could make one more noise, or engage in one more antic, I conveyed with my very best *teacher look* that he would do well by quietly following me out.

And surprisingly, he did. Of course, at this point he certainly had command of everyone's attention.

"I farted," he stated loudly as we stepped outside of the room. "I'm a real character, huh?!" he added, with a wide smile that was not so much a smile of satisfaction, as it was a smile of simple amusement with himself.

From that point on, Christena and I were on a mission. Twice a week, I was in the classroom for an hour, sometimes two. We co-taught lessons, we taught all the kids how to handle Ernie's behaviors—which to ignore, which to reinforce—and we taught Ernie how to go about seeking attention more appropriately. It was a lot of work. A *lot* of work. It involved a comprehensive intervention plan that required nearly one hundred percent consistency on Christena's part, and she and I talked every day, regardless of whether I was in the building that day or not.

Both Christena and I found the time investment paying off. Ernie was learning important skills, he was developing friendships with peers, and things were definitely running more smoothly in the classroom.

A month or so into our program, after being in the room for a few minutes, I quietly asked Christena who the new boy was. She looked at me curiously, saying, "Who?" I pointed out the new boy, and she turned to me, stating, "Debra—that's T.J."

T.J.? T.J. is a boy I know well...how could he not look one bit familiar to me?

This was happening so often, I thought. *Did he get a haircut? Is he sitting one seat over?* I hated this. Kids knew. They picked up on it when they would hug me on the playground, or I would run into them at a store and have no idea who they were, no sense of familiarity. Even though I did my best to fake it, I could feel that the kids knew, and it broke my heart to crush even a hint of that unguarded affection and enthusiasm they were always sending my way. But I couldn't help it. So few things ever looked familiar to me anymore.

The day with Denney—that day when the man driving the van full of children spoke to me and I had no ability to put face to voice—that was the first. I have since learned to anticipate these awkward encounters and deal with them somewhat gracefully, but the gut-kicking, panicky feeling that occurred that first time remains tethered to my soul—deeply carved into my emotional memory bank.

How could I possibly not recognize people I know?

Three Musketeers and the Subjectivity of Brilliance

My dog, BoBaily, had been scheduled to start chemotherapy in Durango on April 14—exactly one week after my accident. Bo was a sensational dog—young and strong, but with a cancerous form of a venereal-like disease (contracted on the reservation prior to his rescue) that had a ninety-nine percent cure rate given proper treatment. Bo had been part of my world since I stumbled upon him in Bluff, starving and rail-thin, six and a half months earlier—and he had weaseled his way deep into my heart. He was probably about eight months old when I first took him home, and with his big white body, expressive brown eyes, wide forehead, and large jowls, Bo looked like a cross between a Great Dane, a Burmese mountain dog, and a Saint Bernard. And he could run like no other dog I had ever known. Bo could maintain a fifteen-mile-an-hour pace for eight to ten miles as he followed me while I drove the car down an isolated dirt road.

Whatever his mix, I always said that Bo howled like a hound dog, ran like a greyhound, and loved with the heart and loyalty of a lab.

Strangely enough, just one month prior to my accident, Bo and I—along with my then three-year-old dog, Teek—were running in the early morning darkness when a car came racing out of nowhere, hitting and throwing Teek a good fifty feet down the road.

If Bo's to be described as a sensational dog, then I think Teek has to be categorized as a spectacular example of a boy in a furry, four-legged outfit. When I first stumbled upon him, the vet figured he was about two or three weeks old. He didn't even weigh a full pound. Teek and I found each other in the fall of 1999 in Galena, and I had to wait until my next trip into the city of Anchorage before getting him proper medical care. Until then, I mixed up the best formula I could, and did my best to feed him. Despite all odds against him, this remarkable dog survived, and I carried him next to my heart in a homemade *tzute*—one of those South American type sashes—until he was big enough to transfer into a ferret pouch that hung from my neck and down my chest. Teek (his name is short for Teekona—an Athabascan Indian word for wolf) went nearly everywhere with me, every day for the first year of his life (much to the delight of schoolchildren and occasionally to the angst of my supervisors).

And this now-eighty-pound black-lab-and-husky mix of a dog had absolutely no idea that he *was* a dog.

Most people figured I didn't know it, either.

When Teek was thrown down the road that icy cold morning in March, we were fortunately less than half a block from home, and my adrenaline kicked in at an all-time high. There was no small-animal vet in Blanding, and the nearest vet I felt confident in lived one hundred and fifty miles away, in Durango, Colorado. I drove to Durango in my truck in just under ninety minutes. Teek lay on my lap not making a sound, and Bo stood behind my seat and threw up over my shoulder. I never was sure if Bo threw up from nerves or from getting carsick as we drove over the mountain pass pretending to be Danica Patrick, but by the time we arrived at the Aspen Veterinary Hospital, all three of us were feeling pretty ragged.

In an attempt to save his front leg and shoulder, our vet called in a specialist to provide weekly acupuncture treatments to Teek. It was the acupuncture vet who had told me about Dr. Lee, a respected osteopath she thought might be able to help my brain with its healing.

So every week, Ila's husband, Jimmy, chauffeured the three musketeers—Teek, Bo, and Me—to Durango for our respective chemotherapy, acupuncture, and cranial treatments.

We were quite the crew.

* * * * *

Dr. Lee approached my treatment primarily using acupuncture and cranial sacral therapy. Although, ultimately, it was Dr. Lee who referred me to Dr. Willner, his treatments did help lessen the crushing, white-hot pain of the headaches and the nausea that accompanied them. Unfortunately, they did nothing to combat the narcoleptic fatigue that had me sleeping eighteen or more hours a day; nor did they have any effect on dissipating the fog in my head that made it feel as if I were walking around with a brain smothered in cotton batting.

In June 2003—about seven weeks into my treatments—I had the spontaneous (and, to me, brilliant) insight that the very best way for me to recover would be to take my dogs and do a long-distance bicycle trip for four or five weeks.

Dr. Lee is an intelligent, kindly man, with a gentle but very direct manner that I appreciated. I trusted him implicitly and had been following all of his instructions with the vigilance of the devoted. Still, when he responded to my epiphany with, "Debra—no, I don't think that's a good idea at all. Even though it's your head that's injured, your body's not likely to have the stamina for a trip like you're talking about," I just barreled right over his words, quite sure that I had divined the ultimate in healing opportunities.

"You just don't know me, Dr. Lee! This is how I'll heal. This would be the *best* way for me to heal." Having traveled by bicycle through innumerable states and five countries every summer throughout my thirties, I was quite certain this would be the perfect remedy for anything that ailed me.

"Debra, listen...you're still dizzy. And nauseous. Some days you're sleeping as many as twenty hours...how would you manage on a bike? You, yourself, have said you can't think clearly and that your judgment's impaired. I don't think this is wise. In fact, I think it'd be very, very dangerous."

"No, no, Dr. Lee, I'm *sure* of it. I mean, when I get tired, I'll just throw down my sleeping bag and nap. The dogs'll sleep right beside me for as long as I need to sleep."

Dr. Lee must have shaken his head and prayed that his reasoning would win out over mine. That somehow I would understand that I was neither the physical nor the cognitive person I associated with myself.

Actually, the need for sleep won out—a good thing, since even simple reasoning did not seem part of my repertoire at the time. But I probably put in twelve hundred hours under the covers before I recognized that Dr. Lee was most definitely the wiser of the two of us, and that there was no way I could ride my bike to the corner, much less carry two eighty-pound dogs and gear for several hundred miles in the desert sun.

In reflection, that kind of narrow-minded certainty should have alerted me to some significant changes in my personality. But when you're thinking in a dogmatic, narrow-minded kind of way, you're quite sure you're thinking broadly and intelligently.

It's one of the ironies of a head injury.

Doing Just Fine, Thank You
August 2003

Summer came and went, and school was getting ready to resume. I was still sleeping an incredible amount; still trying to manage more than one task at a time; still trying to remember anything from one minute to the next; still battling the headaches. Sometime in mid-summer, I had started reading novels—beginning with Winnie the Pooh (*House at Pooh's Corner*), and graduating to Joan Hess's tales of Maggody, which had been sent to me by my friend Joyce. I read them all: *Miracles in Maggody, Martians in Maggody, Madness in Maggody, Misery Loves Maggody* (bet I really liked that one). I tried to start and finish each book in one session, even if it took me most of the night to do so, because if I didn't, I had no recollection of the book's characters and only the most fleeting recollection of the plot when I picked it up the next day. I still have a whole shelf of books I read that summer that remain utterly new to me.

Looking back on it, it seems I should have sensed something odd and disquieting about a single-minded focus that allowed me to read for hours on end (though without remembering what I read), and that seemed to be the only thing keeping me from sleeping. Later, and continuing today, writing has the same effect. I am often able to sit at a computer and write for hours and hours, absolutely immersed in the subject matter, and not have to go to sleep. And when I return and read what I wrote a day later or a week later, I am utterly astounded by how intelligent it sounds. I can say this without bragging because I have no real sense of ownership of anything I write. Like the novels that I can read but not remember; I write without remembering what I wrote. It's eerie.

This eerie little glitch became more than a bit disconcerting when I would write a psychological report on a child, only to be unable to discuss it intelligently after it had been delivered to its source. I remember more than once sitting in a car and reading and re-reading one of my own reports, desperately hoping I would hang on to the information long enough to carry on a discussion about my recommendations.

But all this came later. At the close of summer 2003, I had not even come close to being able to write a report. I was still working my way through sophomoric novels and rocking in my bed, holding my head when the headaches hit.

* * * * *

It was August, and Tony had scheduled a back to school meeting for people in my department. For more years than I can count, my calendar did not begin and end in January and December, but rather in August and June. There was always the sigh of relief when another tough but exhilarating year ended in June, just as there was the excitement and anticipation of the new year as it began in August. I had loved the beginning of every school year for twenty-three years as a student, and nearly that many as an educator. This year was no different. I wanted school to begin, and I wanted to return to work full-time.

Tony's morning meeting was scheduled from 8:00 until noon, and I had no doubt that I would be able to sail through it without pause. After all, I had spent April through August doing all the right things to speed recovery; I had been a dutiful patient. True, I was still having trouble with memory, with thinking clearly, with extreme fatigue, and with the headaches, but I was not factoring these things into my enthusiasm. It was August, and school was starting.

As I would only much later identify, a lack of insight into my own situation and a gross overestimation of my abilities would be a consistent and recurring pattern.

Greeting Ila first thing in the morning, I assured her I was confident in my ability to participate in the meeting and was so happy to be back at work. Ila, dear sweet Ila, encouraged me to be realistic and not push myself too hard.

"I'm doing well!" I assured her. "I'm fine. Really, I'm fine."

By 9:00 a.m., my face was tingling and beginning to feel numb. I asked Ila to take notes for me, and also to keep a record of any symptoms she observed.

By 10:00 my tongue felt thick, and I was sure that if I spoke, it would be unintelligible and garbled—and though it wouldn't have been, it felt that way and left me afraid to talk. There was a distinctly metallic taste in my mouth, and Ila's notes from that morning indicate that my word-finding skills had significantly deteriorated by 11:00, as had my receptive language skills. I did not understand what I was hearing; I was getting confused, and it was observable by others.

These physical sensations were all hallmarks I came to recognize as sure signs of cognitive overload—warning signals that my brain was not processing information efficiently and that were giving me time to back away and avoid the payment for depleting my pennies. I must say it took me a very long time—many, many months of headaches and the need for twenty-four, thirty-six, even forty-eight hours of uninterrupted sleep—before I would come to respect and listen to those warning signals.

Until then, I just found myself apologizing a lot and feeling tremendous embarrassment at my inefficiency and lack of stamina.

I came to hate apologizing. I was always apologizing for not being able to finish something I started—for being unable to function at even a minimally efficient level.

I was trying to disguise how little I remembered, understood, or maintained from any interaction. This consumed a tremendous amount of energy, thus exacerbating the symptoms—which increased the painful feelings of guilt, embarrassment, and shame that accompanied the symptoms and my reactions. I hated the feelings. I hated the apologizing. And I wasn't feeling all that fond of this new post-accident me.

It was August and it was time to work. It was just that simple.

* * * * *

Not making it through the morning meeting was devastating. The fact that simply sitting and listening in a low-keyed meeting resulted in such dramatic side effects stunned me. What was I going to do? I mean, it was one thing to take the summer to recuperate— summer was a time I had free to do with as I chose—but now it was time to return to work. How was I going to function in such a high-intellect job when I still could not *think* without my face going numb, without simple conversation resulting in blinding headaches and the need to sleep for hours on end?

It's amazing the amount of stimulation that exists in one's environment without any realization of it at all. With the exception of short visits from friends, my life had been essentially still. I did not have music on in the house; I did not have background noise of any kind. My windows remained covered with their curtains and blankets.

Suddenly, there was more than one person to look at and attend to; conversations took place between two or more people. There were bright lights and colors, posters and music, sounds outside the room. Either I zeroed in on one person at a time and blocked everything else out, or I got lost in the clamor. Either way it was costing far more pennies than my daily cup allotted. I was shocked, and the panicky feeling that lodged in the core of my being was nearly paralyzing.

Work is what I did. In many ways, it was who I was. It defined my time, my passions, and my sense of identity. I couldn't use a power tool effectively to save my life, but give me a school full of problems and dilemmas, and there were few situations I didn't have a box full of tools I could effectively utilize.

Yet it was clear I was not going to be able to manage the environmental demands and stimulation found in my job, much less the cognitive ones. While Ila and Tony helped me reconcile this and encouraged me to accept this fact, I couldn't help but think I should be able to just *buck up* and pull it together. I still held the mind-set that this was, after all, *only* a mild concussion, and surely I could work if I put my mind to it.

It didn't take long for me to realize that no matter how hard I tried, how tough and *bucked up* I attempted to be, I was not able to responsibly carry out the demands of this job I loved so much. At least not yet.

This realization brought with it the threat of a nearly incomprehensible depression at the thought that the smells, sounds, and energy of each school would carry on while I sat home, wrapped in blankets of silence.

So, instead of sitting in the house for one more day, lamenting the fog in my head and fear in my guts, I decided to do what I knew always restored me: I would go camping. I could sleep outdoors in the wilderness just as well as I could sleep in my darkened bedroom, and I could do it feeling a whole lot less afraid.

I wouldn't do it on a bike, but I would take the dogs, drive only rural, unpopulated roads, and we would go camping.

Ready to go! We packed us up!

Dirty Devil

My decision to pack up my car and go camping for an indefinite period of time must have worried many people. Most of my friends and acquaintances probably knew that psychologically it was something I felt that I had to do, yet I can't imagine anyone believed I should be heading out alone. The best I could offer was the commitment that I would get a cell phone and stay connected. A friend's husband helped me get the car ready for the trip, and on the last day in August, I headed away from Blanding on Highway 95.

Had I been capable of analyzing anything clearly, my first day on the road surely would have made me question the wisdom of my trek—but analysis of any kind (clear or not) was not among my current cognitive strengths. Perseverance, on the other hand, was present in copious amounts.

Heading northwest, within an hour of starting out in late morning, I found myself beginning to feel tired and a little bit dazed. I turned west onto a gravel road that I thought would take me into the million-acre Glen Canyon National Recreation Area. It's an area filled with the Anasazi Indian ruins and the red slickrock so well-known to outdoor enthusiasts in the southeastern Utah area. I had been there several times with friends of mine who were teaching me the basics of rappelling into the slot canyons, and I was quite sure it would offer the isolated and quiet camping I was seeking.

I must have driven back a mile or two, and I was having difficulty negotiating the potholes and washboard contours of what appeared to be a washed-out, unfamiliar road. Somehow (and to this day I am not sure how) I found myself on a small, dirt side road, parked precariously close to the edge of a drop-off.

My dilemma was that I was facing the edge of a steep cliff, and I was at a complete loss for getting myself out of such a predicament. I was afraid to back up—afraid if I pushed in the clutch and the car rolled forward even one inch, it would tip over the edge and plummet several hundred feet downward—most certainly ending my odyssey before the middle of the first day. I couldn't go forward, and I couldn't bring myself to put the car in reverse, so Bo, Teek, and I sat there in silence.

The three of us sat like the see-no-evil monkeys, staring out of the front windshield, with me having no idea how to resolve this situation.

I contemplated getting out of the car, but was afraid changing the weight factor might send the car barreling over the edge, and I didn't want that to occur if the dogs were still in it. In my logic of the moment, I decided, instead, to let the dogs out of the car first—not reasoning, of course, that if weight were the factor, then their combined one hundred and sixty pounds to my less than one hundred twenty pounds probably meant I should go first. Either way, it was a silly contemplation because while certainly close to the edge, I had very much misperceived the "wiggle room," and our being in or out of the car was not going to affect it a bit.

But I didn't know this at the time, and was quite certain we were in mortal danger of barreling over the cliff and plunging to our death—Thelma and Louise style—hundreds of feet below.

Suddenly, I noticed another car driving slowly by on the main gravel road. Racing out of the car, oblivious to the fact that I had just determined getting out of the car would send us swooping toward our demise, I tentatively waved hello to the couple driving. I was unsure if I should flag them down and ask for help, or just pretend I had intentionally parked within inches of a three-hundred-foot drop-off.

Fortunately for me, they made some assumptions and, backing up their car, asked if I needed assistance.

"Well, I feel kind of stupid about this...but see, I'm right at the edge of the drop-off, and well...I'm afraid to push in my clutch, which I need to do in order to start the car...and (taking a much needed breath and slowing down my speech), jeez, I feel *really* stupid about this, but I just don't know what to do."

After I finished explaining my predicament, the wife gave her husband that look that says with no words spoken: *Oh, honey, you help her...go ahead and back up the car for her*. And sure enough—dutifully and without complaint—this good husband got into my car and swiftly backed it up.

"Oh, don't feel bad," said this nice young woman. "We got ourselves stuck up ahead. The road is really washed out, and you probably shouldn't try going back there by yourself."

So much for camping in the Glen Canyon Recreation Area.

The young couple went on their way, and once again, Teek, Bo, and I found ourselves staring out the window wondering what to do next. It was obvious, even to me, that I needed to set up camp soon, as clearly I was exceeding my limit of being able to focus on the road and make defensible decisions. My face was not yet numb and the headache had not yet begun, but I knew I was precariously close to the time when my mental curtain would shut me down completely.

I drove on, passing through Hanksville, Utah, and pulled off on what appeared to be a good dirt road that would take me back to a secluded camping spot. Finding what seemed my perfect headquarters for the night, isolated and complete with a gentle river, I tossed out my instant-release pop-up tent, fed the dogs, and promptly fell asleep.

* * * * *

A hard, driving rain woke me up, and as I peered out the tent door, I could see my glorious little nirvana rapidly becoming a roiling morass. While I love nothing better than camping with Teek and Bo, I must say, there is little worse than having two thundering and sopping wet dogs coated in mud in a tent meant for two (semi-clean) humans. My brain was functioning well enough to alert me that if I waited much longer (like about two minutes), I would be trapped on this dirt road, which was rapidly becoming a sludgy, non-negotiable mess. I knew I needed to get out of there, and I needed to do it quickly.

Leaving the tent, I threw the dogs and myself into the car and headed for the highway. The road was disappearing beneath my wheels, and the rain was coming down in thick sheets, preventing any real view of where I was going. I did notice that my gentle river had risen substantially and was looking like a swirling, angry overflow that I hoped would not swallow my tent before I could return for it.

It was 4:45 in the morning and dark. My brain, not capable yet of generating solutions to problems, left me with absolutely *no* thoughts for how to handle this situation. I headed back toward Hanksville, hoping that once there I would somehow magically figure it all out. The rain was diminishing, but so was my ability to stay awake.

My problems magnified when my single-minded focus took over. The sun was coming up, and a beautiful double rainbow appeared to my right. It seemed logical to try to get closer to it, so I turned off on a side road and drove in its direction. My thinking—and I use this word loosely—was that I would get closer to the rainbow, find a good spot to park, and figure out what to do.

What did *not* occur to me—besides the fact that I certainly was not going to get closer to the rainbow—is that I had veered off onto another dirt road.

Minutes later, I found myself sucked deeply into what I later found out is known as blue clay—bentonite clay to geologists, "gumbo" to locals. Blue clay has a consistency like Crisco—the kind that comes in a five-pound can and makes your arteries harden just to look at it. It's impossible to drive on, and not much better for walking; and like quicksand, it will suck in a car faster than a viper inhales a church mouse. Despite my hundred or so attempts to gun the engine and shift the gear in an effort to extract myself, it was clear that I was not about to be released from the grip of gumbo stew.

Realizing I was going nowhere, I decided to do what came most naturally these days: I would sleep, knowing the dogs would be content to do the same.

Later I was to learn that I had been caught in a flash flood of historic intensity, in an area called The Dirty Devil. I'm sure at the time the irony of its name was lost on me, but in retrospect, I have to admit admiring the coincidence that this all occurred in a place named The Dirty Devil.

* * * * *

It was five in the afternoon, and the dogs, covered in mud, were happily enjoying their new friend, Richard the tow truck driver, as we were being pathetically towed back to Hanksville.

Sometime around nine that morning—after a four- or five-hour nap—I had leashed the dogs and walked into town. Like much of Utah, Hanksville is a small and sleepy community comprised largely of devout Mormons. It's a sin to shop, eat out, or conduct any business outside of the Church on the Sabbath, and I knew from living in Blanding that—this being a Sunday—I was not easily going to find assistance.

Eventually we did find Martha[6], the waitress at the only open café, who knew Joe down the street at the rock shop—who knew Mike, the owner of the tow shop, who would know where to find Richard, the tow truck driver.

This kind of networking is one of the benefits of a small town when everything is locked up tight.

Richard was a fun guy who, at fifty-two, suggested a cross between Jimmy Buffet and Bob Dylan. His wild, curly hair was mashed hippie style beneath a red print bandana meant to keep the sweat from pouring in his eyes; and he had the weathered look of one who spent a lot of time working outside. Richard and I got to know each other quite well that day—in the way people do when it takes one of them six straight hours of digging before a car can be extracted from blue clay, and the other one stands around feeling guilty. Not only had I managed to sink the car deeply into the gumbo guck, I had done it at an angle that required Richard to dig out the *road* before he could get the tow truck in the right position to hitch and pull out the car.

It took the entire day, but Richard was finally able to hook up the car, and with the very filthy Teek and Bo complaining loudly about riding shotgun in the Subaru, we retreated to Hanksville.

Richard charged me twenty-eight dollars, and when I protested, he stated, "Hey, we charge by the mile from town, and you were only three miles away, so twenty-eight dollars is what it cost you." He then checked over my car, which surprisingly seemed in working order. After apologizing sixty more times for the backbreaking work he had to do to get me there, I waved a grateful farewell and put the three of us back on the road.

After all, we had a tent to retrieve.

Four miles and five minutes later, the car died. It simply stopped running in the middle of the road; and only because I was on a downhill slope was I able to roll it to the side of the highway. Sighing and wondering if maybe I hadn't thought this trip through quite as well as I should have (well, okay, I hadn't thought it through at all), I put Teek and Bo back on their leashes and once again began the walk toward town.

I was becoming very familiar with the four-mile strip between Hanksville and nowhere.

Just as I was wondering what I would do once we got to Hanksville, since it was still Sunday and now after five when everything would be closed, I spotted the yellow tow truck heading right toward us. Pulling over to the side of the road, Richard leaned out the open window, grinning.

"Need a ride?"

"Richard! Oh, boy—am I glad to see you. Do you have a call out this way again?"

---

[6] The names of the people who helped me in Hanksville have been changed, with the exception of Mike, who really does own the tow trucking shop, and Richard, who really is Richard the tow truck driver.

"Nope," he said, smiling.

"Well, what are you doing here?"

"Well, Curly..." Despite his own rather rebellious hair, Richard had begun calling me Curly several hours earlier as the ninety-degree heat turned my long and very wavy hair into a frizzy mass of ridiculous and unmanageable spirals. "...I just didn't have good feelings about you and the dogs in that car. I thought I would follow at a distance for a little while and make sure you made it where you were headed."

With that, Richard plopped us all into the front seat of his truck. Teek and Bo were ecstatic, happily licking Richard-their-new-best-friend, and laying their muddy paws and bodies over every inch of the cab.

Pulling into the parking lot of a small, run-down motel clearly in the process of remodeling, Richard walked into the tiny lobby with the three of us—caked in mud and surely looking like something out of a comic strip—following closely behind.

"Martin, this lovely lady and her dogs are going to need a room for the night."

Martin, a man of substantial size and questionable orientation, stared at us, clearly speechless and at a loss for responding.

"You got one, don't you?" Richard asked.

"Well, yes, but..."

"Well, then, set 'em up with one!"

I *liked* the way this Richard guy worked!

Martin eyed Richard grudgingly and looking at us said, "Well now, just a minute...I need to talk to Robert about this."

Robert?

Robert, apparently Martin's partner and in charge of decision making, had wandered out from their attached apartment and was looking us over with a bemused eye. I imagine I looked pretty desperate at this point. I certainly know I felt it.

"Mmm. Well, you can see we're remodeling and aren't really set up for guests...but if you're willing to clean up after yourself and not leave a mess, I guess we can put you up for the night. Just one night, though."

Oh, you betcha, I thought, the mental fog taking supreme domination over all else. *Just one night.*

I just need to sleep.

The next morning, as if I had called and ordered a giant yellow taxi, there was Richard waiting in the parking lot, ready to tow us to Richfield, Utah—the closest place to order the new clutch I would need if I wanted to go anywhere independently. Teek and Bo—bathed, mud-free, and happy to be riding with their new pal in the cab—curled up and slept while I calculated how much it was going to cost now that the towing mileage was one hundred and thirty instead of three.

After two nights in a motel, with a new clutch installed and some intense reservations about whether or not I should continue, I decided to push forward with my plans. I stopped to get myself a cell phone before leaving Richfield, after wondering if even *camping* was something I could no longer manage independently.

The hard pit of fear lodged deep in my belly.

What if there hadn't been a Richard to bail me out?

Let the Dogs be the Trail Guides

Leaving Richfield, we headed north without any idea where we might end up. I could not drive more than a couple of hours at a time, so finding a place to camp really had more to do with what I spotted after about ninety minutes of driving (so I had thirty minutes left of functioning to utilize for setting up camp) than with any planned destination. As it turned out, the timing took us right to Fish Lake, a perfect spot to begin my healing journey.

I prefer to think of the official start as happening after the new clutch was installed.

Fish Lake is beautiful. Six miles long and a mile wide, it has a walking trail that surrounds it. The aspens were just beginning to turn, and their gold and red leaves provided vivid accent to the spruce and fir trees that thickly framed the crystal waters. It was early September and the nights were cold—frost quickly covered the ground once the sun set, but the days were warm, and the sky was a cloudless, brilliant blue.

Other than the camp hosts, Teek, Bo, and I had Fish Lake to ourselves, and it was indeed serene and restorative. We spent two nights camping there—the only time on the seven-week trip that we stayed in an actual campground—and given that I had become more than a little insecure about my thinking and planning abilities, it was nice to know that camp hosts were just down the road.

We spent our days walking around the lake and napping, and in the evenings I would write by the fire while the dogs rested at my feet. When Bo wanted to go to bed, he would quietly remove himself from our little camp circle and place himself squarely in the middle of my sleeping bag. Bo loved that sleeping bag. It seemed he knew how to time it just right so that he snatched his position before I did, and when I would ask him to please move over (a command Teek has always readily responded to), Bo would look at me with those huge sun-kissed brown eyes and emit just the slightest of groans, indicating he was quite content where he was, thank you very much.

"Bo. Move over," I would say. This, of course, yielded absolutely no response, so I would try a more commanding approach, saying *"Bo!"* while giving him a little shove. If dogs smile, this one was doing it then. Trying to move Bo when Bo didn't want to be moved was like trying to shove an eighty-pound bag of wet cement off a table with both hands tied behind your back.

"Move *OVER*, Bo. You have your *own* sleeping bag," was generally the gist of my last plea. In Bo's mind, I am quite sure he believed that my sleeping bag *was* his sleeping bag. Ultimately, I would squeeze in beside him and push him over just enough that I could zip us up. Bo would heave a happy sigh, at which

point Teek would leave his sleeping bag and lie down on the other side of me.
   Such is how we spent our nights under the stars.
   There is something to be said for routine.

Journal Entry, early in the camping trip:

A recollection: 1973. Me: age 19. Home from college for the weekend. My brother home from his college in Tucson as well. And with him the marijuana brownies he had brought for us to share (well, actually I don't think he thought about me in regards to the sharing part, but being one who had constantly sought his approval and willingness to include me in on something he and his friends did, I prefer to remember it as something he planned for us to do together).Because I desperately wanted to share an experience with my brother—any experience— eating them seemed like a good idea at the time. I thought it would be a bonding experience.

Of course I did not know at the time that he was planning to stick around for all of five minutes before departing for the weekend with friends. Turns out that I had the house alone, as my parents had gone to the Toronto Shakespeare Festival and would not be back until Sunday.

Several hours later, after having consumed the "make me cool" brownies, I found myself sitting on my parents' porch, rocking back and forth on a non-rock-able chaise lounge and thinking, "Oh, my God. What if I never come down? What if I am like this forever?" I imagined my parents coming home and seeing me like this: in this seemingly catatonic state from the outside, but with my mind running amok, up and down roller-coaster runways inside. And there being absolutely no ability on my part to latch on to a clear, definable thought or explain what had happened.

"Dear God," I begged, "please let me come down. Please, please don't punish me by making me stay like this forever."

As I recall, I made many promises about what I would never do again if I could just have my brain back. I don't know about all the promises I made, but I sure as heck never touched marijuana again.

Flash forward almost exactly thirty years, and here I am plea bargaining with God for the same outcome. I am sitting here at my little isolated campsite feeling as if I am stoned beyond redemption and plea-bargaining with God.

"Please God; please don't make me stay like this forever."

Another entry (never dated because I rarely knew what the date was):

It's good to be alone because talking with someone feels as if I am talking through a haze; listening is even worse. It's as if my brain needs a major tracking adjustment and a total cobweb sweep. It's good that everywhere I have found to camp has been isolated. I feel more normal if I don't have to say anything out loud.

Next entry:

Who knows what I am or what I think now. Most days I wonder if I even *can* think, and if I do (think, that is), I figure it doesn't much matter because 24 hours later I will have no recollection of having had the thought at all.
Groundhog's Day.

And another:

How come my tongue feels so thick every time I over-stimulate my brain? How come over-stimulating my brain means driving for too long, or interacting with a ranger for too long, or staying awake beyond the moment I have that "I need to sleep" realization?
How come I sleep and sleep and sleep and still feel tired?
I wonder if I look as stupid and blank as I feel.

Near the end of my trip I made a list of "moments," which I extracted from various journal entries over the nearly two months of travel. There are many "Most beautiful" or "Most inspiring" moments. But there are also these:

Most shocking moment: Hiking in the afternoon in the San Rafael Swell and coming upon someone's campsite and thinking how bummed I was that someone else had discovered this area, and that we were no longer alone. Closer inspection revealed that the "someone else" was really us. We had hiked back to our campsite with absolutely no awareness on my part that I was backtracking; absolutely no visual recognition indicating to me that I was on familiar ground. In retrospect I suppose I was very lucky to have found my way back to camp at all, although I suspect Bo and Teek led me there intentionally. It helped that Denney had joined us for the weekend and had a fully functioning brain.

Most "OH NOOOOOO!" moment: Teek and Bo and the porcupine. What a sight. What a PROCEDURE to get those quills out of Bo! I guess there is something to be said for my newly found patience and ability to just sit and do the tedious!

Most disappointing moment(s): Every time I'm flattened by a numb face that is followed by one of those headaches.

During the trip I had written long letters to both Ila and Denney, and when I returned, they gave me those letters back so I would have a journal of sorts (on days I would write letters, I could not also write a journal entry). In one letter I had written the following reflection:

What I am learning from my dogs:

- Nap when I need to. Don't apologize for napping. Sleep as often as I want. Wake up from each nap happy and jubilant, remembering that waking up is the celebration.
- Know where your loved ones are, even if THEY can't see YOU.
- Love like a lab.
- To a dog, it doesn't matter that they are a dog. They will still gallop like a horse and leap in water like a salmon. What matters is the enthusiasm. Do what you love with enthusiasm.
- Snuggle close to the ones you love.
- Drink lots of water. Even if there are other choices, choose water.
- Stop eating when full. It's all right to leave some in the bowl.
- Always let the dogs be the trail guides. Always. They are wayyyy better at it than me (obviously)!
- Run in circles. Do it with total joy and abandon. It doesn't matter that you are only running in circles...it's the joy and abandon that matter.
- Play like you are a child, even if you are not one.
- It's okay to ask for love and attention. Sometimes you get it; sometimes you don't. It's still okay to ask for it when you need it.
- Walk in the shade.
- Protect the ones you love.
- Follow your nose. Chase what is in front of you. It's okay not to catch what you are chasing. It's the eye on the goal that is important.
- When you are scared, curl up really, really close to the one you love and trust the most.
- Love with all your heart. Hold back nothing.

Cliché and poster board cute as they might seem, each one of these provides a memory peg for something on the trip, and had Ila and Denney not returned them, I am quite sure I would have none of these memories at all.

We were strongly connected before, in the way certain people are with their animals, but there is a unique sort of bonding that develops between a person and an animal after spending weeks in the wilderness with no other people or distractions. It's as if they knew what I needed before I did. When I needed to sleep, they slept with me. When I needed to walk, they guided the way. When I needed to laugh, they provided plenty of free entertainment. When they needed to make me more alert, they functioned as two holy-terror watch dogs. And when they needed something from me, just like they did with me, I somehow always seemed to know what it was they needed. We were a threesome, a team; and I felt totally safe and at peace with no other company near.

I never had to apologize to Teek or Bo for sleeping too much.

Ahh-Rooo Mornings
October 2003

It was October 20th; a date that only later would become significant enough to remember. Our days were lazy and serene. We had our routine, which began the same every single morning. Beginning about the third or fourth day of camping, Bo would be the first to leave the tent. He would find an open space nearby and run in wide open circles, howling, *"AHH-ROOOOO."* It was such a fun sound—sort of a cross between a hound dog's yowl and a happy ululation all its own, never before heard. To Bo, it didn't matter if it was cloudy or sunny, cold or blissfully warm. Every day was a celebration, and Bo made his happiness known by running in circles and shouting "AHH-ROOO." Sometimes Teek would join in and surprisingly emit a wailing, wolf-like bay that reminded me I had named him well; other times he would just lie in the tent beside me as we watched our crazy Bo running in circles, greeting the day. We were all happy. We were all content. I thought of them as our Ahh-Rooo mornings.

On this particular day, I had a peculiar feeling—one I couldn't identify. Was it time to leave the Vermillion Castles area in which we had been lounging for over a week? Time to move on? To go home? We were comfortably nestled beneath red sandstone pillars in the Dixie National Forest. It was the peak of fall, and I was in no hurry to leave.

We had created a fabulous campsite. We made a kitchen area apart from the bathing area (this being a five-gallon bucket of water roped to a tree with the spigot just above my head). We had enough space so that I could set the tent up away from the food and water, and we had a fire pit that was just perfect for sitting and gazing at the blazing red and gold aspens that mingled in the coniferous forest surrounding us.

Vermillion Castles is aptly named. All around us spires stood like vivid red pillars rising from castles to meet the sky. Three miles up the gravel road, nestled in a spectacular alpine meadow, we had discovered the Yankee Meadow Reservoir. With its azure blue waters reflecting the crimson and golden leaves of the aspen, maple, and oak trees, and with all of it (and us) resting under a cerulean sky, it was spectacular.

And we had it entirely to ourselves.

But I definitely had the feeling it was time to move on. I looked at Teek, who cocked his head at me, and then at Bo, who was still bouncing around between the fire pit and kitchen area, and said, "Well, boys, I think it's time to pack up. Not sure where we're headed, but I think it's time to leave our little paradise."

I could have sworn Teek's ears dropped and Bo's ahh-rooo turned into an ahh-rats!

* * * * *

Once we were on the road, I just couldn't shake this preternatural feeling that had started early in the day. Heading west toward Brian's Head, I thought we would hike one of the trails we passed up before finding the Vermillion Castles area, but that didn't feel quite right to me, so we turned around and drove back the way we had just come. Landing in Panguitch, a mid-sized town just twenty-four miles southeast of Bryce Canyon and only eight miles from where we had been camping, I stopped to have a roll of film developed while I contemplated our options. Predictably no options were actually occurring to me, but I figured I had an hour to figure something out.

I had discovered early in the camping trip that a peculiarity of the injury was that visual images disappeared faster than drops of water in a hot frying pan. No sooner did I rest my eyes on something—landscaping, a road, a landmark of some sort—than it simply bounced from my memory. It became habit to have film developed every time I went through a town of any size so that I could label and study the pictures every night. This was my way of trying to protect my remarkable journey; my way to hope that some of the images would remain fixed in my mind.

I was having pictures developed of our time in Vermillion Castles, and there were a couple of pictures on the roll of three days we had spent with Denney in an area called San Rafael Swell.

San Rafael Swell is a spectacularly wild area of desert canyons and incredibly rugged beauty located in central Utah. It's a place I never could have negotiated alone at that time, given the challenges I was still experiencing. And actually, I didn't negotiate it all that well even with Denney around. By the time I met up with him at the entrance to the area, I had used up my two-hour allotment of clear thinking, and I found myself entering the Swell at the same time that I was entering that foggy, insipid state of mind that always left me feeling so apprehensive and panicky.

Denney had been to San Rafael before and assured me that it would not take long to find the ideal camping spot. I followed him in my car through an extensive, unmarked labyrinth of narrow dirt roads, and as "not too long" became half an hour, which rolled into an hour, I found myself using every swear word I knew—and some I made up—before my brain went too numb to even curse at Denney. By the time he found a place to park so we could set up camp, I was frustrated, tired, scared, and far too ticked off to appreciate what I was seeing. I couldn't have identified one thing about the area we had just driven through, and it had cost me every ounce of energy and stamina to simply remain awake while I was driving.

My brain felt like the alien had moved back in, and I resented Denney for not realizing that I could not do what he had just required me to do.

"This is great, isn't it?" he said, all smiles and excitement.

I glared.

"What? We're here. It's beautiful. We have it to ourselves."

"F you," I think I might have said. This is not something I remember, but suspect that since it wasn't one of my finer moments, something of this nature might have rolled off my thick-feeling tongue.

Really, I was the one I was so frustrated with; and it was more fear than anger that I felt. Unfortunately, Denney was an easy target for directing my muddled emotions.

Despite any disappointment he might have been feeling, in his quiet, understated way, Denney went about setting up camp. With Teek and Bo thrilled to trail after him as he built a fire, pitched the tent, and organized the campsite, Denney let me remain alone and comatose until I was ready to interact. Several hours later, when my brain had at least somewhat cleared, a full moon had risen and I realized we were nestled in a canyon. The moon's light was reflecting off the towering rock walls surrounding us, and for the first time I was aware of the magnificence of where we were. Looking around, I was experiencing one of those profoundly inspiring moments that occurs when you are immersed in something truly worthy of the overused word awesome.

"I'm so sorry," I told Denney. "This is beautiful."

I really was sorry. It's impossible for anyone else to contemplate how frightening and overwhelming life becomes when the pennies are all gone—I needed to work harder at not letting my fear contaminate everything around me.

Denney stared at me across the fire, his muscular frame and angular features outlined in the combined glow of the flames and the moon.

"Guess what?" he said, smiling.

"What?"

"Guess."

"*DENNEY*. I can't guess. I can't even think, much less guess. What? Tell me."

"I brought you a present," he said, drawing this out in a quiet, teasing kind of way.

I looked at him.

"Shower. As in solar. I brought you a solar shower. I stopped by Brenda's and borrowed it for the weekend." Brenda was Denney's sister who lived in Monticello.

"You brought a solar shower? Really? *Really?*"

"Look," he said, pointing up and behind us. And sure enough, by the incandescence of the moon, I could see the silhouette of long towels, functioning as privacy curtains, surrounding a large black bag hanging from the branch of a tree.

"Oh, my God! Oh, you are so wonderful." I practically slobbered as I thought about warm, clean water pouring over my head. "Hey, do you think the *moon* supplies enough solar power to warm that water?"

"Sorry. I think you'll have to wait until tomorrow afternoon," Denney answered. "Unless you want a very cold shower," he deadpanned.

"I knew that," I said. "Just so you know, I was joking about moon solar power. That wasn't a head injury question."

I wanted to be sure to clarify that point.

"I knew that." Denney smiled, looking at me across the campfire.

The next day, on a hike, Denney snapped a picture of me, one arm around each dog, sitting in the hollow of a rock wall. It was this picture I stared at as I sat in Panguitch debating what to do. It was the only picture ever taken of me with both dogs, and it gave me this warm, goofy feeling of happiness. Noticing one of those Kodak machines, I blew it up, cropped it, framed it, and splashed "All kinds of family love" across the top.

I made five copies, went out to the car, and said, "Boys, I think it's time to go home."

Flooding

Fifteen miles outside of Moab, I pulled onto a dirt road. Driving back about half a mile, I let the dogs out of the car, and we all took a stretch and bathroom break. I knew we would have to camp one more night—my brain would not manage another ninety miles of driving—but this was definitely not the spot. From where we were romping I could see the highway, though it was a bit distant, and I could hear the deep, droning engines of the massive trucks carrying freight to Salt Lake City and beyond.

We would have to find a more remote site than this.

"Teek, Bo, come on! Time to go. Hop in."

Teek jumped in the car with Bo right behind him. But with half a paw in the door, suddenly Bo was off and running. The hound in him caught scent of something, probably a rabbit, and despite his usual desire to obey commands, Bo was not listening.

"BO...

"BO!"

I saw it from where I stood, and somehow I knew. At the top of the distant hill was a giant tanker, full silver body gleaming in the sun, its deep, grinding engine sounding ominous even from here. I knew in my heart that Bo was going to collide with that tanker. I knew because Bo was that fast of a runner.

Bo ran across a field and under a fence with me sprinting behind him and crying out his name, hoping that the sheer volume of my voice and depth of my despair would stop him.

It didn't.

When I reached the highway, the tanker was far past the spot where Bo lay in the road. Running to him, I dropped to the ground and held his head on my lap. Those soft brown, sun-kissed eyes looked right at me as I said, "Please, oh, please, Bo. I'm so sorry..."

And then my beautiful hound dog, who ran like a greyhound and loved like a lab, closed his eyes and died.

* * * * *

A phenomenon quite common to individuals with a TBI is something called *flooding*. Like many experiences with a brain injury, it isn't that flooding is alien to everyone else—rather it's the frequency and intensity of it that distinguishes it so much, making it such an impairment. At some point in life, everyone feels too overwhelmed to think; too exhausted to make good decisions; too angry to trust their usual ability to inhibit what they might say or do. However, generally, it takes a pretty full plate to get most people to the point of feeling so overloaded that their behavior is compromised.

When you have a head injury, it doesn't take much to render you confused and disoriented—resulting in an uninhibited response, an overreaction, or an inability to back up and think along different lines. For those with a head injury, the phenomenon of flooding can occur frequently, leaving a person feeling powerless and overwrought in everyday situations. Because when the brain floods—when it overloads—there simply *is* no ability to think through to logical solutions or options. It takes so much less stress, so much less stimulation and frustration to set off a monster flood in the brain—that when the stress truly *is* great, it can generate a situation that renders you, well, *stupid.*

* * * * *

I was sitting at the edge of the highway, Bo's head in my lap and sobbing with the apparent mind-set that the harder I cried, the more likely he would be to revive, when two twenty-something girls stopped and got out of their car to console me.

"Ohhh...I know exactly what you're going through," said one of the girls—a girl with a long blond ponytail that rode high on her head. "When my dog died last year I thought I'd never survive it."

"How can we help? What can we do to help you?" This came from her friend, a girl with short brown hair.

"I don't know... it's... Bo... it's... Bo." I buried my face in his fur, making the kind of guttural and clipped noises one makes when sobbing at a nearly out of control level, but trying to contain it.

"Do you have a car?" asked the blonde, her ponytail swinging as she glanced around.

I managed to nod, but it was sorely overridden by my heaving, and I'm not sure I communicated whether I did or did not have a car somewhere nearby.

"Oh, gosh... here, take a deep breath... We can help you. Where's your car? How'd you get here?"

I looked up at these girls, these really nice, caring girls who stopped to help me, and all I could do was whisper, "I think Bo died."

"Oh, I'm so sorry..." The ponytailed one looked at her friend before adding gently, "Do you *know* where your car is?"

"*TEEK!*" I shrieked this so suddenly that the girls jumped, screeching *"What?"* almost as loudly as I had shrieked Teek's name.

"Teek!"

The girls looked at one another, not sure if I was speaking gibberish, suffering from a mental breakdown, or perhaps just on weekend release from the state mental hospital.

"Teek. My other dog. He's in my car."

"Ohhhh, okay. Good." The one with the ponytail smiled. "You *do* have a car. Maybe we can help you get your car."

"Oh, it's over there somewhere." I flopped my arm in the direction of the side road. "I don't know...we were peeing." Those poor girls—I was not offering them the kind of information that was at all helpful.

The girls stared at each other. "Do you see her car?" the short-haired one asked.

"It's down that...that road somewhere. It's back there somewhere..." Apparently, my arm had lost all muscle tone in the span of twenty minutes, and the best I could do was flip my wrist in the general direction of the railroad tracks that separated the main highway from private land.

By this time—seven months post injury—I knew enough about overload and flooding to realize that I had to make myself slow down; had to make myself try to think through the steps that I needed to take in order to gain some control over my brain. I breathed. I breathed again. "I'm not...not sure where my car is, actually. It all happened so...fast. I just know I ran from that direction."

"Okay, listen...are the keys in it? We're going to get in our car and look for yours. One of us will drive your car back here, and we'll put your dog in the car so you can go into Moab."

Oh, this seemed like a good idea. I liked that these girls could think and give me a plan.

The girls went in search of my car, and I stayed, holding on to Bo, my face buried once again in his fur.

* * * * *

At some point the girls returned, the blonde with the ponytail driving my car and her friend driving theirs. We wrapped Bo in his beloved sleeping bag, put him in the backseat, and moved Teek into the front with me. For some reason, I thought it would panic Teek to be in the back with Bo, and oddly, although he watched Bo over the seat's edge, he made not a sound. With many, many truly heartfelt thanks to these two for stopping to help, we headed into Moab.

Brain flooding does not easily recede. I was driving the car in the right direction, but I had no idea what to do once I *got* to Moab. What should I do with Bo? Worried, I stopped at the first convenience store I saw and bought the largest bags of ice available. Stacking several of them, I laid Bo on top, and then I packed the remainder of the bags around him. I continued the drive to Moab, hopeful that I was at least keeping Bo preserved while I wandered around not knowing what to do.

Long before I left Alaska and moved to Utah, I knew about Moab. It's famous for the slickrock trails that challenge even the most experienced mountain bicyclist, and I had seen slides and photographs of friends who vacationed there often. Once, I saw a picture of a friend of mine in midair on his bike, at an angle that truly defied gravity. It looked to me like a photograph from some other planet. In fact, though for different reasons, to many longtime Utahans, Moab does indeed seem like a place on another planet. For one thing, it has restaurants that serve *alcohol*—it even boasts a small restaurant brewery—and for another, its newspaper, *The Times Independent*, is one hundred percent wind-powered. Utahans, especially those in rural parts of the state, are not exactly known for making conservation high on their list of priorities.

Moab may be the Devil's playground to many Utah natives, but it is a Mecca for the cyclists, artists, environmentalists, and outdoor enthusiasts who live and visit there. Even so, I didn't think it was such a good idea to drive around with my beloved dead dog nestled in a sleeping bag and riding high, packed on ice.

It is just that I could not think of what else to do.

But I love this sleeping bag...

Dr. Freud

At some point, though I've no recollection when, I called Denney at work and asked him what I should do. As always, calm and encouraging, he told me he would not be able to leave until the end of the day, but that he would come to Moab and we would find a place to bury Bo. I have absolutely no memory of where I went or what I did during the hours before Denney arrived, shovel in hand.

Denney drove my car, with Bo still packed in the back on top of the now melting ice and Teek sandwiched between us in the front. He spotted an area away from the highway, beneath red sandstone walls. We buried Bo in his beloved sleeping bag. This may not have been the most environmentally responsible choice, but for some reason it was comforting for me to place Bo beneath the earth zipped up in that bag. I figured I would do something extra good for the soil for the next twenty years to help compensate for it.

Denney used to love to rile Bo up before we left to go on a hike or walk. He would look at him and with excitement in his voice, say, "Bo! Are you *ready* to go?!" Bo would buoyantly run back and forth between the door and the living room, beside himself with enthusiasm, while Teek would race for the door and turn in circles—his own anticipation piqued. No matter how many times Denney instigated this scene, it never failed to amuse us both.

So, when we found the right stone, Denney carved, *Bo—are you ready to go?!?* at the top, and I followed, etching: *My BoBailey, 10-20-2003. One last Ahhh-rooo journey.*

We placed Bo's makeshift marker atop his grave, and then we had to walk away and leave him there on his own.

Quite some time later, Denney, returning from a trip to Moab, told me that the formation of the rocks towering over Bo's gravesite resembles the profile of a dog's head.

And indeed, on my next trip to Moab, I could clearly see red- and cream-colored sandstone that had somehow bucked and shifted over geologic time to form a giant canine head. A guard dog watching over my Bo, making sure I would always know just where to find him.

* * * * *

After returning home, the remainder of the fall was spent sleeping, keeping appointments with the neurologist, and agreeing at her request to undergo a neuropsychological evaluation in order to more specifically pinpoint cognitive weaknesses and strengths.

I am reasonably familiar with the neuropsych evaluation. As an educational psychologist, I have had a fair amount of experience with conducting parts of such an evaluation with children, and the neuropsychological underpinnings of a child's disabilities have always been a special interest of mine. Did I want to know just how significantly my attention span, ability to reason, and memory had been impacted? Did I want to know if the cognitive effects I was experiencing were real and able to be validated by a specialist?

Of course I did. I wanted the same kind of specific information that I had always sought in order to develop intervention programs for children.

Did I want someone *else* to do this assessment and put into black and white the extent of my impairments?

Absolutely not.

The very thought of someone else performing tests that would quantify and substantiate deficits made me hate the person doing the testing before we even met. In this case, the person was a man named Dr. George Feinsworth[7], PhD, ABPN, American Board of Professional Neuropsychology, Certified.

Lots of initials and certified to boot. Lucky me.

Before actually meeting him, I canceled my scheduled appointments with Dr. Feinsworth several times. I canceled them until I finally ran out of excuses to cancel them. There can only be so many colds, bad weather days, traffic jams, and unexpected crises in a person's life.

If I could have found a way to avoid the evaluation entirely, I would have. Given that I couldn't avoid it, if it had been possible I would have cheated. I am not proud to admit this—I prefer to pride myself on having a commitment to honesty and integrity, but the truth is I would have cheated. That's how panicked I felt at the thought of being evaluated. I just couldn't figure out how anyone could do that. It's pretty hard to look up the answers when you're alone in the room with a test giver.

Finally, having run out of excuses, I found myself sweating and swearing, but entering the office of Dr. George Feinsworth at the scheduled 8:00 a.m. time.

A slender, fairly tall man in his mid-forties with a beard and dark hair introduced himself to me.

The interloper here to document the newfound dullness of my brain, I thought.

I am quite sure I all but scoffed out loud when I noticed Dr. Feinsworth carrying the proverbial clipboard and yellow legal pad. When he sat down and crossed his legs, smiling pleasantly as he asked his first question, I sarcastically wrote him off as a fraud.

Of course, all of my sarcasm and rebellion were conducted silently in the privacy of my own head. I knew what power this man had. I was not about to present myself as a *"difficult patient,"* a *"resistant subject,"* a *"hostile individual."* He had a final report to write that would contain observations of my behavior. I would make sure to present myself in a way that belied my

---

[7] Name changed.

hostility and disdain.

I smiled, silently reminding myself to just answer the questions. *Don't elaborate. Don't say any more than is necessary. Just answer the question.*

"So, Debra, I see here you've been in a car accident."

Brilliant. Figuring I would sound hostile if I said anything at this point, I simply nodded and smiled (though not *too* broadly lest he mark down that I had inappropriate affect).

One step ahead. Always stay one step ahead, I counseled myself, pleased that I knew enough about these things not to become trapped in questions that might reveal any neuroses I had carefully tucked out of others' sight for most of my life.

"Tell me about it."

For some reason, that *really* ticked me off.

What do you want to know, you idiot? What it felt like to somersault down a highway? Or, maybe you want to know what it feels like to walk around in a constant state of subpar alertness? You want me to talk to you about my suffocating PANIC that this inchoate mass of vague thoughts is how I will THINK FOR THE REST OF MY LIFE?

Or, gosh, Dr. Freud, perhaps all you're really looking for is just a nice pat answer like, 'Oh, my...it was a very frightening experience.'

I could just see it: "The patient presented as remarkably sarcastic and hostile during the course of the initial interview..."

"Well," I said carefully, "what can I tell you? It's probably all there in your notes. I was driving to an early morning meeting, and I fell asleep and rolled my truck."

"Did you lose consciousness?"

"No, not that I remember."

For crying out loud... the neurologist referred me here, you piece of shit psychologist. You must already know that I don't remember being unconscious because I was UNCONSCIOUS, YOU FUCK.

I smiled, smoothing the seams of my shirt with attention it had never before received.

Just as I was telling myself to chill out, that I needed to relax and trust in this man's ability to conduct the evaluation, Dr. Feinsworth shifted his leg position and, crossing his other leg without ever dipping his clipboard *lest I see his notes*, he asked: "Are you married, Debra?"

Oh, shit.

Now why's he asking me that? He has several reports right there in his little packet that state that I'm single and divorced. What could this possibly have to do with my current brain functioning?

"No," I said benignly, determined to sound neither desperate nor delighted by this fact.

"How many times have you been divorced?"

"Oh, um...just once. Well, actually twice." I took a deep breath. I have always been a terrible liar.

"Three. I've actually been married three times."

Bet he writes that down in a hurry. "Subject hesitantly indicated she has been divorced three times, appearing embarrassed and uncomfortable with this disclosure."

"But I don't consider them failures," I quickly asserted. "I prefer to think of myself as an optimist."

Oh, good Christ all mighty, I thought. *Just strike me dead. Just strike me dead right this minute. Please tell me I did not just say that.*

I could feel the sweat beginning to trickle down my armpits.

Dr. Feinsworth, switching subjects, said, "Well, tell me a little about your background, Debra. Where were you raised?"

"What?"

"Where did you grow up? Do you have siblings? Where did you go to college?" Dr. Feinsworth threw out any number of examples for me to answer.

Where was I RAISED? Are you going to probe into my childhood, you psychoanalytic, psychobabbling freak? *You're supposed to be testing my cognitive skills, not psychoanalyzing me.*

"Client was evasive and challenging when asked about her early background..."

Maintaining careful eye contact and keeping my voice steady, I mentally reminded myself to be brief. "Well, I was raised in the Midwest. I'm a solid Midwestern girl. I lived with my parents in Ohio until I went to college."

I practically looked around to see if someone else had spoken for me. *A solid Midwestern girl?* A solid Midwestern *girl? Why would I even* say *something like that? 'Oh, you betcha, Uncle Henry, I'll just go right out and fetch them chicken eggs for you...'*

Holy shit. I mean, I grew up in the suburbs for God's sake.

I wanted to shut myself up—or at the very least, stand in defiance and tell Dr. *Freud* just what I thought about his probing and questioning.

Instead, maintaining what I hoped was an appropriately modulated demeanor, I said, "Excuse me, could you just explain...I mean, I thought I was here for you to conduct tests that would help determine if there's been damage in my brain. I'm not trying to be rude or anything, but what does all this have to do with finding out about my current cognitive abilities?"

"Well, Debra," he said, offering me what I think was supposed to be a reassuring neuropsychologist smile and direct eye contact, "I like to look at each client as a whole person. So before I dive right into the testing, I like to find out a little about their background."

OHMYGODDIDTHEYTEACHYOUTHISINNEUROPSYCH GRADUATE SCHOOL? If you want to know about my background, Dr. Freud-FREAK-Feinsworth, why don't you ask me what I consider to be the important or significant events of my life? Ask what I think have been my achievements, my failures. You're not going to see any "whole person" here in fifteen minutes by asking me these inane questions, you fucking, fucking freak.

I smiled pleasantly, as if *so* pleased this man was willing to look at me as a whole person.

The thoughts of condemnation toward Dr. Feinsworth were coming fast and furious, and each one was leaving me feeling angrier, more hostile, and more resentful than the last. *What nerve. What* arrogance *this man possessed!*

It never occurred to me that this kind of anger, this internal ranting was a stunning new dimension to my personality.

I was working very hard to keep my face looking neutral, but I was beginning to feel a twitch develop in my left eye, and I'm quite sure I was gritting my back teeth—because that is what I do when I'm feeling extreme tension. If one is looking closely enough, a telltale sign of my anxiety is seen in little flinches at the back of my jaw, right by the base of my earlobes.

The fact is, while Dr. Feinsworth could have been a little less stereotypic in his initial interview, the questions he asked were not so out of bounds. There was nothing so horrible about the manner in which he was conducting the evaluation process. What was out of bounds was my own anxiety over being tested—my fear of appearing deficient, of having lost intelligence. My fear of someone else not only knowing this, but actually having the power to write it up and make it public. Lifelong insecurities about not being intelligent enough were being poked, and like dormant ashes that suddenly receive a little bit of air and burst into flame, my very deep-rooted fears of discovery were igniting. Not only could this man say I had lost cognitive skills in the accident, he could attest that I hadn't been very smart to begin with.

In my mind, the less I liked and trusted Dr. George Feinsworth, the less I would have to accept his test results as valid. This, along with the fact that I was no longer thinking as flexibly as before the accident, and that my range of emotions had been reduced to one of two extremes, led me to see things only one way: my way. I had a script for Dr. *Freud* to follow, and he simply was not following it.

And *that*, in my book, made him wrong and me right.

* * * * *

What was supposed to be conducted in one six- to eight-hour day ended up taking several months. Part of the reason for this was that my brain simply would not let me concentrate on anything so intense hour after hour. Part of it was that I would get nauseated and dizzy when I had to look at too many black and white designs and patterns (of which there were many as part of the evaluation process); and part of it was that I used every little bump in the road as an excuse to cancel a follow-up appointment.

What? The roads are a little icy between Cortez and Blanding? Ring, ring, ring. *Oh, hello, Dr. Feinsworth, I couldn't possibly ask someone to drive me there in this kind of weather! Can we reschedule for a later date?*

Eventually, I did complete the entire process, and one of the advantages of it extending over a long period of time was that I lost some of my defensiveness with Dr. Feinsworth. I even came to rather like the man, though I wasn't willing to admit that too loudly until I read his final report. I wanted to keep my options open for dismissing him as a Freud wannabe, whose professional judgment could not be trusted.

What Dr. Feinsworth said in his final report was this: I presented as cooperative and without any psychiatric distress, other than some anxiety in relation to (my) change in neurocognitive abilities. He also spelled out difficulties I was having with specific tasks, stating that no previous medical or psychological factors accounted for these difficulties. In other words: I was not a hypochondriac; I was not making up my symptoms; and impairment following the accident could be quantified.

The report Dr. Feinsworth wrote also contained some of the scores (but not all) for the various tests he had administered—scores that displayed a stunning discrepancy between what I *can do* and what is challenging for me to do.

For example, my abilities on tasks that involve understanding words and using and interpreting language fell into what's called a Superior Range. Somewhere around the ninety-fifth percentile compared to other people my age, thus explaining how I am still able to write comfortably and put thoughts together using words. However, tasks requiring spatial memory, tactile perception, and/or processing certain kinds of information quickly didn't fall anywhere *near* a superior level. Those skills hovered somewhere between the *sixteenth and thirty-second* percentiles.

In the world of statistics and psychological evaluations, scoring between the sixteenth and thirty-second percentiles is considered to be within a Low-Average Range. For more than twenty years, I had comforted hundreds of parents whose children scored within this range, assuring them it is still within an average range, and that *average is respectable*.

And I, probably like a lot of those parents, did not find myself one *bit* comforted by the assurance that these impaired skills and abilities still fell within a *low-average* range. It did not matter to me that many of my skills still reflected superior abilities. In my mind what screamed loud and clear was that I performed worse than sixty-eight to eighty-five percent of my peers on all those *other* tests and tasks. Scores in the *sixteenth percentile*? God help me, how will I manage to function?

The worst part about it was that by the time I got this information, I was thinking clearly enough to realize Dr. Feinsworth knew what he was doing, and I couldn't write him off as any kind of Freud wannabe. The man had earned his credentials fairly.

I was grateful that Dr. Feinsworth did not describe me as hostile and resistant during the interview, and that he substantiated that I actually did have post-accident changes. And I was deeply appreciative that he was insightful enough to look beyond whatever outward presentation I offered during those painful testing sessions.

The good news about the results was that I had believed so strongly that I was being weak, spineless, and exaggerating the deficits, that it relieved a lot of stress to see my challenges confirmed in black and white.

The bad news was that in my mind it also confirmed that I was now a dullard, just as I had always feared.

Only now I might be stuck with eternally wandering around with a blanketed awareness of every event transpiring in my life.

In the concluding paragraph of his report, Dr. Feinsworth recommended that if it was possible for me to continue traveling to Cortez, I should schedule sessions with him in order to develop some compensatory skills and tools for managing the anxiety that accompanied awareness of my impacted abilities. Unfortunately, by the time I got the results of the testing, it was mid-April 2004. I was alligator deep simply trying to manage working, living, and figuring out how to get through my days without sleeping them away or having the details of each one fade into dreamlike oblivion. Finding a weekly ride to Cortez for "therapy" sessions or for clarification of the test results was not high on my list of priorities at the time.

Looking back, I wish it had been.

Hindsight is, as they say, twenty-twenty. Perhaps had I taken Dr. Feinsworth up on his suggestion to work with him, I would have had an objective, dispassionate influence to help me analyze the events of the next eighteen months—before they avalanched into the stunning debacle that define the memories of my post-accident life as an educational psychologist. And had I continued working with Dr. Feinsworth, it might not have taken me four years to figure out that without engaging in Stage Four sleep, my memory and fatigue problems could do nothing *but* increase, exacerbating what might have been only mildly impaired abilities.

But, like I said, hindsight—as we all know—is twenty-twenty.

PART III:

Inside The Box

"But I don't want to go among mad people," said Alice.
"Oh, you can't help that," said the cat. "We're all mad here."

Alice and the Cheshire cat

Evan

January 2004-March 2004, Blanding, Utah

It was January 2004, and although Dr. Willner would not give me a release to return to work—not until she saw results of the completed neuropsychological evaluation—I returned anyway. Financially I needed to work. I had taken out a bank loan to get through all the months without an income, but even more obvious to me was that from a psychological standpoint, I really needed to get back to the schools. I worried about the kids, and I felt enormous guilt knowing that Ila and Alta were having to add the responsibilities of my job to their own.

I hoped to return to my previous levels of responsibilities, which would have meant going to several schools. Fortunately, Tony and Ila were far more realistic than I was, and they limited me to two schools with one condition established. The schools were San Juan High in Blanding, and Mexican Hat Elementary. The condition was that I did not drive myself to Mexican Hat, but would arrange to carpool with one of the several teachers who commuted between Blanding and Mexican Hat every day.

They got no argument from me on that one. I was not too anxious to drive that route myself.

The first couple of months back challenged me in many ways, not the least being staying awake. Within three weeks of returning to work, the doctor prescribed a medication often used in cases of narcolepsy, and this helped a great deal. I would set my alarm for 5:00 in the morning, take two pills, and go back to sleep. By the time the alarm rang at 7:00, there was enough of the time-release drug in my system to help me wake up and stay awake. While I had some concerns about being on a stimulant medication, in my mind the benefits far outweighed any side effects. It allowed me to think more clearly and remain awake without expending half my energy just keeping my eyes open.

One morning in late March, I returned to my office and found a message asking me to call Bob Peterson—the principal of San Juan High School. Bob was new to the district this year, and since I had not been at school from August until January, I was still getting to know him. My experiences with him so far led me to suspect there was a good reason to return the call promptly.

"Hey, Bob. It's Debra. I just got your message—what's up?"

Close to my age, and with plenty of experience under his belt, Bob had already impressed me with his intelligence and knowledge of effective teaching strategies. I liked the way he interacted with both teachers and kids, and I had come to respect and enjoy working with him. I was particularly appreciative of the support he extended as I tentatively worked to discover what I could and could not do.

"Oh, hi, Debra," he said pleasantly. "I wonder if I could run something by you. Do you have a few minutes?" I assured him that I did. "I have a kid over here—a freshman, that I think I'd like to have you interview."

"Sure. Who is he? What do you need?"

"His name is Evan Thom, and to tell you the truth, I'm not sure what I need. I can't really put my finger on it, but he's missed a lot of days—a real truancy issue that came to my attention this morning." Bob was thoughtful for a minute. I could tell he was trying to find just the right words to explain his thoughts. "I called him in earlier today and talked with him. Debra, I don't know, there's this red flag going off in my head, and I thought maybe you could interview him. See what you think."

"What kind of red flag?" This sounded interesting—certainly unusual. I get plenty of requests to interview kids, but usually it's an event such as a suicide attempt or weapons violation that precipitates a request for my involvement. Although all students with a special education label who require psychological services are on my caseload, the high school has several counselors trained to handle most non-special education situations that arise; and they only refer kids to me when the situation feels out of the realm of their expertise or experience.

"I don't know exactly. I don't want to stereotype or jump to any conclusions—it's just that he struck me like one of those kids we hear about that ends up committing some sort of school violence—you know, the loner, quiet kid that nobody really pays attention to. Like I said, it's just a feeling. I thought it might be good to see what your impression of him is. You could let me know if you think I need to be concerned or not."

"I have no problem with that at all, Bob, but let me clear it with Tony first— make sure I don't need any parent permission or signatures. I don't think I will just to conduct an informal interview at your request, but I'd like to make sure."

It can be a little sticky sometimes if the psychologist talks with a child before informing the parents.

In this case, Tony had no problem with my interviewing Evan Thom, as long as it was just an initial contact. Anything beyond that would need a signed permission.

* * * * *

A slightly heavyset boy, wearing a gray hooded sweatshirt and baggy jeans, knocked on my door later that afternoon.

Shaggy blond hair hung down over his eyes—not so much that he appeared insolent or unkempt—just enough to provide a small barrier against people looking at him.

He introduced himself and told me he had moved to Blanding from Nevada the previous month.

"Do you have family here?" I asked him.

"My grandparents live here." His voice seemed modulated. Flat. "I live with them." There was little inflection to reveal whether Evan considered this to be a distressful or a positive living situation.

Despite his lack of affect, Evan and I connected with ease, and conversation between us flowed without difficulty. He seemed surprisingly relaxed with me, and I suspected I was not the first of my field to interact with him.

"Evan, why do I get the feeling that you have talked with psychologists before?" I asked, smiling as I looked at him.

"I've talked to you guys a lot," he said. "I like to mess with your heads."

I figured my head had been messed with enough for one lifetime, but I refrained from mentioning this to Evan. Instead I just asked him in what way he liked to mess with our heads.

"Oh, you know, figure you guys out before you try to figure me out. I can figure out your games...mess with your heads a lot better than you can mess with mine." He explained this without belligerence, but rather with a certain tone of pride—muted as it was.

"Well," I said carefully, "you are obviously a very bright kid, Evan. Can I assume you've been referred to psychologists due to some troubles you've experienced?"

"You could say that," Evan said, his eyes looking dull and a bit glazed over.

"Are you comfortable telling me about some of those troubles? It's up to you—I don't want to pry into your personal business," I added respectfully.

I had an intuitive sense that treating this boy with respect was, above all else, important.

"Well, it's no big deal. I mean, nothin' all kids don't deal with."

I noticed his fingers twitching.

"What kinds of things do you think most kids have to deal with, Evan? It sounds like maybe you've had some experience with very difficult situations." I was proceeding cautiously. At this point, I suspected Evan had a fairly significant psychiatric history under his belt, and I wanted to make sure he would be comfortable enough to tell me more.

"Oh, you know—family stuff."

"Well, I know that family stuff can be pretty tough stuff." It seemed important not to zoom in too quickly—to give Evan plenty of room to dance vaguely around the family subject if he needed to do that. "Did you live with family before moving here?"

"Yeah, I lived with my aunt in Wyoming."

"Wyoming?" I asked, a little surprised since he had mentioned moving here from Nevada.

"Well, I lived with my aunt in Wyoming, but my mom is in Nevada. She has a drug thing...so I kind of went back and forth between Wyoming and Nevada. I was in some hospital in Nevada before coming here." Evan tacked on this last bit of information somewhat hesitantly.

"Well, I imagine you've learned to be very independent and self-sufficient, Evan. I know that it's pretty hard to live with a parent or guardian who's struggling with their own drug issues."

"It was no big deal," he said dismissively. "I was used to it."

"And your own history with drugs; what's that been like for you?" "I've done every drug there is since I was ten," he said. "Except needles. I never used needles." Evan looked at me, and when I displayed no reaction one way or another, he said, "But I never got the drugs from my mom. She never did drugs in front of us kids. I'll say that for her."

Over the years of working with boys abandoned by their mothers, I have found that the most effective approach is to find some thread of decency, no matter how violent or abusive the mother. Once acknowledged, the boys have less need to defend them and are usually more open to disclosing the not-so-decent aspects of their lives with a woman who chose to move forward without them.

"It sounds like your mom tried hard to be a good mom even though she was struggling with her own issues," I said.

"She was a good mom."

I paused for a moment before saying, "I sure believe that she tried to be, Evan. One thing I believe for certain is that few people set out to hurt their children. Even if that's what ends up occurring, not many parents start out with that intent in their minds." Looking at Evan, I continued. "So, okay... You've done a lot of drugs...and you mentioned a hospital. What kind of hospital were you in? If you're comfortable talking about that."

"It's okay. I'm okay telling you about it. They sent me to the state hospital to deal with my anger." After a second he added, "It was a stupid place. I did what I had to do to get out of there."

"Did something happen that resulted in someone putting you there, or was this a voluntary commitment on your part? I mean, again, Evan, I don't want to pry into anything that you consider private. It's really fine to tell me you don't want to talk about something."

"I tried to kill myself," Evan said, looking directly at me. I didn't get the sense that he was trying to shock me; it was more like he anticipated that his disclosure would elicit a major reaction of some sort from me, and he was waiting for it.

"I'm sorry, Evan," I said gently, but rather matter-of-factly. "Things must have seemed pretty intense for you to want to make a permanent exit."

Evan half nodded, half shrugged, but overall, my response seemed to pass whatever test it was that I was taking.

"How about your dad?" I asked. "I mean, a biological dad. Has there been a dad in your life?"

"Well, my mom's been married six times, but the one who is my biological dad is in jail." Evan returned to that flat and even tone. "We lived with him for a while. We lived with my mom until I was eight, then we went and lived with Stephen."

"Stephen being your biological dad?" I asked, making sure I was following this correctly. "And because you said *we*, does that mean you have siblings?"

"I have a brother and sister."

I was thoughtful for a moment before saying, "Okay, let me see if I'm putting this together right. Your mom and dad had three kids, and somewhere along the way they were no longer living together. Your mom was involved pretty heavily with drugs and hooked up with other men, so when you were eight, you went to live with Stephen." Evan gave me a nod, and I went on. "I'm thinking you're the oldest of the three, is that right?" Again Evan nodded, looking at me with interest now, as if he were curious just how much I might be putting together. "...and I'm guessing you have pretty strong feelings about your dad—I mean, the fact that you call him Stephen kind of tells me that."

"You're good," he said, one eyebrow slightly lifted.

"Well, it helps to have a bright student to listen to," I said, smiling. "I could be way off, Evan—but you strike me as the kind of kid who maybe acted as a protector of that younger brother and sister of yours. I am going to make a leap for a moment and guess that Stephen was abusive." I said the latter with a questioning tone. Everything I was hearing and seeing suggested this boy had been through some serious abuse issues.

"He's in jail for molesting my sister." A slight red flush surfaced under Evan's chin.

"I'm sorry, Evan. That must have been very difficult for you. I imagine you felt very responsible for keeping them safe." It was quiet for a moment, and I went on. "How about you and your brother. Was Stephen abusive with both of you?" I was gently probing, trying to find out just how wide and deep a history Evan was shouldering.

"He put me in the hospital a couple of times. I took all the physical stuff, so my sister and brother didn't have too much of that. I have scar tissue on my brain from him beating me in the head." His eyes affected that spiritless look again, and his voice had returned to its colorless tone, devoid of inflection.

"I imagine you got very good at figuring out what sorts of things provoked Stephen."

"*Everything* provoked him. One time when I was about eight or nine, a kid in school beat me up. When I got home, Stephen busted my jaw and three ribs telling me, 'No kid of mine is gonna be some pussy.'" Evan looked at me before saying, "I'll tell you one thing...that was the last time any kid in school ever beat me up."

Evan's voice had taken on a new tone when impersonating his father, and I suspected that what he was telling me was hard-core truth. Later I would come to know much more about this man's abusiveness and cruelty, and criminal records would substantiate the truth behind Evan's words.

"How does that scar tissue on your brain affect you now?" I asked.

"Well, I have a hard time concentrating. I can do five things at a time, but not one. And I'm not good at math, but I like to read. I like to read Anne Rice books." He paused and I didn't say anything, hoping he would continue to talk, but he just looked at me with that same pallid look filming his eyes.

"Well, I can understand about scar tissue on the brain," I said. "In fact, I'm just returning to work after being gone for almost a year because of a head injury—so I know how hard that can make things. I don't know about you, but I still get wicked headaches."

"Yeah, I get headaches, too. I black out sometimes. You ever do that?"

"What, black out?"

"Yeah."

"Well, describe for me what you mean and I'll be able to tell you better. I'm not sure I know what you mean when you say black out."

"Well, it happens when I get angry," he said slowly.

"You mean like you get really mad and then don't remember what happens?"

"Yeah."

"Well, no, I don't have those kinds of blackouts, but I'm familiar with them. Sometimes they're caused by head injuries, and sometimes they're the result of someone in an extremely stressful situation. Have you had experiences of hurting people in anger and then not remembering?"

"I beat a kid with a lead pipe once—put him in intensive care for a month. And I tried to choke my brother, and probably would have killed him except my sister hit me from behind with a lamp and knocked me out."

"Wow, Evan. Your head has taken quite a few hits," I said, smiling gently before asking, "The kid with the lead pipe—do you remember what set you off?"

"He was saying things about my family. I didn't feel bad about it at the time, but now I feel kind of bad about it. I mean, I think he has permanent damage from that. I never remembered hitting him. I just remember picking up the pipe and going after him." Evan was quiet and thoughtful before saying, "I'm a lot better now at knowing when people are making me mad."

"Sounds like you were feeling a lot of rage and that you were very protective of your family. How long ago was that, Evan?"

"Sixth grade. I was eleven, I think. Maybe twelve."

I was wondering if I would be able to remember all the details of this conversation in order to write them down after Evan left. I felt fairly certain that taking notes at this point would stop the conversation entirely, but the amount of information I was gathering was astounding.

"And how do you manage it now?" I asked him. "Your rage, I mean. Do you still get blackouts?"

"Well, not so much. My gramma is really good about telling me…like she'll say my eyes are glazing over and I need to go take a walk and cool down. That helps. And she bought me a punching bag."

"It sounds like you have a wise gramma, Evan." I smiled, quiet for a minute as I digested all that he had just disclosed. "It sounds to me like you've learned a lot about yourself. You know that you're capable of feeling a tremendous sort of anger, and you recognize that it has the potential to be a dangerous kind of anger."

Evan looked at me, seemingly curious to see what else I might say.

I paused for a minute, partially to give him a chance to add more, partially to simply allow him some time to process what I was reflecting back to him.

"Some people take a whole lifetime before ever figuring that out about themselves, Evan." We looked at each other, and I could see behind those lifeless eyes to a very bright and very wounded child looking out, wondering if he ever dare reveal himself.

"Let me ask you something, Evan. Is one reason you skip school so much because you don't want to put yourself in a situation where teachers or other kids can make you mad?"

"Yeah. That and there's nothing they can teach me here." He stated this in a tone falling somewhere between smug and defensive.

"Well, I know you're very bright. And it sounds to me like you are also a kid with a lot of compassion."

Evan looked up at me with surprise when I used the word compassion. It's probably not a word he was used to hearing associated with himself.

"I mean, Evan, it requires both intelligence *and* compassion to recognize one's own instinctive reactions and to make a conscious choice not to go there. It takes intelligence to recognize it, but it takes compassion to choose not to display it. And that is not necessarily an easy choice to have made."

He looked at me.

"It *is* a compassionate choice, Evan, and I respect that a lot in you." I was quiet for a minute before asking, "Is it on target if I'm thinking that you avoid *all* social situations so that you are not in a position where other people make you angry?"

"That's on target."

"That must get lonely for you." I said this gently.

"Not really. I'm used to it." Again, I noticed Evan assuming that muted tone. A tone that casually dismissed any connection to feelings beyond a few bleached out and watery sentiments.

At this point, I knew it would be impossible for me to write all this information down from memory. I was happy if my memory held out for fifteen minutes, much less the sixty minutes or more that we had already been talking. Taking a chance, I looked at Evan, saying, "I have a favor to ask of you."

"What's that?" he asked, suspicion girdling his voice.

"Well," I said, "generally, out of respect, I try not to take too many notes when I'm first talking with someone. I think what you have to say is important, and I prefer, if possible, to just listen and talk with you, not spend my time looking at my paper and scribbling away. I mean, that seems so *shrinky* to me— you know what I mean?"

Visions of Dr. Feinsworth and his yellow legal tablet were dancing around in my brain.

"Yeah," Evan said, allowing a half snort, half smile to replace suspicion. Apparently, Evan had experience with one or two Dr. Freuds of his own.

"Well, here's the thing, Evan. My brain just doesn't always work right anymore, and something else that is important to me is that I do you the honor of remembering what you tell me accurately. I mean, I don't want you to come back in here sometime and have me say, 'Oh, yeah...you're the kid with the mom in Detroit and the dad in New Delhi!'" I looked at him with mock horror on my face.

This time Evan allowed himself to emit an almost out loud laugh, and I said, "Would you be willing to help me jot down a few key things and make sure I'm remembering them correctly? I guess what I am asking is if you will help me make some notes."

"Sure, I can do that," Evan said, and as I had hoped he would, he took some pride in helping me jot down names, dates, and events correctly. I noticed at that point that he was left handed and that his foot, which had previously been doing a rhythmic tap dance under the table, was still.

"I'll tell you what," I said when we were done making notes. "We've been talking a really long time, and I appreciate how much information you've shared with me. I like talking with you—you're bright and insightful. I'm wondering if you would be interested in talking some more at another time. I'd like to get your grandparents' permission, and if you are willing, spend some more time with you."

"What would we do?" he asked, caution saturating his tone.

"That would be up to you, really," I said. "I'm not much in the business of trying to mess with kids' heads—I figure they've had their heads messed with enough already." I smiled before going on.

"It's been my experience, Evan, that kids who have been raised in really troubled households often think they're crazy when they're not. Most often what I find is that kids in these situations have developed all kinds of intelligent strategies for surviving the craziness in their world. But when their world changes, they aren't quite sure what to do. I mean, sometimes it's hard for kids to actually function well in a world that isn't filled with chaos and violence, if that's all they've ever known." Looking at him, I added, "I'm usually pretty good at helping kids figure out new strategies for surviving in their new, gentler world. If they're interested, that is. In here the decision will always be yours whether you want to participate or not."

I made sure to tack on that last part, certain that Evan feeling in control of what happened would be critical to the success of any intervention established with him.

For the first time since he arrived, Evan's eyes did not appear glazed over, and his voice took on some expression. Though still flat, there was a hint of happiness, perhaps even relief in his voice when he said, "Yeah, I'd come back and talk with you again. When? You mean like tomorrow morning?"

Smiling, I said, "Well, maybe not quite that soon—but only because I need to get your grandparents to come in and sign permission for me to talk with you. How about if I talk with Mr. Peterson and we get some paperwork together? Then we'll invite your grandparents to come in, and we'll see if they'll sign permission for us to spend time together."

"They will," he said. "They'll just be surprised that I want to."

After Evan left, I sent a memo to Bob, stating, among other things, the following:

Per your request, I met with Evan Thom today (3-31-04). If the information he has disclosed to me is accurate, then I would respond to your question regarding whether there is a risk of him committing some sort of violent act by saying that yes, there is risk of an episode occurring that could be of a violent or aggressive nature. The <u>immediate</u> risk factor appears low, as Evan is aware of his history of violent episodes, and of ongoing difficulties with managing anger.

Currently Evan copes with stress and resulting aggression through use of avoidance. That is, if he is not around people, then people cannot make him angry, and he will not end up in a situation involving violence.

My impression in this initial meeting is that Evan appears to have a very limited repertoire of strategies to cope with frustration and anger, although he has a strong awareness of his propensity toward reacting in aggressive and violent ways. Thus, if you intend to pursue putting pressure on him to increase his school attendance, this will place him in far more contact with both peers and authority figures. This, I believe, will increase the risk factors of an explosive or aggressive encounter occurring.

I am guessing that we will need to build a strong team of supportive adults around this student, and to modify his educational program in a way that can accommodate some of his immediate needs while we gather more information about his educational, psychiatric, and social history. If he does not already carry a special education certification, we may want to explore evaluation in order to determine if he is eligible for services. I suspect that with or without the special education label, however, we need to look at developing substantial wrap around services in order to make sure he is both successful and safe in this environment.

Please let me know how you would like to proceed at this point. I would suggest we document all contacts and concerns.

Bob's referral, his gut instinct, proved to be remarkably insightful. Evan and I initiated a therapeutic relationship that day that would become increasingly intense and would last until the day I left Blanding in June 2005. It would prove to be a relationship that challenged me—perhaps more than any other I had experienced—as both an educator and as a therapist.

It would also prove to be one of several significant cases that would become polarizing forces with me on one end, and Bob, Tony, Ila, and the special education teachers on the other. Cases that would pit their questions concerning the effects of my head injury against my questions concerning the ethical and legal maneuverings of district policy and procedure.

But that all came later. In March 2004, everyone was happy that I was back on the job, and it appeared that things were moving along quite smoothly.

Will the Real Debra Please Step Forward
Summer 2004

The 2003-2004 school year ended in late May—somewhat to my relief, as I was exhausted by the energy it had required to manage things. Summer brought a welcomed reprieve from having to remain alert and organized each day, and except for bi-monthly sessions with Evan, I was not involved in any school-related activities. I was quite sure that Evan was experiencing symptoms of acute and chronic posttraumatic stress syndrome, and I had ordered myself several hundred dollars worth of books and materials to study over the summer as I developed his treatment plan. Other than that, I did not attempt to learn any new information or participate in any of the usual continuing education classes I always attended in the summer. It frustrated me that I seemed to forget what I read, and I would make notes that later were nothing but a confusing mass of words. Somehow, however, I managed to keep moving forward with Evan, and our relationship had begun to develop some real momentum. He followed through with every appointment and every assignment I gave him, and I was impressed by his motivation to become healthier.

My own life felt like a series of snapshots out of context to me. I moved through my days with a muted awareness and recollection of things, and each experience I had was only dimly remembered. Even with photographs and notes, reading about my days felt more as if I were reading a dream journal than recalling real connections to daily events.

Sleeping still dominated my time, although somehow (and I honestly am not sure how) I did manage to take each of Denise's twins on their "age fourteen" trips. Between those trips, I would be back to sleeping eighteen, twenty hours a day in order to recover. Unlike in summers past, I did not spend several days in the Lindsey household, which was a home filled with the normal hustle, bustle, and rowdiness of any house containing five exuberant people. Instead, I would get there the night before a trip, and return to Blanding the day the trips ended. For the first time in years, I did not make a trip to see Joyce and her family in their small town outside of Salt Lake City.

Throughout the summer, I allowed minimal distractions within my environment. Denney and I continued to spend time together, but our relationship was becoming increasingly strained, and one night in late summer things came to a head as we were taking an evening walk.

"Denney, I just feel like as I get better, things between us get worse. It's as if you don't want me to rejoin the world. Like you're happier when I just want to sit silently in my little house." I had begun seeing Denney through a new filter. What for so many months had comforted me—that quiet, understated way of his—was beginning to take on an annoying shape. I found that Denney in any sort of social setting appeared tense and awkward; and he was perceived as stiff and uncomfortable by my friends if they would drop over when he was at my house. I certainly knew from past experience that I had a tendency to veer toward men who ended up wanting to monopolize my time and focus, and I wondered if I had again connected with someone who was happier if we isolated ourselves from the rest of the world.

"That's *not* it, Debra. I just... I'm just so...frustrated. I'm so..." Denney was struggling for words, and his agitation was evident. "...I just don't know what is *you* and what is the head injury." I had never seen him like this before—this emphatic in his expression of emotion.

"You remember San Rafael Swell?" he continued. "When I couldn't find the turn-off and you raged at me? Do you remember that?" A fiery edge was barely reining in his words.

"Well, I remember being frustrated," I said, feeling myself starting to pull inward.

"You *raged*, Debra. '*What the fuck is the matter with you?*' is what you said, to be exact. You got out of your car and asked me what the fuck was the matter with me. I was stunned, speechless. To me, Debra, that was the beginning of the end."

I was the one stunned and speechless at this point. This wasn't my recollection at all. I remembered our having a nice time after the initial poor start, and I certainly didn't remember *raging*.

I turned and started heading toward home—wanting to get away from Denney; wanting to get as far away as possible from the image of myself he had just laid out before me.

"Debra. Wait! Slow down."

I kept walking. As if somehow I could outrun this information, outpace it and make it fade away.

When he caught up with me, Denney was nearly frantic, saying, "Talk to me about this, Debra. Don't just walk away. Talk to me."

"I am not going to have a fight with you out here on the street, Denney, not for all of Blanding to watch."

"Then go inside with me." We were in front of my house by this time.

Walking into the house, I turned on him, livid. "Denney, you have *no* idea." My words spit out angrily. "You have no idea what it's like being inside my head or what it's like to drive on dirt roads when I can't even feel my *lips* they are so numbed out, much less *think* about keeping a car on the road. You have no *clue*, Denney, what it's like to live inside a head I can't even *depend* on anymore. It's not like I have a choice in this, Denney; this is what I can do. *All* I can do. You forget that I don't have an endless cup of pennies anymore... and there were no pennies left in my cup that day, Denney. *None*."

Words were spewing out of me, fueled by a lethal cocktail of emotions that had remained bottled up far too long. My emotions threatened to dissolve into tears that might wash away the anger, but could leave nothing in its place other than a mountain of pent-up fear.

Denney sighed. He was quiet before saying gently, "You're right, Debra. You're right. I don't know."

I looked at him, breathing deeply and trying to calm myself down.

"I don't know what it's like in your head, Debra. But you have to try to understand that I also don't know what is *you* and what is the TBI. And that's hard on me, too."

We looked at each other, each of us wanting to work our way back to that space of tranquility we had once found within one another.

"Debra, just...try to understand from my perspective, too, okay? I knew you only a few weeks before the accident. I mean, we had very little time together alone before that day. You were vibrant and perceptive and alive and funny. That's what I knew. I knew what I saw when you interacted with children, and what I saw on the few hikes we took.

"Now you display these *moods*, Debra. You create this distance that I feel from you at times; it's like you erect an emotional *moat* that I can't get across. I don't know what to do with that...is this *you*, the *real Debra*—were you like this before the accident—or is this the TBI and something that will get better? Is this something new that will go away, or is this something old that is resurfacing?

"I don't know how to tell, Debra, and I just don't know what I'm supposed to do." Denney's voice trailed off as he looked at me, and I felt a profound sadness accompany this understanding of what I was causing him to experience.

How could I explain that I *was* the real me, and *not* the real me? That every undesirable trait I have seems magnified a thousand times since the injury. Magnified a thousand times and a million times harder to anticipate or inhibit.

For a short time, things were better between us, but eventually, trying to sort out the TBI from the real me became too difficult—for both of us. Denney's job ended at the counseling center, and he took advantage of the opportunity to move to Moab.

Summer was over and school was ready to begin.

Maybe it's better, I thought. *I need just to be by myself and not try to manage a relationship on top of everything else. This is too hard on someone else, and it's too hard on me. It's just too hard.*

Still, it was painful to watch him go.

Sleeping Dragons
September 2004

The 2004-2005 school year began in mid-August, and despite the ongoing TBI issues, I was anxious to return to work. Prior to school ending in the spring, we had interviewed and hired a licensed educational psychologist with several years of experience. I was excited that we would have a second psychologist on staff, and I looked forward to collaborating with Vernon. During his interview, he presented himself as a level-headed professional who felt passionately about issues in the field. The father of five young children and with extended family in the area, Vernon was quite likely to remain with the district for a long time, and that pleased me immensely.

Of course, this was because I assumed that I would remain with the district as well.

Even with two of us, it was going to be difficult to meet the needs of the district's twelve schools (one school closed since I first began working for them). The most distant school, located in Navajo Mountain, was a four-hour drive south of Blanding. Just north of the Arizona state line, Navajo Mountain had less than four hundred people—more than ninety-five percent of whom were Navajo. Although such remote schools always interest me, anything involving a long drive was out of the question, so Navajo Mountain was assigned to Vernon, along with the two schools in Monticello and the middle school and elementary school in Blanding.

Vernon volunteered to add the small but remote school located in La Sal— a town of three hundred located an hour northeast of Blanding. Navajo Mountain and La Sal were both small enough that they only required intermittent services, and Vernon wanted the opportunity to experience the distant schools. He would also have the elementary school in Montezuma Creek.

Montezuma Creek is located forty minutes southeast of Blanding. A small town of about five hundred people, ninety-seven percent of whom are Navajo, part of the town resides inside the northwestern border of the Navajo Nation, and part of the town resides outside its borders. Navajo Nation, a Native American Sovereignty, is 27,000 square miles of reservation that is home to more than 173,000 Diné, as the Navajo often refer to themselves. The Diné— meaning *People* in the Navajo language—still maintain a strong connection to their native culture, even as they attempt to merge traditions with the innovations of the twenty-first century. It's a complicated and conflicted struggle that is often played out in microcosm in the schools.

There are two schools in Montezuma Creek, and I had worked in both of them prior to the accident. The elementary school houses the preschool through sixth grade students; and Whitehorse High School, a few blocks away, serves the seventh through twelfth grades. The latter school bore the reputation as the toughest, most needy school in the district, and it was a well-earned reputation. It was certainly the only school I had ever worked in where teachers lock their classroom doors any time they leave the room, even if it is for brief moments. It was often said laughingly, though it was no joke, that rarely a day or two passed that there wasn't some crisis or intense issue that needed addressing at the high school. If the word-of-mouth hotline spread the information that a principal had been assaulted, a lockdown had occurred, or some sort of meltdown had taken place, before we were even told, we would assume it was an incident at White Horse. And generally, we were right.

To my knowledge, no principal had remained in this school beyond a couple of years. While nobody ever said it outright, it appeared that working at White Horse High was considered hard-core duty. Once served, dues to the district were paid, and a person could look forward to a more desirable assignment. Indeed, there would be a new principal there this year, since the previous principal had been moved into a central office position in Blanding.

Whitehorse High was assigned to me, along with Mexican Hat Elementary, Bluff Elementary, San Juan High in Blanding, and Monument Valley Middle/High School. I was distressed and worried about having Whitehorse. Although my relationships with staff had been excellent in the past, I knew the kind of intensity and the amount of time necessary to be effective there. I was not sure I had what it would take to handle Whitehorse. Tony and Ila assured me they would provide backup support if needed.

Being assigned to Monument Valley, on the other hand, thrilled me.

Monument Valley Middle/High School was a fifteen-minute drive south of Mexican Hat Elementary. The entire area was within the boundaries of the reservation, and the school itself was just a mile north of the Arizona border.

I always loved the drive between the two southern schools. After leaving the elementary school, the road winds south, merging into the wide, desolate landscape that is familiar to anyone who has ever watched a John Ford/John Wayne movie. Monument Valley has provided the backdrop for more of their films than any other location, and for good reason. It's a land filled with towering monoliths and sandstone columns, of square buttes, spires, red sandstone mesas, sand dunes, and canyons. It is the land of legends. Each spire, each column, each butte has a name and a story.

Three Sisters, Sleeping Dragon, Ear of the Wind, Mittens.

Mittens, according to one of my more traditional students, was so named because the giant mittens with the thumbs pointed skyward are said to have belonged to the gods, who would leave them there so they could come back and reclaim them.

Spending time in Monument Valley made me wish I could be itinerant in the way I had been in Alaska. I would have loved to spend four or five days focused intensely in the school all day, and then wander the roads as the sun set in the evenings. There was something about the sunsets in Monument

Valley that made me feel as if I could weave my spirit into the landscape as the contrasting shadows transformed the stark spires into darkened silhouettes. When the sky moved through its smoldering shades of red and orange before settling into darkness, the visions and mirages from which shape-shifting legends must have been born would surround me, and I understood so much more about the *Yei's*—ghosts—kids at school would tell me about.

There was an entirely different feel to the Monument Valley School than to Whitehorse High, though both were reservation schools. Walking into Monument Valley felt like going home to me. Like my hot Alaska. Entering the building, one was immediately enveloped by an ambience of Navajo culture—a feeling enhanced by the elders who were nearly always present in the front office, gossiping in their native language. The students were respectful, and though many were taller and bigger than me, they did not feel threatening or imposing, such as when I was in the halls of Whitehorse and kids pushed and shoved their way around me.

The principal of Monument Valley High, Pat Seltzer, had been there for twenty years. Her husband, Jack, was a teacher and the athletic director, and they had raised their own children in the community. This commitment was reflected in the way the school operated, and while there were the familiar signs of poverty, gang conflicts, and academic barriers created by cultural and language priorities vastly different from those of an Anglo culture and curriculum, things ran efficiently and smoothly in this school. The need for psych services was minimal, and I figured it would be no problem to trade an hour or two of Mexican Hat Elementary time if they needed me occasionally in Monument Valley.

Once Vernon and I had our assignments, the 2004-2005 school year officially began for each of us, and while most years begin with the psychologist hitting the decks running, the pace of this year would prove relentless.

The middle of September found me deeply immersed in the needs of each one of my schools. Mexican Hat, as always, had children and teachers with intense needs for my time, but the principal, Val Roberts, and staff developer/teacher, Barbara Silversmith, were highly skilled and equally committed educators. We worked well together, engaging in the kind of teamwork I had experienced in Alaska.

Prior to my accident, Val, Barbara, and I had been training teachers to run a special kind of intervention team that would provide support to other teachers in the building who had academically and/or behaviorally demanding students in their classrooms. I had been developing and training teachers to effectively operate these teams since the early 1990s, and I was a passionate believer that when empowered with skills, creativity, and the appropriate support systems, teachers could solve many of their own problems without referring students to special education for testing or to me for counseling intervention.

Over the years, I had observed teachers involve everyone from a student's peers to the school's cooks, secretaries, custodians, and bus drivers in implementing creative and innovative plans that helped students learn the necessary social and academic skills to be successful. It's probably the area in education that most excites me; and I had been surprised that nothing of this nature existed in any of the schools in the San Juan School District.

The administrator and staff at Mexican Hat had been enthusiastic about learning how such a team operates, and it thrilled me that in September of 2004, it was actually up and running after the lengthy delay due to my absence. Although initially developing such teams requires an enormous commitment on my part, over time the teachers independently manage the team in their building, and the results are such that it makes it well worth the initial time investment.

Ernie's program, in Christena's room, was the most involved, and it required the bulk of my time, along with Petey Begay's program and treatment plan. Petey, the boy whose meeting I had been in such a rush to attend that April morning when I rolled my truck, was now in sixth grade, and we still had much to accomplish before he would be ready to head over to the "big school" in Monument Valley.

Monument Valley had a surprise student for me—a boy by the name of Monty, whose deep emotional troubles concerned the teachers and principal immensely. The amount of time I was spending there far exceeded what I had anticipated, but doing so was a joy. Collaborating with a team of more than ten staff members, we developed an intervention plan that had genuine potential to help Monty; and while the plan was intensive, everyone was following through with their own piece, and, so far, no one seemed to be feeling overwhelmed by the demands. Rarely had I worked with a more committed and intelligent staff, and when working at Mexican Hat and Monument Valley, I often found myself experiencing the familiar rhythm known in my Alaska days. My relationships with both principals and all the teachers were mutually supportive, and it brought me great pleasure to spend time in both schools.

My only problem was the drive.

Because of the amount of time I was spending in Monument Valley, carpooling was not always an option since I would finish up at school much later than the teachers who were commuting from Blanding. There were days when I would drive the sixty plus miles between Blanding and the southern schools, and it was not uncommon to see my district car parked on the side of the road, or in a pullout. I slept when I had to, and although it felt weird to sleep on "company time," I figured that since I always worked five or six (or more) hours beyond the normal school day, I could feel okay about my thirty- to forty-minute naps here and there. Even with the stimulant medication, staying awake remained challenging.

In contrast to Monument Valley, Whitehorse presented itself as a school that truly required its own full-time psychologist. And a Herculean one at that. My relationships with the principal and the general education teachers were strong, and I enjoyed working within the building when my responsibilities involved collaborating with them. While I very much *liked* the teachers within the special education department, I had not developed much respect for the quality of services they provided, and like in any system when there are weak links, it seemed to me that their lack of training affected the entire school.

Five, maybe six weeks into the school year, one of the seventh grade science teachers, Kathy Keene[8], contacted me about a student. Kathy was a new, young teacher who had started the year full of enthusiasm, but within seconds of our meeting her feelings of stress and overwhelm were evident. Her concern, she said, had to do with a boy in one of her morning classes who did not seem to grasp the subject matter and was disruptive every day with his inappropriate behavior and remarks.

According to Kathy, she had talked to the teachers in the special education department, but had gotten no response or help. Yes, they confirmed, he was a special education student, but they told her not to worry—that he was just in there for socialization purposes.

"I don't know what to do with him," Kathy said. "What does that mean: he's in here for socialization? He disrupts every class, and I feel like I'm spending more time trying to manage him than I am teaching. Not to mention that I don't think he understands a thing we're doing in here."

"What are you working on?" I asked, wondering why Kathy had gotten no assistance from the special ed. department.

"We're studying planets. But, Debra, I don't think he can read the text book. I'm not kidding, I honestly don't think he can read it. And I'll tell you, I have modified and modified for him, and he *still* doesn't seem to grasp what we're talking about."

"What's his name?" While I didn't know all the special education students at Whitehorse, I knew many of them. If this was a student familiar to me, I might be able to offer some insights and strategies even before doing observations or pulling files.

"Germaine."

I was stunned into silence. I knew a Germaine, but it was not possible that we were talking about the same boy. The Germaine I knew was of very limited cognitive ability, with an IQ falling somewhere in the mid-forty range. An IQ of 100 is average, and while not everything should be based on the number obtained from an IQ test, in this case the number conveyed an important fact—a fact that should be driving his instructional program.

"You're not talking about Germaine K. are you?" I asked, working hard to contain budding feelings of outrage.

"Yep, that *is* who I'm talking about. *None* of my management strategies work with him, Debra, and I've had to move his seat half a dozen times." As she gestured toward the student area of the room, made up of small tables allowing partners to work together, her face conveyed the obvious: there was no place to put Germaine that did not put him in close contact with other students, and unless he was to be entirely isolated, he was disruptive wherever she sat him.

I had worked with Germaine before my accident, when he was in the fifth

---

[8] Name changed.

grade. At the time we met—somewhere around February of 2003—Germaine already had a thick file of documented aggressive and violent acting-out behaviors. He was so disruptive that Tony had placed him in an isolated setting, one-on-one with a special education teacher. Part of my job had been to help develop the behavioral intervention plan that would help him gain the skills to move back to the self-contained—but more inclusive—setting of the special education room.

"Who comes in here with him?" I could not fathom that Germaine would be placed in here without support. *Any* time a student with such intensive needs is included in a regular classroom, it is with well-developed support services, either from a trained paraeducator or one of the special education teachers.

"No one has *ever* been in my classroom with him." Kathy looked directly at me, and her tone held the absoluteness of one who has been in the skirmish alone far too long.

"Well, who's modifying the curriculum for him?" I asked, working hard to keep my voice steady and neutral, wondering how a boy with an IQ of forty-five is supposed to function with a seventh grade text. Or, how a teacher without special education training is supposed to manage a child with both cognitive and emotional impairments, along with her twenty-seven other students.

"Me," she said. "And not well. Nothing I've tried works. I have no idea what his disabilities are. Nobody has told me one thing about him, and I don't know how to simplify the information any more than I already have."

"Okay," I said quietly, a wave of heat flooding my system and forcing me to remind myself that a display of outrage would not, in any way, be useful. "I can tell you a few things about Germaine, and I can help you with a few initial strategies to get things more under control. If he stays in here, Kathy, and I have to say that I'm not sure I think it's appropriate that he does, but if he does, I'll work with you much more and help in any way that I can."

Noticing the open door, I asked if we could talk privately and got up to close the door. More than the privacy, which we certainly needed, this was my own strategy for giving myself a few seconds to check my temper outside the room.

"Without even looking at his file, I can tell you that you are absolutely right in that Germaine cannot read the text book," I said. "I don't know exactly what his reading level is, but if he can read at a primer level, I would be very surprised." Kathy looked at me, stunned. "Germaine is a student identified as having an intellectual disability, meaning that limitations in his ability to think and learn information are directly responsible for his academic delays. The term mental retardation is probably more familiar to you."

"Well, how am I supposed to teach a student like that?" Kathy asked, near tears.

"You aren't. Not without support, anyway." I thought for a moment before asking, "Have you ever heard of something called a *parallel curriculum*, Kathy?"

Shaking her head she indicated no, which didn't really surprise me. While all special education teachers have—or should have—a clear understanding of this term, until a general educator has an intensive needs student in their classroom, it's rare for them to have familiarity with it.

"Okay. Some kids do need socialization skills, skills that will be required throughout life. Things like paying attention, not interrupting, using appropriate language. That sort of thing. One of the best places for them to gain those skills is with their age-appropriate peers, who provide wonderful role models for them while they are getting instruction in mastering these skills. That's what they meant, I think, when they told you he was in here for socialization.

"The thing is," I went on, "you can't just stick a kid in a classroom and expect him to independently gain these skills, so one strategy is to develop a *parallel* curriculum. In this way, a student like Germaine can participate with his peers, but with material at his ability level—and with different goals and outcomes than you have for the other students. Am I confusing you yet?" I smiled.

"I'm with you. Sort of. Go on."

"Okay. For example, let's say you're having your students write a letter to NASA to convey their support of the colonization of Mars. Obviously Germaine can't do that, but if his goal is to attend to a task for fifteen minutes without disrupting, then he could be doing something like making a paper-mâché model of Mars, or choosing pictures out of a book of things that might be needed to live on Mars. He would still be participating in the same subject matter as his classmates, but with a different goal and different materials. Does that make any sense at all?"

Explaining parallel curriculums takes more than the two minutes we had left together.

"Well, it does, but am I supposed to find time to develop that, too? I have no idea how to go about doing that, Debra. I wouldn't even know what's appropriate for him to be doing." Her stress level was escalating exponentially.

"No. I mean, absolutely, positively no," I reassured her, smiling. "Take a deep breath. I am sure this is some sort of mix-up. If they keep Germaine in here, it isn't your responsibility to develop his program for him. That's the special education teacher's job in collaboration with you. And usually, especially in the beginning, it requires that a second person—the special education teacher or paraeducator—is in here with you guys."

Students were beginning to wander in for her next class. "Let me do some checking and talk with the special ed. teachers and see what's going on." As I started gathering up my own things, I said, "Whatever happens, I can tell you that you deserve a medal of honor for managing as well as you have. Germaine can be a very endearing kid, but I also know how challenging he can be. I'm really sorry this happened, Kathy. You've done a great job—I mean that. You have really done well."

I thought she was going to hug me right there in the classroom.

Walking out the door, I thought I was going to blow a gasket. Placing Germaine in a core science class with no support services and giving the teacher no information is inexcusable. Regardless of what I said about a little mix-up, this was no little mix-up. It was not even a forgivable oversight.

The issue with Germaine turned out to be only one of what quickly surfaced as problems with several students. I was rapidly becoming overwhelmed by what appeared to be an entire system of dysfunctional and archaic practices, with no one to anchor the program with any kind of order. Conversations with the principal revealed that he, too, was feeling enormous frustration with the department of special education in his building.

No one could explain to me why Germaine was in the science class, and no one in the special education department was familiar with any of the techniques and strategies that maximize the chance that an inclusion model (including a student because it's age appropriate to do so) could work. When I offered to help them develop a parallel curriculum for Germaine, they smiled and pretended enthusiasm, but when it came time for them to follow through independently, they didn't. I had the suspicion they were frustrated with me and felt I was asking them to do something above and beyond the scope of their job description.

So, I was finding myself in the wee hours of the morning developing materials and parallel lesson plans to go with the seventh grade science curriculum.

I spoke with Tony about all this.

"I know, Debra. I know. We've always had problems getting competent teachers there. No one wants to move to Montezuma Creek," he said, commiserating with me. "It's just so hard to find trained professionals interested in living down here."

I found that odd, knowing the Stanford graduates and four-star chefs Carl had been able to lure—and keep—in Galena. I wisely refrained from mentioning this at the time, however.

Short Fuses

The problems were not just cropping up at Whitehorse. They were becoming apparent to me in each one of my buildings.

About two months into the school year, Tony called me at my office asking me to stop over sometime during the day for a chat.

"How come you want to talk to me? Did I do something wrong?" I immediately felt anxious that Tony had called in the middle of the day for no apparent reason.

"*Sanders!* You worry too much." Tony always called me *Sanders* in an affectionate, endearing sort of way. I considered it a Tony-hug—sort of a hug with words.

"Just come over whenever you can. I want to touch base with you," he said.

I don't remember how long it took, but my guess is—not counting the two-block walk—that I was in his office within about five seconds flat. I am not one to sit on anxiety comfortably.

"So, how are you feeling? How do you think things are going?" he asked, after I arrived and sat down in a chair facing his. He smiled, but I knew Tony well enough to sense that he was uncomfortable.

"Good. Fine. I feel pretty good. Why?" I *didn't* feel that good, but I wasn't going to admit that. I was tired and my brain felt stressed. I still struggled so much to remember things and keep things in any kind of order, and it seemed like all I did when I was not in school was sleep.

"I just wanted to check in with you. See how you felt you were doing."

"Why are you asking me this, Tony? Are you *not* feeling like I'm doing okay?"

"No, you're doing okay. It's just that...well, people are feeling like you're a little short with them. A little...abrupt."

"*Abrupt*?" This took me momentarily by surprise. But then I said, "You're talking about Sherry, aren't you?" Sherry was the district physical therapist and a nice woman in her early fifties. I liked Sherry, and she was an excellent therapist who cared about the kids, but she could really annoy me sometimes.

Recently, I had requested a meeting of the various people involved with Daniel, a student in Blanding. Daniel was fourteen and recovering from a year-long struggle with cancer. Things were looking much more promising for him than they had in the past year, which, between hospitalizations and chemotherapy treatments, had left him unable to attend school since the previous November. Daniel was living in Blanding with his grandmother, a woman I guessed to be in her sixties, and now that he was doing better, they had contacted me to talk about his return to school.

With a sprinkling of freckles running across his face, and copper-colored hair sprouting back now that his treatments had ended, Daniel appeared to be a kid who desperately wanted to be around people again. A bone marrow transplant had necessitated that he remain quarantined to the house for the last two and half months, and he was tired of treatments, tired of being sick, and tired of worrying about dying. He just wanted to feel like a normal kid— just wanted to go back to school. In a couple more weeks, if Daniel's blood counts were good, his quarantine would be over.

Prior to his illness, Daniel had not been a strong student. Whether this was due to a chaotic childhood that interfered with his learning, to learning disabilities, or to what was then about to be diagnosed as cancer, was not clear. Whatever the reasons, Daniel had struggled enough in the first three months of eighth grade for his teachers to refer him for testing to determine if he was eligible for special education services.

"Am I going to go to the high school or back to middle school?" Daniel had asked me one day.

"Well, let's talk about that, Dan. What are your thoughts on this?"

"I dunno. I guess either would be okay," he said.

I sensed this wasn't how he really felt.

I looked over at him, this fourteen-year-old boy who had lived a lifetime in the last twelve months, and I asked, "Daniel, during all that time in the hospital, what kinds of things did you think about? I mean, what did you *dream* about? Decide you wanted to do if you ever got out of there?" I was making the assumption that fourteen-year-olds, just like thirty- and sixty-year-olds, start setting goals for themselves, hoping they can just survive long enough to go after them.

"Well, I decided I want to go to college." He looked at me, hazel eyes thoughtful and a little wary, as if I might laugh at this.

"That's a huge goal. It's a wonderful one."

"I never thought about going to college before," he added.

"Okay, let's look at that for a minute, then. What kinds of things will you need to do, to think about, in order to make that goal happen?"

"Well, I have to get stronger. Stay healthy. And I have to be more serious about school." He looked at me and smiled in a mischievous sort of way.

"Daniel!" I teased. "Are you telling me you never took school *seriously* before you got cancer?"

"Well, yeah. I mean, not really, I didn't. I wasn't really *bad* or anything. Just, you know...I used to do stuff with my friend..." His voice trailed off as if unsure if he should continue.

"Go ahead. I can handle it. Throw it at me, Dan," I said, smiling.

So Daniel told me of various exploits, and of certain choices he had made, and at the end he said, "And I just think, you know...now...I really want to go to college. The thing is, I'm worried about ninth grade. I mean, I didn't even go to much of eighth grade."

"What is it that worries you the most?"

"Well, see, if I went back to eighth grade, I could take some time and get caught up, and if I do get bad grades, it won't be on my transcript. But if I get bad grades in ninth grade, it will be on my transcript and I won't be able to get into college."

I was impressed that Daniel had thought this through so carefully; that he had even realized that eighth grade transcripts would not affect college admissions.

"Wow, Dan. You've obviously thought about this a lot," I said. "Okay, so that's one plus for going back to middle school. Tell me some other thoughts you've had about it."

Over our next few meetings, we revisited the topic several times, going over the many pros and cons of each option. Lockers were a big plus on the high school side, but he was new to the area and did not know any ninth graders, and that concerned him. Daniel had cousins at the middle school who he felt would be supportive as he returned to the classroom, and who could help him in the subjects he found most difficult. He figured the teachers were about the same at both schools and would help him if he was struggling. I was the psychologist at the high school, but not the middle school, and this, in his mind, was a plus on the high school side. On the other hand, he knew and liked the principal at the middle school, and thought he could talk to her if he was having trouble. I told him about Mr. Hatch (Vernon), the psychologist at the middle school, a man I thought he would be very comfortable talking to if he wanted to continue working with a psychologist. So, that became a plus on the middle school side.

There are a lot of people involved in making this sort of educational decision for a student, and I wanted to be sure everyone was in agreement about the best course of action. I had requested a meeting of all the significant adults involved, and Sherry was one of the people at the meeting, as were Tony, Ila, the principals of both schools, the two school nurses, Daniel's grandmother, and Sandra.

"This is about the Daniel meeting, isn't it?" I asked Tony, feeling a little defensive all of a sudden.

The meeting had gotten intense right away when Sherry began by adamantly stating that she was against the retention option—against having Daniel repeat eighth grade. She had launched into a monologue about how we should *never* retain kids, and how the research is *very* clear that retention doesn't work and results in a higher rate of students dropping out later. Sandra, who was also opposed to the retention option, was nodding her head in agreement, and it infuriated me.

I put my hand up to interrupt her. "Sherry! *Stop. Just stop for a minute*. You haven't even listened to the various pros and cons of each side yet. I know all about the research behind retention issues, believe me," I said, thinking how in twenty years I had only supported one retention. "But remember, we are not looking at a regular retention here," I continued, feeling perfectly justified in having cut Sherry off. "This isn't a student who went to school, failed, and is going to repeat the year with the same materials and the same teachers against his will. First of all, Daniel never went through eighth grade at all—he left in November. Were he to return there now, it would be at exactly the same time as when his education was interrupted. And he himself *wants* to complete the eighth grade."

"But he's going to be older than the other kids. It's not a good idea," Sherry stated firmly. Other people were nodding in agreement, and my level of impatience and irritation was rising.

"Wait a minute. Just *wait*." I could not believe how closed-minded people were being. "At least let me run through the pros and cons on both sides before we all just state 'no' to a possible retention."

"Well, I don't think kids should be calling their own shots and determining whether or not they're retained," one of the other team members stated.

"Oh, *come ON*. I am not saying to keep him in eighth grade just because he wants it—I am saying let's look at the whole picture here. However, the fact that both he and his grandmother want him in the eighth grade, *is* a factor that should be considered, although obviously, not the only factor."

To me it seemed like people were not being reasonable, and while I was not aware of it at the time, this must have been conveyed loud and clear through my tone.

I had arrived at the meeting with copies for everyone of the pros and cons of each option, hoping this would be a starting point for discussion. It seemed obvious to me that no one really wanted to have any discussion on the matter, but I went through the list anyway, reading each point aloud.

As I got to the end of the list, Sherry stated matter-of-factly: "Well, we need to retain him. I think he should stay in eighth."

I looked at her.

"Well, I changed my mind," she said, shrugging nonchalantly. "I mean, now that I've heard all those other things, that option makes sense. I can support him staying in eighth."

Nods around the table indicated that everyone either was in agreement with this, or could at least live with it.

"So...what, Tony...you're telling me I was too abrupt, too short in that meeting? I mean, everyone went into it with their minds set—what was I supposed to do, sit back and let Daniel be promoted to the high school and then fold my hands quietly and watch him fail?"

"No," Tony said. "I'm just saying that people are feeling like you're coming across a little too intense. Too strong. Like you're not listening to what they have to say."

"I'll listen to what they have to say, if they have something to say that makes *sense*, Tony. I mean, Sherry started that meeting stating emphatically that she would not support a retention, and then she did an about-face. I didn't force her to do that. I didn't coerce her into changing her mind on that."

Tony stared at me, clearly feeling awkward.

"Do you think I was wrong in that meeting, Tony?"

"Debra, I'm saying that you can get intense. I just wanted to talk to you about how you're approaching people. You need to ease up a little bit...back off a little bit, okay?"

I was quiet for a minute.

"Okay." I felt bad. It wasn't like me to offend people, much less alienate them.

"Okay. Enough on that." Tony smiled a little and leaned back slightly in his chair. "Tell me how you're feeling about your driving."

"Oh, *whaaat...*now you're going to tell me you're getting complaints about my *driving*?" I asked in exasperation.

"Not complaints, Debra. Just...concerns."

I stared at Tony. *Concerns.* I thought about this for a minute before saying, "Well, I will say that driving is still hard for me. Especially if I'm tired. Why, what have you heard?"

"Just that you're weaving a little bit." Tony smiled. A nice smile. An empathetic one that made me feel back on higher, safer ground. "I don't want you to drive if you're tired, Debra. If we have to, we'll figure out a driver for you. Okay?"

"Okay," I said, looking at him before adding, "Really, Tony? I'm *weaving*?"

"Really, Debra," Tony said, looking at me for the first time that day without appearing uncomfortable.

I felt better when I left Tony's office, although it was uncomfortable to think people had spoken to him about both my driving and my behavior.

I mean, I wasn't that *short-tempered. I just wanted people to consider the issues, and make sure the right thing happened for Daniel.*

Tony and I made several agreements before I left his office that day, among them that I would stop working so much overtime, that I would not drive when tired, and that I would work at being more patient with people. I would try my best to honor those agreements, although not working overtime was a tough one. The only way I seemed to be able to get things done was to work hours and hours after school.

Not long after this meeting with Tony, I received a memo from him stating that since Daniel would be attending the middle school, he no longer had reason to be on the high school campus and should be discouraged from being there. Daniel had gotten in the habit, now that he was no longer under quarantine, of dropping by to say hello. My impression was that he didn't know many people in town, and he felt connected to me after the time we had spent together. Daniel was lonely; I was someone he could talk to who understood the whole cancer thing without him having to talk about it or explain it.

It was not going to be comfortable for me to tell him that he was no longer supposed to be on the high school campus.

The next time Daniel stopped by, I tried explaining the situation to him.

"Well, I'll just come by to say hi when I'm on my way home from school," Daniel said to me, smiling in the guileless way of one who believes the solution to a problem is an obvious and simple one.

"Well, actually, Dan...you can't. I mean, it's not that I don't enjoy your visits—I certainly do. I think everyone just wants you to be comfortable with the decision of staying at the middle school and spending time talking with the psychologist over there."

"Yeah, but I like talking to you. You're fun to talk to." Daniel grinned, smiling in a way that always made me think of Tom Sawyer getting someone to paint the fence for him.

"I like talking with you, too, Dan, but I think we should respect this request...okay? I'll make sure to keep tabs on how you're doing, and I'll see your gramma in town and check in on you. For now, though, it's probably best if you don't keep stopping in on your way home."

I inwardly cringed at the look I saw in Daniel's eyes when I said this. It was a pure kid-look. The look on the face of one who knows so much about matters of the heart and so little about matters of politics.

When I asked Tony about it, he said, "He has no business there. He needs to be at his own school."

There was not much I could say at the time. It just didn't seem reasonable to me.

Not reasonable at all.

On the other hand, I thought, *what if it's my own judgment that is off? What if I don't perceive situations accurately anymore?*

That thought scared me more than anything.

* * * * *

It wasn't long after both the Daniel meeting and the issues that surfaced regarding Germaine that Tony asked me to attend another meeting—this one at White Horse. It would be attended by Ila, the special education teachers, and the principal, as well as Tony and myself. The purpose of the meeting was to talk about the issues that were generating my frustration as well as theirs.

By the time the meeting was over, it would no longer be my school. Tony and Ila (who was a licensed educational psychologist) would together pick up responsibility for Whitehorse High School. I was not in trouble, I was assured— Whitehorse just required more time and energy than I could give them.

The principal and the general education teachers would be forthcoming with many verbal and emailed expressions of disappointment that I would no longer be serving the building. The special education teachers would assure me they never said a word of complaint to Tony or Ila. I appreciated the former; I have to admit, I did not believe the latter.

I, myself, had mixed feelings. I didn't think I had been *that* impatient. I certainly never asked anyone to put out more than I myself was willing to give.

On the other hand, I was not leaving the office most nights until after midnight, and I was working both weekend days. I was feeling so scattered and overwhelmed that I didn't know one day from the next, and everything still took me *so much time*. I was amazed how long it took me to do everything, to label it in a way that I could see it and keep it organized, and organize it in a way that was effective for me.

Maybe I was wrong on the Germaine thing. Maybe I shouldn't have expected the special education teachers to know about parallel curriculums, or how to effectively place kids with disabilities in regular classrooms. It's just that Mary Rubadeau had taught me about these things beginning in 1984, and the professional literature has been saturated with both research and opinion articles since at least the early nineties.

Still, maybe I really am way off base here, I thought. *Maybe I am being far too judgmental.*

How weird is that? Not being judgmental has always been one of my trademark qualities.

This constant second-guessing of myself exhausted me and immeasurably eroded confidence both in myself, and in my competence as a psychologist. It never occurred to me that the issue might not be my competence or ability to judge a situation appropriately, but rather it might be that there were changes in my countenance—in the way I both communicated and responded to and with others.

That thought did not occur to me at all. Not, in fact, until almost four years later. At the time, I simply thought it peculiar that I was being perceived as impatient and critical.

I did find out later that Kathy resigned at the Christmas break and went back to Montana. I have to admit that hearing this news helped dispel some of my anxiety that it was my own incompetence that drove me out of Whitehorse, although it made me feel very sad for Kathy.

She could have been a very good teacher.

Silver Linings
October 2004

"I'm overwhelmed." I looked at Merrilyne in frustration.

"What can I do to help?" she asked. As if she hadn't done more than enough already.

Merrilyne was a young, second-year language arts teacher at the middle school in Blanding. I had met her at a summer workshop, and we shared a love of dogs as well as a love of the outdoors. She was a gifted naturalist, and hiking with her was always a treat, as she could name just about everything that grew, flew, flourished, and flowered in the desert wilderness. She had become somewhat like an adopted daughter to me and had been spending more and more time at my house.

Partly Merrilyne was around so much to help with Teek and Meka—a rescue puppy that had wandered into our lives about two months after we returned from the camping trip. Partly she was there so much because the demands of teaching were overwhelming, and I could help her with developing lesson plans and with feeling more confident in herself as she grew into the role of teacher. But I think mostly Merrilyne was around because she saw the day-to-day ways in which I was struggling, and helping me gave her a needed feeling of importance.

Whatever the reasons behind our mother-daughter type of partnership, more and more Merrilyne was managing the details of my life—getting things completed that I simply did not have the time or the organizational skills to manage. I cooked for her, helped her develop lesson plans, and provided a nurturing home environment. She kept my dogs well tended and fed, made sure my bills got mailed on time, made grocery store runs, and did almost all those tasks I felt myself too overwhelmed to take on.

Or simply didn't remember to take on.

There had been many nights when Merrilyne would come to the office and work on her own lesson plans. When she finished, she would spend time helping me, and eventually would apologize, saying she needed to go home and sleep.

"Don't ever apologize!" I reassured her. "No one else should work like this. It's ridiculous." Despite my promise to Tony to try to work fewer overtime hours, I could not work less and still stay on top of the demands of the job. Or, at least the demands of the job as I perceived them.

The residual effects of the head injury had left me with an odd combination of over-focusing and cognitive fatigue. I remained unable to wake up in the morning if I did not take the 5:00 a.m. dose of stimulant medication, and if I did not take it, I would still sleep twenty hours at a crack. As long as I took it, however, I could rise and go to work, and for about two hours, I would do very well—more if I was really engaged in what I was doing and moving around physically. Somewhere in mid-morning, my ability to stay alert would begin to wane, and I would become less and less attentive to my physical surroundings. The symptoms of cognitive fatigue would begin, and although far less severe than they had been, I was still prone to a numb face or the feeling that my head had been stuffed with cotton. Sometimes a nap in the car would help; sometimes it didn't. Sometimes it might have, but was simply not possible given how packed my schedule always seemed to be. That was more often the case than not.

No-Doz was becoming a routine backup to my morning stimulant.

The oddest aspect of my new brain would show up in the evenings when I would sit down to write a report or work on lesson or therapy plans. Writing was the one thing I could do better than any other—the one thing that somehow engaged my brain in a way that kept it awake and in focus. *Over-*focused, in fact. I simply could not end a task until it was completed, and I could not handle any interruptions whatsoever. In absolute silence, I would sit hour after hour after hour and crank out the required written reports.

I would read them in the morning, or a day later, and be so impressed with myself. Having little recollection of the details I had pieced together in order to understand the complexities of any child I had evaluated, I was always amazed to read these well-written, well-researched reports, with solid recommendations attached. Of course, this is part of the reason I could not stop before they were finished—I never could pick up where I left off. If I did, I would have to start all over again in order to make sense out of the data.

The same held true for therapy plans, lesson plans, or any intervention plans I was working on. If I didn't complete the task at the time, I had to start over. If I did complete it, then all I had to do was study it and learn it, in order to implement it effectively or talk to teachers about it knowledgeably. Never mind that I always had to do that right before "show time." I figured it was like being an understudy to my own life script.

"So, how can I help you?" Merrilyne repeated. "Why are you overwhelmed?"

"Well, for one thing, I think I might be getting another new student," I said. "A high school boy, here in Blanding. A boy with a head injury, oddly enough."

"Is that Simon D?"

"How do you know that?" I asked, a bit surprised. I myself had only heard about Simon recently.

"I have his sister in my English class. She is brilliant. A wonderful student."

"Wow," I said, thinking about what I knew about Simon at this point. "Do you know much about him? Did you have him last year?"

"No, I only had the seventh grade students, and he was an eighth grader. All I know is that he was in an ATV accident and is in the hospital. His sister hasn't really said much."

"I don't know too much more myself," I said. "Just that his family was on an outing over Labor Day weekend. Apparently, he flipped over the four-wheeler and slammed his head into a rock, and I think he was helicoptered to St. Mary's in Grand Junction. Now he's in Salt Lake at Primary Children's Hospital."

I looked at her, thinking about my last student with a severe head injury—an eleven-year-old boy named Joey who had accidentally shot himself in the temple with his father's gun. I had thought about Joey a great deal over the last year, knowing how differently I would have developed his program given the insights I had gained from my own experience.

"Will he be your student? I mean, what would you be doing with him?" Merrilyne asked.

"I really don't know. I mean, I don't know if he will be a student I work with, evaluate, consult on...or have no involvement with. I do know that I want to be prepared when he comes home because one thing is certain—if he does not go to a pediatric rehabilitation center for head trauma victims, then whatever rehab he gets, he is probably going to have to get from us here at school."

"Do you know how to work with a student like that? I mean, I know you know from your own experience, but from what I heard, his injury is a lot more serious than yours, right?"

"Well, I don't know the extent of his injuries yet," I said. "But, yes, I am assuming that his is an injury with far greater impact than mine. As far as knowing how to work with him, I know to some degree what needs to be done, but I don't know enough. I mean, I've had training, and I had a student in Alaska with severe head trauma who I worked with for years. I learned a lot during that whole experience from the other professionals on the team, as well as from him. I learned a *lot* from him."

Working on a team with other professionals who were dedicated to a student's program had always provided wonderful learning opportunities, and I missed this type of teamwork in my current job.

"I got really interested in the neurological side of learning disabilities after working with Joey, the boy in Alaska; and somewhere along the way I started going to as many workshops as I could on how the brain learns and how to apply neuropsychological principles to assessing and educating kids. Kind of ironic, isn't it? I mean, that I would wind up with my own head injury." I paused for a minute, thinking for the hundredth time about the irony of this. "Anyway, I'm no expert, that's for sure. But if I'm needed, I will do my best to become one, you can bet on that."

I smiled somewhat wearily at Merrilyne, both of us knowing my propensity for doing whatever it takes to learn what I need to learn to work with a student. The reality of life in remote locations is that you simply do whatever it takes to responsibly offer educational services to a student. There was no doubt in my mind that some of my strongest areas of expertise became so simply because if I didn't learn about something, or master a specific technique or type of service delivery, a student didn't receive it. It was one of the challenges of living so far from any sort of medical, rehabilitation, or psychological service providers.

It was my understanding that Simon had been a star athlete, a straight-A student, and one of those kids everybody liked. What I knew about the injury so far indicated that he had been in a coma for weeks and that the brain had swelled so much that surgeons had to open the skull to relieve the pressure. There was some speculation that part of his brain had been removed, although this information came my way sketchy at best.

My heart ached for these parents, who must be overwhelmed by the magnitude of their reality. I could only hope that Simon would attend a rehab hospital for several months before returning to Blanding, and that his parents and sisters could participate so that all of them would be able to reconcile the inevitable changes that surely were to be seen.

"I'll find out more soon," I told Merrilyne. "The parents signed a release so that I can call the hospital and get more information. I'll know more after talking with people at Primary Children's Hospital."

"What do you have to get done tonight? Want me to go take care of the dogs?"

"Would you? I feel bad asking you to do that, but I have to admit it would be a huge help. If you would take them for a run, I could do a little research and develop the questions I want to ask when I make the call to the hospital in Salt Lake. Plus, I have another report to write."

Running the dogs had always been one of my greatest joys. It afforded us a special kind of connection to each other and to the outdoors; and walking, running, hiking, and biking with them was as natural (and necessary) to me as breathing. But since the accident, it seemed like even though my *spirit* wanted to go, I simply did not have the energy to propel myself outdoors. There was no distinction in my cup of pennies between energy used for thinking and energy used for anything else. I needed all my pennies to think...to work...to perform in my job. As important as I knew exercise was to my emotional, physical, and psychological health, it just kept getting harder and harder for me to get myself outside. It was unhealthy for all three of us, and yet, I seemed unable to walk away from the office and close the door until things had been completed.

"A big one?" Merrilyne asked, referring to the report I had to write, and familiar by now with my need to write it all in one sitting.

"Yeah, a big one," I said. "But a really, really *interesting* one!" I added, smiling.

Despite the hours it cost me and my frustration with not remembering much, I still loved the process of figuring it all out in the first place. I loved gathering the information and data, looking for patterns that explained deficits, and then developing solid and manageable recommendations that made both teaching and learning less stressful and more rewarding. This sort of challenge gave me an electric kind of charge, and even before the accident, I had been known to work late into the night on a case that had people stumped.

The difference now was that I worked on it a lot longer and remembered it a lot less—but my ability to conduct the analysis and put the pieces of the puzzle together seemed mostly (though not entirely) unimpaired.

If I could just retain the knowledge of what I figured out, life would be a lot less of a struggle for me, that was for sure.

On the other hand, I was able to give myself an unbiased pat on the back for work well done—something I had not known myself to do previously. I could look at my reports a day or a week later and unabashedly think, "Whoa, this is good stuff! This is right on the mark in terms of what's going on with this kid!" Then I would study it as if seeing it for the first time so I could talk about it as if I had actually written it. Which I had, of course—but it never *felt* like I was reading my own work, so I really had no ego or sense of ownership invested in it. The good part was being able to give myself credit for it anyway.

I looked at this as sort of a skewed silver lining to the accident.

That night I left school at 3:00 a.m., my list of questions done and my report completed.

Before I left, I wrote a heartfelt letter to Simon's parents, just to let them know I was available—if and when the time came that they needed to access my services.

I simply could not stop thinking about how very difficult this must be on Simon's parents.

Right Brain, Left Brain, Whose Brain
October 2004

"I spoke with the people at Children's Primary in Salt Lake City, and it looks like Simon will be back in Blanding by Thanksgiving. I thought it would be a good idea if we got together now and developed a game plan for when he returns."

We were in the conference room around the long table. I had asked for a meeting with the people most likely to be involved with Simon, given what I had learned about his head injury. Steve—the district's occupational therapist—two of the speech and language therapists, the school nurse, and Sherry were present, along with Sandra, Ila, Tony, and myself. I had done my homework, and felt relaxed and prepared for this meeting.

I knew that of all of us, Steve had the strongest background in head injury rehabilitation, and I was excited about an opportunity for us to work together in an integrated way. I had learned so many skills in the past through collaborative relationships with other team members, and I found this oddly lacking among the itinerant service providers in the San Juan District. Knowing how critical it is to work in synchronicity when providing assessment and treatment for a student with a recently acquired head injury such as Simon's, I was excited about our team doing this.

"According to Elaine—the woman I spoke with—Simon is doing remarkably well considering all that he has been through, and what the initial expectation was. He's had a right temporal lobectomy, meaning they removed a piece of his right temporal lobe, and he has been getting several hours of speech and physical therapy every day. Obviously, he has a long way to go, but according to Elaine, their team is really pleased with his progress." I used my notes, making sure to accurately convey the information and ensure that I didn't forget to communicate anything significant.

I was giving team members as many facts as I could from my lengthy conversation with Elaine, when one of the team members stated, "Well, the bishop told our ward he'll have a full recovery..." as if to dismiss any need on my part to convey the significant impact of Simon's injury.

"He did?" I was very surprised that this kind of information had been communicated publicly, and I immediately felt concerned about the expectation this set up both for the family and the community members. While no one could say what Simon's recovery would ultimately look like, it didn't seem realistic to believe there would not be some permanent changes.

"I think he's doing well, but I can't imagine that he's going to return to us with full recovery. I mean, he's had a piece of his *brain removed.*"

I couldn't help but think how many residual effects *I* was still trying to manage, and I had not had my skull cut open and part of my brain removed.

"The bishop's in touch with the family, and I know Simon's mom pretty well. I think we should just wait and see how he is when he gets home. I don't think we should approach them assuming that he won't be fully recovered."

I could feel myself begin to flush with the heat of irritation.

"Well, I'm not sure I'm comfortable with that. The primary team said they aren't going to be doing any assessment. There isn't going to be any neuropsych testing done at all before he's released. I asked if they would be sending a team down here to help transition Simon back into the home and community and to work with us. Elaine said they wouldn't be doing that, although they would be available to us by phone. So, that means it's up to *us* to do an assessment and develop a program for him." I paused, adding, "I think we need to start working on this now. It's going to take a lot of collaboration time, and I think we need to plan for it." I looked around, surprised that I even had to defend my thinking on this.

"What do you mean by a lot of collaboration time?" someone asked.

"Well, I mean we can't approach this assessment like we do other assessments. We can't each do our own little piece and write individual reports the way we usually do. Or, at least I don't think we should. I think we need to determine exactly what information we're seeking, and plan an integrated evaluation. Simon is not going to have the physical or cognitive stamina to go through testing with each one of us. I think there's a way to do this assessment differently, more efficiently." I looked around before continuing. "I know this takes a lot of planning time, and everyone is stretched really thin, but I think this is the only responsible way to conduct this assessment on Simon."

An uncomfortable silence permeated the room. I simply could not believe everyone wasn't enthusiastically agreeing with me on this.

"This is a *fourteen-year-old kid with a piece of his* brain *removed*. Whatever Simon is going to get he has to get from *us*. We're it. *We're* his rehabilitation team." I could hear my tone taking on that razor-sharp edge I found myself assuming so often lately when other people seemed to miss the obvious. "Why *wouldn't* we work together on this?" I snapped. "I mean, why wouldn't we take whatever time is needed to do this right?"

I was unaware at the time just how challenging a tone I must have projected. A tone that disallowed anyone the opportunity to disagree with me unless they wanted to appear as a less-than-caring professional and team member. All I could see was a fourteen-year-old boy who was going to need an approach outside the box, and a group of professionals who seemed to me to be unwilling to go there.

"Has the team up north done any academic assessment?" Steve asked, interjecting a voice of calmness that might perhaps dispel the chill that was building.

"No, they haven't," I said, taking a deep breath and urging myself to slow down. "And apparently they aren't *planning* on doing any. Elaine said their concentration is only on his physical recovery right now. According to her,

Simon is hemiparetic—he has paralysis on the left side of his body. Also, he is unable to speak—although he can whisper. And, of course, he fatigues very quickly. She did say that he's making remarkable gains every day, but they have no idea when that might plateau."

"Well, I can tell you right now that his parents are not going to want him in special education," one of the people sitting at the table said.

"Well, whether he is identified special education or not, he's going to need a comprehensive assessment and intervention plan. Elaine also mentioned that he demonstrates left visual field cuts, so obviously the occipital lobes are involved. And we know at the very least the right temporal lobe is involved. There are *dozens* of unanswered questions that we are going to have to address in order to develop any kind of educational plan that's realistic and that will help him be successful. And I don't think it should depend on whether he is labeled Special Ed or not. It's what Simon is going to need, and we need to provide it."

I looked around the room, not understanding why I seemed to be the only one feeling this intense need to plan all this out. The less I felt everyone's agreement, the more fervent my tone became.

"I mean, *think* about this for a minute. Given the information we have right now, we *know* that in addition to anything physical that Sherry and Steve will be evaluating, we'll have to assess Simon's abilities in terms of new learning, concentration, attention, memory for previously learned information, visual spatial thinking, working memory..." I was clicking these areas off on my fingers at a rapid pace, continuing with, "...not to mention assessing for all the possible *behavioral changes* we might see with a kid who has had part of his temporal lobe removed." The temporal lobes are associated with both memory and emotions.

"With damage to both the temporal and occipital lobes," I went on, "my guess is there is also damage to the frontal lobes. We won't know this until we receive the medical reports, but I will be more surprised if we *don't* find that information in the report than if we do. And if Simon has sustained frontal lobe damage, then he is probably going to be demonstrating things like increased impulsivity and irritability, difficulty with flexible thinking and problem solving, a decrease in his ability to empathize, difficulty in modulating his temper or emotional outbursts...among other things."

I knew I should be less strident in my presentation, but I found it impossible to sedate my tone. In my mind, I shouldn't have to defend any of this...it should be automatically accepted by everyone sitting around the table. This is the price we pay for living in a beautiful, but remote area. We have to learn what we don't know, and do whatever it takes to learn it right and do it well, so that a child's life is not compromised because of our inadequacies or lack of sophisticated services. I had learned this lesson during my first couple of years in Alaska, and it's a philosophy by which I'd lived my professional life ever since.

It never occurred to me that in describing possible impairments in Simon, I had just described many of my own deficits. No one had ever suggested that I might have sustained frontal or temporal lobe injury, yet that would certainly be consistent with the effects of the kind of rapid acceleration and deceleration of my head that would have occurred if my truck really had rolled, and the rest of my body had been restrained by the seat belt. Dr. Willner had told me emphatically that I did not need to have hit my head to sustain damage. She assured me that the impact of my brain slamming against my skull could cause tearing or stretching of tissues that may not show up in MRIs and CT scans, but cause people all sorts of problems, nevertheless.

Had I followed through with Dr. Feinsworth's suggestion to participate in sessions aimed at teaching me some compensatory skills, I suspect that as I reported the series of events that were transpiring, he and Dr. Willner both would have talked to me about possible frontal and temporal lobe impairment. The classic textbook symptoms of such impairment involve hyperirritability, disorganization, memory deficits, loss of social graces, and sleep disturbances resulting in chronic fatigue. Hindsight tells me that had I talked with Dr. Feinsworth about the series of impaired personal relationships that were occurring, about people's complaints of my abruptness and lack of patience, he would have quickly made the association and helped me run interference with my own behavior. The only explanation I have for my own lack of follow-through is the continued sense I had that this was *only a mild concussion,* and that if I just tried harder, I would supersede any weakness.

That, and I never once thought the weakness had anything to do with personality—only intellect.

The meeting continued, and not once did I believe that my reactions, tone, or responses were out of line or inappropriate to the discussion. An icy tension was building, and when the meeting ended, I left the room feeling confused and angry. I could not imagine why such edginess and hostility had surfaced. To me this was a straightforward no-brainer: we had a student with a severe head injury, and we were going to be his only access to healing. We needed to dig deep and put every ounce of our efforts and collective skills toward maximizing our effectiveness. *Why wasn't everyone on board with me on this?*

It simply never occurred to me that the atmosphere in that room might have had very little to do with Simon, but a great deal to do with my own deportment.

Or that everyone in the room was making an association I would not make for another four years.

At some level, I must have known I owned some culpability in the strain of the meeting because I sat down and wrote a long memo to team members, apologizing for my intensity and attempting to explain in writing what I had hoped to convey in the meeting.

The fact that I typed a five-page, single-spaced memo did not seem excessive to me at the time.

Not one person on the team responded to or even acknowledged receiving the memo (of course, no one in their right mind had time to read, much less respond to a five-page memo). I was especially disturbed not to get feedback from Steve, whom I respected as the brightest and most levelheaded of all of us. In the back of my mind, the fact that *Steve* (with whom I had always shared an easygoing professional camaraderie) did not respond left me with the nagging feeling that I must have done something very wrong, but when I looked at it myself, it seemed that I had done nothing other than advocate for the right thing to happen for a kid. I simply had no flexibility in my thinking or analysis of this. My motives were pure; what I was requesting was the right thing to do for a student; therefore, I was right and everyone else was wrong. It was that simple.

I just couldn't figure out *why* everyone else was approaching this so wrong.

About the same time that the issues were surfacing regarding Simon, another student in Blanding came to my attention. This was a student named Heather, a ninth grade girl identified as having learning disabilities. Heather, along with Daniel, Evan, and Simon, would become central to the conflicts that were about to explode in Blanding.

But before meeting Heather, I met her mother.

And before I met her mother, I heard about her mother from the teachers.

One Mother

"She enables Heather," one special education teacher said. "I really don't think there is anything wrong with the girl, but her mother is so strong that no one has wanted to take on the battle."

"Are you saying that she doesn't really have learning disabilities?" I asked. "That she was diagnosed and placed in special education to appease the *mother*?" I couldn't imagine any professional, much less a *team* of professionals, engaging in such an unethical practice.

"Well, she didn't meet the criteria for eligibility for special education services—she was one point away from meeting it. Her mom was adamant that she get special help, and they are a very influential family in town here."

"She's a very strong advocate for her daughter," the other special education teacher said, her voice trailing off.

We were in a meeting about upcoming evaluations. Whenever a student is in special education, a comprehensive evaluation is required every three years in order to make sure they are appropriately placed, making progress, and that there is a continued need for services. Heather was due for such an evaluation.

"Well, what are her learning struggles?" I asked. "I mean, what kind of learning disabilities does she have, or does the mother *think* she has?"

"No one knows." The teacher shrugged.

"I mean, really, this is a bright kid who gets all A's and B's. She does fine in school," said the other. "We aren't even modifying things for her."

"She gets all A's and B's?" I asked, incredulous. *Why is a student who is getting A's and B's, with no modification in the curriculum or teaching strategies, in special education*? This made no sense to me at all.

"Well, I think I'll meet with the mom first," I said, "and find out what it is she hopes we can accomplish in this assessment. I can tell you right now that if this girl does not have learning disabilities, I will not say that she does to appease a parent. I just won't do that."

"Well, I talked to the mom about you and told her I thought it would be good to contact you," said one of the special education teachers. "I think she is very willing to meet with you." It was silent for a moment before she added, "Good luck, Debra. I have never seen anyone stand up to Peggy[9] yet."

Well, I am not going to call a kid learning disabled just to calm her mother down. Of that, I have no doubt, I thought.

* * * * *

---

[9] Name changed.

I watched a woman get out of her car and walk toward the building. *So this is Ms. Formidable*, I thought to myself. *She doesn't look so intimidating.* She was wearing a blue-jean dress, and wavy, strawberry blond hair fell well past her shoulders.

Probably in her late thirties, I thought. *Good. I'm older.* It was one advantage of having more than twenty years of experience—I could always remind myself that I really did have the credibility that justified speaking up and staying true to what was ethical in terms of students.

Peggy came into my office, and I was surprised to sense how nervous she was. I had expected a bolder, more forceful woman. What I encountered was a somewhat shy and hesitant woman, although one who was quite articulate in voicing concerns about her daughter's education.

I was perched on the chair in my usual position, listening to Peggy as she talked about Heather.

"She is very bright...but something is off," she said. "I can't explain what I mean...it's just that something isn't right."

"Well, maybe it will help if I ask some specific questions," I said. "If we can pinpoint your concerns a bit, then I'll have a better idea of what we need to look for in an assessment. My usual approach is to define the questions we want to have answered and then go about the testing to answer them. Once we do that, we can develop a much stronger intervention program. Does that make sense?"

I could feel this woman relax as our conversation went on, and I found myself liking her very much. She struck me as intelligent and insightful, and as far more insecure than overpowering.

"Let's start with some basics, Peggy. How about any history of ear infections, head injuries, sleep disturbances...anything like that?"

"Well, she did have ear infections, but we were unaware of it until she was about four, and that was when we found out she had been having them since she was an infant. She never did have tubes, and she does still complain of earaches on occasion, and sometimes she seems to have trouble hearing. Heather has a lot of trouble sleeping at night, which makes it hard for her to get up in the morning. And yes, she did have a concussion—she got dumped off a four-wheeler when she was eight. She had a small puncture-type wound on the back of her head and was hospitalized for three days. We limited her activity for several weeks, and then she seemed fine. No personality changes or changes in her abilities at school. Not that we noticed, anyway."

I was very impressed with the information Peggy was able to give me. It was beginning to give me clues about Heather's background that might turn out to be quite important.

"What about academics? Reading, writing, math? Things that require memory?"

"Oh, boy," Peggy said, a sigh accompanying a facial expression suggesting a long history of frustration. "Math has been the worst. She has just never gotten it. I can't tell you the hours and hours we have spent at home trying to supplement what the teachers have given her, trying to help her with her homework.

"And her fine motor skills are funny...I know that isn't very helpful, but I don't know how else to describe it. She has terrible handwriting, and she doesn't like to do things that require fine motor skills." She paused for a moment before adding, "And there is something very wrong with her information processing...it's out of whack, but I can't exactly say how." Peggy sighed again before continuing. "I'm sorry, I know this doesn't help you...it's so hard to be specific. It's like I can tell you that something is wrong, but I can't tell you exactly how or what."

"No, no, you're doing great," I assured her. "Actually, this is very helpful. Tell me about her grades, Peggy. My understanding is that Heather is an *A-B* student. How is she obtaining these grades if she is struggling so much?"

"Well, for one thing, we spend hours with her every night on her homework. So she gets the assignments turned in. A huge part of their grades is just having turned in homework. If you look, you'll see that she does terrible on all the quizzes and tests, but she gets the assignments in, and so she gets good grades. Well, that, and they use a modified grading system."

I had recently become aware of the grading system used with kids in special education, and I was not only surprised by it, but stunned to discover that there were no indications on the report cards that the grades received were modified in some way.

I was finding myself moving from a position of thinking we had a student inappropriately identified as having learning disabilities, to one who had them, but they simply were not identified specifically enough for anyone to know how to treat them.

"You know something else?" Peggy said. "She can't read cursive. She has never been able to read it, and learning to write in cursive was a nightmare. She still prints if given the choice. She does get some occupational therapy from Steve, but I'm not exactly sure what he's doing with her right now. He's been very good with her, though." Peggy added this last statement as if to assure me that she was not being completely negative.

I didn't think she was being negative at all. I thought she was simply being very forthright, and I appreciated it.

"Do her teachers know she can't read cursive, Peggy?" I was thinking about all the confusion Heather would experience if teachers put the daily objectives and homework assignments on the board in cursive.

"I honestly don't know," she said. "I know that Heather is so embarrassed about it that she would never be the one to tell them."

"This is very interesting. I mean, I'm beginning to sense a pattern here...the difficulty with numbers, the fine motor problems, the inability to read cursive." I pondered all this for a minute before asking, "Can Heather tell time, Peggy?" It would not surprise me at all to hear that she could not.

"Well, I'm not sure, to tell you the truth. She had a terrible time learning to read a watch or clock, so all of ours are digital. She does fine with a digital clock."

"Can she read music?"

Peggy's eyebrows arched in surprise. "Funny you would ask that. No, she has a terrible time reading music, although she has a beautiful singing voice and loves to sing. She has had piano lessons, and it has been so *frustrating* for her. Not only does she have trouble reading the music, but she has trouble coordinating both hands."

"How's her spelling?" I asked, anticipating that this would be another significant weakness.

"Horrible. It's awful. And I'll tell you, we spend hours and hours on that kind of stuff. We always have. And she'll have these meltdowns because she is so frustrated." Peggy was thoughtful, looking at me with an expression I had seen before. A look that conveys such a feeling of helplessness in a parent who knows something is truly wrong with their child, but is unable to fix it and make it better. "I can't tell you what homework time is like in our house."

I could only imagine that it was more than a little stressful.

"Peggy, you are giving me such great information. This helps a lot. All of these things…not being able to read music but being able to carry a tune, the problems with numbers, with cursive, telling time…these all give me some ideas about what to look for. How about if I take some time and plan out the assessment, run it by you, and then start meeting with Heather? That way, you'll know what tests I'm going to give and why, and hopefully both of you can feel more relaxed about the whole testing experience."

Peggy had already disclosed to me how nervous both of them felt about testing, based on their not-so-positive past experiences.

"I feel so relieved," Peggy said. "I mean, I always feel like I'm so pushy…such a loud mouth. I think the teachers all think I'm the problem and that I should just be quiet. But it's hard to do that when I watch her struggle so much."

I was surprised that Peggy had an awareness of the teachers' perceptions, although I shouldn't have been. This was not the first time I had encountered a parent advocate who had been made to feel ashamed of using their voice to speak out for their child. It had always been a bit of a pet peeve of mine, since one of the rallying calls in education has been for parents to speak up and become actively involved in their child's education.

"Well, I can't speak for others, Peggy, but I applaud this in you. I think it's great. I mean, you know your child better than any of us ever will. I trust parent perceptions a lot. I'm not saying you're right about it all—we won't know that until the testing is completed—but I trust your perceptions, and they've given me clear information that will help me develop a really solid assessment protocol."

"She'll like you," Peggy said. "I really think she'll like you." Looking at me shyly, and with a bit of embarrassment, she added, "You are not anything like I expected you to be."

"No?"

"No. I mean you are so easy to talk to…so relaxed. I guess I expected someone more intimidating." She smiled at me when she said this, and sort of nodded toward my seated position.

I suppose perching with both feet on a chair does lessen the intimidation factor, though I had never thought about it before.

"Well, you know what, Peggy? I thought the same about you. I was all prepared to feel intimidated, but I find you equally easy to talk with. So, we are both pleasantly surprised with the outcome of this meeting, and that's a really good thing." I smiled back, feeling genuinely pleased to have met this woman. I enjoyed how articulate and concerned she appeared, and it was wonderful to talk with someone so well educated. Peggy had mentioned at some point that she had a master's degree in early childhood, which explained her awareness of things like Heather's difficulty with processing information. In my mind, there was no better combination of traits for a parent to have to ensure good home-school collaboration than this level of concern, insight, and knowledge.

I was certainly looking forward to meeting Heather and conducting this evaluation. If my hypothesis proved accurate, this was a girl with quite *specific* learning disabilities. And if this turned out to be true, then we could develop the kind of intervention program that could have a very positive impact.

What a shame if everyone has written her off as an overprotected and enabled child, if it turns out that she is experiencing the disabilities I'm hypothesizing, I thought after Peggy had left.

And what a shame that it's been communicated to Peggy that she's the problem, instead of encouraging her as a partner.

Funny thing about us school people. We are always saying we want parental involvement, but when we get it, we have a tendency to label the parent as overbearing and a pain in the butt. I suspect that our response is rooted in our own insecurities as educators regarding how to teach kids with complex learning challenges.

Oh, well, we'll see what comes of the evaluation, I thought. *Until then, everything is merely speculation.*

I stayed until 7:00 writing out detailed notes from my meeting with Heather's mother and organizing assessment tools that I would utilize. If I waited until the next morning to do this, I wouldn't remember what it was I had been thinking in terms of Heather's patterns and issues.

My poor dogs, I thought. *They are being so neglected. It really isn't fair to them for me to work like this every day.*

I knew, even as I was thinking this, that I would return later in order to write reports on kids I had already evaluated. Fortunately, the dogs were able to come to school with me in the evenings.

My days just kept getting longer; my nights shorter. No doubt, this did not help my own impulsiveness and level of irritability. I just didn't feel like I had much choice in the matter.

Not if I wanted to be the least bit effective, anyway.

Hypotheses and Heartburn

"It was difficult working with her, actually," Mr. C. said. "I mean, she's a really sweet girl...she wasn't hard to work with. It's just that we would go over and over and over something, and she couldn't seem to get it. And when she did get it, she wouldn't retain it. By Christmas we hadn't even mastered four chapters."

I was talking with the middle school teacher who had individually tutored Heather in math for one period every day of the previous year. I had recently interviewed five of Heather's current teachers and two of her middle school teachers in order to gain more information and insight about their perceptions of her strengths and weaknesses in each subject area. Consistently, each teacher indicated that Heather was a sweet and cooperative student, capable of better work than she was producing.

"So, you're saying that you would individually go over the processes and concepts with Heather, but she wouldn't understand them?" I asked him.

"Right. And you know...I know she didn't like math," he continued, "but it was more than that. She just...I don't really know what it was. She just couldn't seem to hold on to the concepts even though we were going over and over them in as many ways as I could think to present them. She was very frustrated and would find ways to avoid coming to our sessions. I mean, I don't blame her—she really couldn't seem to grasp it, but I worry about her emotional stamina and ability to persevere under stressful conditions."

This was interesting information to me, as Heather's current algebra teacher had mentioned that she didn't think Heather had the basic number concepts mastered, and that she appeared very confused about positive and negative integers—which was making it impossible for her to be successful in this level of academic work. Her science teacher also thought Heather's skills were behind her peers, yet, just as Peggy had described, the homework was submitted on time, and so Heather's grades were solid.

Heather's language arts teacher described Heather as very creative with average grades, although she felt Heather was capable of better than average work. Handwriting and spelling were mentioned as areas of significant weakness.

All of the teachers commented on Peggy's involvement, or—as it appeared to each of them—her over-involvement.

Heather's drama teacher noted her exceptional talents, adding, "I don't believe there's a thing wrong with that girl. If her mother would just back off and let her be, she would be just fine."

School records dating back to early elementary school documented a longstanding history of academic struggles and equally longstanding observations of her cooperative and sweet nature. Year after year, there were comments on Heather's report cards indicating that teachers were concerned about her struggles with math. Teachers encouraged her to study harder at home or to keep up with her efforts over the summer. Test scores, when analyzed, suggested that basic math concepts had never been mastered.

The initial referral for testing had been initiated by Peggy, and it was Peggy who advocated for Heather to be identified as having a learning disability when she was one point from meeting the stated criteria. Not one teacher interviewed appeared to have considered the possibility that Heather was experiencing genuine learning disabilities, and none of them knew why she carried a special education label or what they were supposed to do with that information. It appeared that the belief that the problem resided in Peggy's advocacy was passed from teacher to teacher more consistently than were the written records.

My initial reaction to Heather's referral—that she was in special education to appease a parent—was rapidly being replaced with a hypothesis that I had just stumbled onto a girl with classic indications of developmental dyscalculia. Kids with this disability are frequently very good with creative language (Peggy had mentioned that Heather wrote beautiful poetry, and Mrs. Moon, Heather's language arts teacher, commented on her creativity despite her poor mechanics). However, these children can never quite grasp the language or concepts associated with math. Spatial and quantitative references confuse them, and in early elementary years, words such as *before, after, between, more than,* and *less than* seem to elude them. They just don't get it, and it is common to watch children with this disorder grasp a concept one day only to forget it a day or two later. Difficulty with handwriting, left-right confusion, inability to learn sequences (spelling, dance routines, months of the year), and problems with reading music and mastering a keyboard are commonly observed challenges for children with developmental dyscalculia.

The more I studied Heather's historical records and talked to teachers, the clearer I became on what I was hoping to ascertain through her assessment. My hypothesis that Heather was a girl with a very clear disability could be easily proved or disproved by utilizing the tools available to me. Either Heather would score well on certain tasks and poorly on others; or if I was wrong about this, she would score well within average ranges on all tasks presented.

I looked forward to meeting Heather and beginning this assessment. This was just the kind of testing I loved to conduct, and whether I was right or wrong in my hypothesis was not particularly important to me. What thrilled me was that I was clear in what I was looking for in the evaluation and could proceed in a scientific manner to look for answers. Answers that would hopefully guide us in developing a useful and appropriate intervention program for this girl.

* * * * *

"Hey, how's it going?" I asked. I had walked into the classroom of one of my favorite special education teachers. "You look frazzled," I added. "What's up?"

"Grades," she said, rolling her eyes. "I hate this."

"Sorry," I said, commiserating. Filling out progress reports each grading period was always a tedious chore for special education teachers. "But since we're on the subject of progress reports, can I ask you about a couple of your students?"

"Sure."

"I'm doing triennials on Sam and Kevin. In looking at their IEPs[10] over the last year, it looks like they have met or exceeded their goals in all areas, but when I talk to their general education teachers, it sounds like they are both failing miserably. What's up with that?" I asked, knowing that this was a teacher who always had insights on each one of her students.

"Well, Sam can't read, for one thing," she said. "And Kevin never comes to school."

"What do you mean Sam can't read? Can't read as in, can't read at all?"

"Yep."

"So, do you have his textbooks on tape?" I asked, incredulous that a tenth grade student who had been in special education for his entire school career was still not reading at all.

"No, actually we don't. I know his younger brother sometimes reads the texts to him at home. They're both really good kids."

"Well, what are you doing to teach him to read? And I mean, how are you and the teachers adapting the materials so that he can learn them—so he can access the curriculum?" I felt that familiar flush pulsate through me. "And why do his special ed. grades indicate that he is at or exceeding his goals?" I found this hard to reconcile with what my friend was telling me about this student's abilities.

"Well," she said, looking a bit uncomfortable, "I'll tell you the truth, Debra...I gave all my students threes[11] on their progress reports. I just wanted to be done with it." She looked at me, waiting for me to respond.

I didn't know what to say. I adored this woman. She was my friend and my teaching colleague; yet she had just disclosed engaging in one of the most unethical practices I had encountered in my years in education.

"Oh, wow...I mean, jeez, if he transfers to another district, they're going to think he's mastered all of these things, and in truth, you're telling me he hasn't made any gains at all." I hardly knew what to say. It felt like concrete had settled in my midsection. "Well, what about Kevin?" I asked, hoping to engage in a more encouraging dialogue. "On his IEP it indicates that the only service he gets is through attending the after-school tutoring program."

"Which he never shows up for," my friend noted.

"Well, I didn't figure he would, looking at his attendance records. I mean, if he did he might be the first kid in *my* history in schools to attend after-school

---

[10] Individualized Education Plans

[11] Three on a four-point scale, which means that the goal is nearly met.

tutoring, but skip school." I said this smiling—hoping to dispel some of the tension that had arisen. "My question with him was more why that is his only modification or accommodation. I mean, if all he needs is to master the same curriculum as other students in the after-school tutoring program, well then, he shouldn't be a special education student. I mean, by law, the definition of eligibility involves not only having a disability, but requiring specialized instruction, methods, or accommodations. Is this a kid that could actually be exited from special education?"

It would be wonderful to think a student had actually achieved to the level of being able to shed the special education label.

"Well...no. I don't think he can be exited. I mean, I think he only reads on a third or fourth grade level."

Silence stood between us for a minute, with me not knowing quite how to proceed. My mind was racing, and I felt saturated with frustration and anger over finding yet two more students with such inappropriate programs in place.

"Debra...nobody has ever talked to us about these things before. I mean, no one has ever told us anything regarding a student's assessment results, or why a student can or cannot do something; and nobody has *ever* talked about all the various interventions that you've presented as possibilities for us to implement. It's not that I don't care. I just...I just don't know how to go about all of this. It's all so new." She was quiet for a minute before adding, "Sometimes I think I should go back to being a para," referring to the fact that she had been a paraeducator in the district for more than a decade before becoming a certified teacher.

As he had done for several others, Tony had made it possible for this woman to complete an online program in order to obtain her special education teaching certification. She was a wonderful person, a dedicated child advocate, and she loved these kids with all her heart.

She just had no idea how to teach them.

* * * * *

"I'm telling you, Merrilyne. I just don't get it. I mean, I love Tony. I love these teachers. But this is outrageous. I mean, the stuff that goes on here is just not right." I was still pondering my earlier discussions about the two high school boys. "Does this go on at your school? I mean, what are your IEP meetings like? Don't you guys sit down and look at the testing, and then as a team consider what deficits can be remediated, what needs modification, and what skills need to be bypassed before writing goals and objectives and developing the individual education program?"

"I don't know," Merrilyne replied. "I've never been to an IEP meeting."

"What do you mean you've never been to an IEP meeting? How could you not go to meetings with the high number of special education students placed in your classroom?" For months, I had been helping Merrilyne develop lesson plans that addressed the needs of her many special education students with their various learning disabilities.

"I mean, they never have them. At least not that I'm aware of. The case manager just comes by and has us sign the forms."

"Don't tell me this," I said, a sick feeling lodging in my stomach. "I mean, that's illegal. Are you aware of that? These decisions need to be made by a team, Merrilyne. IEP goals are developed *collaboratively*, not by some special education teacher who writes them up and just walks around and gets the paperwork signed. Please don't tell me this is the standard procedure in your building, Merrilyne."

"It's illegal?" she asked, a look of concern etched in her expression.

I looked at the face of this young woman who was well into her second year of teaching and struggling every day of it to make things work for her students. "Well, yeah," I said. "But don't freak out. I mean, you had no way of knowing that." I paused, thoughts racing through my mind and colliding with one another midway. "Just don't sign IEPs that way anymore. Okay?"

She nodded, a serious look on her face.

"If you want, I'll role play with you how to stand your ground and say you won't sign...and that you want an IEP meeting to take place that includes the parent and appropriate teachers."

"That'd be good," Merrilyne said, looking both relieved and anxious. "That'd be really good."

Assertiveness, we both knew, did not happen to be among Merrilyne's many gifts and strengths.

Buzzed Heads and Skewed Perceptions
November 2004

It was November, and things were moving along at an incredible pace. Even without going to Whitehorse, it seemed like there was so much to do and never enough time to do it as well as I would have liked. And it seemed like every time I turned around, I was in conflict with somebody over a student.

As I spent an increasing amount of time with Evan, I came to know his grandparents better, and the extent of his grandmother's own emotional challenges had become evident. One day, I went to Evan's home to pick him up, and his grandmother opened the door to my knock.

"*Whoa.* Wow. Mary," I stuttered as I glanced at her. "That is a very new look for you."

Her head, shaved and bald, had taken me entirely by surprise. It was hard to know where to settle my eyes. As they reflexively traveled away from her fuzzy scalp, they landed on a breast. A naked, hanging, pendulant, *exposed* breast. Oh, God, two breasts. She was wearing a jumper with no shirt or underwear underneath.

Oh, my, I thought, eyes ricocheting wherever. *Ohhhh, my, my, my.*

Mary is not a tall woman, but she is a large one. Seeing naked breasts on Mary is not like coming upon the naked breasts of, say, Twiggy or Kate Moss. Not that it would be any less shocking, I suppose, if one were to stumble upon a bare-breasted skinny model, but the sheer bulk of Mary's bosom made it hard not to stare.

"Oh, I look terrible," she wailed. "I look terrible."

"What *happened*?" I asked, wondering what could have transpired to turn this sort-of-normal woman into the shrieking, bald, half-naked, and wailing creature I was seeing right now. I looked around at the usually neat home and was shocked to find it in complete disarray. They were a very poor family, and they did not have much, but I had been to the home several times before, and it had always been tidy. Mary had definitely displayed some odd characteristics and behaviors over the months I had come to know her, but nothing that prepared me for this.

Mary's wailing amped up a decibel or two.

"Well, Mary, look at it this way...it could be worse," I said, not knowing exactly what was going to spill from my own stunned lips. "You could be bald, braless, and flat-chested. I mean, if you're gonna flaunt, I guess it's good to have something to flaunt. Right?!"

This got a laugh out of her, and as quickly as the wailing began, it ceased.

She smiled a sweet smile, looking at me from beneath her eyelashes like a naughty child who knew she was more cute than bad. I would later learn that Mary had been diagnosed with a severe psychological disorder, and that *several* distinct personalities resided within her. At the time, however, I didn't have this information, and before I could do more than register the oddity of this sudden switch in demeanor, Evan's grandfather, Donald, stepped into the room.

"Oh, holy...gosh!" were the first words to pop out of my mouth, although not the first ones to cross my mind. That was one thing about working in elementary schools—early on, it trains spontaneous cussing right out of a person.

Cue ball bald.

Donald was standing there with a stark naked head.

"Well, I didn't want her to feel bad," he said, shrugging nonchalantly. "So after she went crazy and whacked off all her hair, I shaved it for her and then told her not to feel bad, I would shave mine, too."

Wow. Wow, I thought. *This family certainly sticks together.* I wondered if Evan would show up without any hair as well.

As it turned out, Evan had retained his hair, preferring his over-the-eyes look to a naked scalp.

* * * * *

As I first witnessed during the shaved head incident, it was clear that Mary shifted rapidly between states of rational, logical thinking and irrational, explosive behavior. After she signed a release of information, her therapist confirmed a diagnosis of Dissociative Identity Disorder, indicating that she had seven distinct personalities. This helped explain why on some days Mary would badger and berate Evan for his relationship with me (showing extremely jealous behavior), and at other times be lovingly supportive of his efforts toward better mental health. While this certainly was the healthiest home situation Evan had ever experienced, it was not by any means an optimal environment for him, and the fact that he was working so hard on his therapy goals (almost never missing an appointment) pleased me.

Evan, unfortunately, was not putting the same kind of effort into academic work, although for the most part he had been showing up for his classes and silently participating. To be a good student requires far more risk-taking behavior than most people realize, and Evan was nowhere near healthy enough to risk turning in papers, volunteering answers, or following through with assignments. In his mind, it would be better to fail than to appear stupid, as long as he could write off failure to not putting in effort. To put in effort and fail—that would be a public shame Evan would not chance. I understood this about Evan, and I felt confident that if we stuck to the intervention plan developed, over time he would feel secure and trusting enough to take the risks necessary to engage in academic work.

This was not a viewpoint held by many.

The special education teachers increasingly raised questions about whether it was appropriate for Evan to be in a public school setting; and, unfortunately, they were not following through with generating the lesson plans or approaching academics in the way we had agreed upon when designing his intervention plan. I had developed initial lesson plans for Evan, hoping that, provided with a model of a different way to approach academics, his teachers would be more comfortable in stretching out of their own comfort zones. I did not, however, have the time to continue creating lessons, and Evan felt like he was "floating" in his classes—biding time until the teachers figured out how to teach him. He was bored, and his attendance began to be erratic. This was disconcerting to me as I already felt that Evan spent far too much time isolated at home engaging in aggressive video games, reading, and/or lost in fantasy of a violent nature.

A very stressful meeting occurred in mid-October at the request of one of Evan's special education teachers. In attendance was the principal (Bob), Ila, myself, the two special education teachers, two of the paraeducators who worked with Evan, the school's at-risk coordinator, and a man I had never met who was apparently from a social service agency. The repetitive disquiet about Evan's placement came up early in the meeting.

"I just do not think we have the skills to handle a student like this," one of the special education teachers stated. "I think maybe he needs a more institutionalized setting."

"*That* would be the worst thing for him," I instantly retaliated. "There is nothing good that will come for Evan by being locked up in some psychiatric institution, and a whole lot of harm that could come from it. He's making progress; he's working his buns off therapeutically, and that's huge for a kid like this."

"But we're not equipped to deal with him," one of the teachers stated.

"What if he gets violent?" another asked.

"Has he *shown* any indication of violence?" I snapped. "To my knowledge, he hasn't. Frankly, considering that the plan we laid out isn't being followed and that he has no structured academic program, I think Evan has managed his emotions quite well. I can hardly blame him for skipping classes at this point when there's no viable instruction going on for him in those classes." My level of frustration and anger was exponentially increasing with each statement the teachers uttered. Looking back on it, I had probably not been subtle about my feelings that they were not putting in the necessary effort to be effective educators with a kid like this.

"Well, Debra, I can't teach him one to one. I have other students in the classroom."

"I realize this," I said pointedly, "but it's not like you have to sit there one to one with him. It's a matter of setting up assignments like we discussed, and then checking in to make sure he's on the right track—and simply to communicate that you're aware of his presence. That's really all this kid wants right now...to know his presence is felt and appreciated. Well, that and to know that his teachers are willing to put in some extra time in order to teach him in the way he can learn."

I discovered early on that the harder I worked to develop effective treatment interventions for him, the harder Evan worked to complete them. At one point he had asked, "Why do you do this? I mean, this must have taken you a lot of time. Don't you have a life?"

Laughing, I had simply responded, "Fair question, Evan. I sometimes ask myself the same one. Yeah, I have a life, but you're important to me. It's important to me that I work as hard at teaching you as I ask you—or any of my students—to work at learning."

I was convinced that this encounter early in our relationship was at least part of what propelled Evan out of bed and into our sessions multiple times a week.

"Look how well he's doing with Briana," I continued. Briana, a student with severe impairments, was self-contained in Sandra's classroom. She was a medically fragile child who looked and functioned much younger than her twenty-one years, and she was dependent upon others to move her, comfort her, entertain her, and provide for her. Evan had noticed her sitting in her wheelchair, placed in front of cartoons on the television, and he had begun to pay attention to her. Rolling her a ball soon turned into his taking her for short walks in her wheelchair, and although Briana had no intelligible speech, she was clear in her communication of joy when Evan entered the room. An immense smile would unfold over Briana's face, and she would excitedly clap her hands when she spotted him coming through the door. Briana knew Evan would interact with her, and her delight was unmistakable.

Like many children with significant emotional issues, Evan was remarkably tender with and toward those underdogs more obviously handicapped than himself. I had been extremely pleased to see Evan display the kind of empathy and gentleness he showed toward Briana, and I knew that he was deriving important feelings of confidence through his role as Sandra's helper that hour.

"Speaking of that...I'm not comfortable with that situation," Sandra stated. "I think it's great that he wants to be a teacher's aide fourth period, and I'm okay with that, but I think we should tell Briana's mother about Evan."

"Excuse me?" I asked.

In retrospect, it is possible I barked rather than asked this question.

"I mean his history of abuse," Sandra said.

"I will tell you right now, that would be illegal as hell and a blatant violation of Evan's right to privacy," I said, horror punctuating my every word. "The purpose of my disclosures about some of Evan's background has been to help you understand him, to give you insight into his behavior, and help you understand our treatment goals in therapy. It was *not* to provide ammunition against him."

My hands were shaking, and I could feel my face hot with repressed outrage. In this small Mormon community, making that kind of information available to parents just about guaranteed that it would become public and evolve into a volatile source of conflict, not to mention idle gossip.

"I would like you to give me one good reason that Briana's mother should be told anything at all about Evan," I continued. "He has no history whatsoever of inappropriate sexual behavior, and we have no reason to believe that Briana is not safe with him. He has been responsible and caring in acting as your aide, Sandra, and he has given Briana much needed attention." My words were tight and slicing, cutting through all social conventions and spitting out my disagreement with little regard to professional protocol.

Ila, ever the peacemaker, stated that she agreed we could not violate Evan's rights by disclosing information, but she said that we would need to have two adults present in the classroom at all times so there would always be at least one adult supervising when Evan was around Briana. In other words, if one adult had to make a bathroom run, the district would be able to attest that there was still an adult present with Evan and Briana at all times.

I was livid. In my mind, this was a ridiculous use of resources already spread too thin. And I knew that with his hyper-perceptiveness, Evan would figure out without a word being spoken that the level of trust in his attentiveness to Briana had been questioned.

The tension level in the meeting intensified, and, by the time it was over, my relationship with Sandra had taken on new and uncomfortable dimensions.

But it wasn't only with Sandra that my relationship was becoming increasingly strained. It was happening with the special education teacher and the speech and language therapist in Mexican Hat as well.

A second grade teacher had approached me about one of the students in her class who was receiving special education services, but who did not seem to be making any progress. In reviewing the girl's file, it turned out that she had been going to the resource room and receiving reading instruction every day—which would have been fine, except that her disabilities were in the areas of math and articulation disorders.

Somehow, the people in charge had missed that little detail when developing her program, and she was receiving neither articulation therapy nor math intervention.

Another student, a sixth grade boy, was reading on a primer level despite having been in special education for the past five years. I had not interacted with him for long before it became evident to me that severe *auditory* processing disorders were a significant part of—if not at the root of—his academic struggles. I could not imagine how the speech therapist, who had conducted numerous evaluations on this boy over the years, had not identified this. He, like many others, was receiving a generic and ineffective intervention plan, when instead, specific strategies should have been developed to address the issues at the root of his academic failure.

Several other children with equally intense needs came to my attention via their general education teachers—each of whom expressed frustration by the lack of effective help through the special education department; and each of whom had these children in their classrooms the bulk of the school day. More and more, these teachers began referring children already identified and placed in special education to the intervention team, because despite their special education placement, the children were not making behavioral and/or academic progress.

I had become especially concerned about Willy (the twelve-year-old with the megawatt grin) because unless Eleanor was in the room, it seemed he was left on his own a great deal with little in the way of a structured skill-building program in place. Eleanor was a full-time (and very gifted) special education paraeducator, but she was not a certified and licensed teacher. It concerned me that Willy was isolated in the special education room from the time he entered school in the morning until he left at the end of the day, even eating lunch in there in the absence of peers. He would be off to Monument Valley next year, and eventually he would be an adult community member. Willy needed to develop the kind of socialization and adult living skills that would allow him to live as independently as possible; and while Eleanor was fabulous about weaving such training into his day, it was not her job to be the educator responsible for developing or overseeing his program.

This was the job of Eleanor's direct supervisor, who was the only certified special education teacher in the building.

Several months later, I would discover paperwork in Willy's file that made it clear the program implemented was a violation of the law and his educational rights. At the time, however, I was not directly involved with Willy and therefore had no reason to go through his paperwork. I only knew, from observing, that his program seemed substantially lacking, and it concerned me.

Christena was doing a fabulous job with Ernie in the second grade classroom, and his progress was evident. She had not, however, been receiving the special ed support she had been assured of when we developed the program as a team. I worried that Christena would burn out quickly unless she had additional assistance with his program on a daily basis.

We had scheduled a meeting regarding Ernie's program to address this and other issues. When the time came for the meeting, besides me, only the special education teacher and Christena were present.

"This is weird," I said. "How come no one else is here?"

"Who else should be here?" the special ed. teacher asked.

"Well, you're the case manager. Didn't you invite the rest of the team members?"

"I wasn't sure who was on his team."

Looking at her quietly and with absolute frankness, I said, "Well, that is just not acceptable. You're the case manager. It's November—we've been meeting on Ernie since August. It's your *job* to know who's on the team and to inform them about meetings. My gosh, at least his *mother* needs to be here, not to mention the nurse and the occupational therapist. It's not even *legal* for us to have this meeting without his mother being here." I stated this with the frankness of a child who had not yet learned the conventions of social interactions. Spoken with the frankness of a child, but sodden with the glaring disapproval of an adult.

There was an uncomfortable silence between us. I found it inexcusable that this woman would be so lax; this was one of our most challenging students, and for his program to continue successfully we needed to collaborate among all the team members.

Four years later, I would cringe to think how she must have wondered who died that day and made me the Special Education Gestapo. But, at the time, all I could fathom was that this boy's program was likely to falter unless we provided the support to the general education teacher that she needed to maintain the current level of intervention. My reaction was entirely colored by an overwhelming sense that we all needed to work harder and do better by these kids, and that there was no excuse for doing less.

Although it was never my intent, I suspect that in my single-minded and dispassionate way of communicating the truth, I both embarrassed and chastised the special ed teacher on that day. That sort of approach was dramatically out of character to the way I had performed my job as a consulting educator for the previous twenty plus years, and must have taken her (as it took others) by complete surprise.

Regrettably, it was yet another example of the less-than-venerable moments I displayed that were recognized far too late to correct. I liked this particular teacher a lot—she was teaching me much about the Navajo culture, and I respected her immensely for her traditional ways and involvement in community. However, like many of the teachers in my buildings, she was "home-grown." Tony had arranged for these individuals to get their degree through an online program, and none of them ever had the opportunity to experience teaching under someone who was effectively implementing special education services. I was not blaming them as much as I was blaming Tony for not exploring creative opportunities by which they could experience the necessary modeling and guided practice we all need before obtaining competency. For not having higher expectations. For what appeared to me as an acceptance of mediocrity based on a belief that it was the best we could hope for in our little pocket of America.

As October drifted into November, services at San Juan High did not seem to be improving. Each evaluation I conducted revealed students who had made no academic progress despite being served through special education. I was amazed to discover that the general education teachers received little or no information about each individual student, and had no idea why the kids were struggling and what they, as educators, should be doing about it. And despite our having a significant percentage of Native American children in the schools, the speech department appeared to do very little to distinguish between the children struggling because of language-based learning *disabilities* and those struggling because of their language *differences*. I was uncovering appalling gaps in services to children, along with what appeared to me to be an equally appalling lack of motivation to correct this.

As I had found at Whitehorse, and indeed in all my schools, the principals experienced as much—or more—frustration as I did.

"We've never had any support through special education," one principal told me.

"Special ed is my weakest department," I heard repeatedly from these administrators.

"No one at my school knows about the things you're talking about, Debra.

When you use terms like *parallel curriculums*, or talk about *inclusion* versus *mainstreaming*, I don't think any of our people know what you're talking about," a principal said to me one day.

This took me by surprise. First of all, these are terms and approaches that have been considered legal and ethical "best practices" for many years. Secondly, there is a huge difference in the strategies and support services needed when a child is *included* in the classroom because it is age appropriate and those strategies needed for a student who is *mainstreamed* into a classroom after reaching a level of mastery indicating they can handle the academic work with minimal modifications. Or, between the child who is failing in the curriculum because they do not have a well-developed English language base and one who is failing because auditory processing disorders are making it impossible for them to correctly hear the sounds in words, distinguish background noise from instructional noise, or process syllable sequences correctly (thus causing the student to mishear the words being spoken).

If no one understands or pays attention to the reasons behind academic failure and behavioral problems, it would be impossible *not* to set both teachers and students up for disaster.

"Tony, these kids are *failing*," I said to him one day in his office. "They are failing miserably. We need to do something. These teachers, all of them— special education and regular—they need training."

"They've had training, Debra."

"Tony, I don't think they have. They might have had exposure, but that is vastly different from being *trained.* I mean, Tony, there hasn't been one person I've talked with who has a *clue* how to *differentiate* instruction; or who understands that there are various kinds of learning disabilities that require different kinds of intervention. It's as if every kid receives a modification that states they get more time to do less work, but not one of them is receiving instruction in a way that allows them to grasp the content. More time and less work doesn't help them learn the curriculum if the information isn't presented in a useable format." I paused for a second before adding, "I mean, *jeez*, Tony, we'd never say to a deaf child, 'Here, you only have to do half the amount as the other students, and you'll get a week longer to turn it in, but we're still going to teach you by speaking.' We'd provide an interpreter, for God's sake, and then we'd maintain the same high level of expectation for them as we have for a bright, hearing student."

"I know what you're saying, Debra, but you have to be patient. This is the problem down here—we don't get educators who have been through strong university training programs or who have had experience implementing these things. People don't want to move here—they'd rather be up north where they're near cities, and where there aren't the issues that we have in terms of poverty and ethnic diversity and language issues. You should have seen what it was like when I first got here. We are so far beyond where we were."

"Maybe so, Tony, but come on. Teachers down here are capable of reading current literature in order to know what is ethical and intelligent educating. My God, they are using this *absurd* grading modification system that's making me crazy. The only thing it does is give kids A's and B's who are obtaining classroom averages of *forty, fifty,* or *sixty* percent." I took a breath, though not a very deep one, before continuing my diatribe.

"Tony, I had a teacher tell me last week that he never knew if a student was identified as special education or not until it was time for grading. He said he only needed to know so he could plug in the grading modification formula. I asked him if that was true, then how was he modifying the material or differentiating the instruction so that it addressed a student's learning disabilities, and he said he wasn't. He said he's never been told *to* do that, much less *how* to do that.

"That's outrageous, Tony. It's unethical, if not downright illegal."

"Well, the grading modification is a sound one," Tony said. "It's based on a mathematical formula."

"I don't *care* what it's based on, Tony. If that's *all* that's being done, then it does nothing other than give a very false impression about what a student is achieving. It makes a kid who is mastering only forty percent of the work look like they are above average. As far as I can tell, there is not **one** special education teacher—at least in my buildings—who understands how to help general education teachers use different teaching strategies so that a kid has an opportunity to *learn* in the general education classroom. That may not be true for the teachers in the other buildings, but it is definitely true in my buildings. It's as if they think they're leveling the playing field by watering down the curriculum, when what they should be doing is leveling it by teaching the information in a different way, but maintaining the same standards and expectations. The way things are being done out there communicates to everyone that kids with learning disabilities are not *capable*, and that's wrong, Tony. That is just wrong."

"Debra, these teachers have had all this training. I'm telling you, they've had it. Welcome to San Juan. We don't get the quality of educators here you're talking about. It's the price of living in our remote corner of the state."

I could feel an increasingly familiar reaction of intense outrage and anger surfacing, and I knew better than to vent these feelings to Tony. He was too defensive. Over the last eight years, Tony had brought this district from a place centuries behind the rest of the world to where it was now. I reminded myself that he was probably not particularly open to my less-than-subtle criticism over the current practices.

On the other hand, I am not the best one to tell that no one wanted to move here, or that good special education teachers couldn't be found.

For God's sake, I thought, *if Carl could get highly competent people to move to the bowels of Alaska, where milk costs nine dollars a gallon and it stays below zero degrees and dark for months at a time, Tony should be able to entice equally educated and passionate people to a place where the sun shines 320 days a year and there is access to some of the country's best recreational areas.*

"Well, Tony...all I can say is you may have trained them, but they didn't get it. You've given them *drive-bys*. Exposure. The teachers have *not* had the kind of modeling and guided practice that we know everyone needs to master new information. And these teachers, Tony, your special education teachers, they have *no clue* how to help the general education teachers who have all these kids in their classrooms. They send a paraeducator into the classroom with a kid and tell them to 'help them.' *Help* is never defined for anyone, so most of the paras are ineffective. Not because they aren't competent, but because they are untrained and misdirected. You know what a teacher said to me last week? She told me having the paraeducator in there made things harder for her, not easier. She said it was like having another disruptive student in her classroom."

I was a snowball on a roll without anything in its path to slow it down.

"The kids are paying the price for all this, Tony. You're graduating kids who have been in special education for eight, nine, even ten years that are still reading on a *third or fourth grade level* but have grade point averages of *3.5 or better*. That's *absurd*."

Despite my earlier internal warning to hold back and not confront Tony about all the failures in the system, I seemed to be doing exactly that. And doing it with that tone of righteous indignation that seemed to constantly overtake me when dealing with these issues.

I was so adamant, so outraged, so *angry* about it all, and—although I didn't realize it at the time—there was absolutely no restraint or diplomacy in how I presented my thoughts. I felt them intensely, and I presented them intensely. I felt things were wrong, and I conveyed that things were wrong. And hindsight suggests that I did so in a way that must have made everyone feel as if I thought I was the only passionate educator on the planet. Or at least in the San Juan School District. I didn't understand why people were responding to me defensively, because all I could see was that what was happening for students was *wrong,* and I felt everyone should embrace that understanding and work to change the system.

Even though I might have been correct and these things *were* faults within the system, unlike in the past, my communication of this information was such that it could do little beyond alienate the people who needed to hear the information the most. For twenty years, my ability to bring "dead wood" back to life had been a trademark skill. I had long been known not only for working effectively with the most resistant teachers and administrators, but for getting them to participate in innovative and creative approaches to teaching with enthusiasm and, even sometimes, with passion.

It never occurred to me that my line of attack was vastly different now than it had been in my previous two decades of work in education. I truly did not see or sense that I approached anything differently from the way I had for my entire adult professional life. I was years away from understanding that while my passion and advocacy for children with special needs was unchanged, my ability to communicate, motivate, and shape viewpoints had not only changed, but had become significantly impaired.

At the time, my interpretation of the unfolding events was that people were being obtuse, lazy, unreasonable, and resistant to stepping outside the box in order to approach education differently. My thoughts centered on how absurd it was that Tony was telling me that we were "too remote," "too small," or "too underfunded" to provide the kind of services for which I was advocating.

I wanted to rail, yell, and chastise people. I wanted to tell them to stop giving me all the reasons we *couldn't* and start thinking about ways we *could*. But no one was listening, or so it appeared to me (of course, who wants to listen to railing and chastising?). And no one beyond the principals and a few of the general education teachers seemed interested in taking the extra time needed to learn the necessary strategies to effectively teach these children.

So, I did what I always do when I think others are not completing their share of the work.

I worked harder.

The Letter

December 2004

"I have a meeting with Tony today." I was talking to Vernon during a rare and quiet moment together in the office. "I think I'm in trouble."

"Why? What'd you do?" Vernon asked me this with an affectionate smile on his face. I adored Vernon, and I respected him immensely. He was everything I was not as a psychologist: he was even-keeled, professional, level-headed, and he somehow managed to snap his briefcase shut and walk out the door every single day at 4:00. Not 4:01 or 4:02, but exactly 4:00. And not a.m. either. But 4:00 in the afternoon. Vernon had a beautiful wife and five young children, and while he loved this work deeply and performed his responsibilities with great integrity, his work did not consume him.

Vernon had balance in his life; something I was sorely lacking.

"I'm not sure. But I think some of the teachers are mad at me. I think they think my expectations are too high."

"Are they?" Vernon asked fairly.

I thought about that. Maybe they were. It was so hard to say. I had been having one stressful meeting after another—something I had rarely experienced in the past, no matter how complicated a student or a situation. I couldn't figure out if it was me that was the problem, or if the problem was that I was no longer in Alaska, and the kind of creativity and drive I was used to seeing in teachers and administrators just wasn't endorsed here, much less encouraged and applauded.

"I know Tony has been working on something for the last few days that has him really preoccupied," Vernon said. "I've never seen him this stressed before."

"Really? Do you think it's this meeting?" I asked, looking at Vernon with concern.

"I don't know, and that's the truth. Let me know how things go, okay?" Vernon was getting ready to leave the office for the nearby middle school. It was nearing the Christmas vacation, and while our schedules had slowed down a little, neither of us could afford much down time.

"Oh, you can count on that," I said. Vernon had been a good listener over the last few months, and more than once I had vented my frustrations over the events that were unfolding.

* * * * *

Tony had called earlier in the week and asked me to come in so we could talk over our "Four Agreements" and take stock of how things were going. As I had said to Vernon, I had the feeling that I was in trouble, but when Ila walked into Tony's office moments after I arrived, and closed his door, I felt my anxiety level escalate beyond anything I had anticipated.

"What's Ila doing here?" I asked, looking at Tony.

"I just thought she should be here," he said. He looked uncomfortable. Tony did not enjoy confrontations. That much I knew for sure.

"Is this a disciplinary meeting?" I asked, tension running through every part of my body.

"No, Debra. It's not. I just want us to go over the agreements we made earlier in the fall and take a look at how things are going."

In the next few moments, silence laid the foundation for the wall that was to grow between us. I looked at Ila as she sat perfectly still, notepad in front of her, poised to record all that transpired.

"Why do I feel like I need a written agenda for this meeting, Tony?" I looked at him directly, both wary and challenging at the same time. I had long ago learned that the best way to approach a meeting that was likely to be emotional was to have a written agenda that everyone agreed upon, and then stick to it.

"We don't need a written agenda," he said. "But I did write this out in a letter to you." Tony handed me a formally written letter—one that had been cc'd to the superintendent.

Little beyond the sound of Tony's and Ila's breathing could be heard in the minutes it took for me to skim through the letter, although it wouldn't have mattered if Snoop Dogg, the Beastie Boys, and the Gregorian Chanters had all banned together in the next room. The hammering in my ears would have drowned out even the most disharmonious of ensembles.

"...concerned because you have used hyperbole to describe student issues"; "...engaged in aggressive and confrontational behavior toward colleagues"; "...overstepped your role as a consultant and itinerant school psychologist"; "...implemented interventions and evaluations which are too intensive." I suddenly knew why people write that their heads were spinning or that the floor seemed to disappear beneath their feet. Both held true for me at that moment.

I looked at Tony as he quietly said, "This was not an easy letter for me to write, Debra. I thought about these things a long time before putting them down on paper."

"I believe that to be true, Tony," I said, my own words sounding echoic and like they had been spoken by someone else. "I'm sure this was very difficult for you to write."

We all sat mutely, no doubt each lost in our own misery and discomfort. A feeling of humiliation began to weave its way through the cracks in my quickly erected armor.

"Tony, I am not prepared to respond to this right now. I need time to read this and think about it. I can't talk about this right now." I could no longer look Tony in the eye.

"Okay. Take the time you need," he said, probably relieved to have a reason to end this meeting. "I need to present an in-service to teachers this afternoon. We can talk about this later, whenever you're ready." He got up and headed toward the door.

"Tony?" I asked. "This is copied to the superintendent. Is this going in my file?" I had never had a letter of admonishment in all my years of working. The closest I had come was one time when Jim Foster told me if I brought Teek to school one more time, he would be forced to write a disciplinary letter and put it in my file. He never did, of course, and much later—after I had stopped bringing Teek to school for good—he laughingly told me that he figured the only thing that would keep me from bringing that dog with me everywhere I went was to put the fear of God in me.

Jim was right about one thing: placing a disciplinary letter in my personnel file would certainly put the fear of God in me.

"No. No, Debra. It's just policy to cc any written correspondence to an employee to the superintendent."

"Okay," I said, glancing toward Ila, who was still sitting motionless and silent.

Tony left the room, and I know Ila and I sat there and talked for at least an hour. I have absolutely no recollection of what either one of us said, though I know I felt a little better after leaving her. I was in the habit of writing down as much as possible after I had conversations with people so that I would remember what was said or be able to refer to my notes before the next encounter, but that day, I wrote down nothing that was said between Ila and me.

I think I was too shell-shocked to remember that I wouldn't remember unless I made notes.

* * * * *

That night I talked with both Joyce and Denise on the phone, hoping to get some feedback from them.

"You're rocking the boat, Debra. People in schools here aren't used to that," Joyce said. "It's threatening to them when you point out all the illegal and unethical stuff that's going on."

"Holy shit," said Denise. "Sounds like a disciplinary letter to me. You better make sure that doesn't go into your personnel file."

Both of them wondered what I was going to do.

That made three of us.

* * * * *

The meeting had taken place on Friday afternoon. I spent the entire weekend reading and re-reading the letter, and trying to sort through which points I thought were fairly stated, which I thought were twisted or out of context, and which I thought were out and outright wrong. On Sunday night, I sat down and wrote a response to Tony, addressing his points one by one. I cc'd it to the same people who had been recipients of the letter to me, and emailed it to each of them with the letter as an attachment.

It was just days before the Christmas break.

I hid the gifts I had made for both Tony and Ila, knowing it was no longer comfortable to give them.

* * * * *

"I want to back out of doing the in-service for your teachers." I was talking to Bob a few days after having received Tony's letter. "I just don't feel like I can do it, Bob. Tony wrote me a really strong letter of admonishment about overstepping my boundaries and expecting too much from the people I am working with. I mean, it was *really* strong. I just don't feel like I would have his administrative support if I went ahead and did this in-service."

I had developed a very workable model of how special services could more effectively be implemented in his school, and Bob was thrilled with it. It laid out, in easy to understand language and with clear graphics, a process and procedure that could eliminate a great many of the gaps and glitches now occurring in testing, placing, and developing programs for students.

"Was it a disciplinary letter?" Bob asked, concerned.

"I asked that. Tony said no, but it sure reads like one. I don't know, Bob, I just feel like I need to back way, way off. It sounds from the letter like everyone in every one of my schools is complaining about me and indicating that I'm aggressive and pushy."

"Well, I'm not complaining," Bob said. "I love what you're doing in this building. And none of *my* teachers has complained, Debra. The only feedback I have gotten is that they like you. They're happy to see someone in special ed. actually *doing* something."

"Maybe your classroom teachers like me, Bob, but I suspect that your special education teachers are not feeling particularly enamored with me these days." I was still reeling with shame and trying to reconcile Tony's written statements indicating that I had "*grabbed* a protocol out of the speech therapist's hand"; "*instructed* paraeducators to stay for an after-hours meeting"; and "conveyed to members of (Simon's and Evan's) teams that they were inexperienced in dealing with students manifesting such severe disabilities." Not one of these statements rang true to me, and I could very specifically refute each one of them—but that did not lessen my feelings of abasement.

"Well, think about it over the break," Bob said kindly. "I would still like to have you present the model to my teachers, but if you don't feel comfortable, I will accept that."

"Thanks." I appreciated that Bob was giving me leeway in making this decision. "By the way, I'm going to do Simon's testing over the break, if that's okay."

"Why are you doing that?" he asked. "You need a vacation. You should take the vacation to relax."

"Well, I will," I said. "But I canceled my plans to go anywhere—my brain is just too tired, and I really want to spend the time alone and quiet. So I'll be here. Simon is adamant about us not pulling him from any of his classes once he returns, and no one on the team has expressed any interest in doing an integrated assessment. It just seems like it'd be a whole lot less stressful for him if I take care of my part before he returns to school. His parents are good with it, and he's okay with it, too." I smiled, thinking of my earlier conversation with Simon about him coming in over the break, and added, "Well...Simon is really only *sort of* okay with it. But that's because he has a bit of an oppositional temperament right now. His parents agree it would be a lot less stressful to do this testing over the break."

"It's fine with me," Bob said. "But I still think you should just rest over the vacation. Do something fun."

"Trust me, Bob. I will do only two things over the next two weeks. I'll do Simon's testing and I'll sleep. I can pretty well give you a guarantee on that one."

I left Bob's office feeling relieved that there was at least one coworker I had not alienated.

As they say: *in due time.* Give things a chance and in due time, they, too, will come to be.

Jell-O Brains and the Question of Obesity
Late December 2004, January 2005

"This is stupid. *STOOOOO*-PID," Simon whispered as we were beginning our third day of testing.

"You know, Simon. You are probably right. But if you're going to assert yourself and tell me how stupid my tests are, you gotta use a louder voice than that. I mean, you are going to have to do more than whisper to get me to listen to you tell me my stuff is stupid!"

Simon looked at me.

"Hey, don't blame me. Your parents told me I have to encourage you to stop whispering if you are ever to get your voice back. I just figure if you're going to insult me, you should do it so I can hear you loud and clear!" I smiled sweetly at Simon.

Simon took a breath and, looking me straight in the eye, said in a strong and very audible voice: "STOOOOPID."

"*Ohhh,* that was very good, Simon! And you even looked at me when you shouted it." Making eye contact was another area that Simon's parents hoped we could work on, as since the accident, Simon not only slumped and sometimes allowed his jaw to go slack and drool to form, but he wasn't looking at people when speaking with them.

"Of course, we still have to *do* these stupid things," I continued, "but, hey, I thank you for insulting me so audibly. I didn't even know you could speak that loud, Simon!" I smiled and watched as he rolled his eyes and grimaced.

"You're weird," he whispered.

"Good thing you whispered that one, cowboy," I said, as I set up more testing materials. "My feelings might have been **reeealllly** hurt if I had heard that." I noticed Simon had a slight grin on his face, despite his attempts to ignore me.

Over the last month, I had developed quite a comfortable rapport with Simon and his family, and I was enjoying the uninterrupted, quiet time that testing over the Christmas break was affording us. While his injuries were extensive, Simon's recovery was nothing short of miraculous. He was walking, albeit with his left side dragging, and he was talking, albeit in a whisper. He did not have use of his left hand and arm, but his family was hopeful that time and physical therapy would provide what was needed for significant improvement to occur. What were the most difficult aspects of the injury for the family—and I anticipated what would be most difficult for his friends—were the changes in Simon's personality and demeanor.

By everyone's description, Simon had always been an easygoing, bright, funny, and well-mannered kid. A tall, lanky boy with sandy brown hair and a ready smile, Simon had displayed none of the teenage posturing so common to fourteen-year-old boys. He attended church with his family without complaint, and he participated in the Monday *Family Home Evening* activities that were a part of every devout Mormon family's schedule. He adored his two younger sisters, and they idolized him. Simon was every parent's dream child. He was the son who wrestled, played basketball, and worked on restoring old cars with his dad. He was nurturing and loving with his mother, and watched out for his sisters, including them in his life and always making sure they were safe.

No one was prepared for the effects of this head injury, which altered not only Simon's physical abilities, but also his personality. Gone was the easygoing, compliant child everyone knew. The Simon who returned from Children's Hospital in Salt Lake City was a much more impulsive, disorganized, stubborn, and socially challenged boy. A boy whose manners were no longer reflecting his strict upbringing, and one who did not perceive his own rude behaviors when they were displayed.

While Simon recognized some of the physical limitations of his post-injury self, other than short-term memory deficits and early morning fatigue, he did not see the changes in his personality. Initially, Simon didn't want anything to do with me, thinking that as a "psychologist" the only reason I would be involved is because I must think he's crazy. I certainly didn't think Simon was crazy, but I needed to be involved with him both for purposes of trying to help him manage the emotional ramifications of his injury, and to assist with the cognitive retraining that needed to start taking place. Ultimately, I was able to convince Simon that I was more brain coach than psychologist, and that just like Sherry and Steve would be helping him train and strengthen the left side of his body, it was my job to help him "train the brain."

It was a responsibility I took very seriously, and one that I knew was going to cost me many, many after-school hours as I studied the books I had ordered to help me learn everything I could about right hemisphere damage in the teenage brain.

* * * * *

"Whatcha doing?" Merrilyne asked as she watched me mix an ugly concoction of Jell-O with red, blue, and green food coloring.

"Making a brain," I said, with a triumphant smile.

"You're making a brain?"

"Yep. See? I ordered these brain Jell-O molds, and I'm making brains to use with Simon's friends. We're going to be having a brain party, but I wanted to practice everything first and make sure it would work."

Merrilyne looked at me, her curiosity aroused.

"Well, it's been my experience that kids with head injuries—especially kids with some of the challenges Simon is experiencing—really confuse their friends. I mean, in some ways they seem the same except for the obvious physical limitations, but then there are all these odd behaviors they display...and a lot of the time, what happens is that the friends start to disappear. Not all of a sudden and not all at once, but suddenly you've got this teenager who no one wants to hang out with." I was thinking of Joey in Alaska and how confusing and lonely things became for him after the novelty and drama of his injury had worn off for his friends.

"So, I thought maybe we should have an *Everything you've wanted to know about Simon's brain* party and, in a fun way, start teaching his peers about the injury. You know, so they'll understand more and...maybe not disappear quite so fast." I looked at Merrilyne as I poured this horrible-looking gunk into the mold. "The more involved they are in his healing process, the more I figure they'll stick around and support him. So, *this*," I said, pointing to my brain mold, "is my little prop for station number one: a Jell-O brain!"

"Sweet."

"Go look in my bedroom," I told her with a grin on my face.

As Merrilyne headed off to my bedroom, I started making a second mold—this one anatomically correct also but showing a different perspective of the brain. It was my intent to have the kids slice into these two brains as we identified the various lobes—and if they were so inclined, once we figured out what role the lobes played, they could eat them.

Merrilyne came back into the kitchen with a puzzled look on her face. "Ummmm, you have twelve pairs of white tennis shoes in there." Merrilyne had this way of saying *Um* that cracked me up. It had its own tune as she drew it out into three or four syllables, and the funny part was that she was never aware of saying it.

"Welll!" I said, grinning. "What I'm *planning*—If things work right—is that I'll divide the kids into small groups and send them around to stations. Each station will have a simulation that will help sensitize them to something that Simon is experiencing. Except the last station—that one will be run by me and will allow the kids an opportunity to ask questions or talk about their concerns regarding Simon."

"Will he be there?"

"He will," I said. "Although I've already worked it out so that he goes to all but the last station. That has to take place without him in order for the kids to feel comfortable talking about what's annoying or irritating them. Or just to ask questions."

"Are his parents coming?"

"Oh, most definitely! Not only coming, but I'm putting them to work. Each of them is willing to run a station, which is great because I think it gives the kids permission to *talk* about this injury. To acknowledge its reality and not just pretend that everything is the same."

"Wow, that's so cool," Merrilyne said. "What are the other stations? What are you doing with the shoes?"

"Well, the shoes are in a station where the kids pair off and interlock their inside arms, which will leave them one right hand and one left hand between them. The kid on the left is going to function like the left hemisphere of the brain, and since that is where most of the language centers are, that student will be able to talk. But the other kid on the right is *not* allowed to talk. Their mission will be to figure out how to tie the shoe using the one student's left hand and the other student's right, and only one of them is allowed to use words to communicate. Later, we'll process through how frustrating it was to accomplish what usually is a mindless task. I won't have to tell them how this all relates to Simon—they'll each have their own *A-ha!* experience over the course of the afternoon. At least I hope they will."

I smiled at Merrilyne, obviously tickled by my own creativity.

"If you grab that notebook over there, you can read what I'm setting up at the other stations."

By this time, I had moved on from making Jell-O brains to making pipe cleaner neurons, using beads for dendrites. I had found a fabulous website operated by Eric Chudler—a professor at the University of Washington—and he had dozens of recipes and models for teaching kids about the brain. I was so excited to discover this wealth of information and ideas, but with my own challenges, I knew I had better try out everything before using it with kids. I had already discovered that following the eleven steps of making a string neuron contained about nine more steps than I could handle.

"So, what are these?" Merrilyne asked, holding up a couple of Baggies stuffed with purple squishy-looking things.

"Oh, well, *those* are Gummy Brains! If I don't *eat* them all before the party, Simon and his pals will get to eat Gummy Brains of their own." I was well known for my peculiar affinity, not for chocolate like most normal people, but for anything that was sweet and gummy. Jelly beans, Swedish fish, Hot Tamales...and apparently, my newly discovered Gummy Brains.

Merrilyne looked at me.

"Help yourself," I said. "It's very good brain food."

The two of us chewed on a few brains for a while as I went about seeing if I could manage to string forty-five beads for each neuron.

* * * * *

Other than testing Simon, I did very little over the Christmas break except wallow in some sort of cave of despair and despondency. I vacillated wildly between feelings of anger and frustration, and those of insecurity and complete devastation. I would read and re-read Tony's letter and wonder how I could be so *off*, so *wrong* in my perceptions that teachers were happy with what I was doing in their buildings. By the time school started in January, I was reluctant to go into any of my buildings. I was convinced that I had grossly misperceived teachers' reactions to me, and that everyone I worked with thought I was aggressive, overpowering, and imposing.

"Val, can I talk to you in private?" I had run into the principal in the hallway at Mexican Hat Elementary.

"Sure," he said with a smile. With his white hair and kindly blue eyes, Val looked like he should be wearing one of those T-shirts that said, "Number One Grampa," or "My grandkids went to Florida and all they brought me back was this T-shirt!" He just had that *grampa* look about him.

One of the things I most respected about Val was that for all his good cheer and warmth, when it came down to holding kids accountable for their behaviors, he was clear and unhesitant. And most importantly—at least to me—he had been willing to listen to my fifteen-year-old speech about why we shouldn't suspend kids from school, but should come up with more effective consequences that taught rather than just punished. Despite thirty-some years as an educator, Val was enthusiastic as he learned about an entirely different approach to discipline. And, as the results spoke for themselves, his passion as both an educator and as my supporter was unmistakable.

Working with Val was a joy, and it had been nagging and uncomfortable for me to think I had perhaps misperceived how relaxed and comfortable our professional relationship was.

Walking into his office and sitting down, I looked at Val before hesitantly saying, "I need to ask you something, and I need you to be truthful with me, okay?"

"Sure," Val said, looking a bit surprised. He wasn't used to seeing me so subdued or serious.

"I would like you to give me some feedback about my work in your building. Like, if I've been too aggressive, or if you think the teachers think that the interventions we have developed are too intense."

Val looked at me. "What brought this on? My teachers have nothing but the highest respect for you—they love what you're doing. You must know that. I mean, everyone in this building thinks you're amazing. We wouldn't know what to do without you."

I could feel tears pooling behind my eyelids, and I knew I did not want to sit in this office and cry. On one hand, I was so relieved to hear Val affirm that the work I was doing was valued and within reason of what was "do-able" in a classroom. On the other hand, my emotions were raw after two weeks of second-guessing myself and my ability to continue being effective in this job.

"For real?" I asked Val. "I mean, you would tell me if I was too aggressive or overbearing or something?"

"You know I would," Val said, looking at me with concern on his face. "I would absolutely pull you in here and tell you to slow down or back off, or whatever, if I felt the need for that. I've never had any indication, Debra, that I had a need to do that. What's going on?"

I looked at Val, wondering if I should tell him more, if I should explain why I was asking. At the time, I decided it was best not to say too much, so I simply said, "I got a letter from Tony before the break. Apparently there have been a lot of complaints about me."

"Well, they didn't come from anyone in this building," Val said. "I'm happy to tell Tony or write him a letter attesting to that."

"Oh, jeez, no, Val! I mean, I really appreciate that...you have no idea how much I appreciate that. But I don't think it will help, and I think if Tony thinks I got you to champion my case, it would *seriously* tick him off. I really did just ask you this because I need to know if I am mis-performing in your building, and, if

I am, to ask for help in modifying my behavior." I looked at Val, horrified to think he might go back to Tony and advocate for me.

"Okay. But, I mean it, Debra. We need you in this building, and we love what you're doing. If I need to make that clear to Tony, I will."

"Thank you, Val. Thank you so much." I looked at this dear man who I had so come to admire and trust over the last two and a half years. "If I need you to go to Tony with your impressions, I'll tell you, okay?"

As I left his office, Val smiled at me, a worried look in his eyes.

* * * * *

"I don't get it," I said to Denise over the phone. "I mean, I've asked each one of my principals for honest feedback, and not one of them feels like their teachers think I am aggressive or that the interventions we've developed are too intense."

"Well, what do you make of it?" she asked. "I mean, why would Tony write that in a letter if it isn't true?"

"Well, I've thought a lot about that, Denise. I think it probably *is* true—but only from the standpoint of the special ed teachers. The general ed teachers and the principals have been really open and excited about what I'm doing; they just seem more willing to stretch out of their comfort zone and learn new techniques and strategies. At least of few of them do. But the speech and language people, and the special ed teachers... I just think they're resistant. *Really* resistant."

"Why? I mean, why are they so resistant?"

"I don't know, actually. Maybe because they don't feel like they have the skills to anchor the plans or to follow through on a daily basis so that consistency is ensured. Maybe they don't want to keep data on the plans. Who knows? Maybe it's just too intimidating to them, and they feel like they should already know all this stuff. Or maybe it's just because I get short-tempered and confrontational. I don't know..." I sighed, exhausted by the energy all of this was costing me.

"*Are* you short-tempered and confrontational?" Denise asked.

"I am. I know I am. I hear it in my voice. And in the letter of response that I wrote Tony, I owned that piece. But I don't think I'm *aggressive.* I mean, maybe it's semantics, but to me, there's a line you cross that takes you from being short-tempered or impatient to being aggressive. And I don't think I've crossed that line."

"Well, what does Tony say?"

"Here's the odd thing...he hasn't said anything! I mean, here it is the middle of January, and not one word has been mentioned about my letter or us getting together and talking more about it or anything. I've been in our regular weekly meetings with him, I've seen him in the schools—but not a word has been said. It's stressing me out in a big way."

"Did you ever find out if the letter went in your personnel file?" Denise asked, knowing as a teacher that such a letter could result in devastating consequences if I had to look for a different job.

"Just what Tony told me that day…that it wouldn't, and that it was just routine to cc it to the superintendent."

"I would check that out and make sure, Debra. I would make very sure that letter is not in your file."

We were quiet for a minute before I said, "Okay, enough about me. I'm tired of talking about me. How do *you* feel?"

"Pretty good," she said. "A little tired, but not bad." There was a split second before Denise added, "I think I'm going to have intestinal bypass surgery."

"What? What for? Why would you do that?"

"Because I read an article that said non-smoking fat people die sooner than thin smokers, and I want to maximize my chances of seeing my kids graduate from high school and go to college, get married…"

"Oh, Denise, you can't do that," I said, horrified. "They take your whole stomach out when they do that. It's *major* surgery. I know two women in Kenai who had it done, but they weighed at least four hundred pounds. I mean, how much do you weigh, for God's sake? Not enough to put yourself through a major surgery like that!"

"Well, I weigh enough to be considered obese, and that means I'm at least a hundred pounds overweight. And if I can increase my lifeline by doing this, I'm going to do it." Her voice held that tone of absoluteness I had heard so often throughout our years together. There would be no point in arguing with her if she had her mind made up.

"Well, send me some links so I can read about it," I said. "And while we're on the subject of your ample and loving frame, how is your back?" Denise had mentioned a week or two earlier that she had some pain in her lower back.

"It's there," she said. "It's not bad. It's just a little uncomfortable."

"Get it checked," I said. "I'm not kidding, Denise. Get it checked out."

I did not have a good feeling about that pain. And I definitely did not have a good feeling about the idea of her having an intestinal bypass.

As if taking out her intestines hadn't been enough. At this rate, she wouldn't have any organs *left* to become diseased.

Racks of Chips and Reams of Confrontations
January, February, March 2005

"*Sanders!* You're in big trouble now!" Tony said, with good humor and a face full of smiles. It was an early Saturday morning in late January, and I had just bumped into him and his infant son in the grocery store.

"Well, that seems to be where I reside lately," I said dryly. "What'd I do now?"

"You missed the UAA in-service yesterday!" He was grinning.

"Oh, shoot, Tony. I did! Oh, wow. I am so sorry!" I was eyeball deep in developing a plan for a boy in Mexican Hat. A sixth grader named Leroy had blown a gasket and smashed the window in front of the receptionist's desk while screaming that he was going to get a gun and kill everyone in the school. I hadn't even gone into my office yesterday morning. I made two early home visits in Blanding, and then went right to Mexican Hat to meet with the boy and his parents before sitting down with Val to develop a discipline plan to submit to the school board.

Any time there is a weapons violation—or any violation of the Safe Schools Act—a student is at risk for expulsion. Rarely did I support expulsion as a tenable response to most violations, but it takes a lot of thought and time to develop an alternative plan. It is no simple task to find consequences that hold a student appropriately accountable for his actions, ensures everyone's safety, and yet provides an opportunity for the student to learn and practice more appropriate and acceptable ways of managing their behavior.

Over the years, I have spearheaded the development of quite a few of these plans, and I was always pleased when they were approved by the school board involved. In many ways what I would propose would be much more difficult for a student and their family than an expulsion or suspension. Sometimes it's easier to just get kicked out of a place rather than be held fully accountable for restitution and learning better skills. But in the long run, I think everyone (including the kids) ended up respecting the value of these alternative plans.

Somewhere along the way I had heard, and adopted, the belief that punishment is something we do *to* a child that makes us (the adults involved) feel like a kid is appropriately paying his dues. Contrarily, a *consequence* is something we put into place when we want a kid to learn something from the experience—and it may or may not leave the adult feeling like the kid is suffering sufficiently. There's a lot of truth in that differentiation, although initially it is often a hard sell to more traditional administrators who tend to believe that suspensions and expulsions are the only viable options in cases involving severe behavioral infractions.

"Tony, I feel terrible. I mean, I never even went into the office to look at my calendar…I was just so preoccupied with the Leroy thing." I was glad to be involved in developing a proposed plan, but I really did feel badly that I had completely spaced out a Friday afternoon in-service.

"Don't worry about it. You weren't the only one. There were four or five people not there. It's not a big deal, and we can catch you up in about an hour."

"Well, that's good. But still, I really am sorry."

No mention had been made of the December letter since Tony's brief acknowledgement that he had received my response and would "review it very closely." In addressing Tony's statement that I had "implemented interventions and evaluations that were too intensive," I had provided a list of the principals, parents, and general education teachers who were involved with each intervention plan he cited in his letter. I requested that he get written feedback from each of these individuals since all plans were developed and implemented not only with the special education teacher but with these members as well. In my letter, I stated that I would take full responsibility and work with him toward improvement if, as equal members of the team, the others also expressed concern. I had become increasingly stressed as time passed with no word from either Tony or Ila regarding the status of the situation, and my angst and anxiety had risen exponentially as the days and weeks passed without any sort of resolution. This was my first encounter with Tony since December, outside of our weekly staff meetings.

Following our brief interaction, Tony and I each continued our shopping. I was standing by a tall rack of potato chips when Tony came up next to me and, grasping my hands inside of his, said very sweetly, "Sanders! Don't be saying that you are always in trouble. You're not! One time! Just one time!" Tony looked at me, a friendly and teasing expression on his face.

Disbelief swept over me, fed by the casualness with which Tony was referring to something that had been both personally and professionally devastating. On one hand, my heart was melting at the sincere and caring way in which Tony had just looked at me and taken my hands in his. At the same time, it infuriated me that he would blow this off as if it was inconsequential.

"Tony, you don't want to have this discussion with me here," I said, pulling away.

"One time, Sanders! Just one time!" Tony said, still in a teasing kind of mode, still feeling secure in the history of relaxed familiarity that had defined our relationship until recently.

"Tony, I am telling you, you do *not* want to have this conversation with me, standing in Clark's Market." An iceberg of fury was quickly overtaking any melting of my heart that I had been feeling.

"Oh, Debra!"

"Tony! Do you not *know* how devastating this whole thing has been for me? You hand me a letter that makes it sound like I'm unprofessional and disliked by everyone in all my buildings, and then I hear nothing from you. I asked you in my letter to contact the other team members and get feedback from them and..."

"And you expected me to get that done by now?" Tony said, interrupting me.

"Well, *I* got it done, Tony. How'd you expect me to work in my buildings thinking that I had totally misread everyone? I've met with every *one* of my principals, including Kit." Kit was the principal of Whitehorse High School.

Seeing Tony's look of surprise, I went on. "Tony, I had to. I came back from the break a *mess*...worried sick about performing adequately in my buildings. When I heard nothing from you, I finally realized the only way I was going to be able to function was to be very direct with the principals and ask them if they perceived me as aggressive, or if they felt my plans and reports had seemed overwhelming to them or anyone on their staff."

Tony was staring at me.

"You know what I found, Tony? I found that without exception, the response was surprise and shock. Each principal assured me that they were *more* than happy with what I was doing in their building, and that they had never heard a word of complaint about me or my behavior."

I knew I should stop myself, should calmly suggest we meet next week to talk about this, but the floodgates had been opened and the words kept pouring out.

"You know what *that* told me, Tony? It told me that ninety-nine percent of the people I work with on a daily basis are very happy with what I'm doing...but your letter made it sound like I'm some sort of nightmare. And you haven't even *mentioned* it since—"

"You told me you didn't want to talk about it," Tony interjected.

"Tony! When you handed me that letter and knocked me flat on my butt, I told you that I did not want to talk about it *then*. But, I followed that with a very detailed letter addressing each of your points, and I assured you that I would discuss them further. Then I hear nothing from you *or* Ila, not even a cordial, 'I know you were upset before the break, how are you feeling now?' *Nothing*, Tony. This is so not right. This whole thing is so not right that I have applications out to other districts." I took a quick breath before adding, "I have a meeting with the *superintendent* Monday morning, Tony, and I've called the Union for advice."

I had been on my way to school with Merrilyne when we decided to stop by the market. Our plan had been to work for several hours and then take the dogs hiking. Although Merrilyne had been standing next to me throughout these interactions in the store with Tony, at this point, she backed away, saying she would just "go out to the car and wait." Confrontations were not on Merrilyne's list of favorite Saturday morning activities. They aren't even on her list of favorite *any*time activities, and this was definitely becoming a confrontation.

"Tony," I continued, looking at him intensely, "I think the way you and Ila have handled this is inexcusable, and it makes me sad because I love living here, and I love my job, and I think I've done good things for teachers and families and kids. But I can't work for you if I don't trust you, and, Tony, this totally impacts my ability to trust you as an administrator. Not as a friend, I might add, but as an administrator."

Tony was looking at me with an expression I could not quite read.

"And just so you know…I did not ask for a meeting with the superintendent. I wrote him a letter requesting confirmation that your letter was not going into my personnel file and that it was not a letter of reprimand, and…"

"Well, I don't know if the letter goes into your file or not. Once the copy goes to the superintendent, it's up to him. I don't know what happens to it."

I stared at Tony, stunned. "Tony, you flat-out assured me that it was not a letter of reprimand and that it would not go in my file."

"Well, I don't know what Dr. Wright does with those copies. It's up to him what happens with them."

"Well, Tony," I said, my voice becoming quieter and more controlled, "it's your *job* to know what happens to it. As a director, if you're going to write a letter like that—and especially one that contains unsubstantiated accusations and misinformation—it sure as heck is your responsibility to know what is to become of it."

"Debra, I spent a lot of time laboring over that letter…"

"Tony, I don't doubt that it was a difficult letter for you to write, but I'm sorry you put so much time into something that I think misquoted me and that I feel was accusatory in tone. Tony, I felt *humiliated* by that letter."

"Well, Debra, I just don't know if we can work together," Tony said, all the fun and friendliness gone from his face and his voice.

"Wait a minute, Tony…you began this conversation assuring me I had *only been in trouble once* and trying to make me feel better, and now you're saying you don't know if we can *work* together? That hardly makes sense."

Tony and I looked at each other, his son fortunately oblivious to the tension that had to be obvious to anyone passing by.

"Well, I hope your meeting with the superintendent goes well Monday morning," Tony said, as he literally—and figuratively—began to move away.

I imagine that I just stood there, half dazed and half crazed by how stupidly I felt Tony was handling this whole thing. I mean, from the beginning, why hadn't he just called me in and *asked* me if the things he listed in the letter were true? Given the incredible amount of time I had invested in doing the *right* thing for kids, why on earth wouldn't he have at least given me the courtesy of asking if certain things were true before writing them in a letter of reprimand as if they were facts?

I just did not understand this whole situation. And, I'm sure, neither did Tony.

Whatever occurred the following Monday morning with the superintendent, it must not have done much to diffuse the situation. As I recall, he listened politely, but was noncommittal. Mostly he just encouraged me to work with Tony and see if we couldn't smooth things out.

I do not have notes from that Monday morning meeting, but I suspect I was a little frustrated by the bland reception. I wanted Dr. Wright to listen to me—

to ask questions about why I had so many concerns and what my suggestions were for improving services. To his credit, Dr. Wright *did* do this the day before I left Blanding, and at that time, he expressed genuine regret for not "hearing me" earlier. But on that Monday morning in March, Dr. Wright was still looking at me as someone who was out there making trouble.

If I tried to smooth things out in my relationship with Tony, I certainly did not do so successfully.

* * * * *

"Oh, boy, Denise...this is just getting worse and worse," I said during one of our ever-increasing phone calls.

"Why? What happened now?" she asked, and I could hear a note of concern edge her voice.

"Oh, my God...I slammed out of Tony's office today. I mean, I *slammed* the door—so hard it's surprising all the glass didn't shatter."

I had been in Tony's office, hoping to talk about the tension that was growing between us. In hopes of helping Tony understand my perspective, I had given him one of my personal journal entries to read. It was a very lengthy journal entry—one mostly reflecting on Carl's approach to education in remote places, and on what I had learned from working for him, and from working in Alaska for so long. I sat on the journal for two weeks before giving it to Tony, deciding in the end that maybe it would help him understand why I was so frustrated. He sat on it a week before calling me into his office.

"I will tell you right now that I am no Carl Knudsen and neither is Dr. Wright," Tony said as soon as I sat down. His voice was rife with defensiveness and more anger than I had ever observed in him. Tony was not quick to display any sort of temper, and while I had seen him display feelings of irritation or frustration—even anxiety and sadness—I had never seen him angry.

"Tony, that's not what I meant. I didn't give that to you because I want you to be a Carl or a Jim Foster. I just wanted you to see what can be *done* in remote places...how *innovative* programs can be. How *easy* it would be to recruit passionate, experienced educators if we were offering the kind of programs that tapped into their excitement about education." I looked at Tony, recognizing instantly how very wrong I had been in giving him a copy of this personal journal reflection.

The meeting went downhill from there, culminating with my extraordinary exit from his office.

"Well, what happened then?" Denise asked. "I mean, how did it end?"

"With me shouting that he would have my resignation on his desk in the morning," I said, still stunned by both my own impulsiveness and the explosion of anger I had displayed.

"Are you going to do it? Resign, I mean?"

"Well, considering that it happened to be a day when all the principals were in for a meeting, and half a dozen of them were milling around Tony's office when I stormed out, I would say, yeah, I'm turning in my resignation."

"Oh, Debra."

"I know," I said, sighing deeply. "I know."

At the time, I don't think I recognized what had become a pattern of unusual emotional volatility when confronted with situations that left me feeling overwhelmed and frustrated. But I certainly recognized the consequence of this incident.

Denise and I were quiet for a minute before I asked, "How's your back? What's happening with that?"

"The doctor says it's arthritis."

"*What?* Arthritis! Denise, that doesn't make sense to me. Did they do an MRI or CT scan?"

"No, he said there isn't any need to. He knows what it is." Denise had told me earlier that there was so much pain when she moved, she was teaching sitting down. Denise not only never *acknowledges* pain, but it's my guess that in all her years of teaching, she could count the number of times she taught from a static, seated position. It was when she told me this that I knew something very bad was happening in her body. That and the fact that she said she was sleeping downstairs in the recliner because it hurt too much to stretch out on the bed.

"Well, it will get better," she assured me. "I just need to go easy on it...not overexert. It's okay."

I doubted very much that it was okay, but I knew better than to push too hard. I could only hope she would either go to another doctor or insist upon an MRI.

She did neither.

* * * * *

It was a Saturday, and as had become routine, I was spending the whole day in the office. On this particular day, I was trying to rewrite the ninth grade earth science textbook using a larger font and fewer words. Heather had been struggling in her science class, and although she was a good reader, like many students with learning disabilities, she often found herself overwhelmed by too much text. The result was that her comprehension really suffered, and frequently, she shut down in the face of frustration and simply gave up trying to complete the task. Modifying textbooks was not a realistic long-term option, but I thought if we could use the modified text to teach Heather more efficient strategies for reading any textbook, then in the long run it would have been worth this initial time investment.

Once starting on this project, it became clear pretty quickly that it was a far more ambitious task than I could accomplish by myself in a day's time. I called Peggy and begged for her assistance. It wasn't in my nature to ask teachers, much less parents, to help me with creating lessons or modifying texts, and I was feeling rather proud of myself for actually asking for help.

I had completed Heather's testing in October, and indeed the results had validated my hypotheses about her learning disabilities. Unfortunately, she still did not have a written IEP on file, and no program had been developed to address her needs in the academic setting. There is a legal timeline specifying how long the school has from the date a parent signs permission for the child to be tested to when the team must have all the paperwork completed and on file; and we were months beyond that timeline. There had been a meeting in January, but Peggy had found the IEP document unacceptable, and to her credit she would not sign it.

It is unusual for a parent to stand up to a team of teachers and refuse to sign agreement with the IEP, and although I was surprised by Peggy's advocacy for her daughter, I was pleased by it. Although I had not mentioned it to her, I happened to agree with Peggy's decision that the IEP was not acceptable, and I respected the fact that she had not allowed herself to be intimidated by either the special education process or the special education team. Over the years, I had observed far too many meetings where even the most confident and outspoken of parents found themselves reduced to silent dissention.

After the meeting, Peggy worried that she had been too outspoken, and although I did not indicate at the time how much I agreed with her, I strongly affirmed that she was well within her rights to have asked for a revised document. Since that time, we had exchanged frequent email communication regarding Heather. The more I worked with Heather directly, the clearer I had become on her learning style and the kinds of strategies that would be most effective for a teacher to utilize in the classroom; the more communication I got from Peggy, the better the therapy progressed.

While Peggy and I worked on rephrasing, typing, and copying pages of the science textbook, we talked about Cassie Moon—Heather's language arts teacher. Cassie and I had recently attended a workshop in Salt Lake City on differentiating instruction, and we were both excited to collaborate and put the strategies in place that would work for Heather. I was excited by this teacher's willingness to stretch well beyond her comfort zone. I explained to Peggy that differentiating instruction meant that Cassie would be using the same coursework with all the students (in this case, a unit on Romeo and Juliet), but by being very clear on what she wanted the students to *know*, to *do,* and to *understand*, she would be able to create choices in the ways students could *demonstrate* their proficiencies. As I talked with Peggy about how this concept worked, I found myself coming up with innumerable ideas that Cassie and I could integrate into the unit that would maintain a high level of expectation and accountability for Heather (and all the students), and yet tap into each student's specific learning style and strengths.

By the end of the day, Peggy and I had assembled four extra-large three-ring binders with all the important information from the science text and none of the fluff (not to mention that she got an abbreviated Education 500 class in differentiating instruction!). It wasn't until 6:00, when Sandra popped in to pick something up from her classroom and came into my office to say hello, that the issue of my having asked Peggy to come to school became problematic.

It became problematic because in the coming week, somehow the rumor would circulate that I had Peggy in my office on Saturday, copying Heather's file.

But when I left school that night, despite feeling a cold coming on, I was feeling mighty pleased with the day's work. It was definitely a good day's work. And it had been fun.

* * * * *

Over the next ten days, the cold I felt beginning that Saturday night would develop into a full-blown case of pneumonia, forcing me to stay home from school for three days. When I returned, the rumor was not only that I had copied Heather's file, but that I had copied *several* files and taken them to the state special education office in Salt Lake City. I was not to learn about this until a week later, and by that time, Heather's IEP meeting had taken place.

By agreement I had not attended Heather's IEP meeting, both because I would be leaving the district and was therefore not involved, and also because there was so much tension between me and Tony and Ila (both of whom would be at the meeting) that it was in everyone's best interest if I stayed away. I would regret this decision later, because I still do not know exactly what transpired in that meeting; however, when it was over, Bob was no longer my ally.

* * * * *

"What?" I said, incredulous at what I was hearing. "You have got to be kidding me." I was talking to my friend—one of the special education teachers in Blanding. It was 7:00 at night, and seeing my car in the parking lot, she had come by my office to talk to me. I was hearing for the first time what the rumors were, and why Bob, and others, were so angry with me.

The absurdity of it all, the outrageousness of the accusations, began to suffocate me as I drove home to feed the dogs.

* * * * *

"I kid you not," I said to Denise, not fifteen minutes after getting home. "She told me that Bob and Tony both think that I have been encouraging parents to litigate. I have never encouraged a parent to sue a district in my life!" I said, my anger escalating. "I have worked my *ass* off in this district to *keep* parents from litigating." I could not believe that anyone thought I would encourage parents to sue a district. My whole approach centered on empowering parents with the knowledge and confidence they needed to *advocate* for their children, not to go to court.

"What else did she say?" Denise asked.

"Oh, you won't believe it. Let's see... Oh, get this...apparently there is to be a special ed Audit, and everyone thinks when I was home sick that I was actually in Salt Lake City turning over copies of files to the auditors. Jesus, Denise, I have been as up front with this whole thing as is possible. I have never said one word to anyone that I have not first said to Tony. Not one."

Denise muttered something comforting, I am sure, before I barreled on, saying, "You know what else? And this *really* pisses me off...apparently Peggy presented a written document of all the accommodations she wanted to see on the IEP, and they thought *I* had written it. Can you believe that? I mean, I definitely sat down with her and helped her articulate what she hoped to see on the IEP, and I *did* suggest she write down her thoughts so other people could have a written copy of her input, but I did not write this list or letter or whatever it was. I haven't even seen it."

"What, they don't think a parent is intelligent enough to write a letter on their own?" Denise asked.

"Apparently not," I snorted. "Which is what I've been saying all along...that the whole campaign to involve parents is just lip service, and people really don't want it. But what really ticks me off is their assumption that I would draft such a document. I mean, I told Peggy that writing them down did not mean they would all be accepted and put into place, but that it would help everyone if they could see what she was requesting. I did not write anything for her. And I sure didn't put the words in her mouth that apparently came out in this document."

"Do you think that..." Denise started to ask, but I interrupted her as another complaint flashed through my mind. "Oh, oh, oh, Denise...you *gotta* hear this part. Sorry to interrupt, but this is unbelievable." I could feel my anger escalate as I spoke.

"Merri Shumway, she's the president of the school board, had come to my office a few days ago. I was really surprised—I had never met her before. Anyway, she came to ask me why I submitted my resignation and if I was willing to discuss it with her. Apparently, a bunch of teachers and parents and principals have written letters expressing distress that I've turned in my resignation. Anyway, I was just leaving the office for a meeting, so I only spoke with her briefly. But the rumor is that I spent the DAY with her and gave *her* files to look at!"

"Holy shit, Debra. How do these rumors get started?"

"Who knows. I can make some guesses, but I don't know for sure. All I know is that Sandra saw Merri leave my office."

"So, are you going to talk to her—the president of the school board?" Denise asked, clearly astounded by the magnitude of what was occurring.

"Yeah, I set up an appointment to talk with her next Monday, but before I do, I'm going to write out everything so that I am clear and, hopefully, not too emotional." I was silent for a minute before adding, "Gosh, Denise, I just cannot believe what this is turning into."

"Well, it's big all right." Denise was quiet before asking, "People have really written letters?"

"Apparently," I said. "Oh, and I was also told that Doug Wright—the superintendent—thinks I went out and stirred up a *Debra Sanders fan club*...as in, I solicited these letters."

"Well, they wouldn't want to think someone could actually have a major *impact* in education. Speaking of impact, how's the job search going?"

"Oh, I don't know, Denise; I'm so torn. I feel like my guts are being ripped to shreds lately. Last night there were two mothers sitting in my office, crying. *Crying,* Denise. They said that if I left, nothing would ever change, that the system would have won, and that my voice is *needed* here. Then I saw Simon's parents this morning and heard more or less the same thing from them—as well as from teachers and the principal at Mexican Hat. Part of me wants to stay and take this on. I like these people so much, Denise. I *care* about them so much. But the other part of me ...I don't know, Denise...my brain is just fried, and it seems like everything in my entire life is total chaos."

"Would they let you retract your resignation?"

"I doubt that!" I said. "Actually, Bob and Val and I had been working on a proposal for a grant that would pay me to work as a coach in their schools. I mean, to train and coach teachers in utilizing differentiated instruction and strategies for teaching challenging students, not to coach-coach. But I don't even know about *that* now...since apparently Bob is no longer happy with me."

"Well, you sure do know how to stir the pot," Denise said. "You go, girl," she added, sympathetically. "You just stand your ground and go!"

I had been so upset that night that I forgot to ask Denise about her pain level. When I called her back, I found out that it, too, had escalated.

Everything was intensifying. Everything, it seemed, just kept getting bigger and bigger and bigger.

More Letters Than in the English Alphabet

April, May, early June 2005

"Listen, you guys...everyone, I mean, *everyone* is replaceable."

Peggy and another parent were sitting in my office one evening in late April.

"Who knows," I continued, "maybe there's someone out there just waiting to see the ad for this job; someone who can come in and take this cauldron of bubbling muck that I seem to have stirred up, and help this district move forward."

Both of these women had seen my car in the parking lot and, independently of one another, had come in to talk with me about reconsidering my resignation.

I looked at these two mothers, both of whom had become so dear to me; both of whom sat there with tears ready to flood a room already submerged in emotion. There was not a fiber in me that did not ache from the last several weeks of escalating tensions. It was boggling to me how one person—*me!*—with the honest intention of trying to increase the level of ethical and effective services for kids, could have seemingly polarized nearly an entire community. I was at a loss for explaining how the current situation had evolved, and my own emotions felt like a room filled with Ping-Pong balls that dropped every few seconds from an upper level balcony, with anger jigging around sadness, and confusion bashing into overwhelm. And with each bounce and hit, I could feel my brain taking one more step toward a major crash. Each guess and each second guess exhausted my brain, pushing me faster and further into that place where I knew my brain would simply shut me down.

On one hand, I would chastise myself for being weak, for not being able to stand up to the stress that comes with the territory of taking an unpopular stand; for being a coward who was slithering away instead of holding strong to what I believed to be right. And I would ruthlessly lecture myself about how badly I was screwing up—how I had managed to take my passionate advocacy and belief in the ability of systems to change and make a mess not only of my professional relationships, but of my friendships as well.

And then, just as I would be about to call *Uncle*, someone I respected would tell me that I was doing the right thing; that I was fighting for the rights and resources that were supposed to be a part of every child's education. So, I'd press forward and remind myself that even Erin Brockovich and Karen Silkwood must've had self-doubts and bad days.

Of course, in the back of my mind, I'd also remind myself that Karen Silkwood had been run off a road and most likely killed for the position she took against the lack of safety at the plutonium plant in Oklahoma. I'd think about Karen Silkwood every time I needed to remind myself not to romanticize unpopular position-taking. The truth is, Julia Roberts and Meryl Streep could make anything seem doable, and I—unfortunately—was not cast in their molds.

The reality for me was that quite often, this simply did not *feel* very doable.

Yet each time somebody—whether it was Joyce, Denise, a parent, a teacher, or a principal—encouraged me not to give up, it infused me with a little more energy and confidence. Each time someone I respected assured me that what I was doing was a good thing, or that my brain really was still functioning and I was indeed thinking clearly, I pushed forward. Never mind that cotton batting was being harvested in my head, while sticky notes and random scraps of paper containing miscellaneous ramblings and crumbs of conversations were threatening to overtake my life.

Prior to meeting with Merri Shumway regarding my decision to resign, I composed a ten-page letter that outlined my concerns regarding the way special education services were being carried out in my schools. I backed up each statement with the facts and examples that had led me to my current position. It was a hefty and potentially explosive document in response to the question of why I had chosen to resign. The number and specificity of examples of students whose programs and rights had been violated at worst, and unethically carried out at best, was staggering.

As was my documentation of the paper trail attesting to my repeated (although unsuccessful) efforts to work through the system's pecking order in hopes of resolving the concerns.

In my letter to Mrs. Shumway, I acknowledged my belief that, because Tony and I did not seem to share a vision for the district's special education program, I understood that I was the one who needed to move on. I understood that my responsibility as an employee was to carry out the vision of the director by "working the front lines," not by imposing my view of how services should be delivered. This acknowledgement, however, probably did little to soften the blow that every school board member surely must have felt, realizing that not only was the district at risk for liability in every example cited—but each one of them was at risk for being held personally responsible should a family ever decide to pursue litigation.

What I probably did not make clear, in writing or in direct conversation, was that I had no intention of encouraging parents to sue the district; in my mind, litigation was never a viable option for working on this problem. My intent was to make administrators and board members aware that what we were doing was *wrong*; it was illegal in some cases, unethical in others, and simply the use of outdated or mediocre practices in others. In my mind, we should all be sitting at a round table, taking a hard look at the system and developing a five-year plan for doing it better. And when that didn't seem to be happening, it was my intent to empower a group of intelligent and concerned parents and teachers with the confidence and information they needed to advocate for the children in a way that would be heard. Not by suing the district, but by using the law and their knowledge of the field as constant reminders that the changes they were asking for were not only reasonable, but entitlements granted by law for three decades.

I wanted the parents to speak up. I wanted the teachers to speak up. I wanted to empower them all by walking them over to a window they had never looked through and letting them see the possibilities that existed.

I did not want anyone to bring a lawsuit against the district.

Hindsight suggests that I was too blinded by my outrage and lack of awareness of my new, in-your-face-personality—and the people in charge were too blinded by their defensiveness and fear of litigation—for us ever to come together around a table.

Square, round, or rectangular.

* * * * *

Following my encounter with the two mothers that evening, a new flurry of rumors and accusations surfaced, which incited more letter writing on my part in order to clarify what was truth and what was not. At the same time, several parents and teachers had taken it upon themselves to write their own letters. Their topics ranged from feeling disheartened that the district would let me leave to requests to participate on any committee that was interviewing for a new psychologist.

One night in April, at 11:45 p.m., I emailed a letter to Peggy. In part it read:

> …Do you remember when I encouraged you and other parents not to focus on me, but to keep your eye on the kids…that sometimes when people hear someone's name too much, too often, and with too much praise, the natural human response is to either dismiss the person talking as not being objective, or to simply get oppositional and shut down in the face of the "saint"?
>
> Well, methinks maybe you are all too passionate about me and my leaving. Not that I do not totally appreciate what you are doing and how hard you are trying to get in a position where you can right some of the wrongs which have been done to your and others' kids…because I DO appreciate that. More than I can ever express. But this is what I fear:
>
> You (all) have incredible potential to start a grass roots movement that will truly benefit the kids in this town. I mean, a real, genuine, make-a-true-difference in the way services are delivered movement. I don't want you all to diminish your credibility in the eyes of administration because you are perceived as my champions… You all want—and need—to stay in a position of influence where you are respected as the intelligent and informed parents that you are. To do this, you might need to distance yourselves from me in terms of any conversations you have with the board, Tony, Dr. Wright, or Ila. I think

they all need to perceive you as parents who know the law and expect to be treated as intelligent, thinking parents who know their kids; and **NOT** as someone who likes me so much that you can't see past the disappointment of my leaving. Because you know why? If by chance they hire someone who does <u>not</u> do a good job, the more you are affiliated with me, the less the people in charge will listen to you if your kids' needs aren't being met. They will simply write you off, dismissing it as a: "Well, no one would please them after Debra."

I think you need to turn your campaign around and focus not on being **passionate**, but on being **dis**passionate. Does that make sense? Be more neutral about my leaving. No one is ever going to beg me to stay, and most likely, no one besides Mrs. Shumway will ever even ask me why I am leaving. I know this makes you crazy...it's making a lot of people feel a little nuts...that the district would just let me walk away. But they have, and I will, and it will be okay.

It will be okay as long as you can keep your fire where it needs to be—and that's in really looking at how things are done here, and on helping them do it better.

Maybe there will be someone out there (educational psychologist) who will be better than me to help you take everything where it needs to go. Sometimes a person can be good for moving something from one place to another, but the same person is not the best one to take it to the next level.

I love you all for your own passions and for making me feel so loved and valued throughout all of this. You have no idea how much you have helped me survive what might otherwise have been a devastating experience that could have permanently driven me out of the field.

Save your passions and energy to support a new person when they get here. They will need you. And you will need the district to listen to what you have to say.

That letter was written around the same time that I inadvertently discovered Tony was not planning on advertising for a licensed and nationally certified school psychologist. Apparently, he had already begun the process of interviewing a school counselor he thought he could put through a school psychology program while she worked on the job. For all the dispassion I encouraged Peggy to display, I most definitely did not take my own advice. I wrote a letter to the school board outlining my objections to any plan that did not involve hiring a licensed and certified educational psychologist. Included in the letter were the following paragraphs:

...There is a difference in the demands of a school psychologist and that of a school counselor. I have been both; and while I am quite certain that most certified school psychologists have had the training required to function as school counselors, counselors are not generally given the training to function as educational psychologists. Let me ask you this: **are your certified counselors ready to assume responsibility for carrying out the following activities?**

- Setting up research-based interventions and monitoring/evaluating the results, such that a student's response to intervention (RTI) can then be considered in the context of a total evaluation to assist in making eligibility and programming decisions;

- Helping parents and teachers understand the complexities of _specific learning disabilities_ and assist in the _diversifying of lesson plans such that a student has reasonable access to instruction_ in a curriculum that might be anywhere from two to eight years above their current academic functioning level;

- Administering psychoeducational assessments that can reliably and validly separate out the issues of limited _English proficiency and cultural differences_ from the issues of _learning disabilities, cognitive impairment, and other disabling conditions_ so that valid eligibility and programming decisions are made;

- Assisting teachers and administrators with the academic and emotional issues that come with serving students who are struggling with _traumatic brain injuries, severe mental health issues, emotional disturbance, intellectual impairments,_ and/or syndromes such as _fetal alcohol, fragile X,_ and/or _visual_ and _auditory processing disorders_?

- Participating as an active member of, and often in a leadership role in, such meetings as the _manifestation determination meeting_?

...I have said this to Mr. Done and I have said this to Dr. Wright: **this district is currently violating federal laws surrounding children being served under I.D.E.A. And (I) have worked to troubleshoot situations in order to prevent this district from being involved in litigation.**

...In my role in this district, I have spent countless hours helping teachers differentiate instruction so they can more effectively teach kids with special needs; and I have spent hours upon hours, week after week working with children who have been raped, brutalized, burned, and/or victimized to such an extent that they now present themselves as possible violent offenders within your doors.

Does this district need counselors to assist with the intervention and treatment of children at risk for learning and behavioral issues? Absolutely.

Can any counselor, no matter how bright and dedicated, be placed in the position of functioning as a school psychologist and expected to succeed in an on-the-job situation? It is doubtful. That is why accredited school psychology programs require two years of coursework and practicum experience beyond the master's degree before _ever_ placing someone in the position of educational psychologist—and then, doing so only under intense supervision for one year...

...I repeat what I have been saying for months: **the children of San Juan County are not being effectively served through the special education program, and this district is at risk of being sued because of it.** _**Qualified and experienced psychologists**_ offer you significant protections against the risk of misdiagnosis and/or inappropriate placement and/or services...and of violations of the rights of children and parents under the Individuals with Disabilities Education Act (I.D.E.A.).

What is the harm in mounting an aggressive recruiting and advertising campaign to bring experienced and qualified educational psychologists to this district? Surely, the children and teachers of the San Juan School District are deserving of your hiring the best and the brightest out there.

And they **_are_** out there.

The good news I suppose is that the scheduled interview with the local school counselor was canceled, and Tony was required to place an ad with the National Association of School Psychologist's career center.

The bad news is that this did nothing to endear me to Tony or Ila, and our already strained and deteriorating relationships were not even close to being able to withstand another bout in the ring.

* * * * *

As April moved into May, the emails and letters continued to fly, and my outrage and anger were fueled with each one directed toward me. Although I do not, and did not, agree with much of what was said in some of these letters, distance and hindsight have helped me see that several valid attempts were made to help me see that I was *not the me* I used to be. That my short-temperedness, my irritability, my unwillingness to let any error go unattended were not of help to anyone, least of all the children. And that my quickness to anger when I felt stymied or frustrated only compounded an already volatile and stressed situation. Both Bob and Sandra sent me email letters to this effect, and while I can read them now and hear the concern and the caring behind their words, at the time they only inspired anger in me. Sandra pointed out the similar challenges that both Simon and I shared, the similar difficulty we both displayed with backing away and changing approaches, but I was not ready to listen to or see that yet. I could only hear her saying that my head injury was a factor in the situation, and all I could imagine doing at that point was slamming a door as literal and figurative as the door I had slammed in Tony's office in March, and shutting out the cacophony.

Denise's pain levels were rising; she was insisting on going through with the intestinal bypass surgery, and there was a school psychologist job opening eight miles from their home.

I flew to Colorado for an interview.

Urdu Weddings and Warped Floors

Late May, early June 2005

Not everything was stress and volatility. While I had been battling my inner demons and attempting to slay all the wrongs in the school district, Sharon and Dan had been moving from that first awkward date to the wedding ceremony that was about to take place on the mountain overlooking Bluff. It was a quintessential Utah springtime-almost-summer day: the sky was a deep cerulean blue; the sun was hot and dry; and the birds were preceding the music of the ceremony with their own special brand of song.

Somehow, through all that had transpired, Sharon managed in that unique way she possesses to maintain a steady friendship with both Tony and me. I never asked her what he might have said, and she never offered to tell me. On the few occasions I asked for her input or insight, Sharon was somehow able to convey a response that neither supported nor denied my viewpoint; and I assume she was somehow able to do the same with Tony. At one time, we had all been friends. At this point, we were both still good friends with Sharon. So, now for the first time in weeks, Tony and I would be standing within proximity of each other. While it certainly crossed my mind that I should miss the wedding and avoid the inevitable encounter, the joy over Sharon and Dan's wedding was one of the few things that clamored more loudly than the anxiety, confusion, and angst that ran through me.

The wedding was magnificent in its simplicity, allowing the beauty of the surroundings and the freshness of the air to set the scene for the entrance of the bride and groom. Sharon—having forgone her traditional peasant-like skirts and baggy tops—was resplendent in a gorgeous, fitted gown that probably surprised everyone but Dan at just how petite and lovely a figure she has. With her long, wavy hair and unmade-up face, on that day Sharon could have graced the cover of any bridal magazine and represented wholesome beauty the world over. Certainly, both she and Dan radiated the kind of joy that makes all those around them tear up while participating in their sacred commitment of forever.

Watching Tony that afternoon left me with such conflicted feelings. He looked so *Tony*, walking around with his young son, drinking a beer, laughing with people. I wanted to throw my arms around him and make the words and the angst of the last eight months disappear. I wanted to hear him call me *Sanders*, and know that we would work together to provide incredible services to the kids we both cared so much about.

But, I also knew that the time for this to happen had long slipped by, and as Bob had said to me in his letter, it did seem that I had "burned quite a few bridges." So, while Tony and I did say hello to one another, we did not speak; we did not clink beers; and we did not share our joy over Sharon's happiness.

It would be the last time I would see Tony before leaving Blanding.

* * * * *

My last weeks at school were spent making sure my files were up to date, and that I had written a useful summary for each student I was involved with. Just as when I left Alaska, I wanted a new person to be able to walk in and quickly gain knowledge about what interventions had been implemented, how successful they had or had not been, and what treatment methods had been utilized to help a student move from Point A to wherever they were currently standing.

Writing those summaries and saying good-bye to all my students took up the better part of my last two weeks in Blanding.

The most difficult student to leave was Evan. Partially this was because my relationship with him was so intense and focused; partially because I knew that while he had moved well beyond Point A, he was nowhere near where he needed to be; and partially because this very tough and still potentially violent boy had shown me his most tender and vulnerable sides. Somehow, saying good-bye to Evan left me feeling as if I had failed. Failed him; failed the system; and failed myself. There was so much left unfinished, and I did not believe that Evan would choose to return to school in the fall and give someone new the chance to work with him. Nor did I believe anyone from school was going to take on the task of encouraging him to attend. Evan had turned eighteen. He no longer had to be there.

In our last session, Evan had asked a provocative question. With no urging and for no apparent reason, he looked at me and said, "If today is after yesterday, and if tomorrow is beyond us, then what is yesterday?" I thought about that for a minute; thought about all the choices this boy had made over the last eighteen months: his choice not to harm anyone; his choice not to end his life; his choice to be kind to Briana; his choice to work so hard on facing his own demons. And without really knowing how I was going to answer, I said, "Well, Evan. I guess yesterday would be that moment in time when you decided to conquer, survive, and embrace life, instead of destroy it."

I had thought about this a lot over the last few days, and as a good-bye gift to Evan, I made a computerized version and framed it.

It really was quite lovely.

* * * * *

After dropping the gift off at Evan's house and saying good-bye to both him and his grandparents, I headed home to continue packing. Fatigue and headaches had dominated the last few weeks, and nothing stood out clearly in my mind. I knew only that I had somehow managed to interview for a job in Colorado Springs, accept it when it was offered, and spend a very brief afternoon with Denise the day before she underwent the surgery that would remove most of her stomach.

The phone was ringing when I entered my house, and stepping around boxes and more boxes, some packed, some half packed, and some empty, I picked it up in time to hear a click. I had missed whoever was calling.

Hanging up the phone in frustration, I looked at the chaos surrounding me and suddenly realized something was very wrong in my living room. It took a moment for the reality to register, and when it did, a gasp barely escaped my lips before a feeling of utter despair took over.

My living room floor had buckled under the pressure of all my boxes. The very foundation of this house I had been living in was collapsing.

All I could do was sit down on the sagging floor and cry. No matter how many pennies the tears would cost, it was quite simply the only thing left for me to do.

* * * * *

The call I had missed was from the Lindseys, telling me that Denise was in the hospital. I hurriedly tossed the rest of my belongings into boxes, gave away as much as I could, sold what little could be sold, and without ever saying good-bye or making amends with the people who had embraced me and cared for me during all those months when not a clear thought passed through my brain, I left for Colorado.

I wish I could say that I was able to leave Blanding behind.

Blanding's ghosts, as well as the very real phantoms that still plagued my brain, went all the way to Colorado Springs with me. The truth is I would have traveled the circumference of the world if it meant I could have left them behind. But the reality was, there was no way to outrun them.

No matter how far or how fast I traveled, they followed.

PART IV

The Gordian Knot

It would be so nice if something made sense for a change.

Alice

Gordian Knot:

Part of Speech: Noun

Definition:
- An intricate knot tied by King Gordius of Phrygia
- An exceedingly complicated problem or deadlock
- Any very difficult problem; insoluble in its own terms

To cut the Gordian knot signifies taking drastic action to solve a difficulty.

Good to Great by 2008
Fall 2005, Colorado Springs, Colorado

The summer passed in a blur of rapid changes and too many crises. By the time I arrived in Colorado Springs and jammed the contents of two U-Haul trucks into a storage unit, Denise had been in the hospital for several days. As it turned out, one week after her intestinal bypass surgery, Denise's right leg was three times its normal size. The doctors, at last doing a CT scan, discovered not arthritis but a tumor—a fifteen-centimeter tumor to be exact. One that wrapped with octopus-like tentacles around both her femoral artery and her bladder.

An aggressive protocol of chemotherapy and radiation was to begin immediately, despite the reality that with her newly-sized stomach, Denise would be able to consume only four tablespoons of food a day and two ounces of water at any given time.

"Oh, she'll be fine," her doctors assured me when I expressed significant concerns regarding how she would receive enough nutrition to withstand such a treatment protocol. "She'll be getting vitamin supplements."

Merrilyne, who by this time had moved to Wyoming, flew in to help me with the dogs and unpacking so that I could spend my days at the hospital until school started.

* * * * *

"Hey." I smiled at Denise, hoping to hide my shock at her appearance. I had just seen her three weeks before when I had flown in on June 8th for my interview with Fountain-Fort Carson District Eight. The changes were stunning.

"I know why you're here," Denise whispered to me, her blue eyes instantly pooled with tears.

What is this? I thought. *I mean, Denise **never** cries.*

"And why is it you think I'm here?" I asked, taking her hand. "Besides the fact that I've permanently moved here and will be able to move into my own house in just a few days."

"Because God sent you here to take care of my children." She nodded her head as she whispered this, although she was so weak, or perhaps so medicated with pain killers, that it was clear that even this small movement required effort.

I thought carefully before responding. I was taken aback by this display of emotion. By what she was saying underneath and behind those words.

"No," I said slowly, "no...God didn't send me here to take care of your children, Denise. He sent me here to help *you* take care of them. Only you can take care of your children, you know."

She stared at me, still holding my hand.

Tethered, tethered, tethered. The filament that kept us tethered shortened a notch at that moment, drawing us closer, with unspoken words strengthening the connection.

I wonder if the implication hidden behind those words will ever be spoken out loud, I thought, not sure that I ever wanted it to be.

"I'm glad I'm here, Denise," I told her. "I'm supposed to be here, and I'm not going anywhere."

Nodding, Denise silently mouthed "I know" before shutting her eyes and drifting off to sleep.

* * * * *

Officially, my job was to begin on August 1, 2005—about three weeks after I arrived in the Springs, and less than a week after I was able to move into the home I had purchased. In the evenings before school started, Merrilyne and I would tackle the unenviable task of opening boxes, making a cursory attempt to put order to what had been packed with an apparent lack of rhyme or reason. It shocked me to find blenders packed with pictures, toiletries packed with underwear, artwork mixed with appliances, and bedding thrown into random boxes in an obvious (but unsuccessful) attempt to cushion fragile objects. It was stressful just seeing how my mind must have been working (or not, such as the case clearly was); and I couldn't help but wonder how I was ever going to manage my life without a Merrilyne to help me.

School began with a one-week orientation for all new staff and teachers. On the first of five days, the superintendent, Dr. Jones, spoke to the audience as a whole.

An African American man in his mid-forties, Dr. Jones approached the group with ease. He was adept at creating an intimacy with the audience quickly, speaking in a conversational and relaxed manner. He appeared likeable and intelligent, although my newly tarnished view of public education administrators kept me from being overly engaged in his presentation.

In the early part of his welcoming address, Dr. Jones, while telling an amusing anecdote, used the word *hell*. The sound of it actually startled me out of my half-engaged listening state as it reverberated (or so it seemed to my ears) through the microphone. Three years in Blanding had accustomed me to hearing nothing stronger than *Oh, my heck*—the common phrase adopted in lieu of verbalizing any words considered sacrosanct or impious. I looked around to see if anyone else appeared electrified by the superintendent's bold articulation, and as far as I could tell, there was not a single visibly raised eyebrow among the crowd. I suddenly felt like Dorothy when she said, "Oh, Toto...I've a feeling we're not in Kansas anymore." I had this overpowering urge to turn to someone and laughingly pop off with a similar phrase, but I didn't know anyone and thought perhaps it best to remain quiet, seeing as no one else appeared to be having such an astonished and cheerful reaction to the word *hell.*

Dr. Jones, becoming more passionate in tone as he started talking about the school district, said, "Fountain-Fort Carson School District Eight has been on a continual path to maximize student learning at every grade. Our motto is **Good to Great by** *2008,* and we are on our way!" As he continued to talk about the district's accomplishments, he smiled the triumphant kind of smile one would associate more with a recipient of the Heisman Trophy or Stanley Cup than with an educator talking about lowering the achievement gap for minority and students of low socioeconomic means. I was listening to a superintendent who was *excited* by his own leadership and by the philosophies that drove his administration.

I had not heard this tone—this *fervor*—from an administrator since leaving Alaska. Not only was one not to be admonished for expressing such vehemence of opinion and philosophy in this district, this superintendent was making it sound as if it were a requirement to be hired here. Embarrassingly, my eyes filled with tears as I listened to Dr. Jones say, "We simply will *not* accept the notion that ethnic background or financial status is a valid hindrance to student success. The district is proud of the gains it has recorded. We can boast a ninety-six percent graduation rate as well as minority achievement scores forty percent above the state average. *Forty percent* above *the state average!*" he emphasized, driving home to everyone that just because these kids were African American, military, poor, handicapped, or all of the above, there would be no lowered expectation for their academic accomplishments. Under his stewardship, not only had the minority gap lessened, the district had nearly eliminated it.

I felt ridiculous, foolish, and nearly giddy with emotional excitement. People sitting around the room were nodding; they were smiling—smiling in the way people smile when they are hearing affirmation of something they have long known or practiced.

As Dr. Jones began to wind down his presentation, he said, "Let me close with three powerful thoughts. First, whether educators believe all students can learn is 'right' or 'wrong,' they are in a position to prove themselves correct. Second, the public is much like a baseball umpire when it comes to assessing a great school. A pitch is neither a ball nor a strike until the ump calls it. Similarly, a school is neither good nor bad until those who send their children make the call. Third, in school, as in life, you may not get all that you want, but often you will get what you expect."

With those words and a wave to his captive audience, Dr. Jones stepped down from the podium.

I wanted to throw my arms around the man and hug him as he walked by my table. I had a nearly overpowering urge to enfold him in the way I had locked on to Dr. Willner's ample frame when she validated I was not crazy on that first visit to her office. Fortunately, sixteen months post injury—while there were still plenty of residual side effects from the accident—I was in a little more control of my public displays of emotion.

Presentation after presentation, day after day, this feeling of exquisite relief and unreserved joy would sweep over me. I was a bit dumbfounded when each new speaker would evoke the same dewy-eyed response in me, and I kept my distance from people. I was afraid I would introduce myself as Carson Middle School's new psychologist and immediately burst into tears while trying to articulate my blithesome elation at having been hired in District Eight.

The only exception to my feeling that I wanted to commit a dog-like loyalty and lifelong devotion to this district came with my assessment of *how* the presenters had delivered the information all week. Although the speakers *talked* about the need for teachers to utilize a variety of strategies other than lecturing, no one actually modeled any of the strategies they were referencing. As a trainer myself, I always felt that the most important thing I do is model the strategies in my own presentation, rather than just talk about them. It took me a little by surprise that day after day, hour after hour, each speaker talked *at* us, but never really used the strategies that maximize engagement of all participants.

Oh, well, I thought, *at least these people are passionate about kids and current research! At least they are not threatened by people who think outside the box!* I did make a note of my observation in the end-of-the-week evaluations we needed to complete.

The Director of Secondary Programs, an administrator by the name of Tim Holt, was aware of my comment, and in a brief conversation, stated: "You know, you're right. I want to start justifying and explaining why we all did this, but the fact is we *did* all present in a lecture format while talking about it not being the most effective way to engage people in learning. You're right...we should have done more modeling." Mr. Holt did not seem the least bit offended by my thoughts, and I felt good about our conversation as I walked away.

In what was to become a nightmare of administrator hypocrisy and disappointment for me, Mr. Holt would prove himself a worthy ally.

At the time, however—with absolutely no idea of what was to occur over the next eight months—I knew only that it felt like I was back among administrators who believed in an ethical, legal, and passionate approach to educating children; and it felt safe and very, very comforting.

Like I had, at last, come home.

Rigor Mortis, Two Chopsticks, and a Ball of Yarn
October 2005

A cardboard box flew past my windshield as I drove down I-25 South, heading toward Fort Carson Army Post, where I was working at the middle school. Immediately following the box, a large plastic, pale-blue trash can on wheels hopscotched across the highway, causing cars to swerve and horns to blare as everyone attempted to focus on the road and keep their bobbing cars steady.

This is some wind, I thought as I continued toward Carson, wondering if my classroom—located in a trailer next to the middle school—would still be in an upright position when I got there. *Wow.* I half expected to see the wicked witch, with her green face and striped stockings, furiously pedaling a bicycle alongside of me. I probably would have looked around for her were it not for the fact that driving was still nerve-wracking due to my continued difficulty with dividing my focus—along with my continued lack of awareness of anything not directly in my line of vision. Unless the sportily clad witch pedaled right by my front windshield on her way to Oz via Colorado Springs, I would most likely miss her entirely.

Whoa! I mumbled to myself, startled as I watched a branch—leaves still intact—blow by.

Flashing my identification for the soldier at the Gate One entrance, I drove the short distance to the middle school and noticed that the intensity of the wind seemed to be increasing. *Maybe it just appears that way,* I thought. The school, undergoing a complete renovation, was full of construction materials—fragments of which seemed to be executing an unchoreographed ballet as they went catapulting across the school grounds.

A slab of what I think might have been asphalt roofing whizzed by, making a dull slapping sound as it smacked and then bounced off the walls of one of the other trailers.

Three portable trailers lined both sides of a wooden boardwalk. This area, designated as the sixth grade wing until everyone moved into the new multimillion-dollar building in the fall of 2006, was where the principal had placed me for the year. This was a tough set-up for a teacher with thirty kids trying to conduct science experiments, or a language arts teacher trying to put kids in cooperative learning groups, but for me, it was like landing in educational nirvana. I was beginning to think maybe those guardian angels of mine—the ones who did nothing but make sure I resided in professional heaven—had returned from their overly long sabbatical.

Each trailer was set up to accommodate two classrooms, and while some trailers had one bathroom in a hallway that connected the two rooms, in my case there was a wall separating the two classrooms, and we each had our own bathroom.

Even in Galena, I didn't have *windows* in my room, much less my own bathroom.

The angels had definitely returned.

It made me smile every morning when I walked into this room. I'd created some fabulous offices over the years, always very kid-friendly and embracing—but this room—well, this one was *sans pareil*. It was, as the kids said, *"bad."* This was a *bad room* and I loved it.

A small round rug with a blue and red circle screaming **ROCK ON** was there to greet kids at the front door. Behind it stood a tall lamp with five different-colored globes that could be twisted and molded into any variety of shapes. It was a very funky, fun lamp, and by situating it near the front door, on nice days when the door remained open, it always drew kids in for a quick peek and a hello.

We divided the room into sections, with one area containing tables for students to sit in pods while completing assignments and listening to instruction. In my way of thinking, the only way to teach the kids to work cooperatively (or to work alone without *poking* one another) was to put them in that situation and teach the skills in context. It was in this area that we started each day—after the kids came in, read my white board of morning news and instructions, and put their belongings in the designated area. I'm big on process and procedure, and it was remarkable how it stabilized everyone's morning to follow the same routine every day. Me included. My whiteboard of the morning's schedule was as much for me as it was for the students.

We referred to another area of the classroom as the *Living Room,* and it was defined by its leopard- and zebra-striped chairs, a couch with soft throws and squishy pillows, a zebra-striped rug, and my ancient, but well-loved lava and little monkey lamps. It was here we had intimate conversations, solved disputes, and gathered together for small group discussions.

The third area contained a tall purple cabinet (one of my all-time best thrift-store finds) that contained all the items in my *School Store.* Items in the store were utilized with those kids that were still at a level of needing tangible reinforcement to learn and master new skills—but it provided much more than just prizes and rewards. By implementing the store program, the kids got plenty of opportunities to practice math skills, as they had to do daily, weekly, and monthly graphing of their progress. They also gained valuable experience in developing goals for themselves and working toward them (their progress was rated daily by their teachers); and maybe just as importantly, the store program provided a way for the kids to cheer each other on and encourage one another to be successful. Built into the system was a way to celebrate as a class, each time the boys collectively achieved a certain level of accomplishment.

Unlike in both Alaska and Utah, I had no budget here, so the store, along with my ongoing purchases of new educational training and teaching materials, were expensive undertakings for me. I had no doubt, however, that all were worthwhile investments.

We affectionately referred to the last area as: *The Office.*

The Office had been the object of the kids' first lesson in respecting personal space. Once set up, it was off-limits to all students unless they were invited in or given permission to enter. The kids were great about respecting this. Rarely did anyone enter without first knocking—a very definite improvement from the beginning of the year. Their respectful approach was heartwarming and endearing to me, and it inevitably brought a smile to my face each time a student knocked and requested admittance.

Mostly because there were no doors.

This classroom, like all my offices and classrooms in the past, smelled of vanilla, had soothing music in the background (or rock 'n roll depending on the time of day), and managed to project an air of warmth and comfort that embraced people the minute they entered the doorway. Kids loved it. Parents loved it. Teachers loved it. And as I always hoped, instead of the room being identified as a *special ed room*, it was considered the "coolest" room in the school. That was always good for my students, who had far too many years behind them of being labeled and scapegoated. For once, they were the ones considered lucky, and I liked that.

I liked that a lot.

It appeared that my administrators were a bit put off by my room, which surprised me. Having not lived in a large city for some thirty years, I was still of the mind-set that I surely must be functioning centuries behind the rest of the world. That my room might be considered out of the ordinary or particularly odd had never occurred to me. Certainly, it never crossed my mind that twenty-first century administrators would view a room designed like mine as a place that somehow *enabled* kids, or gave them a crutch of some sort.

About two months into the school year, I was able to talk the two principals into letting me initiate a homeroom class composed of fourteen boys identified with, or at risk of having emotional problems that interfered with their ability to be successful in school. I have never found it very effective to try to teach kids any kind of new skill in an isolated setting once a week. The skills just don't generalize. Teaching social skills and addressing mental health issues are, in many ways, not so different from teaching academic skills. Like with math or English (or any other subject), kids need direct instruction, guided practice, modeling, and independent practice if they are going to master new skills. And I needed to have them every day in order to offer them that.

There has always been debate over whether teaching is a science or an art—whether teachers are born or made. From my observations, teaching is both science *and* art; and while some individuals do seem born to the profession, they are *made* into great teachers. Behind their élan—behind the heart, soul, and passion of every truly exceptional educator—one inevitably discovers the scientist in them. Beneath their magic, there is nearly always the systematic implementation of research-based strategies that a teacher has had to learn and practice before capably incorporating them into daily instruction.

It is not initially easy to teach using the strategies that maximize the effectiveness of instruction. This does not mean, however, that one must resort to tap dancing or performing stand-up comedy routines in order to teach effectively. There are dozens of research-based techniques incorporating the principles of good instruction that fall somewhere between seating students in rows and talking *at* them for forty minutes, and standing on a desk shouting, *"Oh, Captain, My Captain!"*

Of course, on occasion, tap dancing and stand-up comedy are not half-bad ideas when one is faced with twenty-seven middle schoolers seven hours every day.

* * * * *

While the rest of the homerooms were following a curriculum based on the (very worthy) Sean Covey book, *Seven Habits of Highly Effective Teens*, the fourteen boys in the school's only non-coed, multi-age classroom were experiencing learning in a different sort of way. The principles underlying our weekly units and daily lessons mirrored the Covey principles (be proactive, take responsibility for yourself, practice synergy, etc.), but the actual topics were different from what was being presented to the kids in the other homerooms.

Specifically, we focused on topics such as stress management; controlling one's hyperactivity and maintaining focus; keeping oneself organized and on track; managing emotions and temper, etc. Generally, we focused on everything and anything related to these boys becoming successful learners.

For fifteen years, I had been incorporating—and training and teaching others to incorporate—the basic tenets of current brain research into lesson planning. It didn't matter if the subject matter was geography, history, Romeo and Juliet, or using active listening skills. The same research-based principles apply. I have always believed teachers can—and should—design and build lesson plans using what we know works to maximize both instruction and learning, and I certainly tried to do this in the lessons taught during the homeroom period.

Although my classroom might have appeared to be a bit too much fun for serious learning to take place, in fact, little happened in there that was not by design. My college-level teaching experiences, along with my years of working in elementary, middle, and high school classrooms, had validated the truth behind the research. I was a confirmed believer in the powerful and positive effects on learning generated by introducing novelty into lessons, creating a safe and nurturing environment, teaching to various learning styles and intelligences, and making sure that enough movement, feedback, and interaction were woven into daily lessons.

It took me awhile to figure out that my new administrators might not be quite up to date with their reading. They did, after all, talk the talk. It would be a few months before I got it through my own head that they might not be walking it.

* * * * *

One of the twenty-first century buzzwords in education has been *rigor*. It certainly was a frequently used word in my new school—a word that initially excited me. *Rigor* implied student engagement; *rigor* implied high expectations; *rigor* implied that teachers utilized the research to develop their lessons and teach to the way children learn. Not once in my three years in Utah had I heard the term *academic rigor* used with teachers in a staff meeting or during a district-wide in-service (this is not to say it wasn't ever used; it's just to say I personally don't recall hearing the word bandied around).

Of course, rigor also tends to be associated with rigor mortis—a certain stiffness and inflexibility that is incompatible with change. Initially that thought did not occur to me; later it would not leave. I would begin to think of rigor as a sort of blue clay. Academic gumbo stew. A slick-textured directive that had the potential to suck teachers down faster than a viper inhales a church mouse.

I must have heard the word rigor five hundred times in the first weeks of school after moving to Colorado. *Rigor*—and—*bell to bell*. They went together. Kind of like the three little pigs and the big bad wolf.

The witch and Hansel and Gretel.

Snow White and the red apple.

* * * * *

"Bell to bell, teachers! Remember: bell to bell!"

In the hallways, in staff meetings, in informal conversation with our administrator, this phrase was repeatedly spoken. The idea of *bell to bell*—that kids are engaged in learning from the minute they walk through a classroom door to the moment they walk out—is a concept I wholeheartedly embrace. The amount of "down time"—of kids disengaged from learning, and of instructional time lost to nonacademic activities—had been a source of enormous frustration for me in Utah.

Suddenly, I found myself in a school where there was tremendous focus on the research that identified the amount of lost instructional time if teachers were not managing their classrooms well. A great deal of attention was placed on making sure teachers understood just how much time was lost to nonacademic tasks such as maintaining discipline, getting kids seated, taking attendance, passing out papers. To this end, *bell work* was set up. The first ten minutes of every class were structured so that students independently engaged in an academically related activity while the teacher took care of these important, but non-instructional duties.

Good in theory. Excellent in theory, in fact.

Unfortunately, *academic rigor* and *bell to bell* teaching became as problematic for me in Colorado as the lack of them had been in Utah.

* * * * *

Early in September, a teacher asked if I would spend some time in her room, observing. Her concern, she said, was that none of the students seemed very engaged, many of them appeared very slow to grasp concepts, and several of them were disruptive.

Few things excite me more than being able to share my experiences and knowledge with other teachers. Probably to a fault, it gives me pleasure to spend my free time helping teachers redesign lesson plans to incorporate the research and enthuse kids about learning. I was thrilled that this teacher had invited me to engage in this process with her, and after spending time in her classroom, I went home and wrote a memo summarizing my observations and suggestions. We were to meet the next afternoon to talk about the ideas.

The following is a portion of what was contained in the memo:

...Eliminate rhetorical questions and try utilizing **choral responding** instead. This really eliminates the problem for the **slow processors** and for the ones who **do not know the answer, and keeps 100% of your students engaged**...

...*make sure they are talking at least every ten minutes and moving every 15. TTYP* (turn to your partner) is a talking activity, as is choral speaking (I'll go over ways to use both of these when we meet)...

Think **28/3**! Most people need to do something correctly (or work with a concept) approximately **28 times, spread out over** *a period of about three weeks,* in order to learn it in a meaningful, lasting way...

...we shouldn't let them gather knowledge for **more than 10 minutes** without giving them **2 minutes** to process the information in a different manner. That's the **10-2 rule!**

When I met with this teacher, she enthusiastically praised the ideas and strategies identified in the memo; and then, promptly told me that she could not implement them in her classroom.

"Why not?" I asked her, genuinely surprised.

"I can't. I just can't." She said this looking uncomfortable.

Thinking she was underestimating her own abilities, I said, "These won't be hard for you to implement. I'll help you with ways to integrate them into the curriculum, and I think you really will see a huge gain in terms of the kids' engagement and understanding of the concepts." I was so impressed with this woman's teaching, and I wanted to support any effort she made to try some of these ideas.

"That's not it, Debra. I love these ideas. I believe they would work...I *know* they would work. It's not that, it's that..." She looked around the room as if worried she could be overheard.

"Close the door and talk to me," I said. "Tell me what's going on."

As she closed the door, this wonderful, energetic, intelligent teacher said, "I know these techniques work, Debra. But, the people who evaluate me do not. If the principal came in here and saw my kids engaging in a lesson like this, I would be written up." She paused, looking at the page I had offered before saying, "He would *not* perceive this as *rigor*."

Most likely, she was referring to a strategy that involves kids having a "walk-talk"; or a Kagan Cooperative Learning strategy known as *Fan-N-Pick*[12], which encourages higher level thinking skills but could look like a modified card game; or perhaps a Spenser Rogers of PEAK[13] Learning approach, which involves using rock 'n roll music in the classroom. The strategies I suggested were all research-based methods for reviewing or learning new material, but they did not generate a quiet, studious-looking classroom.

"I just can't risk him coming in here and seeing me teach like this. It's my first year here. I'm not tenured. I can put some of your suggestions in, for sure. But not most of them. I'm sorry, Debra."

It was my turn to sigh, thinking about the many opportunities Jim Foster and Carl had provided in order to promote these same strategies in Galena. In fact, that entire district had been fully trained in PEAK strategies, and every teacher was provided with a stereo system and a remote in order to foster incorporating music into lesson plans.

I had been wondering what it was about the administrators in this school that had teachers so stressed. At the time, I was so smitten by the principal's enthusiasm and talk of *rigor* that I missed seeing that teachers were reluctant to employ alternatives to bell work that did not require students to be silently engaged in writing tasks. I knew that fully a third of the staff was new this year, and I knew that a similarly high turnover had occurred the prior year, but I had no insight regarding the reasons behind such high teacher turnover. In my mind, I thought perhaps this principal simply steered people away who did not want to work so intensely every day.

Of course, teachers are no different from students. If they fear judgment and admonishment, they are not going to risk stretching out of their comfort zone in order to learn and then incorporate new strategies into their teaching. And while I desperately wanted to see some of these strategies and techniques implemented in the general education classrooms, after all the problems in Blanding, which grew from my desires to see people stretch and reach beyond the comfort of teaching in autopilot mode, I was hesitant to push too hard at this new school.

It was so hard to make salient judgments about how and when to push through resistance. That, of course, is true in any working situation, particularly a new one—but for me this difficulty was magnified a thousand times because I never knew if the problems that arose were due to me, to the head injury, or to a faulty bureaucratic system and weak leadership.

* * * * *

In developing the homeroom program, I determined that the first thing these boys needed to master was the ability to sit, listen, and process information without their bodies, feet, and mouths appearing as if they were leading the half-time marching band during the Super Bowl. Of my fourteen

---

[12] Spencer Kagan, Cooperative Learning, c 1998

[13] Spenser Rogers, Performance Excellence for All Kids

boys, twelve of them were master fidgeters of Olympic caliber, and each day it became clearer to me that they were not likely to experience movement every fifteen minutes, or have the opportunity to verbally process information every ten minutes anytime soon in their other six classrooms. Turning into a Zen master is a worthy target goal for any Tigger-like student with attention deficits; however, in a school where the sun rises and sets with the CSAP[14] testing process and the scores, it was not just a worthy goal—it was an imperative one.

I started by introducing them all to two chopsticks and a ball of yarn.

Don't let anyone ever tell you that middle school guys don't like to mess with yarn. Once trained properly, my *Fourteeners* could concentrate, listen, and remember information with the best of them (i.e., with their feet on the floor, air bubbles stifled, and drumming fingers stilled). And *nobody* makes creative memorabilia like teenage boys who are mastering cognitive information while their fingers are busy with two chopsticks and a ball of yarn.

There weren't many rules in my room, but the ones that existed were adhered to with the consistency that Emily Post practiced good etiquette. And because middle-schoolers by nature just have to break rules, we never referred to them as such. We called them *Guidelines for Success* (with thanks given to a man named Randy Sprick, who first taught me this); and they applied to me as much as to the students. One of these guidelines was *Be Kind*. Another was *Be Respectful*. The third was *Do Your Best Work.* And the last was: *You may fiddle with it as long as it 1) doesn't distract you, the teacher, or your neighbors; and 2) you can* demonstrate *that you are listening and learning.*

We had colorful ornaments accessorizing all parts of that room, and not once in all those days, weeks, and months of lessons did I have to remove two chopsticks and a ball of yarn from a student.

True, the boys weren't able to utilize this strategy in their other classrooms, but using it in ours allowed them to learn and practice some very important concepts and skills that *would* generalize into their other rooms.

The boys might have looked like they were in a Japanese knitting class, but they were listening, learning, and staying on task without distracting themselves, me, or their neighbors.

And I must say, those boys graced my Christmas tree that year in a way I will very likely never see again.

---

[14] CSAP: The state of Colorado's testing program that students participate in each year.

Jess

"*Ms. Sanders!* Whoaaaaa, Ms. Sanders! It's **really** windy out there," Jess said, smiling as he blew into the classroom—hair and clothes rumpled and disheveled.

Later we would discover the wind was blowing at a fierce eighty miles per hour, but at that moment, we only knew that it was strong enough to be rocking the portable trailer that housed our classroom.

"Well, good morning, Jess! I'm so glad the wind didn't blow you in the wrong direction. I was afraid I wouldn't get to see any of my favorite *Fourteeners* today!"

"The wind couldn't blow me in the wrong direction, Ms. Sanders," Jess commented quite earnestly. "And you would have to see us, because it's Thursday. You only don't see us on Saturday and Sunday."

Tall and strapping, Jess was a handsome eighth grader, with a sweet smile and a clear desire to be liked. He wore the same coat every day (a Broncos jacket), and he carried the same pack in the same way and dumped it in the same place every morning. Despite this kind of precision, Jess somewhat resembled a walking tornado, and inside the bag so carefully situated, one was likely to find about two hundred miscellaneous papers with absolutely no order whatsoever to them.

When I first met Jess, I had approached him with the mind-set that he was a teenager with a bipolar[15] or oppositional disorder[16], which—according to his records—were his official diagnoses. Conversations with past teachers indicated that Jess was known to throw legendary tantrums and exhibit major "shut downs" that had not been responsive to medication, psychotherapy, or behavior management and intervention. His behaviors perplexed teachers, who, despite these difficult and challenging outbursts, really liked him. Although odd and quirky, teachers found something about this boy quite arresting and enjoyable. At least, some of the time.

Observing Jess in other classrooms as well as mine, I found there was something about the cadence of his speech and an odd tilt to his walk that began sending off signals in my head. And when he lost his temper, erupted into what appeared to be an out of control, inappropriate display of "bad sportsmanship" or

---

[15] Bipolar Disorder: An affective mood disorder once known as manic-depression, which refers to a mental health condition defined by periods of extreme, often inappropriate, and sometimes unpredictable mood states.

[16] Oppositional Defiant Disorder: A condition characterized by a pattern of negative, defiant, and hostile behavior that develops in childhood or early adolescence, lasts for at least six months, and causes significant impairments in everyday functioning.

absolute *defiance* in response to a teacher's request, I was beginning to detect a pattern. A pattern that to me seemed more fitting of a child with Asperger's Syndrome than one with a bipolar or oppositional defiant disorder.

I first noticed this concerning *time*. Shortly after we started the homeroom class, I was working with another student when Jess came over, interrupting what we were doing.

"Jess, I'll be with you in a couple of minutes," I told him patiently. "Go ahead and sit back down, and I'll come on over and help you shortly."

Jess sat down, but in no time at all he popped up and came back over to us.

"Ms. Sanders, you said two minutes," he said, expecting me to attend to him immediately.

"Yes, Jess, I know, but we're not through yet. I'll be with you as soon as we're through."

"But, Ms. *SANDERS*," Jess said emphatically, a near panicky look on his face. "That's not *right*. You said *two minutes*."

Thrusting his arm in front of me, Jess jabbed his finger at the face of his watch, and his own face contorted into what I knew signified the beginning of a major meltdown.

"It's not *right*, Ms. Sanders," he said, wagging his head back and forth. "You said two minutes. It's just not right." Plopping down in a huff, Jess then refused to do anything at all.

It didn't take too many of these encounters before I realized that for Jess, "a couple of minutes" *meant* two minutes. One hundred twenty seconds. Not one hundred twenty-three seconds, and certainly not *three hundred* seconds. One hundred twenty seconds. Two minutes.

Jess's awareness of when those two minutes expired was uncanny. He had the most remarkable awareness of time I had ever seen—a characteristic that became invaluable to me once I learned how to channel it properly. After being repeatedly admonished by the assistant principal for the kids being late to their next class (due to my own *impaired* sense of time), I made Jess my official timekeeper during homeroom. It was a brilliant role for him to have, and once assigned, the students were never late again.

"Five minutes until the bell, Ms. Sanders," he would point out in our prearranged manner, a wide smile on his face.

"Thanks, Jess! Okay, everybody...start packing up to head out."

Saved us all from getting into trouble a number of times!

It occurred to me one day, as I was watching Jess in another classroom, that perhaps when he said something like, "That's not right," what he *really* meant was, "You are breaking a *rule* and that's wrong."

Individuals with Asperger's can be very rule-bound, and often, they are the watchdogs in every classroom, making sure the teacher knows when someone does something outside the boundaries of the stated rules. The problem for kids with Asperger's is they can be very literal, and often do not understand the *nuances* of everyday interactions—like, "a couple of minutes" may well mean five or even ten minutes. Often, this student can come across as a real tattletale and busybody, and is frequently reminded (by both teachers and peers) to mind their own business.

To a person with Asperger's, that makes no sense at all—because after all, *a rule is a rule,* and breaking it therefore *is* their business.

Life becomes a very frustrating and exasperating set of experiences to people who think in these absolute and literal terms.

Not long ago, Jess stormed into the room, heading to the living room area with a huff and a grunt and an expression on his face that my mother would have said "could sour milk."

"I *hate* Mr. C," he stated absolutely. Arms folded across his chest and slumped in the chair, Jess had his face in a contortion somewhere between a scowl and a pout that I knew was signaling the potential start to a very rough day.

"Wow. Want to tell me what happened? It's only seven forty-five. You haven't even had him for class yet!" I said, thinking *Uh-oh,* not *a good way to start a day.*

"Errrghh," he responded, emitting a sort of drawn-out growl.

"Errrghh, meaning…?"

"Errrghh. I *hate* him. He should be fired." Jess's eyebrows knit together, forming a long line that barreled across his forehead, punctuating his indignation.

"Well, tell me what Mr. C did, and perhaps we can figure out together if it's worth him getting fired over. Maybe I can help you sort through it a little bit. Because you know, usually he's one of your favorite teachers."

"I'm going to get my mom to get him *fired*. It's not right what he said."

It took a great deal of time and some serious digging, but what finally emerged was that the Broncos had lost an important game the day before. Jess wore a Broncos jacket that he dearly loved and was very proud of owning. Apparently, when he got off the bus, Mr. C, who was on bus duty, teased Jess by telling him he should *burn that jacket.* And Bronco fans everywhere (meaning the bus and the Youth Center that Jess attended before and after school) were making nasty little jokes about the rather substantial margin by which the Broncos had lost the game.

Jess was very literal, and he navigated through life by following a strict set of governing rules that he had somehow gathered together. In his mind, when you support a team, it's rather like having taken marriage vows—through sickness and through health, through good times and through bad. *It's not right* to make fun of your team and say you don't like them anymore, just because they lost the major game of the season.

That's *wrong.*

Mr. C. had told him to burn an important and costly piece of clothing, and *teachers* are supposed to know better than to tell students to burn their clothes. Therefore, Mr. C should be fired because he did not follow the rules, and students needed to be punished for saying bad things about the team they support.

This was all very clear in Jess's mind, and it allowed a very confusing world to make sense and have some predictability. When rules like these were violated, it would affect Jess in a way very similar to how the rest of us might react upon finding out that our spouse lied or cheated, turning our predictable and safe worlds upside down.

"Jess," I said to him later that day, "tell me about you and your sense of humor. What kinds of things do you find funny?" Because they are so literal, and because they miss the subtle inflections in tone and voice, individuals with Asperger's almost always miss the humor in the things others find funny.

"I don't," said Jess. "I don't have a sense of humor."

"Really? You don't ever laugh?"

"Yeah, I do. But not when other people do. I never laugh when other people do. I don't get why they're laughing."

"Well, *that* must be frustrating," I said, thinking about how hard that must be, especially in the world of peer-driven middle schoolers.

"Well, yeah...but I've *never* had one. That's why kids don't like me." Jess was quiet for a minute before adding, "Kids are mean."

"Let me ask you something...do you ever feel like you're trying your very, very best to fit in with those kids...I mean, *really* trying hard...like here at school or over at the Youth Center, but no matter what you do, it just comes out all wrong?"

Jess brightened, his face registering complete understanding of what I was talking about. "All the time, Ms. Sanders. And not just kids...it's teachers, too. And my mom. That's why we fight all the time. Nobody believes me." The eyebrows were cascading downward and toward one another again.

"Explain what you mean, Jess. What do you mean when you say that?" I was really interested in what his perceptions were about how other people interpreted his behaviors.

"I mean, they never think I'm trying. But I am. I always try. I try to do my best. Just like it says in here: 'Do your best work.' But nobody believes me."

"Well, I believe that's probably true, Jess. I've seen you in here long enough, and in your other classes, to know that you are genuinely trying." I pondered this for a minute and then asked, "Jess, what do you think other kids your age like to talk about?"

He was silent, an absolutely blank look on his face.

"I don't know." He shrugged, those expressive eyebrows rising high this time. He looked a bit surprised—as if it had never before occurred to him to wonder what other kids thought or talked about.

"That's okay, that's why I'm asking. It's good to know what you know and don't know. How about this: What do you think your face looks like when you're tense or angry? Can you describe it to me?"

Silence again.

"I don't know. I have no idea." Clearly he was thinking about this and trying to figure out what his face *did* look like.

"How about your mom? Can you tell me what hers looks like when she's mad?"

"No. But I *know* when she's mad!" he said. "She screams."

I couldn't help but smile.

"Hmm. Isn't that interesting, Jess? I mean that you don't know...because I know *exactly* what my face looks like when I'm mad...and you know what? I know what yours looks like, too. You knit your eyebrows together like this." I imitated with my own eyes what he does when angry or ready to pout.

He laughed, more because I looked silly than out of recognition of his own expression.

"You know what, Jess? People use their faces and their bodies a *lot*. People tell us a ton about how they feel without ever using words. And we do, too. We communicate a lot of information to other people about how we feel and what we're thinking—without ever actually saying anything."

We looked at each other for a moment while I contemplated the enormity of what needed to be taught directly to this boy.

"You know what, Jess? I think we forgot to teach you how to read *people*. Reading people is every bit as important as reading books. You're a *great* book reader...but I think maybe we forgot to teach you how to read people."

This seemed to spike his curiosity.

"Jess...you ever hear of something called Asperger's syndrome?"

"Nope," he said.

"Well, just listen for a minute." I got up and grabbed a folder I had that contained a number of statements about Asperger's syndrome. I started to read:

> Martin is seen as weird by his classmates. His social skills are poor. For example, he'll continue to talk about a subject (e.g., tarantulas), unaware that people have lost interest...

"*That's* me," Jess interrupted matter-of-factly.

> ...Martin doesn't understand when someone's making a joke, and takes things very literally. For example, when a fire broke out near the school, one of the students joked that they could toast marshmallows. Martin believed that she really was going to do this and told her it was dangerous. When she laughed, he got very upset, and went and told the teacher that the girl was going to roast marshmallows and then all the kids told him he was weird.

"That's me, too," Jess stated, his eyebrows furrowed, not in anger but in concentration this time.

> ...However, Martin *isn't* weird. He has a condition called Asperger's syndrome. That's a kind of disability that affects the way people communicate and relate to people around them. People with Asperger's may want things to be the same all the time. For example, they may find it difficult to cope with changes to their school timetable or a different teacher...

"Oh, that's *really* me!" Jess said, his eyes widening. "That's really, REALLY me!" I was smiling at Jess's reaction. He was so amazed by the fact that what I was reading was describing somebody else, and yet it was so very much like himself.

He was captivated. "What else does it say in there?" he asked, pointing to my folder.

> ...People with Asperger's find it *really* difficult to make friends. That doesn't mean they don't *want* friends, but they're often the target of bullies. One young person described how bullying left him in tears for hours every night. What made matters worse, was that he was being bullied by someone he thought was his best friend.

"I *have* that, Ms. Sanders. That's me." Jess was as serious as I had ever seen him. "I have that thing. What's it called again?"

"Asperger's syndrome, Jess."

"That's me. That is exactly me!" His face broke into a wide smile.

"Maybe so, Jess, maybe so. It's certainly something we can explore."

Jess stood up, shaking his head back and forth in amazement, that wide, open smile never leaving his face.

"But, Jess...I have to tell you something," I said in earnestness. He looked at me, and I continued. "If you do...if you *do* have Asperger's, then we have a lot of work to do."

Jess tipped his head way to the side, scrunching up his face. "*Huhhhhhhhh?*" (No one ever said that individuals with Asperger's syndrome couldn't also be dramatic!)

"Well, having Asperger's...*if* you do have Asperger's...means you have to *learn* all these things...these things that you don't know, like how to tell if someone is getting bored with what you're saying. Or how to figure out when someone is joking." I looked at Jess and could see he was listening carefully. "It doesn't mean you can't ever be better in the way you interact with people—it just means you'll have to do a lot of work to figure it all out. Like math...only you have to learn *people* formulas...stuff other people just seem to get without having to study—you're going to have to learn and practice.

"And, Jess, you can't ever let it be an excuse for bad behavior," I added. I could just *hear* Jess telling his mom or a teacher that he blew up because he has *Asperger's syndrome*, and I didn't want him to walk away from this conversation thinking it was a ready-made excuse for inappropriate reactions.

"That's okay, Ms. Sanders."

"What's okay, Jess? What do you mean?"

"I mean it's okay if I have to be taught that stuff." Jess gathered his books and headed toward the door, saying over his shoulder with utter confidence, "You're a really good teacher, Ms. Sanders. You'll teach me how."

And with that Jess left for his next class, which was, after all, beginning in exactly four minutes.

That night I spent three hours and four hundred dollars ordering materials online that would teach me how to teach Jess.

And I paid extra to have them shipped overnight.

High Winds But No Tsunamis, Please

One by one, the wind blew in the boys. Jack—followed closely by Joey—blasted into the room, laughing and making jokes about the weather.

"Hey, boys! Welcome to Oz," I said, as the door slammed shut with a loud thwack.

"Hey, Ms. Sanders!" Jack waved as he put his backpack away. Joey, as he did on most mornings, rushed over to give me a giant bear hug.

"I am *so* glad the wind didn't blow you into the wrong room!" I said, smiling and returning his hug.

Josiah came in next. With his rich coffee-colored skin, this slender, handsome boy always appeared so solemn and watchful. Josiah wore glasses, which made him look studious upon first glance. A closer look revealed one glass eye and one eye that was crossed, and I suspected that his demeanor had much to do with having survived the taunts that such eyes had likely generated over the years.

Conversations with his teachers and school records indicated that Josiah has had poor school attendance and poor grades, but many things conveyed to me that this seventh grader was extremely intelligent, with tremendous potential to be successful.

As it turned out, Josiah would be the one who would decide, by the end of the school year, that he wanted to grow up and be a psychologist. And it would be Josiah who would enter our classroom nearly every day with a smile on his face. The transformation would have much to do with his undergoing surgery and getting the crossed eye straightened, but it would also have to do with the relationship that not only he and I developed, but that he developed with the other members of this homeroom class.

"*Winnnnn…deeee!*" laughed Tyrone as he whipped into the room, all neon white flashing teeth and boy energy. He took off the powder blue ski cap pulled low over his forehead, and shook his closely cropped, tightly coiled black hair in an exaggerated and goofy fashion. The kids around him laughed in a supportive, friendly sort of way. It was so nice to see Tyrone enter happy. Whether he would be that way in thirty minutes I had no way of knowing—but at this wild and windy moment, he was all Cheshire cat grin.

There were mornings when I'd look over and see Tyrone with his head bowed and his hands knotted together between his knees while silent tears splashed onto the table. I had never seen tears like Tyrone's—a literal *curtain* of them, which, as far as I could tell, would appear without provocation. I adored Tyrone almost as much as I worried about him.

Michael, a sixth grader like Tyrone, came in next with a huff and a puff not unlike the big bad wolf. Throwing himself into the leopard-covered chair and pulling his hood over his head and face, Michael refused to look at anyone. Just as I was debating whether to intervene or wait and see if he would work through this on his own, I noticed Josiah, fleece blanket over face and body, curled into a fetal position under one of the tables.

It was then that I remembered that Josiah had a severe—a very severe—storm phobia.

"What's wrong, Josiah?" Tyrone asked, looking under the table.

"He's having a bad morning," offered Jack. "I don't think he likes the wind."

"It's okay, Josiah," Joey added. "I don't like it so much either." From the tone of his voice I half-expected Joey to crawl under the table and pat Josiah on the back in a mothering sort of way.

And people think these boys are so tough! How quickly they've learned to watch out for one another, I thought, not without a small sense of mother hen type of pride.

Before I could give another thought to either Josiah or Michael, Kit, Jonathon, Jess, and Antonio—all seventh and eighth graders—closely followed one another in, leaving the raging wind behind them as the door whammed shut with a ferocious smack.

This is unreal, I thought. *It's beginning to make me a little nervous.* Looking around, I wondered why they hadn't delayed school this morning. *Jeez, even in Alaska they closed the school when winds like these prevailed.*

Antonio was not actually in our homeroom, but every now and then he wandered in right before school started. As I said good morning to each of them, Antonio—in the very loud and singsong, yet strangely monotone voice that accompanied all his words—responded in his typical fashion: "Don't call me Antonio. My name is Eddie. Ed. Eddie. Ed." As if a piano teacher hit middle C for every word, Antonio's tone and cadence of speech made it come out sounding like three long, flat words:

Don'tCallMeAntonio.

MyNameIsEddie.

EdEddieEd.

"Okay, Mr. Ed, Eddie, Ed," I said, smiling. "You need to hustle and get to your homeroom—the bell's going to ring soon." As he turned on his heels and wandered toward the door, looking toward something above the eye level of everyone around him, I added, "Be careful out there, please. There's construction debris blowing around." Despite superior intellectual abilities, Antonio was not always entirely aware of his surroundings, and his mother—a high-strung Spanish-speaking woman—would come to school multiple times every day to make sure he remained safe and uninjured.

Frankly, I was surprised she let him come to school at all today.

The thought crossed my mind that I would really hate for flying shingles to sideswipe Antonio as they went hopscotching by and he proceeded oblivious to them at all. My Spanish wasn't good enough to interpret what his mother would be saying, at the rate she would be saying it, if he were hurt. And while I genuinely liked and thoroughly enjoyed Antonio's mother, when she was upset and speaking in English, I could not understand a single word she said. My Spanish was rusty, but even rusty, I probably did better with her Spanish than her English when she let her Latin temperament get the best of her.

Like Jess (and several other boys in the homeroom class), Antonio had Asperger's syndrome. Although his was a far more severe manifestation of the disorder, Antonio, like the others, was learning to maneuver around and through the myriad of hidden, unspoken rules that can make life in middle school so very difficult for these kids.

The M's came in next—two boys named Marcus. Two keenly intelligent boys. Other than intellect and name, however, they shared few behavioral traits.

Marcus B—a seventh grader—was a sensitive and perceptive boy coping with a medical disorder that resulted in unpredictable and painful outbreaks of blisters on his hands and feet—an inherited condition for which there is no cure. He was a kind, cooperative, and perceptive boy, and though he was prone to some pretty intense depression and some very severe pain, I never heard a short-tempered word from him. Everyone knew who Marcus B was, and everyone liked him—though not many invited him to join them during unstructured or free-time activities. It was his and his mother's request that he join this homeroom class. I knew it had become a very safe and secure place that helped him get a calm start to the day. And it was a place where he could be a part of the genuine connection between the boys. Marcus was a fabulous role model for the others, and the one student in the class without any sort of attention deficit disorder complicating his already complicated life.

Marcus T was a sixth grader who had mastered the art of pushing other people's buttons. He had neither friends nor allies in any of his classrooms due to his many annoying and disruptive behaviors, which ranged from making loud noises with his mouth to outright defiance and surly belligerence in response to teacher (or principal) direction.

One day, Marcus T walked into the classroom, angry before anyone had even offered him a hello. Things were really bustling that day, and I didn't have the time to approach him in order to find out what had happened before he arrived at our homeroom class. Out of the corner of my eye, I saw him sling his pack where it belonged, and then shove his way past the other boys, a scowl blazoned across his face.

Marcus was a funny-looking kid—not in a bad way, but in the way that immediately made him stand out as potential bait for the more aggressive kids. He wore wire-rimmed glasses, and was pale and skinny with ears that—while not Dumbo-sized—were big enough to lend him an air of "geekiness." And he was smart—quick in a way that he could rat-a-tat-tat like an automatic assault weapon of words if something made him angry. Like many kids with hyperactive and explosive anger disorders, Marcus T was very impulsive and not very wise in the way of social skills. Little things set him off easily, in a way totally disproportionate to the situation.

On that day, just as the bell rang and kids were bolting to their seats, I heard a sneering tone mutter, *"Asshole."*

"Ms. SANDERS! Marcus…" Jess loudly tacked on to the end of Marcus's morning utterance.

I looked at Jess, my eyebrows raised, interrupting his disclosure.

"*Sorrr*-rreee. I know… *Who's the teacher*?" A sheepish, half grin replaced the look of indignation that had registered on his face.

Who's the teacher? is a technique Jess and I had been practicing in order to encourage him to let teachers handle discipline in their classrooms—without his collaboration. He had come a long way toward curbing this behavior, which was so annoying to teachers and did absolutely nothing to help him gain points on the peer-popularity meter.

Smiling at Jess in recognition of his backing off, I moved toward Marcus.

"Marcus," I said quietly, "this is a tough way to start the morning. Take a couple of deep breaths and think about how you want the day to go."

When someone is making a poor choice, it's my preference to first intervene with a redirection cue. This is often sufficient to diffuse an impending explosion and avoids the power struggle these kids are so used to creating with adults.

"I don't *care* how the day goes," he snarled in a really unpleasant way. Under hooded lids, Marcus glared at me, spitting out, "Just *leave* me alone. Go a-**WAY**. *Pleeeeeze*." The *please* dripped with punctuated sarcasm.

Slamming his books on the desk, Marcus muttered under his breath, and while I couldn't really hear what he said, it did sound like it started with a **B.**

So much for my attempt to redirect. It's a good thing my management approach always involves a second (and third) step, just in case redirection doesn't work.

Thirteen other boys were watching and waiting to see what I was going to do. This interaction with Marcus was taking place within days of having formed this classroom, perhaps eight weeks into the new school year. Most likely the expectation was that I would get mad, yell, or send Marcus to the office; and while these are three common and understandable reactions observed of teachers, the whole *point* of having this homeroom was to do things differently. To intervene in a way that would teach *new* behaviors, not simply reinforce the status quo in a more colorful environment.

It had not been an easy sell to the administrators to let me set this class up. I knew that this challenge with Marcus was one I needed to manage well. It was important that I validate (to myself as much as anyone else) that I could still manage these kinds of situations in a way that teaches, not just punishes.

Since sarcasm happens to be one of *my* buttons, I was going to have to tread carefully, lest I give in to the instinct to just *react* to Marcus's provocation.

"Okay, Marcus," I said quietly. "I can see you're not having a great start to the day, so I'll give you your choice here. [Step II] I'm going to walk away and give you a couple of minutes to calm down. If you do, that's great…we'll move on with the morning. If you can't, then I'll have someone walk you over to Mrs. A.'s room." [Step III]

Mrs. A. was an eighth grade science teacher—a young, fun, and very structured teacher who agreed to let me set up a desk in the room for Marcus. He might act out in front of his peers, but as a sixth grader, it was highly unlikely that he would do so in front of a whole class of eighth grade students. And if he did, the arrangement was to call his stepfather and have him come into school for a meeting. [Step IV]

Marcus would do anything, absolutely anything, to avoid having his stepfather called into school. Even if it meant taking control of his behavior and calming down. Which, to date, was exactly what he had done. It certainly would have been easier to suspend Marcus for his inappropriate, disruptive, or out of control behavior, but he was learning a great deal more about self-control and personal responsibility by not being given the option of an out-of-school suspension. I was absolutely thrilled that Mrs. A. had been willing to collaborate with me in using this particular strategy, and it did my heart good to know it was working so well. To date, Marcus had been to her room only one time. And his behaviors while in there had been faultless: he had completed his assignments quietly and without distracting other students or drawing attention to himself. Without feeling humiliated or degraded, Marcus had definitely gotten the message that the behavior that landed him there was unacceptable and probably not worth the price he was paying. Neither myself nor his other teachers had had to go beyond Step I of the Behavioral Plan since.

The exchange between Marcus and myself that morning had lasted less than three minutes. I walked away, giving him some breathing space, and we went about our usual morning routine. Although not cheerful about it, Marcus made the choice to put his things away quietly and to participate without expressing sarcasm or frustration for the rest of the period.

When the bell rang, as always, I stood at the door and said good-bye to each student. When Marcus was about to exit, I asked him to stay.

"*WHAT?* I *got* good. I was *GOOD*. I calmed down," he spouted defensively.

"You did, Marcus. And you're not in any trouble. I just want to talk to you for a few minutes."

"I have to go to Ms. K.'s class. I'll be *late*," he proclaimed in a tone that suggested I was merely trying to get him into even more trouble.

"Actually, I have an arrangement with Ms. K., so if you're not there, I just need to flash a smile at her and she'll know not to mark you absent or tardy." Fortunately, Ms. K.'s room was just one trailer over, and this arrangement worked great on days that Marcus needed defusing before heading out into the rest of his day. Almost always, if I took an extra ten or fifteen minutes with him, the rest of Marcus's day went smoothly. As a result, the rest of his *teachers'* day went smoothly.

"I don't see why you want to keep me. I *DID* what you asked." Marcus's voice was intensifying by a decibel or two.

"Marcus, listen to me...you're not in trouble. I'm only asking if you'll stay for a few minutes. It's up to you. If you will, I'll tell Ms. K. so she'll know."

Still convinced he was in trouble, Marcus sighed and slammed his books on the table.

"*FINE.*"

When I returned from Ms. K.'s, I took us both into the living room area. I have this little heart-shaped stool I keep in there that I like to sit on when I'm talking to the kids—it's lower than any of the chairs or the couch, and it puts me at eye level with them. In this case, Marcus had chosen to sit on the couch, and I was on the stool directly in front of him.

"Marcus. All I wanted to tell you was that you did a great job in here today. I was really proud of you. Really."

He looked at me. I didn't say anything else.

"That's it?" he asked.

"That's it," I said. "I just wanted to tell you that I know that was really hard for you to do. But you did it! And the rest of the class went great. That's a big thing. I just wanted you to know that I noticed the kind of choice you made."

Up until that point, Marcus's whole body had been coiled. Shoulders hunched and tension showing in every plane of his face, he had been ready to spring with the slightest provocation. Now, as if a knob had been turned, his whole body deflated as he stared at me.

"I thought you were going to yell at me and call my dad."

"I know you did. And I'm sorry if something I did made you think you were in trouble. I really did just want us to take a few quiet minutes so I could tell you I was proud of you."

Behind those glasses, Marcus had beautiful blue eyes. You didn't always notice them, especially when his expressions were soured by his tension. But at that moment I noticed them clearly, and I saw that they were beginning to fill with tears.

"Would you be proud of me if I was your kid?" he asked. "I mean, your *real* kid, not like your student-kid?" His question took me by surprise.

"Yes, Marcus. I would," I said gently. "If you were my kid and your teacher sent me a note telling me how you handled the morning, I would be very proud of you."

He didn't say anything for a minute. Just sat there.

"My parents are never proud of me," he said quietly. Matter-of-factly.

I looked at Marcus, giving him time to say more if he wanted to.

"I can't do *anything* at home. They've taken away everything. All I have in my room is a *bed.* They took away all my toys, and they make me stay in my room. I can't even use the computer."

Marcus had a near obsession with small toys. And he was a world-class fidgeter. To take away his toys and exile him to his naked bedroom would be severe punishment indeed.

"That must be really hard, Marcus. Sounds like maybe there's a lot of tension there. Did they take your toys away to punish you for some reason?"

"Yes, but I didn't *do anything.*"

I continued to just sit quietly.

"They hate me, actually. They really do."

There was a long pause and then Marcus said, "I think about killing myself. I think about it a lot. All the time."

"Tell me what you think about, Marcus. When you think about killing yourself, what is it you think about?"

"Just wanting to get out of there. To leave them and be gone."

At this point his eyes were pools of tears, but none spilled over. Removing his glasses, Marcus ground his eyes with the palms of his hands, making sure no tears would escape, and then putting his glasses back on, he took a deep breath.

"Well, Marcus, that makes my heart hurt," I said. "It truly makes my heart hurt to know you're feeling so trapped and that things are so hard for you. I'm sorry... I know feeling like this makes everything else just so much harder."

That was quite a morning for Marcus and me. By the time we were through, we had most definitely made our peace and established our boundaries with one another. We had developed a plan to ensure Marcus's safety (and inform necessary adults about his suicidal thinking); and we had a plan that focused on increasing his appropriate behavior in his classes and around his peers. The plans had led to greatly improved behaviors in a short period of time, but there was a long way to go before this child had things under control and in order.

Now, on this unexpectedly windy day, as I watched Marcus put his things away, I was pleased that his mood seemed stable in spite of the weather; and that he didn't seem likely to agitate the already prickly emotions that were surfacing.

Jess had finally figured out who was hiding inside the hood. "What's wrong with Michael?" he asked.

Before anyone could answer, one of the catapulting construction pieces slammed against the trailer, cracking into the window ledge and bouncing away, leaving a sound somewhat like a sonic boom in its wake.

Michael, letting out a piercing wail that rivaled any sound made by flying sheetrock and shingles, dove under the table and landed next to Josiah.

Everyone else was momentarily stunned into silence.

"*Whoaaaaa,*" the boys said, emphasizing the word with a respectful sort of awe in their tones. "*That was* loud!"

Whoaaaaa, I thought to myself. *Did someone forget to tell me about* **Michael's** *storm phobia?*

I herded everyone into the far corner of the living room, and we huddled, having quickly pushed all the chairs together in a tight circle. Everyone was talking at once, the trailer was rocking, and chaos threatened to take over. It took every *bit* of my twenty plus years of experience to pull off calming the boys down quickly, but I was motivated to do so as much for me as for them. I knew already, my head could *not* handle this kind of noise and chaos.

Then the announcement came over the P.A. system: "Teachers, until we know more about the weather situation, we are asking you to keep your homeroom students through the first period. *Do not let students leave your classrooms.* Again, teachers and students: *Everyone is to remain in their homeroom class through the first period.* Thank you. Now let's say the pledge."

Awwww, RIGHT! YESSSSS! the boys said, hands over their hearts as they turned to face the flag.

Ohhhhhhhhh noooooooo, I thought, feeling my heart thump away. *What am I going to **DO** with these guys for the next hour? I had nothing prepared.*

* * * * *

Preparation was the key to my being able to function in this job. It took hours and hours for me to be ready for each day, but it was the only way I could make things work. I think it appeared to other people like I was relaxed and teaching things I'd been teaching for half my life, but that sure was not *my* reality.

Things were so much more complicated than I had anticipated. I thought being in just one school would allow me to accommodate for the areas in which I still experienced weakness, but there were *so* many challenges. Here it was, over two months into the school year, and I *still* didn't recognize the faces of many of the teachers and parents that I'd had numerous conversations with, much less those of all the students I interacted with.

I had been told (off the record) that one of the paraprofessionals was miffed with me because I never acknowledged him outside of my classroom. Apparently, I had completely ignored him while he was on bus duty one day. I had walked right by him without saying hello. Of course, I had no idea I *knew* him. I didn't recognize him at all, which was so disconcerting to me. And, of course, this necessitated that I find him and explain about the head injury so that he didn't feel slighted by my behavior.

It was so hard to know what to tell people up front and what to keep under wraps.

These seemingly little things, like seeking out someone I had inadvertently offended to apologize and explain, took up so much *energy*…so much *time. Ka-ching.* Everything was still costing pennies. Even though I started each day with far more pennies than I had after the accident, the simplest things still demanded payment.

And my cup certainly did not runneth over.

I still didn't seem to have any of the 360-degree perception I'd always had—knowing what was going on in all parts of a classroom; being able to continually scan while engaged with one or a small group of students. Now, I seemed to have no awareness at *all* of someone behind me or to the side of me. I constantly displayed an exaggerated startle reflex each time I discovered someone near me whose presence I had not detected at all. This provided great amusement to the students, who loved hearing my little shrieks or watching my reflexive jump when I would turn and bump into them. But for me, each experience eroded a little more of my confidence and added one more layer of insecurity and anxiety to the already fragile sense of who I had become.

There was a morning when we were involved in a lesson, and Jess interrupted by blaring in a stressed and loudly commanding voice, *"Ms. Sanders, Joey is stealing candy!"* Looking to my left, I saw Joey scooting across the floor, his hand surprisingly close to a large basket of candy I kept underneath a table in the front of the room. Frozen in motion, Joey, with that deer-in-the-headlights look on his face, bellowed in an equally loud, stressed, and commanding voice: *"NO, I'M NOT!"* while I blankly stared at him, wondering how he *possibly* could have gotten from his table to where he was at that moment.

He's two feet away from me, I thought. *How could I not have been aware of his movements?*

These sorts of incidents left me feeling vulnerable, scared, and terribly worried about my ability to be effective. About my ability to safely supervise students.

One of the hardest things about this brain injury was constantly second-guessing myself. About everything: my relationships with people, my recollection of what transpired in a class or conversation, my ability to manage situations. Being unable to rely on my own perceptions and memory in order to give myself feedback undermined my confidence and exhausted my cognitive energy.

And worse, it made me dependent on the feedback I received from others: feedback that only much later was I able to recognize might not have been given in the spirit of assistance or support. Prior to the accident, I think I was much more discerning in how I internalized other people's feedback, having learned—as we all do over time—to recognize that everyone is only able to give us information to the extent that it is filtered through their own lenses. Sometimes we recognize the validity beneath and behind other people's words; sometimes we recognize the need to screen how and what we are told The problem is, when you cannot rely upon your own self-evaluation skills, you quite readily accept all feedback as absolute truth.

At least I did.

Staying organized was an immense challenge, and while I created systems for myself, most of the time I couldn't seem to remember how to use them, or even that I had set them up. I was continually recreating things that already existed, searching for things I needed, or trying to remember what happened two hours earlier in order to stay on top of note-keeping. I was always the last one to leave school, not because I was the most dedicated, but because I had to do so much *undoing*—so much reorganizing. I had even hired the girlfriend of Denise's oldest son Ryan to come in one or two nights during the week and on the weekend to take care of secretarial-type tasks such as making Xerox copies, simple filing, and preparing necessary materials for lessons. Although I had asked about secretarial help, it had been clearly communicated to me that this was not an option; and despite my increasingly dwindling paychecks, this was another school-related expense worth paying for.

Independently and without support and accommodations, the simple truth was I could not handle the demands of the psychologist role and the demands of the teacher role and still remain organized.

On top of the organizational challenges, I had to write out everything— absolutely everything—in order to teach a simple forty-minute lesson. If I did not script *everything*, by the time the lesson or therapy session rolled around, I wouldn't remember the specifics of what it was I had planned on doing (no way would an outline have worked for me anymore). The other advantage of having a written script was that it was the only way I could manage the unavoidable diversions that always occurred, and still be able to continue with the lesson after the question had been asked, the discussion took place, or the knock at the door occurred. I looked like I was teaching off the cuff, but everything was written out word for word. Every session, every class, every day.

So, so much extra time needed for so much less of a return.

I'd already missed a number of school days, and the shame and embarrassment so familiar to me from the months right after the injury had resurfaced with a vengeance. I'd missed more days of school already than I would miss in a whole school year prior to the accident. It seemed like if I made it through Monday and Tuesday, by the time Wednesday rolled around I would wake up in a fog, and realize very quickly that my brain was not processing efficiently. One Wednesday I had been determined to punch through this fog. My *"buck-up-you-are-such-a-weak-sniveling-loser"* voice was barking admonishments inside my head, so I got dressed, ate breakfast, and went out to the car. Sitting in the car, I realized it wasn't safe to drive—I could barely think how to put the key in and get started, much less drive to Carson and responsibly monitor kids—so I went back into the house and called in sick.

Despite the stimulant medication already in my system, seconds after crawling back into bed, I fell asleep. And stayed asleep until Thursday morning.

Sometimes it was a close call as to whether or not I could plow through, and on those days I would go and do the best I could. I think people just thought I was ditzy or spacey or something. Making the choice to go to work on those mid-week days that were "iffy" usually resulted in my waking up on Friday with one of those holy terror headaches that left my face feeling numb. So—hoping I would get the school recording instead of a live voice—I would call in sick and crawl back under the covers.

Generally, it took sleeping until Sunday afternoon in order for the headache and fog to disappear. I was always surprised when people referred to me as "so busy" or as a "social butterfly," because all I did was work and sleep. People made (and still make) the assumption that when my phone doesn't get answered and messages don't get returned, that I'm out doing something fun; and I did (and do) little to dispel this perception. It's embarrassing to say that I'm sleeping at 3:00 in the afternoon, or 11:00 in the morning, or 7:00 at night.

But that's what someone would most often find me doing.

I think my natural enthusiasm and love for what I was doing at school (and I *so* loved it) suggested a confidence I didn't feel. I suspect I projected an image of someone very much in control, who was not in need of any kind of support or assistance. I tried to communicate my struggles, at least a few of them, to the assistant principal, as she was my direct supervisor. But talking with her left me feeling more vulnerable than I had felt before approaching her. Even though all my administrators were aware of my medical history, we simply had not been able to establish the kind of relationship that would have allowed me to sit down and talk about ways that some of these unexpected challenges might be accommodated. It certainly occurred to me more than once that I might do a whole lot better if I could set up a Monday, Tuesday, Thursday, Friday work schedule, but the thought of even proposing something like this to her left me feeling more exposed than a deer in a wide open field during hunting season.

So, now, here I was with the wind rocking the trailer and kids excited to get *Ms. Sanders (!)* for an extra period. I guess I was going to find out if I could still manage to teach without a written script in front of me.

I worried that this would be the day the principal might choose to stop in and spontaneously observe me, but in the two months that I had occupied this room, he'd never been in to see what it was we actually did. Unlike in other people's classrooms, or in my own previous experiences, no one here had ever asked to see my lesson plans or had expressed any curiosity at all about how I was carrying out the responsibilities of my job.

It was probably a good thing that at that moment I was unaware that "keeping the students through first period" would evolve into keeping the students for **all seven periods.** That might have sent me into a full-blown, all-out episode of flooding. As it turned out, the day evolved into one of the greatest teaching days of my entire career (there's a lot to be said for empowering students to become teachers and having them teach their peers a new skill). A remarkable bond was formed that day—not just between me and each one of those boys—but between the boys themselves. Over that seven-hour day, the boys formed a band called the Pillow Percussion People (Triple P's), a poetry center, art center, and a geography center; and we had a dance-off that had even the most reticent of boys boogying down.

Still, I was glad that the morning announcement hadn't given me a clue at 7:45 a.m. that I would be the teacher for those kids for the next seven hours.

Of course, if I'd *had* that kind of prescience, I would have also known that while both the principal and the assistant principal would be observed by all of us as they walked back and forth past the windows—moving in and out of other classrooms to check on teachers and kids throughout the day—not once would either one of them come in and check to see if we were doing okay. Not once.

Apparently, my unconventional zebra-striped and funky-lamped room, with its array of endearing but atypical children, was not, as I had experienced in my past, such a comfortable place for my principals.

The more I thought about that, the more it bothered me. These kids deserved as much concern from the school's leaders as the less challenging students received.

For that matter, so did I.

But, I had a head injury, and I had a history in Blanding. I sure as heck was not going to make waves. I had made enough waves in Utah to sink a battleship—a *fleet* of battleships for that matter. I was going to make sure that my little USS Cruiser bobbed along peacefully in this new school.

At least that had been my intention.

Zoom Lenses and Wide-Angle Perspectives
November 2005

"Okay, gentlemen," I said, waiting for everyone's attention. "Ready? Lights! Camera! *Action!*"

Antonio, our *gaffer* and thus in control of the lights, wandered to the front of the room while our two actors, Jess and Abe, took their places on the set in the back of the room. Our set was not fancy—just a space we had cleared to temporarily represent the eighth grade hallway—but it was functional. The three cinematographers, Kit, Jonathon, and Justin, faced the set with their cameras in hand. I thought the boys had been remarkably good sports about not requiring me to produce real cameras for this particular opportunity to pretend we lived in Hollywood, but had graciously settled for 8x10 white boards that said *Zoom* on one side and *Wide Angle* on the other.

On this day, Abe was playing a tough eighth grader and Jess was playing himself. With scripts in hand, the two boys started walking toward one another, and as directed, Jess accidently stumbled into Abe.

Abe: **Yo, be easy man.**
Jess: **Huh? Whad'you say?**
Abe: **What? You think you're bougie, man? Outta my way fo
    I bust yo grill.**
Jess: **Huh?**
Abe: **What wrong wit you? You some kind of *reeetard?***

I saw Kit move in closer, displaying the *ZOOM* lens. Justin, his eye on Kit, followed suit and similarly displayed the zoom lens as he moved closer toward the actors. This was a nonverbal signal to Jess and Abe that the cameramen thought it a good time to take a closer look at the details of their current situation.

We had been practicing these types of scenarios for the last couple of weeks, and today's session was what I considered an authentic assessment, a way for me to gauge if the boys were really getting this concept we had been working on.

The idea of turning the boys into cameras had come to me after Jess's meltdown over the Broncos situation. I had observed that this particular group of boys seemed to share several characteristics—one of the most obvious being that they did not seem to pay any attention to their own or others' body language, tone of voice, or facial expression. These boys seemed to move through their days in a kind of insulated bubble, never really taking in either the whole picture of what was going on, or the details of a situation. Because of this, they would frequently hook into a piece of a situation and react to that piece. This response on their part resulted in others' perception that their reactions and behaviors ranged from weird or bizarre to grossly inappropriate.

Somehow I discovered that the boys readily grasped the concept of wide-angle and zoom lenses, and this developed into what we were attempting to do today. By asking them to approach a situation as if they were a camera, the boys were learning how to determine if a situation required a close-up shot that looked at details, or a wide-angle shot that took into account the bigger picture—what might have happened *before* they displayed a reaction to the situation.

"TheAliensHaveLandedOnThePlanetAnd..."

"Be **quiet**, Antonio," Jess said loudly, in a stressed and critical tone that reflected his ongoing frustration with Antonio.

"CallMeEddie..."

"Hey, gentlemen. Excuse me—did I lose my *professionals* here?" I asked, raising my eyebrows in gentle admonishment.

"*Sorrrr*-rrryy," Jess said, and turning toward Antonio, just as we had practiced, he said in the more neutral and far less agitated tone of voice we had been working on, "Quiet on the set, please."

"Much better, thanks. Kit," I said, looking back toward the group, "you were moving in for a close-up; you were *zooming in* on the situation. What made you decide this might be a good time to do that?"

"Because Abe will probably get mad?" Kit answered in a questioning tone, looking like someone behind him was giving him a wedgie. Kit's posture ranged between something akin to a rag doll and that of the tin man in *The Wizard of Oz*. He was in Tin Man mode right now—a posture that made him stand out and appear seemingly mechanical to peers.

"Actually," Abe said in his own sort of stilted, though not unpleasant, tone, "I don't really even know what I said to him." Abe was the least affected of the boys in this group, and although his records identified him as having Asperger's syndrome, to me Abe did not seem nearly as affected by Asperger's as by what appeared to be clinical depression. Regardless of his diagnosis, Abe was good for this group and equally good for me. He grasped the concepts much faster than the other boys did. He recognized that other people did not have access to his thoughts—that just because he knew or thought something, this did not mean another person held the same information. Abe provided excellent role modeling for the other boys and was able to help me keep them in focus. And the group gave him a feeling of belonging, of importance, and a venue in which he could explore his own thoughts and feelings.

It definitely worked for everyone to have Abe in this group.

I looked over at Jess, asking, "How about you, Jess? Did you understand what Abe meant when he said something like 'bust yo grill' or 'bougie'?"[17]

"Nope," Jess said, his wide-open, expressive face looking half confused and half entertained.

"So, you don't know what he meant by that, which right away might make this situation difficult, right? Do you guys ever hear language like this around school or in town?" I already knew they did, because I had asked one of the students *"in the know"* to help me write this script.

"Uh-huh," most of the boys said simultaneously.

"So, when that confuses you, does that make you feel like you don't know what to do when other kids are talking and you don't really get what they are saying?"

"Yep."

"Uh-huh."

Pretty much there were nods all around, except from Antonio, who was sort of wandering in circles near the light switch.

"So, boys, when Kit and Justin moved in for a close-up, what do you think they needed to figure out? What questions were they asking?"

"If this has ever happened before," Jonathon said, offering something for the first time that day. Although Jonathon was standing apart from the other boys and might, to a casual observer, appear removed from the interactions, he was actually very much involved. As involved as he was able to be. Like a young child, Jonathon functioned best if he was engaged in parallel activities. He loved being a part of this group, and he considered these boys his newly found friends, but he would rather participate side by side with them than directly interact.

This, too, tends to be a common attribute seen in individuals with Asperger's. It is often mistaken for a lack of *interest* in social interaction, when in reality the interest is keen. It's the individual's ability to successfully *engage* in the interactions that is so glaringly lacking.

"Zoom in to see if Abe's face looks angry," Jess said.

"And to see if, you know, if anyone can tell if my tone is mad," Abe added.

"Good job, boys! Excellent. And, Justin, what do you think? You followed Kit in for the close-up. What could you figure out by zooming into this situation?"

"Maybe...what was going to happen..." Justin said. "Except, I already know that I would be in trouble because he would beat me up." Justin, like many of these boys, had a great deal of experience with having been bullied over the years. And Justin, in addition to displaying very significant Asperger's traits, was also battling intense levels of depression—which stemmed in part from his tremendous social isolation and inability to make and keep friends.

"Well, Justin, remember that by thinking in terms of functioning like a camera and zooming in or zooming out on a situation, you give yourself an

---

[17] My notes did not include the actual scene we used on this particular day, so the dialogue of this particular scene was created for the purposes of this book. The words and actions of the boys, however, are drawn directly from the notes I kept on what transpired in Group that day.

opportunity to think before you react. So, maybe this will help you respond differently than you have in the past...and *that* might just help you avoid getting beat up."

These boys had been told many times throughout their school years to "just ignore" someone, or to "walk away," but as Jess had said one day: "They just follow me when I do that." What I was hoping to accomplish in this group was teaching very specific skills that would enable each one of these kids to modify their *own* behaviors and reactions. It was my guess that, although they didn't realize it (yet), the way in which they responded and reacted actually encouraged those tougher kids to prolong their torment and cruelty.

The boys stood there in various stages of processing what we were doing, when I said, "Okay, one more question for you guys before we move on. At what point do you think the cameramen should zoom out...back away and take a look at the bigger picture?"

"Now," said Justin.

"Okay, tell me why."

"So I can run away."

At the moment, Justin was not thinking in terms of backing off to gain more perspective; he was thinking only about the reality of backing off to gain distance from a bully. Sometimes our role-playing became tangled with real life, and recent experience told me not to pursue this with Justin, but to simply move back into the skit itself.

"Okay, guys. Let's go back and start from the beginning. You're doing great! Two more weeks like this and I might have to call a Hollywood agent to watch you!" Even though I was clearly teasing them, these seventh and eighth graders obviously were pleased by the compliment.

In retrospect, it is possible that none of them picked up on the teasing at all, and were simply pleased that I was going to call Hollywood in a couple of weeks.

* * * * *

This had all taken place in our Tuesday morning group, which had been meeting for about four or five weeks. I was pleased with the effort these boys were displaying, although this was the toughest of all my groups for me to both design and run. One of the hardest things for me about this group was the multi-tasking necessary to be a good facilitator. I had so much trouble attending to all five boys in order to give them feedback about things like their body language, facial expressions, or tone of voice; not to mention just keeping them all focused and connected to one another and what we were doing. By the end of the forty minutes, my brain felt like I had been reading the subtitles of a foreign movie for about forty hours. It was exhausting, and as much as I enjoyed it and got an *incredible* kick out of these very bright, but very idiosyncratic boys, it seemed to stress my brain a lot. It was all I could do to make quick notes about the session as the boys left and my next group came in and got situated.

Truth was, sometimes by the end of the class period I was pretty fuzzy about what had just transpired, and by the time I had an opportunity to make notes or put thought into the next lesson plan, I had long forgotten any inspiration I had regarding what we should work on next. Each time this occurred (which was more often than not), it was painfully frustrating and discouraging to me, and, of course, it was not just with this group that this occurred, but with all my groups.

I longed for the comfort and security I used to experience with principals and administrators who I felt understood and respected what I did. It was this comfort zone—this feeling of security and safety—that had always enabled me to go to them with concerns or dilemmas. Or to just process ideas or worries about what I was observing.

It was this freedom to discuss ideas and concerns that I had so treasured in Chris Reitan during the hardest days with Charlie and Angela; with Val during our Ernie and Petey Begay days; and with Bob, the many times I sat in his office and pondered issues related to Evan. It would have been nice to be able to say to one of my current principals, "Wow, I am freaked out about how fuzzy I am after each session...do you think I'm doing okay?" Or, even just, "You have a few minutes to bounce around some ideas on Antonio?"

My new administrators still had never been in my room to see what I did with students. In fact, a few days prior, the principal had made an offhand remark revealing just how invisible I was to him. I had been summoned to his office for a meeting—a meeting that began with his informing me that I seemed to be "inciting parents," and letting me know just how angry he was.

Stunned and incredibly confused, I asked him what he was talking about.

"It just seems to me like you stir up the parents, Debra. I think your intentions are in the right place, but it doesn't do anyone any good to upset the parents and get them all fired up."

"Um, you are going to have to be more specific with me here," I said, carefully. "I have no *clue* what you're talking about." And I didn't. I had no idea why he would say such a thing to me, and I could feel my anxiety level taking a quantum leap forward.

"The email you sent regarding Jack," he said, holding up an email I had written earlier that morning and forwarded to him, the assistant principal, and the director of special education.

"You sent this email, Debra," he said, waving the paper in front of him. "You indicate that we need to take a look at Jack's program because his program doesn't reflect what is actually outlined in his IEP. That just inflames parents, Debra. We don't need to be creating these kinds of situations."

Now I was the one fired up, and it took all my energy to sit there and not interrupt and barrel right over his words in my own defense. I tried reminding myself that I could *not* afford another Blanding situation, and that I could not afford to be perceived as "hyper-ethical," which had been one of the accusations aimed at me in Utah.

"I know you're passionate about your work, Debra, and we all appreciate that. But we can't be stirring up parents with talk about things not being done right."

"Wait a minute," I said. "What are we talking about here, Steve? *Look* at the memo I sent. It's addressed to you, the special ed director, and the assistant principal. There are no *parents* listed in that address line, Steve. I did not send this email to *parents*; I sent it to the three of you, asking for some assistance in remedying the situation. Look at the subject line, for heaven's sake. It says: *Thinking Out Loud*. It isn't an email to parents; it's to you guys, hoping we could put our heads together and figure out the best way to handle this."

My intent had been to find a way to correct the problem without informing parents—who would have had every right to file a complaint. My interest was in seeing that the student receive effective programming. I figured if I just laid out the problem and asked for some help in solving it, it would be a nice win-win situation all the way around.

Once again, I had either sorely misjudged the situation, or presented my thoughts in such a way as to quickly inflame administrative tempers.

Where did this come from? Why would this principal make the leap and assume that by asking for help in addressing this student's needs, I was going to the parents and indicating that special education wasn't doing its job?

This was making no sense to me at all.

When I interviewed for the job in June, I had been very up front both about the head injury and the situation in Blanding. I had told the director that he was welcome to call Tony and get his input, but that he was not likely to hear anything too positive. In the portfolio I mailed prior to my interview, I had listed several superintendents, principals, and teachers as references, but I had not put Doug Wright's or Tony's name on the list.

As we were driving over to Fort Carson for an interview tour, the director had asked me how I handled parents if I thought programs weren't being properly implemented. I had answered him honestly, stating that I always hoped to empower parents to be active members of their child's team; and that I felt it was part of the ethical code of school psychologists to function as advocates for the kids. This did not mean, I had added, that I was litigiously oriented, as I believed my administrators in Utah had perceived. I was not, and I had assured him that I had never suggested to a parent that they file a complaint against a district.

"Why do you ask?" I had said to the director. "Did Tony tell you that I riled parents up?" I was curious about the phrasing the director had chosen to use in asking me this question. It sounded so Tony-esque. Or perhaps he had talked to Bob, I thought at the time. Bob, too, had come to believe that my approach incited parents and caused a chasm to exist between the parents and the special education teachers.

"I haven't talked with Tony," the director had said. "And, actually, I don't plan on talking to him, unless you think there is a need for me to do so. I've already checked the references you listed on your resume." I had felt incredibly surprised and relieved (and impressed) that this man was willing to look at my long-term history and my current skills without talking to my previous special education director (Tony).

Listening to Steve hurl the words *incite parent*s made me wonder if, in fact, Tony hadn't indeed been contacted, and if my current principal hadn't been given a "heads up" to watch out for any behavior that suggested this might be an issue with me.

I looked at Steve, saying nothing as this entire scenario was playing out in my head. And as the pieces seemed to start fitting together, it felt like kindling being placed on a huge bonfire that was just waiting to be lit.

"Okay, good," Steve said. "I'm glad that this didn't go to parents."

That's it? I thought. *You summon me to your office for the first time and freak me out with your anger, and suddenly it's 'Okay—good. Good-bye'?* This was just so alien to any of my prior experiences with principals that I couldn't walk out the door and let the meeting end on that note.

"Where did this come from, Steve? I mean, how—*out of the blue*—did you make this assumption that I would race to parents and get them all upset about the services? If you knew me at all, you would know that's not the way I work."

"Well, I'm still getting to know you, Debra."

"No, Steve. Actually...you're not. You've never even stepped foot inside my classroom. You have no idea what I'm doing over there or how I do it." I could feel a flush of resentment and irritation pulsating through me.

Calm down, Debra. Calm down. You cannot *afford to alienate this man.* It was requiring a tremendous amount of cognitive energy for me to stay calm, but I was trying very hard not to respond with the kind of intensity I perceived had caused me so much strife in Blanding.

"Well, to tell you the truth, I actually forget you're over there," Steve said. "I mean, you know...you psychologists are like phantoms—you sit in your towers with one student at a time. It's not like you have a regular classroom." Steve's tone was not particularly disdainful or critical; it was more a tone of simple disregard, as if educational psychologists—and, I had to assume, me in particular at this point in time—simply were not worth the attention he would have to put into getting to know what we do.

I had already observed one very clear fact about this man, and that was that there were two priorities in his school: the scores on the standardized tests and how the sports programs were progressing.

I had nothing to do with either. At least not in his perception.

"Well...I resent that a *lot*," I said, in response to his *phantom* remark. I heard a biting edge attach itself to my words, and I could feel another load of kindling being tossed on top of that bonfire. "First of all, I almost *never* have just one student in my room, unless we are testing; and if we are, there's a sign on the door. If kids want to talk to me privately, they can set up an appointment, but generally my approach is to teach them skills and go through problem-solving sessions either in the context of the classroom where they are having problems or in the context of a group of their peers. Both are—in my experience, anyway—more effective change agents than putting a kid in a thirty-minute counseling session once a week. I mean, there is certainly a place for counseling sessions, don't get me wrong...but one of the beauties of being here in a city is that most of these kids have outside psychologists and psychiatrists. I don't need to put my focus into that aspect as long as I connect with the provider of those services. I can concentrate on school-based behaviors so they can be successful here. And if you came in and watched, Steve, you would *see* that what these kids are learning is critical to every aspect of their academic and social success—including improving their test scores."

I probably shouldn't have said this—it most likely sounded challenging, but I couldn't help myself. I was infuriated that I had worked in this building for over three months, and this man had no clue what I did. In truth, I was still simmering over the fact that on the high wind day, no one had so much as cursorily checked in to see if we needed anything.

"So, anyway," I tacked on, "I am almost never in there one on one with a student, and very little of what I do is so confidential that it can't be observed."

Although, I thought, *it would be a heck of a lot easier on my brain if I did just sit in there and see each kid thirty minutes a week individually.*

"Not to mention," I went on, knowing I should stop talking, but apparently unable to stop myself, "there are fourteen students in my homeroom class every day, Steve. That class mirrors the process and procedures those boys are expected to adhere to in every one of their classes, and every day we have well-formulated lessons that are helping them manage the demands of a classroom, their teachers, and their peers. You are welcome to come in at any time and see what we do in there. My door is always open."

I looked at Steve, no doubt, righteous indignation clinging to every line on my face. In reflection, I might have actually been a tad intimidating to Steve at that point—no matter how mucked up my brain might still be in some areas, my ability to spout off a litany of well-articulated rebuttals to his accusations seemed to be resoundingly intact.

Steve looked at me from across his desk. "I suppose I do have my stereotypes about you psychologist types, Debra, and maybe you don't fit what I'm used to thinking of as a school psychologist. I probably do need to make an effort to get in there and see what you do. What you're saying makes sense."

Yeah, well, no shit! I thought as it struck me that the look on Steve's face suggested *he* was suddenly wondering why he had been angry over an email that, in fact, contained nothing inflammatory.

Truth was, I actually liked Steve a lot, and I felt, in spite of his leadership flaws, he really did have a lot of heart for kids. I think I wanted to give him the benefit of the doubt that he was leaving our meeting as confused as I was.

Our meeting had taken forty-five minutes that neither one of us had to spare. I was already late for lunch duty; however, I knew if I waited to write down the notes of this meeting, I would not remember any of the details. So, even though I knew that I would not score points with the assistant principal by being late to my duty, I went to my office and scribbled out notes. Later that night I could refine them and write a follow-up memo to the principal, reiterating my invitation for him to stop by my room at any time.

The forty-five-minute meeting and the extra eight or so minutes that it took to write my notes cost me a lot more pennies than I had to spend. As I had been doing so often, I wondered if the day would *ever* come when I would be able to manage stressful situations, conflicts, or just an excess of interactions without having to budget my pennies. I was so tired of budgeting my pennies.

Actually, I was just so tired.

* * * * *

The very next day, Steve poked his head into our room and said good morning to the students and me. He didn't come into the room, much less watch what we were doing, but I told myself it was a start. A start that felt very encouraging to me and left me feeling that maybe, in time, things would smooth out between us.

Unfortunately, that hope was somewhat dashed when later in the day—at a seventh grade team meeting—my principal blithely tossed off a one-liner that *now* he knew why kids wanted to be in *Ms. Sanders'* homeroom. Instead of homeroom, he informed the team with a laugh, *they* got to do art projects.

I suppose two chopsticks and a ball of yarn might look like an art project to an uninformed observer who has no idea of their purpose.

The more I thought about that, the more upset I became. I was new to this school and to this state. In Alaska, having been a past president of the state association and having won awards such as school psychologist of the year and adjunct college faculty member of the year, I had a well-established reputation. Here I was an unknown to all of these teachers. No one in this school had been to any of my workshops or trainings. No one had seen what I do or how I do it with students. Certainly no one had ever seen me teach in the classroom. Despite his joking demeanor, what these teachers had just heard from the principal was that kids got to goof off in my classroom, and that's why they liked being there.

My kindling-loaded bonfire was beginning to feel a little scary to me.

Jonathon
Late November 2005

"So, how's the woman I love to hate?" Denise asked, as we were talking on the phone one evening. She was in her fifth month of chemotherapy, and doing remarkably well. She was tired. She was sleeping a lot and her nutritional issues still concerned me, but overall she was holding up well. Denise's hair, still soft and silky although now cut to chin length, made all of us feel like somehow she was stronger than both the cancer and the chemotherapy. She had lost over eighty pounds, and, admittedly, she looked the best she had looked in years. She was even talking about going back to her classroom after the first of the year.

"I can't believe you call her that," I said, referring to the way Denise always referred to my assistant principal. Despite her Christian charity, sometimes Denise's irreverence just did my heart good.

"Well, I love hearing about her," Denise said. "It always astounds me. So, tell me, what kind of trouble did you get into today, Missy?" It always made me laugh when Denise called me *Missy*—a name usually reserved for use with their daughter when she had cut out on doing her chores.

"Oh, you don't even want to hear this one," I said. "I'd keep you on the phone all night." It had certainly been one of my more trying days.

"I do want to hear. What else am I going to entertain myself with? My cold fingers?"

"What do you mean your cold fingers?"

"Oh, it's a side effect of the chemo. My fingers are so sensitive that I can't even take a carton of milk out of the refrigerator without wearing gloves."

"Are you serious, Denise? Is that normal? I've never heard of that as a side effect before."

"It's not a big deal. Come on...I want to hear what happened today."

I was pretty sure Denise had been getting vicarious pleasure out of my endless kid stories since she was not working in her own classroom for the first time in almost fifteen years. And I was always happy to oblige her because it was a rare day that I didn't have some amusing or outright funny experience or observation to relay. Lately, however, as more and more issues seemed to crop up between the assistant principal and me, Denise had taken to calling me in the evenings at home or at school to get her "daily update" on this woman who so frustrated me. A couple of days earlier, I had been venting my frustration and anger to Denise after the administrator had determined that I would no longer be allowed to place Marcus in a time-out situation in Mrs. A's room.

This had been such an effective intervention strategy because it not only kept Marcus from being suspended and thus home alone, it also required that he work on schoolwork while demonstrating the skills of remaining focused, quiet, and on task. There had only been one time in the last several months when this intervention even had to be used with Marcus (it was a very effective deterrent to his acting-out behaviors!), but on that day he did get into trouble and he was sent to Mrs. A's room.

According to Mrs. A, Marcus was perfect. So perfect, in fact, that she actually forgot he was in her classroom. Marcus completed all of his schoolwork, wrote the necessary apology along with the completed plan of action he had created to avoid making the same mistakes again, and then he returned to his classes and performed beautifully for the rest of the day. Unfortunately, his first period teacher (who sent him to Mrs. A) forgot to tell the second period teacher where he was (not surprising, since it was such a seldom-used intervention), and Marcus was marked absent from his second period class. This created a bit of chaos until it was all straightened out, but instead of helping me or the teachers come up with a more fail-proof system, the assistant principal said we were done using that intervention and from now on Marcus would just be suspended.

Denise had had to listen to me rant and rave over that one for about fifteen minutes, and because she herself had gone through a very stressful time with a similar type of administrator several years ago, she was a wonderfully empathetic sounding board for me.

"Aren't you sick of hearing my sad school tales, Denise?" I asked, figuring maybe after the Marcus story she wanted a break from my trials and tribulations with the school's assistant principal.

"Nope," Denise said. "What happened?"

So, I began to tell Denise about Jonathon.

* * * * *

Jonathon was a seventh grade student who came to my attention very early in the school year. A pale, thin boy with a number of nervous mannerisms, Jonathon had frustrated his teachers to no end the year before and, early on, presented innumerable problems in his current classrooms. He was classified as a student in special education due to what was identified in the records as a severe manifestation of attention deficits and hyperactivity (ADHD). Indeed, those were clearly issues influencing his behavior and impacting his ability to learn. But to me, Jonathon was more than just a child with ADHD.

Jonathon's intelligence was obvious, despite the fact that like many troubled or challenged students, he produced little or no work in the classroom. He would display extreme stress reactions to routine demands. While this also is true of some students with severe hyperactivity and attention deficit disorders, Jonathon exhibited characteristics not generally associated with hyperactivity and ADHD. Children with ADHD are frequently distracted by too many things around them and thus unable to filter out the extraneous stimuli and focus on what's important. But Jonathon seemed more distracted by his own internal world. Teachers perceived him as oppositional, stubborn, and "spoiled"—feeling that he expected those around him to do the work for him while demanding nothing of him. I could see how his behavior would be interpreted this way by a classroom teacher, but my own observations suggested that Jonathon's behaviors were not the result of an indulged child who was simply unwilling to put effort into anything that was challenging or difficult.

Jonathon was as disorganized a child as I had ever seen, and no matter what strategies had been employed in the past, none appeared to have taken root. When Jonathon was pushed by teachers to focus and pay attention, or to adhere to the same academic and behavioral expectations demanded of the other students, he displayed a variety of extreme behaviors such as crying, dumping over a chair, discharging a string of rather surprising expletives directed toward the teacher, and banging his head in frustration. His fingernails were ragged. Peers and teachers both feared that at any moment, this boy was going to either explode or implode, and neither of these options sat well with anyone.

Jonathon fidgeted and he fretted; he obsessed on ideas, objects, and thoughts; and the manifestations of what appeared to be feelings of extreme rage were evident. I wasn't sure what was going on with Jonathon, but I had successfully worked with children with varying levels and intensity of attention deficits and hyperactivity disorders for twenty years, and I felt pretty confident that if, in fact, Jonathon had ADHD, this was but a small part of what he was dealing with.

Early in the school year, Jonathon, along with several others, had been in my room during the lunch period. Because so many kids found themselves wandering into my room at that time, I established a "Lunch Bunch" program, which accommodated the first twenty kids who signed up before school started each morning. While the *Guidelines For Success* were clear and unwavering, as long as they were followed, the kids had freedom during this time to listen to music, work on puzzles, talk in small groups, or play chess or cards; or just wander around and participate in a distant sort of way, if this is what they preferred.

The beauty of the Lunch Bunch program was that although several of my kids were there each day, so were some of the "popular" kids, the "cool" kids, and the "smart" kids. So, not only did this become a time that helped break down the stigma of anything related to special education, it afforded me fabulous role models and real-time situations to refer to when working with my kids on their social skills (or lack thereof). Some great role-playing scripts were created around Lunch Bunch scenarios.

It was about the second week of school when the topic of bullying popped up in conversation during the Lunch Bunch. Jonathon, along with another boy—a sixth grader—tuned right into the discussion. Jonathon made the comment that he was bullied all the time by other kids and that it made him mad. He also noted that he had a problem with anger management. The sixth grade student also spoke of being bullied his whole life and hating it, and having trouble managing his anger. I told both boys that I was thinking about offering a class or group in anger and stress management, and that I would be sure to let both of them know if, in fact, the class became established.

The next day there was a knock at my door, and opening it, I saw Jonathon standing there—so rigid and pale that every freckle stood out as if each were defiantly claiming its dominant position on his face.

"I'm here for your class," he stated, looking for all his assertiveness as if a breath of air would blow him over.

"My class?" I asked.

"Your *anger management* class," Jonathon said, tension punctuating every word. Jonathon's level of tension was so extreme as to seem nearly palpable—as if, like a too-taut guitar string, it would simply snap and pling at the slightest touch.

"Jonathon," I said. "I haven't started that class yet. I don't have a class this period." This was, in fact, my scheduled block for testing students.

Jonathon's level of anxiety instantly billowed and pitched; and as various shades of crimson spotted his face and neck, his fingers twisted around one another like an old woman's. In a voice shaky with what appeared to be barely contained seething, he stated, "But I am mad **NOW**. I am ready **NOW**." The look Jonathon gave me as he stared straight into my eyes seemed to be one of such absolute wretchedness and anguish that it made my heart ache.

It took several days before I could get Jonathon to let go of the idea of coming to my room every day for an anger management class. He obsessed all day long on his need for what he would call "that class," and it was difficult for him to concentrate on anything else. I could only conclude that this boy was in such a state of despair that he had latched on to the notion of *that class* as if it were the last life raft on a sinking ship.

By the time we had initiated the homeroom class, I knew a great deal more about what worked with Jonathon and what did not. I had a strong suspicion that he, too, displayed many of the characteristics of a student with Asperger's syndrome, and about a month after the homeroom class had been in session, this observation was strongly reinforced.

We were in a stress management group that both Jonathon and Abe participated in twice a week. Abe referred to a strategy we had been practicing during homeroom, and Jonathon, in response, asked with genuine curiosity if Abe was in our homeroom.

"Jonathon, are you saying that you don't *know* if Abe is in our homeroom?" I asked him with some surprise.

"Well...I hardly ever look around."

I gently asked Jonathon if he knew how many students were in our class, and he said, "Well, I have heard it said that there are fourteen." He could identify three by name. Given that most of our lessons involved cooperative activities, and that students were expected to respectfully address one another, the fact that Jonathon could only identify three classmates was a stunning piece of information.

This revelation so surprised me that I immediately conducted an informal experiment with Jonathon that I had learned to use with students suspected of falling on the Asperger's continuum. I asked him to watch my eyes and tell me what he thought I was looking at, and to then tell me what he thought I might be thinking about. As I looked at a series of ten different objects, Jonathon missed on both counts, 100% of the time. Sometimes his gaze would land a foot beyond or before where I was looking; at other times, Jonathon's assessment of where I was looking was even further off than that. And, of course, Jonathon could never accurately guess what I might be thinking about, because his eyes were never landing on the same object as mine.

I felt like a coffee junkie after a triple latte topped off with a few chocolate-covered espresso beans. It suddenly seemed so obvious! How could I have missed this? Every one of Jonathon's behaviors fit so perfectly within this framework. This was not a willful and obstinate boy. This was not a hyperactive teenager who just needed to focus more in order to perform appropriately. This was a boy with *Asperger's syndrome*—a child with a qualitative impairment that resulted in his intense and narrow preoccupations, his inflexible adherence to certain topics and routines, and his failure to develop appropriate peer relationships. Jonathon was not intentionally resistive. Jonathon lacked the ability to read the behavior of others, to regulate his anxiety, to integrate sensory information, and to perform such expected tasks as being able to monitor and shift his thought processes in order to perform on a teacher's schedule rather than on his own.

Asperger's syndrome can manifest itself in many different ways, and suddenly I was sure that Jonathon, just like Jess and Antonio, needed to be directly taught the skills he was lacking. Once we gain information about a student, our job as educators is to figure out how to teach not just academics, but all those skills a student must have in order to function in a school (or work) environment—skills we often assume a student has, but which may, in fact, be glaringly absent.

Jonathon's mother had been coming into school at the end of each day to check in with me regarding the events of Jonathon's day. She was a diligent and willing participant in making sure his school program had a good chance of succeeding, and after I shared my insights with her, she was equally excited to try out some strategies that might make life in their household a bit less stressful. Because his dad had been deployed to Iraq, Jonathon's mother was a single parent to Jonathon and his two younger sisters.

It's amazing how many good things can happen once we make that shift from thinking a child *won't* to recognizing that a child *can't*. Suddenly, it isn't about a power struggle between a student and his teachers or a teenager and his parents. It's about figuring out how to help a kid make sense out of his world and develop strategies to function in what—to him—are unbearably anxious situations. It's about understanding that this is a student who is not interpreting such basic things as directions, instructions, expectations, and social etiquette in a way anything like you or I do. And it's about developing the strategies and interventions that will maximize his chances of success.

Although Jonathon required a disproportionate amount of my time and energy, there was no doubt in my mind that the road ahead was going to be far, far more manageable. And to me that was incredibly exciting.

By mid-November, Jonathon was as happy as his parents had ever seen him. His dad was home on leave. Jonathon seemed to feel that, for the first time in his life, he had a peer group that accepted him. He was managing his behavior and stress reactions better in his classes. It was unfortunate that no time could be sanctioned for Jonathon's teachers to receive training in how to approach his learning style and needs; all training time had been allocated to the more traditional topics that focused on increasing student test scores. Still, his teachers were willing partners, and to the extent possible, they seemed to work hard to understand and teach this very complex child.

One afternoon in late October, as we were sitting together after school, Jonathon's mother asked if she could speak with me alone. "I have a question," she said, hesitating and appearing a little uncomfortable.

"What's up?" I asked, after shooing all the stragglers out the door.

"Well, we have an opportunity to move off Post...to move out of our apartment into our own home."

"Oh, my gosh, that's fabulous," I said, imagining that the extra space would be a welcomed addition to their family of five. "Have you found one yet?"

"Maybe. That's what I wanted to ask you about. It's not in this district, it's in District Two, and we don't want to see Jonathon have to start all over. He's getting so much out of this year, and there's never been this kind of help for him before. We don't want to move if it means he has to leave this school."

At that point, I should have immediately suggested to her that she approach the administrators about a waiver, but that thought never crossed my mind. In my homeroom alone, I had several students who did not live within this school zone, but who had waivers to attend Carson Middle School for one reason or other.

"Oh, wow. I can't imagine that would be a problem at all," I said, with my usual unfiltered enthusiasm. "I mean, there are tons of kids who attend school here who live within the boundaries of other districts."

"So, you think he could still go to this school, at least for the remainder of this school year, even if we moved off Post?"

"Well, I can't imagine why not," I repeated. "I mean, we finally have his program figured out, and we know so much more about how to help him—how to teach him. I certainly can't imagine why we wouldn't keep him."

In my mind, watching the relief and joy this family was experiencing, as hope for positive change had begun to factor into their lives, was ample reward for the time it had taken us to reach this point. The hard part was behind us, and we were in the wonderful position of being able to implement a program that truly met Jonathon's educational needs. Of *course* we would keep him! And so, before Jonathon's dad headed back to Iraq, they bought and moved into their dream home.

It had never occurred to me, I told Denise, that I would be alone in my thinking.

* * * * *

"Oh, shit. What happened?" Denise asked, although she had probably intuited the end to this story.

"The assistant principal said no. She said we would not keep Jonathon." I paused for a moment as the full impact of my guilt and anguish over this situation began to emerge. "Denise, they already bought a house in another district's zone. They wouldn't have done that if they thought Jonathon could not continue to go to school here."

I had truly been feeling ill since my discussion with the assistant principal earlier in the day. I had gone into her office to talk about something else that involved Jonathon, when she said, "Well, we won't have to worry about that much longer. He's outta here." She motioned to the door with her thumb. "They've moved."

"Oh, no. We can't *do* that! We can't make him leave now," I said, horrified at the thought of what she was suggesting.

"Sorry, Debra, he is too high a timer to keep when he doesn't live in this area. He's gone!" As she was saying this, she smiled. Not gleefully or in any sort of sinister way, but in the way that indicated this was nothing more than a joke between us, or perhaps that we were merely sharing a casual conversation.

"Listen to me, please," I said. "This is a kid with Asperger's. Every change is literally *painful* for him. His dad just left again for Iraq; they've already moved into their new home—they needed to do that before Pete left for Iraq. Jonathon is already struggling with being in a new and unfamiliar house, not to mention a new neighborhood. We can't ask that he start over in a new school." It was true that Jonathon's behavior had significantly deteriorated over the last couple of weeks since they made the move and his dad left for Iraq. However, I was confident that we could stabilize his behavior once they settled into the new home, and Jonathon was secure that things at school remained constant.

"He's bonded to the kids in homeroom class...they help him. They *like* him, for God's sake; they embrace his idiosyncrasies as a part of him." I looked at her, adding, "He calls them his *friends*. That's *huge*. Jonathan has never, ever had friends at school."

I looked at this woman in the well-tailored suit, with the expensive haircut and groomed fingernails, and in my need to change her mind, I could feel myself on the cusp of some sort of emotional outburst that I was trying very hard to contain. It wasn't anger I felt. Not at that moment, anyway. It was despair.

Despair and a desperation that bordered on panic.

"Sorry, Debra. We're not keeping him."

"But the hard work is behind us. We've *done* all the time-consuming work; we *know* how to manage him now. Surely, what it would cost this school if he stays is nowhere *near* what it will cost Jonathon and his family if we make him leave. Please reconsider this. Please."

"Holy shit," said Denise. "What did she say?"

"Nothing. Absolutely nothing. She just raised her eyebrows and looked at me, shaking her head as if to convey, *Tough luck, Debra.*"

There was silence between Denise and me over the phone—the kind of silence that speaks volumes between two passionate educators who cannot fathom decisions being made that are so contrary to a child's best interests.

"I can tell you this, Denise. I have never felt worse about anything in my whole professional career, and considering the last year, that's saying a lot. And I *don't* want to tell his mother. I really do not want to have to tell this to his mother."

The thought of explaining that Jonathon was not going to be allowed to stay at the middle school was paralyzing. I felt so horribly guilty and responsible. There was no doubt in my mind that if I had never expressed my sureness and enthusiasm, these parents would have approached the administration early on—and, in so doing, would have heard the administrator's position that Jonathon would not be accepted as an out-of-district placement. They may have found their dream home, but I suspect they would have let it pass them by if what it meant was starting over in a new school.

Never, I thought. *Never in one million years would Carl, Jim, Mary, or for that matter any principal I had ever worked for, have made this call. Never.*

Of that, I had no doubt. Not once in over twenty years had I needed to beg for the right thing to happen for a child—beg for what was in a student's best interest. I had worked with plenty of rigid and traditional principals, and certainly I had had to negotiate, bend, convince, and demonstrate success, but in the end, I had never had to beg for a student to remain in their school. Even Tony had somehow found the funds to hire an additional aide for Ernie so that his program could be effectively sustained.

Tony may have frustrated me at times with what I perceived as his acceptance of mediocrity, but never once had I observed him to make a purposeful decision that was not in the best interests of a student.

Not once.

The bundle of kindling on top of the bonfire was becoming frighteningly large.

Brush Fires

"Oh, I am so jazzed about this!"

I was talking with Kathryn, the speech and language pathologist who had collaborated with me on a recent assessment.

I respected Kathryn a great deal, and I liked her immensely. Working with her reminded me of my collaboration days in Alaska—a time when the speech people and I routinely worked together, combining our respective skills to figure out why a student wasn't making progress, and then developing intervention strategies that would help their teachers work with them more effectively.

"This is just so great!" I said. "I mean, this makes so much sense and gives us a whole new understanding of how to approach teaching her!"

We had just returned from the Christmas vacation, and I was conducting an assessment on a sixth grade girl who had been in special education for several years. This girl reminded me of Heather in many ways—she was sweet and pretty, and teachers in the classroom appreciated her quiet and cooperative manner. Like Heather, this girl hadn't been making progress, although her area of challenge was in reading, not math. Studying her records just as thoroughly as I had studied Heather's, it occurred to me that previous testing and teacher comments were reflective of the kinds of scores and comments I might expect to hear about a child who was experiencing an auditory processing disorder.

Unless someone is specifically looking for this, it is very easy to assume that students with auditory processing disorders are simply not paying attention, or are not trying very hard in the classroom and on their homework. Especially because these students can hear just fine and almost always pass the routine hearing screenings conducted at school in the fall, it's easy to miss that academic delays are related to a problem within their ears. Well, not so much in their ears as within their brains. It's the *interpreting* of what they hear that goes so amiss with kids with this disorder. My many years in Alaska and Utah of having to differentiate between students with **limited English proficiency**, ones with a **language-based learning disability,** and ones with **auditory processing disorders** had made me particularly sensitive to catching the red flags suggesting which one of these issues was the likely culprit in impairing a student's academic progress.

Earlier in the week, I had emailed the director of special education and asked him if the district had audiologists who could be consulted in the event that auditory processing disorders were suspected. I explained what my review of this student's records suggested to me, and asked if it was possible to have an audiologist collaborate on her assessment.

His response, indicating that neither he nor anyone else would be so "arrogant" as to assume people had not done their earlier assessments adequately, not only did not address my question about audiologists, but left me feeling embarrassed that he had so misinterpreted what I was asking. I wasn't criticizing early assessments. I was excited to think we might have latched on to an explanation for this girl's lack of progress. In fact, everything I had seen in her records suggested that she had had excellent instruction through the special education program. That was, in fact, one of the "red flags" for me. Finding that a student has had good instruction but has not made expected progress—in combination with seeing a high number of teacher comments regarding lack of attention, poor listening skills, and trouble carrying out instructions given orally—was an exceptionally common pattern in children found with undiagnosed auditory processing disorders.

After receiving what I came to think of as the humiliating "arrogance admonishment email," I had contacted Kathryn, the speech pathologist for the school, to ask if she had any auditory processing assessment or screening tools. She did and agreed to conduct an informal screening. What we found was that this student scored below the first percentile on several of the screening items, and that, in fact, she had particular difficulty discriminating between vowel sounds and end-of-the-word sounds. So, she might, for example, hear the word *grief* but interpret it as the word *grease*. One can imagine how confusing that would get in a classroom when listening to the teacher talk and trying to figure out the relationship between, say, the death of Ophelia and grease.

Kathryn and I were both excited, not that the student had an auditory processing disorder, of course, but that the distinct possibility of one meant we could help teachers develop an appropriate program and put some compensatory strategies and modifications in place.

I wrote a brief report and submitted it to the computer program we all used to enter our respective data. The report summarized a list of characteristics commonly observed in children with this type of disorder, and it summarized the information I had gathered. Only an audiologist is qualified to diagnose an auditory processing disorder, and at the end of my report, I stated that it would be up to the IEP team to determine if an audiologist should be consulted, but that it was my recommendation that we do so due to the number of identified characteristics that this student displayed.

Several days later, I was standing beside the assistant principal following our weekly staff meeting when she told me that she had deleted much of the information I had entered in my report on this student.

"You *what*?" I could not believe that she had just informed me that she had taken the liberty of picking and choosing what went into a psychoeducational report.

"We can't be stating things like you did in that report, Debra. If a district three years up the road reads that and sees that we had information we didn't act upon, they could come back and sue us."

I stared at her, and in that tone that seemed to sneak out when I was truly shocked, truly appalled at professional behavior, I said quietly, "As well they should." A moment later I added, "What is the point in our doing assessments if we don't act on the information the assessment generates?"

"Debra, I've spoken with the director of special education; he has seen your report, and he agreed with me. So it's been deleted. We left in the first paragraph."

The first paragraph simply stated that the reason for the evaluation was that it was part of the triennial assessment, and that previous evaluations substantiated average intellectual ability, so a current IQ test was determined unnecessary.

"He *agreed* with you? I can't believe he agreed with you. I mean...I believe you, I am just so...surprised."

To eliminate the body of my report meant there would be no record of the suspected processing disorder, not to mention that it seemed to imply that we were not going to modify this girl's program to address the concerns or consult an audiologist.

I hesitated, knowing that using the "ethics" word could be risky, but, in fact, everything in me was screaming that what this administrator had done was highly unethical. I didn't even know if it was legal. Could an administrator just delete a professional's report against that professional's recommendation? In the more than fifteen hundred reports I had written over the span of my career, this had never been a consideration. The one and only time altering a report had been requested was the time that Jim and Carl were willing to spend $18,000 to stand behind my professional judgment that no information should be deleted and the report should remain as written.

"I don't know if ethically I can agree to this... This is a military kid... These families move a *lot*... Other schools will need this kind of information so they don't go through another three years of teaching her ineffectively. Once I suspected this as a possible explanation for her lack of progress, I called the special education teacher from her elementary school to see what she thought. She thought it fit *perfectly* with everything she had seen over the last three years and only wished she had known so that she could have approached teaching her differently. We can't just *not include* this in her records..." I said, staring at my administrator, undoubtedly with a look of disbelief on my face.

"Well, Debra, that's the director's decision."

"Well, can I put a copy of the report in her file at least? So that there will be a hard copy of the information in her file when they transfer?"

"No. In the state of Colorado, only the IEP gets sent to a receiving school."

"What? That's not possible!" I said. "I mean, are you saying that we don't send on the whole file that we have? What about a student like Joey?" Joey's file was at least two inches thick. "Are you saying that none of that information would go with him if he were to move? None of my progress reports, or the records from the psychiatric hospital, or previous history collected? Where does it go?"

"It all goes into an archive file, and after a number of years—I forget how many—they get destroyed."

"That's a state regulation?" I asked, incredulous.

"That is a state regulation."

Don't rock the boat, Debra, I said to myself. *Do not rock the boat. You have just returned from Christmas vacation...you do not want to start this semester off with more conflict.*

I walked away without saying more, but this conversation would gnaw and grind at me for several months. It wouldn't be until April, but ultimately I would not be able to quietly ignore the decisions being made that adversely impacted students, and I would begin to ask questions. Many questions. And it would make sense to me to ask others outside of this school about the reliability of the information I was receiving regarding records, transfer of files, and the way business was being conducted with kids with special needs.

And, boy, when I started to ask questions, would the bonfire be torched.

More Brush Fires
Still in January 2006

"Okay, gentlemen," I said, noticing that the assistant principal had entered our room and slid into a chair. "Today we're having a scavenger hunt!"

"All right!" I heard, as several of the boys cheered.

Holding up my hand to indicate I needed quiet, I continued. "The packets in front you contain all the information you will need today." I held up a paper that looked like the one in the front of their packet. "Everybody see this page in the front of your packet?" Fourteen affirmative nods. "Okay, our scavenger hunt is a scavenger hunt of *questions*, and all the answers are in your packets!"

A few groans could be heard as the reality settled in that I wasn't going to send them in search of crazy objects or hidden food.

"Okay, I admit...this is not the most creative of scavenger hunts I have designed. *BUT*...it *is* a scavenger hunt, and I know every one of you can find the answers. So, listen carefully, because this is the last time I can talk for the rest of the lesson! You guys need to read your instructions carefully. *Very* carefully. Your instructions will tell you everything you need to know, and guide you through the hunt step by step. Okay, tell me all at once: what are you supposed to do?"

There was a choral response of something along the lines of *"Read the directions!"*

Good. I knew I had them all engaged.

"And *how* carefully are you supposed to read them?" I asked.

"*Verrrrrrry carefully*," the boys all responded.

Excellent. Not just engaged, but they were actually listening carefully.

"All righty, then! You guys ready? Remember, I cannot talk until the bell rings." I held up my stopwatch. "Begin!"

How each boy performed this assignment would let me know if they were actually able to apply what we had been practicing in homeroom to the general classroom setting. It was actually a complicated lesson to have put together, and I had never tried anything like it before. I didn't know that I would be observed when planning this lesson, and I could only hope it would go well.

I had written out an explanation and an instruction sheet for the two paraeducators I now had in my room most homeroom periods. Because we were given no planning time, the only way I could give them a "head's up" on what I needed them to do was to write it out and hope they took the time to read it. I certainly had learned my lesson in Blanding, and was not about to ask any paraeducator to stay thirty minutes past their scheduled day to receive training, information, or any other extra input. I would not want to make any offer to stay after and work with them to be misinterpreted as a "directive" or as if I was "instructing them to stay."

No indeed. I had learned that lesson well.

For the purposes of today's lesson, each paraeducator had received a set of white boards that contained my drawings (or my attempt at drawings) of amusing cartoon stick figures saying things like, "I am so, so sorry. Your mean teacher will not let me talk today! Take a deep breath and keep reading!" and, "You are doing great! Remember to stay calm and read carefully!" and, "Remember, I am not allowed to answer questions. All the answers are in your packets, I promise!"

In the paraeducator handout, it explained that today's lesson was actually intentionally confusing, *unless the boys read their first page carefully*. If the boys read carefully, as I explained in the handout to the paraeducators, in the first paragraph it told them to *stop reading* and turn to page five. From that point on, instructions were written clearly and would be easily understood by each boy.

This entire lesson had been inspired after watching several of the seventh grade boys try to complete a geography assignment that, because they did not read carefully, resulted in confusion and overwhelm, which ultimately kept them from completing the assignment. After speaking with their teacher, I decided to develop this lesson so that the boys could have their own "Ah-Ha!" experience and identify for themselves the negative impact of impulsively jumping to conclusions, not taking time to read instructions carefully, and forgetting to ask clarifying questions (all skills we had been working on in our homeroom lessons).

The paraeducators' job in this lesson was to observe and record behaviors and to refrain from engaging in any verbal interaction with the boys. To facilitate the latter, they were to display the white boards each time one of the students blurted out or raised their hand to ask a question. My instructions outlined that the paraeducators were to look encouraging and supportive, but under no circumstances were they to engage in conversation with the boys. They were to make notes, if possible, regarding their observations of the boys, particularly if they noticed them using any of the strategies we had been practicing or, contrarily, were exhibiting behaviors we had been working on eliminating.

I was a bit nervous that the assistant principal had wandered in today of all days, but I had no time to focus on my own reaction. Immediately upon hearing me say "Begin!" the boys started shouting out, and my own white boards of encouraging stick figures and cartoons were flashing.

By the end of the period, I was thrilled. Initially the boys panicked, of that there was no doubt. But as white boards flashed before them, they laughed when they read that their mean teacher (me) wasn't letting any adult speak, and they began to calm down. And when I saw them calm and reading, I would hold a board in front of them with a statement such as: "Good job reading carefully!" and I would smile in encouragement. But I would not speak.

One by one as the minutes went by, the boys could be heard to utter, "Oh, jeez," or "I get it now!" and I would see them turn to page five.

"Five minutes to go, Ms. Sanders!" Jess told us in his usual daily role as my timekeeper. I had come to think of Jess as Tonto to my Lone Ranger—I sure couldn't function without him. I had about six clocks around the room, including one that was huge—the face of it being about twelve inches by twelve inches—but nothing worked for me as well as Jess and his precision awareness of time. I had long ago learned that an ongoing side effect for me of my own injury was that ten hours could go by, and to me it would always feel like ten minutes.

Those boys shone like diamonds that morning. Not only was I as proud as I could be of them, I was extremely grateful and relieved. Our daily process and procedure had been followed without a hitch, and the boys had been orderly, polite, prepared, and on task the entire time. Not that I expected differently. I had long been hearing from all their teachers that the change in each of them was very noticeable and that they were, in fact, actually standing out among their peers as models of good classroom behavior. I was just really glad that this morning hadn't been one of those mornings of regression that sometimes happens. After all, it was the first time anyone had come in to watch a lesson.

The assistant principal left, and I was riding high on that feeling of success every teacher has when a class goes exactly as planned. When I got an email to meet in her office the next morning at 9:00 a.m. to go over her observations, I was actually excited. It would be fun to hear her observations of how far the boys had come this year. It was that mother-hen piece of me—I always loved hearing how well my boys were doing.

Before heading home for the day, I composed a memo to the two paraprofessionals, congratulating all of us for the successes observed in the boys, along with information regarding things we still needed to work on. In it, I stated:

> **Best News:** They ALL handled their frustration and ended up working quietly (YaHOO!). Marcus did not get sarcastic; Winston did not get angry; Michael did not put his head down; Kevin did not cry; Joey did not sit, stare, and zone out when he felt confused; Jess did not demand attention or applause and approval when he realized he had figured out what to do.

> **Huge Successes:** Winston found something to do once he finished the Choice page, AND, when he first began and was so frustrated and tried (as he will often do) to distract his neighbors, MARCUS and MICHAEL told him to be quiet so they could focus!!!! (They really ARE learning this stuff, ladies!!!!).

> **Great Insight:** Humor, using the white boards, worked really well as a strategy to keep them focused without getting ourselves engaged in distracting interaction with them, and as a bonus, seemed to really calm them down! Yea! One more new strategy that worked!!! ☺

I finished the memo, ending with the following:

> I am changing some of the things on the lesson plan for Wednesday, based on information gathered today, and I will email it to you when finished. Thanks **TONS** for your help today. It will be interesting a month from now to do a similar lesson and see if they do better in the areas of weakness.
>
> If you made any additional observations, please email them to me, as I am quite sure I missed a **LOT.** And again, you two were awesome and I thank you!!!

I sent the email off to both of them and left for home feeling tired, but still elated over the day.

* * * * *

"Well, Debra," my assistant principal said, sitting behind her desk, wearing a tailored pink suit and accessorized beautifully, "I must say...you certainly gave your paraeducators a demeaning task. I can see why they were upset."

"What?" I was stunned. This was hardly what I had anticipated.

"I mean, Debra, giving them white boards to hold up and not letting them speak? I have to admit, I would feel pretty demeaned if I was the paraeducator in that position."

I stared at her, having a hard time believing what I was hearing. "You thought that was demeaning?"

"Wouldn't you?"

"No! No, I wouldn't have. I mean, it was funny. And it calmed the boys down. Did you see how upset Winston was, and how instead of getting angry and shutting down like he usually does, he actually calmed down and participated?" Winston was a sixth grader in the homeroom class, and a boy who responded to every instance of frustration with anger. Of all the kids yesterday, I was the most pleased by his ability to use the strategies we had been practicing to keep going with the lesson. I stared at my chicly attired administrator, and suddenly asked, "Did you read the lesson plan before coming in there? I mean, do you know what we were doing?"

"I only know that it was very confusing, and if I had been those boys, Debra, I wouldn't have been able to understand what you wanted me to do."

"That was the *point*," I said. I was beginning to feel anger replace my previous feelings of elation. "If you had read the lesson plan, or spoken with me first, you would have realized that the end of the first paragraph told the boys to stop reading and go to page five." I looked at her as I asked, "I don't suppose you have any idea if either of the paraeducators had read their handouts, do you?"

"I don't know, Debra. I only know that it was a humiliating experience for them, and I can't blame them for that. Didn't you see how uncomfortable they were standing there with their white boards?"

Actually, I hadn't. It was hard enough for me to pay attention to more than one boy at a time, much less pay attention to the paraeducators. It was all I could do to force my brain to notice as many of the *boys* as possible. I hadn't paid one bit of attention to the paraeducators. I had been acting on the assumption that they had read their handouts, knew what the lesson was and what their jobs entailed, and were, therefore, having as much fun as I was carrying out the lesson.

"Well, it might help if you read not just my lesson plan, but also the paraeducator handout, and then talk to me about whether or not I treated them in a demeaning way. I might mention that, as I am sure you noticed, I performed in the same role that they did—holding my white boards as a way of communicating encouragement and disallowing verbal engagement with the boys."

"Well, send me what you have, and I will read it. In the meantime, I have to tell you, Debra...the store program you are running...it makes me feel like you are buying good behavior..."

I left her office thirty minutes later, after listening to a lecture about how as a first-year teacher—before she had other tools in her toolbox—she, too, had used behavior modification techniques. But now, as she gained skills in classroom management, she no longer had to resort to using positive rewards. How surely it must be costing me a fortune to run that school store program, and how were the boys *ever* to learn these skills without tangible rewards, if they continued to get them every day from me, and...

She never asked what my plan was for fading and eliminating the tangible rewards (I had one, of course). She never asked if I needed help paying for the program, or if I was aware there were small grants that could be applied for to pay for classroom expenses (I wasn't at the time). She never asked if the classroom teachers had noticed any positive changes in the boys' behaviors. (They had. In fact, I had an entire wall plastered with emailed compliments to me about the students' progress and successes. We called it our *Wall of Success,* and the boys looked every day to see if there were new postings.)

There was not one word mentioned about the boys, their behaviors, or their academic and social/behavioral growth. There was no mention of the use of an authentic assessment to see where the boys still needed work. There was nothing mentioned regarding the value of the lesson, the creativity involved, or how, once the boys calmed down, they remained on-task for the duration of the period.

As the bundle of kindling was piling up on my bonfire, I raised my hand in the middle of her condescending and insulting lecture about behavior modification being a first-year teacher's crutch, and filled the next eight or so minutes with an unleashing of my thoughts and reactions to what she was saying.

According to an email I sent to a friend later that afternoon, I said "a mouthful." Specifically, I said:

> "Excuse me, but I am **_not_** a first-year teacher; I have more than **_twenty years_** of experience, and my toolbox is more than full...but

because you have never allowed time for the teachers to receive any training, I am forced to work with the contents of each of **_their_** toolboxes, not the contents of mine."

And, according to my email, I continued by informing her that:

> "I indeed have a fading plan for the store program; and, if you recall, I have among the toughest fourteen boys in the school in my classroom, and when I began working here, there was not one, **_not one single record, note, or piece of information_** on _any_ of them from the previous psychologist; so I had to start from scratch with each student..."

Assuming my email, dated that January afternoon, accurately reflected my apparently not-very-pleased response to her feedback, I indeed said a mouthful, ending with a statement to the effect of:

> "Personally, given everything, I think the boys have all come a very long way."

I had left her office feeling angry, frustrated, discouraged, and well aware that I had better back off and _shut_ my mouth, or be prepared for the reality that I may well be out of a job at the end of the year.

It seemed my little USS Cruiser was bouncing along on yet another ocean full of waves. Whether I was creating those waves or not, I simply did not know.

I thought about this for several days, working myself into yet another thirty-six-hour nap. After missing still another day of work, it seemed clear what needed to happen. It was costing me so much time (and so many pennies) to explain and justify my every move to this woman, as well as to internally debate how much and when to advocate for students, that my brain was continually stressed and compromised. But stress created from worrying that my outspokenness would result in being fired was one stress I was fully capable of eliminating from my life.

On January 27, 2006, I submitted my letter of resignation, effective at the end of the school year.

I just could not believe I was finding myself in this situation again.

I simply could not believe it.

Seven Bags of Platelets
March 2006

3/21/06 9:09 p.m. email:

They do not know yet what is causing the bleeding. Denise is too unstable and her blood counts and platelets are still too low to allow them to go in and do any GI work. The results of the radioactive tests indicate that it is not in the vessels, and that leaves three possibilities: there is a tumor in the small intestine and it is bleeding; the chemo has basically ulcerated her entire digestive system and all this blood and the clots are the slough off of months of this; or it is mucositis or something like that (and I don't know yet what that is, exactly).

Denise's spirits continue to be really good. I'm telling you, I do not know how she endures so much and stays so centered and dignified. She has mouth sores that make it so she can't even eat Jell-O (it burns); the chemo has made her completely unable to have anything cold (it induces some sort of asthma attack—an apparently common and horrendous side effect of this particular cocktail); her legs and feet are so swollen the skin has split; and she is so prone to bruising that she has bruises all over her butt and back from lying in the bed these last few days.

Yet still she smiles and wants to know about everybody else and how their day is going.

Should I ever be stricken with this horrendous disease, please do not think that you should take care of me in any way other than to shoot me. I would never be so graceful in my walk down this road.

3/22/06 9:30 p.m. email:

Damn if she doesn't insist on sitting in that bed grading papers!

* * * * *

"How's your sister doing?" Steve asked as we were standing outside the lunchroom watching kids head in.

"That's really nice of you to ask. I appreciate that." I paused for a minute, waving at kids who were shouting hello to me, answering others with a cheerful, "You bet, of *course* I'll be in there today!" And, "Yep, I was gone, but I'm back now," as they raced by asking where I'd been and if I'd be inside the lunchroom for duty. As hard as lunch duty was on my brain, often way overstimulating it, I would not have given it up for anything. I loved lunch duty.

It gave me time outside my room to make contact with kids I wouldn't otherwise know. Just by standing at the head of the line and sending the kids through to the food counter four at a time, I had come to know whose parents were divorcing, whose parent was in Iraq, what girl had a crush on what boy, and who was mad at who for saying something mean. Plus, it forced me to stay on top of my one-liner jokes. I was always prepared with a joke or riddle before I would let a downhearted kid pass me and get their food.

No matter how blue or frustrated I might be feeling, having that lunch duty was always an edge soother.

I turned back to Steve. "Actually, she isn't doing so hot. I'm sorry about missing so many days of school, Steve. She was back in I.C.U., and I spent the nights with her so her husband could be with the kids."

"I'm sorry to hear that. Is she going to be okay?"

"I don't know. She's stubborn as a mule, with an incredible will to conquer this thing, but I honestly don't know. This was really scary." I gave two high-fives to kids as they walked by, before adding, "But she's doing a whole lot better than she was a week ago, that's for sure."

"Well, I'm glad to hear that," Steve said, sincerely—if perhaps a bit awkwardly.

Whatever intermittent conflicts I had with this man; whatever failings I thought he had in terms of how he ran this building, he always took the time to ask about Denise, and, in my book, that counted for a lot. I didn't have much overall interaction with Steve—far, far less than with any principal I had worked with in the past—but I always had the feeling that he and I could have worked well together. I was never quite sure why we *didn't* work well together, whether it was his predisposition toward thinking psychologists were of little value; or whether he got inconsistent and negative feedback about me from the assistant principal; or maybe, just that something about me made him uncomfortable. But the truth was, our relationship was pretty tenuous. More than just that first time, Steve had called me into his office and jumped on me, only to back off and have that look I had come to recognize: the look reflecting his own confusion about why he had been so upset in the first place.

In spite of not being comfortable with Steve's particular leadership style, I believed that he had heart for kids. Somehow, I felt that if I had been able to interact with him directly, Steve would have been like many of the principals in my past—individuals who started out skeptical, resistant, or locked into rigid ways of doing things and ended up great collaborative friends. I doubted very much if kids would have been sent away from the school or reports would have been deleted if Steve had been working with me directly. I may have been frustrated with what I perceived as his focus on test scores to the point of detriment, but like with Tony, I felt that Steve had heart.

Heart for the kids; heart for education; heart for what I was going through with Denise.

* * * * *

Denise had gone back to teaching after the first of the year, despite the fact that both Buck and I (and probably many others) felt it was a mistake. And in truth, it was a mistake. She did not have the resistance to withstand the constant exposure to germs, nor did she have the energy to handle the physical and cognitive demands that teaching required (at least teaching the way she did). She was still undergoing chemotherapy. Although radiation treatments had ended, her very rapid weight loss and the inability to consume much in the way of liquids or food left her weak and, at times, dangerously dehydrated. More than once, Denise had wound up in the hospital after fainting, experiencing heart arrhythmia, or displaying some other frightening indication that she was dramatically weakening.

Those of us who loved her—who understood her—knew that in so many ways, teaching defined who she felt she was. Or who she needed to be. To teach meant she was still in control, still the commander in charge, still the dynamo. It wasn't until this last hospitalization that I confronted Denise about her choice to continue teaching full-time.

"I'm okay with teaching. I need to teach," she had said to me.

"Denise. Listen to me. Of everyone, I understand the kind of passion you have for those kids. For teaching. And I know that you at one-sixteenth of your best are still probably better than most people at a hundred percent. But it's costing you. And it's costing your kids. I mean, it's really costing your kids."

It was late at night as we were having this discussion; perhaps one or two in the morning. My days and nights had blurred, much as they had during the time I lived with my dad in his hospice room. The difference was that now I was also trying to work—to keep up with lesson plans and therapy plans, to stay on top of the necessary daily communication with students, teachers, and parents, with remaining connected to Denise's kids, and with keeping up with my own household chores—not to mention spending time with Teek and Meka—my own particular (and to some people, peculiar) definition of family. And do all this without succumbing to the inevitable consequences of pushing my brain too hard.

I knew I was failing miserably when it came to spending time at home when I was doing anything other than sleeping. Journal entries, emails, and notes from that time period all reflect that I was repeatedly assaulted by headaches, nausea, and narcoleptic incidents where I could not keep my eyes open for more than ten or fifteen minutes without needing another nap of several hours duration.

At the time, however, I actually thought I was holding up pretty well.

"How?"

"How?" I was startled by Denise's question. She had been silent for several minutes, and I was sure she had drifted off to sleep—something that happened frequently these days.

"How is it costing my kids?"

"Ahh. Well. Are you really asking me? Or are you just pretending to ask me?" Although Denise and I had engaged in many intimate conversations over the years, and particularly over the last nine months, this was new territory for us. It was rare for me to confront Denise about anything; even more so regarding her children.

"I am really asking you. I want to know what you think."

I was quiet for a moment. The last week had been especially grueling for everyone. Actually, the last three months had been grueling. I did not want my exhaustion, or my frustration with her, to contaminate the opening she was giving me.

"Okay. First of all, as Buck always says: they're not babies. But they're not adults, either, Denise, and this is frightening to them. You guys have wonderful kids—both of you are great parents, and the kids are strong and independent and capable. But you are their mom, Denise, and you have cancer. And they have watched you go from a two-hundred-and fifty-pound mega mama to a what—a hundred-and-ten, hundred-and-fifteen-pound scarecrow? And then you pull something like this."

Denise had begun bleeding into her ostomy bag the previous week. Copious amounts of blood filled with large clots that she did not mention to anyone. The bleeding stopped after the first day, but began again less than a week later. For three days, Denise bled into her bag, saying nothing and getting up every day and going into school to teach. Then one night she had gotten up to go to the bathroom, and Buck heard her collapse on the floor. It was one in the morning, and it took their oldest son and Buck to get her on the bed and call 911, with all three children looking on. It wasn't until the paramedics asked Buck how long she had been bleeding and if there was a *do not resuscitate* order that he had an inkling of what was going on or how precarious the situation was.

Although Denise did not die that night, she came very close to it. It had taken seven pints of platelets, and who knows how many of blood, to stabilize her, and she was by no means out of the woods.

"I know you're strong, Denise," I continued, "but there is nothing strong or admirable about bleeding for days and saying nothing. I mean, you had to know something was wrong..."

"I thought it would just stop. It stopped the week before."

"*Denise!* For such an intelligent woman, you are making my brain look like it's functioning on all cylinders. Come on! Even if you hadn't started bleeding again, didn't it occur to you that something was not right about bleeding at all? I mean, didn't it cross your mind that maybe you should call the oncologist immediately and at least *tell him* you were bleeding?" I was stunned every time I thought about this—about the risks and the foolishness of the choice she made.

"I didn't want to."

"Then explain why. Explain to me why you didn't want to." I looked at her, at this woman with her new angles and boney shoulders, her now thin, wispy, dull-colored hair, and I thought that I could not love her more if she had been born of my mother's womb. She held thirty-four years of my history in her memory. She was the only significant person in my life who had known both my mother and my father, every boyfriend, and each of my husbands. Was her need to maintain control so great that she would risk her life to pretend she still was in charge? Cost her children their mother? Buck his wife?

Me, my "sister"?

"I just didn't want to tell him. Or Buck." She stared at me.

"Help me understand, Denise. Because I'm having a tough time with this one. Is what you are saying...that you didn't want them to *know*; or is it that you think...I mean, did you think by not *saying* it...by not using the words *I am bleeding* that somehow it made it less real? Because, it's real, Denise. I mean, it is so incredibly real. You nearly died. I mean, you really, really nearly died."

We looked at each other before I continued. "Denise, I love you. You are more important to me than I could possibly say...but you cannot always be in control. You just can't. And no matter how much you try to pretend that you are...there are some things that are just not yours to direct."

I was struggling to say what I wanted to say, what my heart and my mind had been trying to sort through during the long hours of the last several days.

"I don't mean that you don't have any control, Denise. You do. But you have to relinquish and share some of it. You have to let *us* have some control, too, and that means, when you bleed, or you have new sores in your mouth, or one of your leg or back sores blisters and breaks open, you have to tell us. Tell Buck, or me, or just *tell the doctor*. But you can't keep ignoring these things and pretend that they don't exist so that you maintain this sense of being in charge. For one thing, it scares your children. It's not like they don't see all of this happening to you."

That conversation lasted for a very long time, and it was a night in which Denise shared more of herself, more of her thoughts, fears, and her worst nightmares than she had ever shared before. It was the night, I think, that I realized how very strong she actually was, and she embraced for the first time that she was not nearly as strong as she pretended to be.

Coded

April 2006

"This is a serious problem, you guys." I was talking to two of the special education teachers during a meeting we were having about upcoming evaluations that needed completion before the end of the year. "Look at this... Back in January there was a manifestation determination meeting[18] on Samantha when she brought that knife to school, and it was determined that there was no relationship between the weapons violation and her disability."

"And...?" Erica, one of the teachers, asked.

"And," I said, "I'm not even sure how that determination was made. Do you believe that's true? I mean, do you think that Samantha has the cognitive abilities to have thought through to the consequences of that action? To have come up with other alternatives in response to the kind of bullying she was experiencing?"

"No way!" one teacher said, while the other shook her head, indicating her agreement.

"Well, Tami, you signed off on this," I said, as I moved the paperwork over to her and watched as she glanced at her own signature.

"I didn't really even know Samantha back then—it was before she was in my class. I was walking down the hall that day, and the assistant principal pulled me in and asked me to sit in on the meeting." Tami is an excellent teacher with high ethical standards for both herself and her students. It was obviously upsetting to her that she might have signed off on something without making sure she knew what she was signing.

"I was out of town," Erica said, almost defensively, as if to justify why she had not been at the meeting. Erica, as Sam's case manager, was the one who knew her best and would have logically been present at this meeting.

"Well, I wasn't there, either, and I *was* here," I said. "I wasn't even *told* of the meeting, which is strange. I've never known a manifestation determination meeting to take place without the psychologist involved—not when there is a potential expulsion at stake. And according to the signatures here, there wasn't a general education teacher present at the meeting, either—and *that's* a legal

---

[18] Manifestation Determination Meeting: a meeting held with IEP team members, which addresses two primary questions: Was the conduct in direct and substantial relationship to the child's disability? Was the conduct a direct result of the school's failure to implement the IEP? This meeting determines whether a student in special education can be suspended from school without services; or, whether alternative disciplinary means need to be developed in order to ensure that student continues to receive the legally required services that are stated on the IEP.

requirement."

Samantha was an eighth grader who was in one of my stress management groups. She was a shy girl who seemed overwhelmed by both the academic and social demands of middle school. I was surprised that Samantha had even approached me about being in the group, and even more surprised that she remained in it. In the first few sessions, her best friend talked for her, and she remained absolutely silent. When her friend moved to another state, I expected that Samantha would drop out of the group; however, she didn't, and over the months that followed, she became comfortable enough to speak up for herself, which pleased me immensely.

In fact, now Samantha seemed to stop by my room every day wanting to talk. Because my time was so limited, I had begun a daily notebook with her; she was very good about writing in it, dropping it off, and then picking it up at the end of the day or the next morning to see what I had written back to her. Sam came from a large family, and there wasn't really anyone in her life who could help her with the myriad of social and emotional issues that were challenging her. I think the daily notebook helped her feel connected to someone who could help her with the daily challenges most girls in middle school experience.

I first became aware of Samantha back in November when Erica approached me with concerns regarding her lack of academic progress. As Erica and I went through Samantha's file, I was surprised to discover that she was identified as a student with learning disabilities, when all of her previous testing elicited IQ scores between 59 and 65—scores that would be far more suggestive of cognitive impairment than of learning disabilities.

"Well," I had said to Erica at the time, "I'm guessing that Samantha isn't making progress because she's of limited cognitive ability. No matter how many strategies you use with her that work for kids with learning disabilities, the fact is Samantha—reading at a second or third grade level—is probably reading at a level close to what she is capable of. There's no way she's going to be able to read an eighth grade text book, Erica."

"Are you sure?" Erica asked, surprised.

"Well, as sure as I can be with just doing a quick record review. I mean, according to past testing, all of her IQ scores place her cognitive abilities at or below the first percentile. If that's accurate, there is no way she could perform at grade level. I can't even imagine why she was ever coded as learning disabled."

Generally, an individual with learning disabilities is one of average or better intelligence who is not learning at an expected rate and has some identifiable processing deficits. If a student is of limited ability, and learning at a rate slower than their peers, that requires a different label and a very different type of programming.

Erica was quiet for a minute before saying, "Actually, this makes a lot of sense. She does fit more with the profile of a student with cognitive limitations. I don't think Samantha is of average cognitive ability." She took a deep breath. "Wow. What do we do now? I feel terrible...she shows up on my records as

PC[19] (which is what learning disabled kids are called in Colorado)... I should have figured this out for myself."

This was only Erica's second year of teaching, and she was struggling in her role as a new special education teacher. I suspected that Erica was wrestling with her own perceptual challenges, and that this made her beginning teaching experiences even harder than is normally expected. But, Erica was a hard worker and willing to learn, and I appreciated that in her. She was like a sponge and would absorb as much information and read as many resources as I was able to give her. We had spent a great deal of time over the last few months talking about kids, strategies, and models of special education. Learning to read files efficiently and effectively was just another part of becoming a good teacher; I was sure Erica would manage this task just fine, in time. Currently, however, her inexperience was causing a student and her teachers a lot of frustration.

"Well, her three-year reevaluation isn't due until this time next year, but that doesn't mean we can't ask to move it up. This is a good reason to do a full evaluation now and not wait. If, in fact, Samantha is more cognitively impaired than learning disabled, we would need to restructure her program a lot—and by the looks of it, that's what we'll need to do in order for her to be successful. I say let's get parent permission and do her testing now."

"Sounds good to me," Erica said.

Unfortunately, when I approached the assistant principal with the information Erica and I had uncovered, her response to my suggestion that we conduct current testing was, "Let it go."

"Let it go?"

"Let it go, Debra. Wait until she's due for testing. We have enough to do without adding this right now."

"But I think she's mislabeled. She's failing without her teachers having a *clue* about how to teach her or what to expect of her. I think we're going to have to restructure her entire program, and we can't do that without having an IEP team meeting and current testing information."

"Let it go, Debra," the assistant principal said, making it clear that the matter was closed.

It was not until February—when Sam approached me about being in a group—that I had reason to become personally involved with her. Without having a major IEP meeting, we were able to add counseling to her program, and I had become increasingly concerned about her fragile emotions, not to mention her academic struggles. There was a meeting scheduled in May to discuss Samantha's transition to the high school, and it was while reviewing her file in preparation for this meeting that I discovered the paperwork on the earlier manifestation determination meeting.

"This really concerns me," I said, looking at Tami and Erica. "In a lot of ways. For one thing, I don't even know if this meeting was conducted legally. I've participated in dozens of these, and I've never known of one conducted

---

[19] PC: Perceptual or Communicative disability.

without a psychologist present, not to mention at least one general education teacher and the case manager. There are just so many pieces missing here..." My voice trailed off as I looked over the paperwork another time.

"Like what?" asked Erica. "I mean, I've never been involved in one."

"Well, it's actually sort of confusing, and there are all kinds of regulations that determine when you do and when you don't have to have this type of meeting. But, the bottom line is that if one is held, it should be composed of relevant IEP team members—not a teacher who doesn't know the student. Certainly it should be more than the school administrators and parents who are present. There should be other members of the team, such as the psychologist or counselor—and definitely a general education teacher should be there. I mean, it should be people who know the student well."

I thought about how many hours of interviewing, reviewing, and documenting I had always completed before participating in one of these meetings, and I looked at Erica, saying, "Plus, at least in my experience, there's a *ton* of preliminary work done before the meeting ever occurs. It's actually a real pain in the butt getting ready for one—although I think it's a necessary pain in the butt. If that makes sense."

We looked at each other before I continued. "It's a legal process, for God's sake. It's not supposed to be a ten-minute meeting in the principal's office where someone says your child brought a knife to school and there's no relationship to her disability, so she is going to be suspended for ten days—and then everyone nods their heads and says, '*Okay.* Case dismissed.'"

"I feel terrible about this," said Tami. "I feel terrible that I signed off on this."

"Well, it isn't good, that's for sure. And what worries me is that it stands in her record that a *team* determined that her weapons violation has no relationship to her disability. I'm not sure after getting to know Sam that I agree with that. I don't think she has a *clue* about how to handle bullying, and I don't think she has the cognitive skills to figure it out on her own. She certainly hasn't had this sort of thing built into her IEP or anything. You guys know how intense it can get with those eighth grade girls...they're *tough*. From what Sam told me, she thought bringing a knife and scaring them away was her only option. Not that that makes it okay," I added. "I just don't think her intent was to use it on anyone. I don't think she has had the training to be able to think through to other options."

"Samantha is not a troublemaker," Erica stated firmly.

"I agree. What I'm saying is that it appears in her records as if she *is* one—a kid with normal intelligence who brought a weapon to school and received a suspension."

"Two suspensions," Tami threw in.

"Two?"

"Yeah, right after she got back, she got into a fight with the same girls and was suspended for another two weeks."

"She was out of school for four weeks without services?" I was sick, thinking what this would do to a girl already so academically overwhelmed. Not to mention that there are legal issues surrounding any kid in special education when they have been suspended for more than ten school days in a year's time.

"Oh, great," I said. "Think about this: She moves into high school next year, and it will probably be a new one since they're likely to be transferred to Ft. Hood, Texas. She hooks up with the wrong kids because she's a follower and unsure of herself, and she gets into trouble. The principal looks at her records and sees that she has a weapons violation *and* an assault violation. What do *you* two think will happen? Not to mention the fact that it's outrageous that she missed a month of school and had no services. It's not like anyone at home can help her."

Several of Samantha's siblings had disabilities, and Sam's mother had told me that she herself was "slow" and had a hard time helping even the youngest of the children with their schoolwork.

Everyone was quiet as the reality of this situation settled in.

"What do we do?" asked Erica. "What are our options?"

"To tell you the truth, I really don't know," I said, shaking my head. "I mean, we could talk to her parents, and they certainly could file an appeal and see if this can be overturned and expunged from the records...but I don't know if they would even understand the importance of appealing it. My guess is, at the time of the meeting, they were just grateful that she wasn't being expelled permanently and 'only' got a ten-day suspension." I was quiet for a minute. "There's plenty of information to validate reasons to appeal the decision. I mean, it doesn't even sound like *any* of the usual process and procedures for holding a manifestation determination meeting were followed. Did anyone even bring up that her records indicate that it might not be learning disabilities causing her academic failure, but rather that Sam is...limited?"

It was always awkward to use the words "mentally retarded" even when it was the appropriate description.

Tami shook her head, and I shook mine, amazed that this crucial information had not been mentioned at this meeting. Obviously, the assistant principal had been aware of this.

"This is a mess. I mean, I've never worked in a district where a parent filed for due process, but I'm telling you, I don't think we want to go there. It can get really expensive for a district, and at least from what I've read, it just can get ugly for both sides."

"So, do we let it stand?"

"Well, I don't think that's a good option, either. I mean, this determination and the resulting record have the potential to dramatically affect Samantha's life. She's fifteen now—if she were suspended next year...she'd be sixteen. I could see her dropping out completely, when, in fact, with the right program in place, she has the potential to go through school and become a really productive citizen."

It was quiet in the room.

"You know," I said, "maybe there's a way out of this. Samantha's transition meeting is scheduled to happen in three weeks. I wonder if we got permission to do the three-year reevaluation now, if the IEP team could overturn a previous manifestation determination if new information was revealed."

"What are you thinking?" Tami asked.

What I was thinking was not exactly on the up and up, since the "new information" was actually available at the time of the manifestation determination meeting, but it was possibly a way to resolve this situation that was both in the best interest of the student and would not put the district in a compromising situation.

"Well...and I don't even know if this can legally happen...but what if we conducted the current evaluation and said, 'Oh, wow, look...Samantha doesn't have learning disabilities, she meets eligibility for S.L.I.C.[20]; and, gosh, her program and IEP have never even addressed these needs...and, hmm...does the team still agree with the earlier manifestation determination?' Maybe the IEP team could determine that a new meeting needs to be held in order to ascertain if the new information results in a different outcome."

"Can we do that?" Tami asked.

"I have absolutely no idea," I said. "But it might be worth a shot, that's for sure."

"What would we need to do?" Erica asked.

"Well, we'd have to get parent permission for testing. The assistant principal has to okay this, and I am not sure she will, because she already told me to let go of the idea of moving Sam's triennial up. I'd hate to be the one to explain to her that we want to do this because she might have screwed up on the manifest determination meeting."

I liked this woman at times, but our relationship was strained from a number of disagreements over students. I could not imagine gaining her cooperation were I to point out that Samantha's manifestation meeting might not have even followed legal protocol, and we hoped to consider overturning the decision.

"I'll take care of that," said Erica, as I looked at her with surprise. "I'll get the permission signed."

"Great! Wow. That's great." Just the thought of not having to be the one to go to the assistant principal on this left me feeling tremendously relieved. "One other thing we might do is whip off an email or call CDE (Colorado Department of Education). Just explain the situation briefly and ask if there's a protocol for overturning a manifestation determination in this way."

"I'll take care of that," Tami said. "I have the time to do that."

"Jeez, you guys are awesome! I'm so far behind right now from being gone that it would help a *lot* if I didn't have to do that."

Just knowing that I would not have to deal with the assistant principal or the state department of education helped me feel like a huge load had been lifted off my shoulders.

"No problem," Tami said. "Like I said, I feel terrible that I just signed off on

[20] Significant Limited Intellectual Capacity—Colorado's coding for children in special education due to limited cognitive abilities.

this without really knowing what I was signing off on."

Tami looked at me, and I could see how bothered she was by this situation. Truthfully, I liked that she was bothered. It reinforced my impressions that she was a conscientious teacher, and it made me feel good to know she was around.

We had more kids to talk about, but we decided things could wait another day or two. The whole issue involving Sam seemed to overwhelm all of us.

Unfortunately, we didn't have the opportunity for any more meetings or discussions. The next day Denise had a heart attack.

Perhaps the good news was that because Denise was already in the hospital when she "coded" as the medical jargon goes, the response team was there within ninety seconds. They were able to resuscitate her, but they could not keep her breathing on her own. She was moved to the cardiac intensive care unit and hooked up to life support.

Instead of being at school getting caught up, I found myself once again standing with Buck at Denise's bedside—this time holding my breath as I watched a machine breathe for her.

Bonfires
Late April, May 2007

4/23/06 8:05 p.m. email:

Denise is heavily sedated—she is on a ventilator as well as many other forms of life support. Even though she is not overtly conscious, we all believe she knows we are here and can hear what we are saying.

It was determined by Saturday that she has sepsis (blood poisoning) and that it is of the most serious nature (septic shock). No one knows for sure yet, but quite possibly what happened is that when she was bleeding into her ostomy bag last month, bacteria seeped into her abdomen, and the infection process began. The infection was causing her heart to simply work harder than it was able, and that's when she had the heart attack.

Her prognosis is very, very guarded. Her dad, one brother, and a very close family friend flew in on Saturday from Ohio, and her older brother who lives in Florida also flew in. Katie, Kyle, and Ryan are spending time each day at the hospital with Buck and myself, and then they go home with extended family. Buck and I have stayed here since she was admitted, and plan to continue doing so.

4/25/06 8:30 p.m. email:

Quick update on Denise. She has a mental and physical fortitude like no one I have ever known. She fights through it all, and, so far, has astounded all the zillions of medical people who surround her. She made it through Friday's surgery, Sunday's surgery, and today's surgery. She is not conscious and is still on life support, but her computer signs read well. The doctors told us today if she cannot breathe on her own soon, they will have to do a tracheotomy as no one can remain on a ventilator for more than 7-10 days without permanent damage to their vocal cords and swallowing mechanisms. That aside, all signs look much, much, much better than when I last wrote—whenever that was (I have lost track of what day it is, if it is night or day, or if I have talked to someone or not).

4/26/06 3:15 p.m. email:

Denise is by no means out of the woods, and she is still in "critical condition" but the doctors say she is stabilizing. They won't say "stable" but they do smile and say she is "stabilizing." They all caution us not to expect too much, but now they add that she is doing unbelievably well and say that if this trend continues, she will survive this.

Recovery will be long and hard, but if she can keep truckin' the way she is truckin' now...she will make it.

I doubt I would have such grit.

4/29/06 3:40 p.m. email:

She is awake! Denise regained consciousness today. She is now considered "out of the woods"!!!! Although she could not speak due to the ventilator, she answered questions by blinking her eyes and then indicated she wanted to write something on Buck's palm. Although her fingers were weak, and I am quite sure her writing was terrible, she made the message clear: "Get this f*@^% thing out of my mouth!"

That's our Denise. She may have almost slipped away from us, and she may have been asleep for ten days...but she woke up with spunk and humor as always.

The doctors indicate that this can now officially be called a miracle. If she maintains like this, I should be back to school soon.

* * * * *

Buck and I had spent the last ten days listening to the sound of the ventilator as it pumped air into Denise's lungs in a manner that was rhythmical, but certainly not soothing. She looked so frail, so very small as she lay attached to more wires than I could count. The days and nights blended into one another, and although I kept in touch with school via the Internet, very little remains clear in my mind from those ten days. I only remember that nurses kept changing shifts, and each time a new nurse came on board, they would look at Denise, check her vitals, and then ask if she was my mother.

My *mother*? May God strike me dead first if Denise heard that through her narcotics-induced coma. She might be battling for her life, but there was no doubt in my mind that she retained a certain level of vanity in the midst of the siege. And looking younger than me was one of those things Denise took great pride in and loved to flaunt.

"It's cuz you're too skinny," she would say. "Fat people don't get wrinkles like you anorexics do."

"Thanks," I would say, "but I'm not anorexic."

"Well, you sure have gotten crow's feet around your eyes!" she would laugh.

Maybe Denise would get well just to come back and swat those nurses. But just in case she did not feel up to the task, I did my best to speak for her.

"She's my younger sister," I would say firmly. "I have her beat by seven months."

"Oh, I am so sorry," the nurses would respond, flustered and embarrassed by their mistake. And then, a moment later, they would inevitably add: "You two are *sisters*?"

"Yes," I would answer. "We're twins."

After the nurse left the room, I would turn to Denise and say, "Ha! Let them try to sort that out! Don't you listen to them, Denise. You don't look like you're my mother. Well, maybe your boobs do...but nothing else!" Truth was, losing more than one hundred and fifty pounds in a year's time does something really unpleasant to a woman's breasts.

Still...Denise did *not* look old enough to be my mother.

Why did people keep asking me that?

* * * * *

After Denise regained consciousness, I began making plans to return to school. It was nearly time for Samantha's meeting, and it was important to me that I was prepared. While emailing with Tami, I discovered that she had inadvertently forgotten to contact the CDE to ask if it was possible to overturn a manifestation determination without going through due process, and so I assured her I would be able to send them an email from the hospital.

The district's school psychologist intern was filling in for me, and I had asked the assistant principal to have him complete the IQ testing on Samantha. I had everything else done. The only other thing I really needed him to do was conduct an IQ test with another student of mine—a seventh grade boy named Lee—who was identified in special education as an *S.I.E.D.* student (a student with Significant Identifiable Emotional Disabilities).

Lee was a complicated kid. Thin and pale-looking, he was an extremely bright boy who had failed academically all year long. Lee had a long history of difficulties and failures in school—not just academically, but with sustaining any sort of positive relationships with teachers or peers. Currently, his teachers had pretty much maxed out on their frustration with him.

Early on, I recognized a younger version of Evan in Lee, and it concerned me immensely. He was an isolated kid, bullied by many and ignored by most. Over time, while working together, I had discovered that Lee harbored deep fantasies of revenge, and his daydreaming life was infused with visions of himself becoming powerful enough to undo the shame and humiliation he perceived he had experienced at the hands of others.

Early in the school year, I had voiced my concerns that Lee demonstrated many of the characteristics associated with kids who end up committing violent acts, and I had pushed hard for changes in his program. For reasons hard to figure out, there was resistance from his case manager, who—despite teacher input concerning his behavior and academic failure—continually asserted that his program was fine and that he was doing well. As the year progressed and Lee's behavior and grades continued to deteriorate, I began promoting the idea of transferring him to the self-contained program located at another school. After having Lee in my homeroom class and two of my groups, I had become convinced that the only way he would invest in academic work, and the only way his emotional needs could be addressed, would be in a small, controlled environment—a structured but informal environment that allowed for plenty of movement during class time—which could address Lee's emotional needs and the specific learning disabilities that he also demonstrated. We could not offer that type of program to Lee at Carson Middle School, but the program was in place at the district's other middle school.

It was time for Lee's triennial evaluation, and I had been collecting my data and working on his evaluation for a month. The only thing left to complete was administering a standard IQ test. I had already written the bulk of my report during the long nights with Denise in ICU, so I entered it into the computerized IEP program, letting the intern know that only the IQ testing remained undocumented. I had written a lengthy and cohesive report that included the results of my interviews with both of Lee's parents and five of his teachers, as well as my observations of him in his general education classrooms, my homeroom, and the anger management and stress management groups in which he participated. Because of my concerns, I had conducted extensive psychological testing with Lee; and, in the report, I thoroughly addressed what my assessments had revealed about Lee's specific learning disabilities, issues of depression, and issues surrounding attention deficits and social skills. I included very specific recommendations in terms of teaching strategies and psychological intervention in each area.

The assistant principal, along with Lee's case manager, strongly disagreed with me regarding his need to be in the self-contained program at the other middle school. Although I am always conscientious when writing a report, in this one I was especially careful to make sure all the *t's* were crossed and all the *i's* were dotted, and that the report followed the Colorado state guidelines for identifying and developing a program for an S.I.E.D. student. I was going to leave no confusion or question regarding the documentation of this student's current failures, and I wanted to be exceptionally clear in the reasoning behind my recommendations for the kind of self-contained environment and instruction I felt was required in order for him to be successful.

It infuriated me that I had to fight so hard for this kid. Despite whatever reasons the two women did not want him to go, there was never anything put into his program all year long to help him succeed at Carson. Every one of his teachers, with the exception of his special education case manager, agreed that his needs were not being met, and four of his five general education teachers clearly stated that they did not feel either safe or comfortable with him in their classroom.

Lee's triennial would be the last opportunity I would have to speak out on behalf of his needs, and I had repeatedly asked the assistant principal to invite the key players from the other school to his meeting. It made sense to invite them, I told her, because they would be able to offer insights that would help the IEP team make the best decision regarding his placement.

Permission to invite them was denied.

The day that Denise had her heart attack, I had taken a bold and probably very inappropriate step. I had sent an email to the IEP team members, outlining my concerns one more time, and urging them to support inviting the people from the self-contained program to the meeting. That part was okay. The inappropriate part came when I cc'd it to the teacher and assistant principal at the other school. I knew this would probably infuriate my own assistant principal, but I also thought that it was my last shot at possibly getting her to back away and allow additional input to be brought into this meeting.

I should have known better. When a person operates from the center of their ego, you *don't* embarrass them publicly and expect affinity to develop.

There was an email from the assistant principal, written to me at the end of that day, telling me to be in her office *promptly* at 8:45 the next morning.

I am not sure what would have transpired between us in that meeting, but I would have liked to have had the opportunity to find out. Unfortunately, that is when Denise went into the ICU, and I was not at school for the next two weeks to meet with her.

The fact is, I never had the opportunity to see the assistant principal again.

* * * * *

5/8/06 9:32 a.m. email:
Well, it has been a scary few days. Just as Denise was getting better, Buck and I made the **wrong** choice and thought it was okay to leave her alone for a night (we had been alternating 12-15 hr. "shifts"). Let this be a lesson to all of you in the event that you ever have a loved one in ICU. **DO NOT EVER LEAVE THEM ALONE WITHOUT SOMEONE VIGILANTLY WATCHING WHAT IS HAPPENING AT ALL TIMES!!!!!!** Long story short: they gave her a near fatal dose of the narcotic Fetanyl. This led to her lung collapsing, which resulted in her having to go back on the ventilator.

5/11/06 8:41 a.m. email:
Denise's primary care physicians are now the pulmonary people. She popped a hole in her lung and it partially collapsed. So, back into surgery—this time to have yet another tube put in her—this one going through her chest into her lung. It did its job and the lung re-inflated, but it has to stay in for now as the potential for the lung to spring more holes is huge. Her lungs are so filled with fluid and so fragile and damaged at this point, that the pressure of the ventilator can easily cause damage, even though it is saving her life at the same time.

Denise is a bit discouraged, I think. She is so ill and she is fighting so hard...I think she is getting tired. One good thing: she has not lost her sense of humor and I see that as very positive. She can't talk due to the ventilator and she's too weak to write, so she communicates with small hand movements, palm spelling, and eye movements. Yesterday the nurse accidentally disconnected her IV, and then in her haste to correct her mistake, she bonked Denise on the forehead. Those huge blue eyes opened wide, and using every bit of strength she could muster, Denise lifted her arm up and made face slapping motions to the nurse's face.

Maybe you had to be there, but it was really funny and made all three of us laugh.

To make life easier for her, I made Denise a communication tool out of latex. I blew up one of those latex gloves and taped all but one of the fingers down (I'll let you figure out which one) and taped a sign to it that said, "Don't make me mad. This is my only communication device!"

Denise, in her limited way, told me that was really, really tacky and that she loved it.

5/14/06 email:

Denise has had another remarkable turnaround!!! A couple of nights ago we had a really frightening experience. Denise indicated through her finger speech that she wanted everything disconnected, and she just wanted to go home and die...that it was all just too much. This is the first time she has ever indicated that feeling, and it scared us all...but we decided to approach it as the natural and understandable cycle it is and just tried to validate her feelings rather than try to talk her out of them. Sandy—her prayer partner and the kids' spiritual godmother—came in and spent fifteen hours in prayer with her!!!

We followed this by bringing the kids in along with a box of crafts, and the kids and I sat on Denise's floor for hours making Mother's Day presents for her. I know she really loved that and even though her eyes were closed through the whole thing, she was very aware we were there and what we were doing (even though we tried to pretend we were keeping it a secret!).

Anyway, things started improving exponentially and they REMOVED THE VENTILATOR TUBE and the next morning they removed the chest tube!!!!! AAAAND...the doctors are talking about removing the feeding tube and seeing if her intestine will absorb nutrition on its own.

This is all remarkably good news and a HUGE boost to Denise's emotional well-being. The ventilator and feeding tube were horribly painful, so to have those gone is HUGE to her. And, of course, Denise not being able to TALK is in itself a near death sentence to her as we all know she is a chatterbox of gold medal quality. So not having her voice restricted is a great boost to her recovery!

The kids and I used window paint to plaster her window with Happy Mother's Day signs, and we had a grand celebration in her room, complete with presents and balloons.

Never was I happier to celebrate a Mother's Day with anyone as I was to celebrate it today with Denise, Buck, and those three kids.

* * * * *

"Debra, this is Henry Gonzales with Human Resources." I was driving down

---

the highway, and although I don't usually answer my phone while driving, just in case it was the hospital I did answer this call. Henry Gonzales was the *last* person I had expected to be on the line.

"Hi, Henry, what's up?"

"I just wanted to call you and tell you that the extended leave of absence you requested has been granted through the end of the year."

"What are you talking about, Henry? I didn't request a leave for the rest of the year."

"Well, I'm sorry I didn't get back to you sooner, Debra. Actually, I had been calling the wrong phone number, and I apologize for that. I'm talking about your leave request that you made on May second."

"That wasn't a leave request, Henry. That was a question I sent to Jo (Jo being the contact in the payroll department). I just asked her if there was protocol in the district to take an extended leave in the event that Denise did not get better. But it wasn't a request, and anyway, I have already arranged with Steve to go back on Wednesday. Denise has stabilized, and I have to get back to school to finish out the year."

"Actually, Debra..." There was a long pause, and clearly Henry was struggling with what to say. "Well, I have to tell you the truth, Debra. You really upset the applecart this morning with your email."

"My email? What email?" I couldn't imagine what he was talking about. I hadn't sent him any emails. I barely knew the man.

"The email you sent to CDE."

It took a moment for this to register—to filter through the layers of confusion and ultimately the disbelief that I was experiencing. *How would Henry know about my email to CDE?*

I had sent an email to the department of education late the previous afternoon, after I found out that Tami hadn't contacted them with the question regarding the manifestation determination. Sam's meeting was in two days, and I definitely wanted to be able to go into it knowing if there was a protocol for overturning an earlier decision. But how would Henry Gonzales in Human Resources know anything about that email? This just wasn't making sense.

"All I can tell you, Debra, is that the director of special education came into my office saying, 'I don't care what you do, get that woman out of there!' And so, you have been placed on unpaid family medical leave through the remainder of the year."

"But, Henry, I don't want to be on leave. I have way too much to do! I need time for closure with my kids, and I have all my write-ups to do for whatever psychologist fills my position next year."

I knew from my experience in leaving Utah and Alaska how time-consuming this was, and I had every intention of leaving the same kind of detailed summaries behind as when I left my other districts.

"Debra. You're going to need to decide how you want to be paid. And if I could give you a little piece of advice...have us prorate this last paycheck through the summer so that you retain your health insurance."

I was so stunned; I didn't know what to say. I could only think that Henry

Gonzales was a very nice man for caring enough to give me advice.

I went home and promptly opened my email and listened to my home phone messages.

* * * * *

"Debra, I only have a minute. I'm just calling to let you know that I think you have been locked out of email and computer access. I'll talk to you later...Bye."

Email message: *"Word has come down from the mountain that we are not allowed to discuss anything with you that concerns students, the school or the district..."*

Email message: *"Rumor is we are being sued by a parent and you were encouraging them...Steve made a point to talk to every staff member individually and in person to let us know we are NOT TO GIVE YOU ANY DETAILS OR INFORMATION ON ANY STUDENTS. Weird..."*

Email message: *"Our assistant principal said, 'This time she has gone too far and I had to put a stop to it.' Were you FIRED????????????"*

Email message: *"Be careful. I think the assistant principal is going to put a block on your home email so that we cannot reach you..."*

It's a good thing that teachers at that school cared about me enough to send me these brief messages. Were it not for those, I would have had absolutely *no* information at all. And indeed, I could not get into my district email or the computer programs that gave me access to student information.

What on earth was going on?

* * * * *

I was never given one word of explanation from the principal, assistant principal, director of special education, or from anyone in the human resources office. One teacher was able to tell me later that when I emailed CDE and sent copies to the IEP team, the assistant principal immediately went to the principal, who went to the director of special education, and within the hour my access to anything or anyone at Fort Carson Middle School was blocked.

I could not understand the problem. My email was not accusatory; in fact, it did not even state for which district I worked. I laid out the scenario and asked if it was possible, given new information, for an IEP team to overturn a previous manifestation determination. After my "lockout," however, I wrote CDE another email and told them apparently the district was very upset that I had contacted them at all, and I asked if they felt that in any way my emailed question had been inappropriate. At that point, I told them the name of my school district, as well as the name of my director of special education.

I promptly received an email back informing me that it would not be appropriate to continue our correspondence, and with the suggestion that I might want to consider getting an attorney.

An attorney? Because I asked a question? This was simply not making one bit of sense to me. None of it was making a bit of sense.

I then received an email from Henry Gonzales, stating that neither the principal of Carson Middle School nor the director of special education had any interest in my returning. Quote, unquote.

I was devastated. Absolutely devastated. *What would my kids think? What would parents think? How would I write end of the year reports if I didn't have access to student files and information? How would I close the year with my kids?* We had become very bonded over the previous eight months, and I knew I was important to my students. It was absurd to think that I would not say good-bye to them or offer any explanation of my leaving.

Surely the district would not disregard the needs of the kids so blatantly.

And then it occurred to me: Samantha's meeting was in two days. Did they think I was going to attend that meeting and disclose all the legal errors that had been made in the initial manifestation determination meeting? Is it possible this was all being done to keep me away from that meeting?

And, of course, there was also Lee's meeting coming up.

Surely, this district was not reacting in such a way because they believed I would push parents into filing for a due process hearing? Not only was that absurd—I had been busting my *butt* to figure out ways to keep that from happening—but I couldn't believe the district would deny teachers the available information I had on students. Or deny students the opportunity for closure with someone significant. What, all because they were *afraid their unethical and/or possibly illegal practices might be made public?*

Never in twenty-three years had I encouraged a parent to litigate, and I had always found myself profoundly loyal to the districts I worked for. But as the reality of what was happening began to settle in, I found myself—for the first time—wanting to sue the backside off a school district. As far as I was concerned, due process was being denied to every student on my caseload whose teachers were being denied access to information that affected their programs.

Not to mention that I personally might have a defamation of character case.

How could a principal and assistant principal walk around a school and instruct teachers one by one not to have contact with me? They made it seem like I've molested a child or something. I mean, what else could be SO BAD that every single person is given the edict not to discuss students, the district, or the school with me?

It is impossible to describe the rage that surfaced from within me. The only description that comes to mind is of pictures I have seen of a backdraft—the phenomenon that occurs when an oxygen-starved fire suddenly receives air and immediately ignites all of the super-heated gases at the same time. It causes an explosion of unimaginable power, and while a backdraft doesn't occur often, when it does, its risks are potentially fatal to anyone caught in its path.

At this point I was no longer sure if I was the one in its pathway, or if I was the backdraft itself.

My first letter went to Henry Gonzales.

Vanished

May 22, 2006, emailed as an attached letter (in part) to Mr. Gonzales:

Dear Mr. Gonzales,

...I did indeed discover that my email was blocked, and my access to Infinite Campus and Excent had been "disabled." On Friday evening and over the weekend various teachers contacted me to express their concern regarding the sudden turn of events and the fact that they were confused over the clear instructions not to speak with me regarding students (several of whom had questions they wanted to run by me). One staff person used the word "socialize," as in, "We were told not to socialize with you or talk to you and that we were to steer clear of you. What the ___ is going on????"

More than one staff member indicated that they had asked the assistant principal what was going on and she indicated that she had fired me. I might add that no one articulated the word "fired" in relaying to me what they had been told, but rather the phrases and words they used were: "She said you had crossed the line and she had to put a stop to it...to get rid of you."

Mr. Gonzales, first of all I would like to clarify for you again that I did not **request** leave on May 2, 2006, and if you re-read the email I wrote to Jo Harris, you will see clearly that it was an email of **inquiry** (and one in which I had requested confidentiality since it *was* only a letter of inquiry). As you know I never received a response from Jo and by the time you had reached me via phone on May 16th, Denise was off life supports and I had made arrangements to return to school in order to complete the work I had to do and effect closure with my students.

I would appreciate it if you would please clarify some specific information in writing:

1. The reason I was not given the choice of four prorated paychecks and benefits (as you had indicated I would have on the phone), but rather was given one paycheck (thus deducting more taxes) with benefits terminating on May 31, 2006;
2. The reason my access to email, Excent, and Infinite Campus were blocked, especially when you were aware I had end of the year reports to write, and to my knowledge I was not being disciplined for improper conduct;
3. The reason teachers were instructed not to speak with me;
4. The reason the assistant principal is telling people that she is responsible for my absence, with clear implication that I was fired; and finally,

5. Whether or not I am being disciplined as would certainly be suggested by #1-4, when in fact I have been gone from school due to family illness and not because of a suspension due to professional misconduct.

I put forth to you that this feels **very much like retaliation** on the assistant principal's part for an email I sent to CDE earlier in the week asking if there was any process for reversing a manifestation determination decision without parents filing for a due process hearing. **In that email I neither mentioned the school nor the district in which I was employed**; I simply stated some facts which led to questions and asked for guidance on how to approach the situation. There was nothing hidden or covert in that email; and in fact, I forwarded a copy to IEP team members who had already verbalized the same questions.

...This email to CDE follows a series of situations which have occurred this year, in which the assistant principal and I have disagreed on what was in a student's best interest, as well as legal and ethical approaches for managing issues related to students. I must say, Mr. Gonzales, the fact that my plans to return to school were suddenly reversed by administration, that an *entire staff of teachers* were instructed not to discuss students with me or have contact with me, and the fact that I was suddenly blocked from accessing any information relevant to my students and which I would need to write responsible end of the year reports, does indeed sound like I have been fired, or at the very least, severely disciplined.

Once I receive a letter from you clarifying exactly what the status of this situation is, I would be happy to speak with you further about the events I believe have led to this situation. If you request documentation regarding earlier professional differences which occurred between the assistant principal and myself, I would be happy to supply these as well.

Thank you for your attention to this matter. With only three days of student contact left, I would like to resolve this as quickly as possible, as students are wondering if I am coming back to say good-bye, and parents would like to know why IEP needs are not being met.

I received no response to this letter.

My next emailed letter was to my principal, and it read (in part):

May 24, 2006
I believe, Steve, that you have great heart for education and kids. I believe that you truly want to be an exceptional leader and to have a school that helps children become successful and productive citizens. My own observation, however, is that instead of approaching situations in a "win-win" manner, you respond reactively; and in so doing, create lose-lose situations that cost people their sense of dignity, among other things.

...I went and read case law; I read through all of CDE's information on manifestation determination meetings; I went to numerous websites and all I could find was information regarding parent complaint and due process before a determination was overturned. I really did not want to see that happen. To me, that is most definitely NOT a win-win situation, as it is always a lose situation for a district when they are subjected to an appeal.

My "brainstorm" was to get permission to do the triennial now instead of when it was due next year; and if the current assessment data supported earlier data, in addition to it allowing us to send Samantha over to the high school with appropriate information and program recommendations, perhaps it would allow us to quietly "revisit" the M.D.

...***There was nothing covert or deceptive in the email, Steve. I did not write it on my school account, did not state the name of my employer; did not give any identifying information. I did not WANT to red flag our district***; I WANTED to know for sure if due process had been violated and if in a non-inflammatory way we could revisit the decision and overturn it, thus doing what clearly was in the best interest of the student.

To me this was a win-win situation. Samantha would not be entering high school with a record that conveyed an incorrect picture of both her needs and her history, and the district would avoid a due process hearing.

Picture this from my end for a moment, if you will. I worked my ***butt*** off (in between my 12-hour shifts in ICU) to research the heck out of something in order to SAVE the district from having a parent file for due process, and suddenly I am punished and publicly shamed, with teachers given information that I am inciting a parent to sue the district, and left with the impression that I have been fired.

...My interest is, has, and always will be in doing what is in the best interests of a student; and in **23 years of practicing in public schools, I have been able to accomplish this without *EVER* speaking to or encouraging a parent to pursue due process.** With collaboration and teamwork there has always been a means of finding a win-win situation—doing what is best for a child and not putting a district (which I have always been loyal to) in a difficult and costly situation.

...I do not think you will find, Steve, that I am the one jeopardizing the district and inciting parents to file for due process. I think if you were to fully evaluate the situation you would recognize that I have protected both you and the district, as I attempted to approach my job in a manner both respectful to the assistant principal's position as my supervisor, but also with respect to carrying out my ethical responsibilities as a school psychologist.

Now I find myself in a position where two things are compromised, jeopardized and of great concern. One is that the rights of every student on my caseload are being violated by denying teachers the opportunity to access information relevant to a student's programming (i.e., in denying them access to me, my records, and my consult, which they have been relying on all year). The other, of course, is the damage done to my professional reputation, the financial cost to me, and the toll this has taken on me emotionally during a time when I certainly did not have the emotional stamina to sustain the assault...

I received no response to this letter.

My next emailed letter went to the director of special education, and contained the following (in part):

May 24, 2006
...As the director of special education, and one of the two names stated in writing who did not want me to return, I am asking you to clarify why. I do not think that is out of bounds... I do not think it is out of line to ask you to clarify for me why it is being communicated that I have been fired, or why sanctions have been placed on me that indicate I am being disciplined and/or considered at fault for professional misconduct...

I received a response informing me only that my medical benefits would be carried through the summer.

I tried again:

Thank you for the information regarding medical benefits.
...I suggest to you that my behavior at CMS was quite predictable all year long. I followed the law; I maintained the professional code of ethics we all adhere to under our NASP credentialing (National Association of School Psychologists); I worked hard; I supported the district; and I attempted to do what I thought was in students' best interests. Perhaps I do not see the correct or whole picture, but I cannot think of a single time in which all of these things were not a part of my professional conduct...
...For the record, not one time during the course of my active employment did I ever, ever speak to any parent about pursuing due process. Not once. Did parents feel supported by me and empowered to play a strong role in their child's program and IEP development? I would say they did. Did I assume a stand of advocacy if I had a disagreement regarding a student's program, identification, or a process utilized to solve a dispute? Probably so, the majority of the time.
...Did I try to talk with the assistant principal about concerns regarding the way things were being conducted? Absolutely. Was I respectful during those discussions? I believe I was. Did I at any time violate a professional code of conduct, act in an insubordinate manner toward a supervisor or exhibit behavior which was in conflict with the school or district's professional behavior codes? I do not believe I did.
Did my questioning and attempts to conduct business thoroughly and in an ethical manner put stress on my relationship with my supervisor? I believe it certainly did. Do I feel that she made unilateral decisions that were not only *not* in the student's best interest, but which violated the letter and intent of the law? Yes, I do.
Do I feel that I should be placed in a situation where teachers have been given the impression that I have been fired and have been told they could not

seek my input as they were making end of the year placement decisions? No, I most certainly do not. I most certainly do not.

I would greatly appreciate any clarification you could give me regarding your reasoning behind the way things have been handled; particularly behind a discipline sanction which does not allow me to meet with my students and put closure to the work we have been doing all year. I would very much like for you to give me the statement *YOU* would like me to utilize with parents and students who are asking why I am not at school.

I received no response to this letter, either.

* * * * *

The school year ended for the students, and I could not believe that I did not march into the school and simply seek out my students and say good-bye. Certainly the pre-head-injury me would have done that. Perhaps even the post-head-injury me might have done that were my brain and physical energies not spent beyond belief. I knew that the kids were leaving school without knowing how important they had been to me and how proud of them I was, but I was unable to find the courage, the clear thinking, or most of all, the confidence that was needed to pull off walking into that building. In my ongoing replay of this saga, it ends very differently, and I walk tall and strong into the school building, tell them to arrest me for trespassing if they want, and then I find each and every one of my kids and tell them what I know they needed to hear.

Instead, I wrote each one of them a letter never sent, crying well into the night as I told them one by one of all the great things they had accomplished over the year. If I had known where to send them, they might have been mailed; instead, after a year of sitting in the same spot, they were tossed into my woodstove.

The flame made by the letters was much smaller than the rage and the love that inspired them.

* * * * *

The last thing I did at Fort Carson Middle School was ask a staff member to do a very big favor for me. Perhaps it was out of bounds. Perhaps it was unfair to ask. Perhaps I would have been better not having asked. But I did, and that is a done deal.

I asked someone to go into the computer program and print out Lee's report for me. I wanted to know if my document remained.

It did not. Not one word I had written, not one paragraph of the results of my interviews, my testing, my observations, or my recommendations were available to anyone who ever looked at this student's file.

It was as if the wind had been sucked right out of me.

More than the wind. The spirit.

My very spirit, at that moment, simply seemed to...vanish.

Never Underestimate a Cat

6/24/06 6:55 a.m. email:

Many thanks to all of you who sent me wonderful birthday messages, cards and phone calls. A special thanks to the trio from Fairbanks who left such a fine, fine rendition of the birthday song on my answering machine! ☺

Sorry for not responding or returning calls. Denise is back in ICU, back on the ventilator, and I have been at the hospital with her or home sleeping. She was transferred to ICU at 1:30 a.m. on the 22nd, and right now is struggling, really struggling, to pull through this latest setback. The culprit at present is pneumonia, and, of course, the fact that at 90 lbs. and unable to absorb nutrition, she simply does not have the immune system or strength to fight off the constant challenges. The ventilator and various machines, tubes and lines are doing their jobs right now, and hopefully (with luck and prayer), she will pull through.

6/27/06 11:49 p.m. email:

Today was a difficult day. They called a family care planning meeting with the two primary doctors (the ostomy surgeon and the pulmonary specialist), the kids, Buck, Denise's dad (who flew in from Ohio), one of her two brothers from out of town, and me.

According to the doctors, the mass in Denise's abdomen is likely a rapidly growing tumor which they cannot possibly treat at this point.

Her ARDS (acute respiratory distress syndrome) is so severe that there is little chance of her surviving without the ventilator. It has shown no improvement over the past week and is not responding to antibiotics, steroids or any other treatment.

Neither of the doctors feels that she can recover enough to leave the hospital, and both feel that continuing treatment is prolonging her suffering. They were quite gentle with us, and her ostomy surgeon (who has been her doctor for the last four years) actually had trouble speaking, as he seemed to be fighting his own emotions. Denise is that kind of person...you cannot know her and remained detached—even if you try to.

One brother wants a second opinion...someone to review her entire file and render their thoughts regarding whether the mass actually IS a rapidly growing tumor, or whether it is necrotic tissue from the old tumor (a distinct possibility apparently).

We are all a bit shell-shocked. I have Kyle here at home with me tonight, and I will take the day and night shift at the hospital tomorrow.

We all sure shed a lot of tears today...and I think we are all trying to figure out where reality, hope and release each exist and need to be acted upon.

What I know for certain is that she is so very, very sick from so many, many directions and surely after 13 months of this her body must be worn down to a thread.

What I don't know is if that thread is one that can be fashioned into a rope, or whether we simply need to accept that asking her to hang on to such a thin line is more cruel than loving.

Journal Entry undated, sometime in late June 2006:

Cancer has no scruples. It wanders around attacking at random, with no regard for the fact that its host is someone else's daughter, wife, mother, sister... lifeline. It snatches at will, shoving its victim onto a roller coaster that winds up and around steep and precarious curves; subjecting its occupant to an onslaught of radiation, lost platelets, chemotherapy, dehydration, low blood counts, and unrelenting pain. And everyone knows that roller coasters are only fun if ridden voluntarily. Ridden long enough against one's will, even the most stoic succumbs to its ravage.

During her years of living with it, Denise rarely mentioned the ostomy bag—and when she did, it was usually to surprise me with something like, "Did you know they have whole catalogues of sexy underwear for colostomy users?" Or, one time—out of the blue and with no warning—she caught me off guard with: "Did you know they sewed up my butt hole?"

"Soooo...what...you don't fart anymore?" I asked, thinking maybe there was a silver lining to this after all.

"Oh, *yeah* I do." She grinned. "It just goes in the bag."

It was impossible not to love her attitude. But I had learned over the past few months that Denise was not as cavalier about her body, her weight, or her colostomy bag as she had led me to believe. Or perhaps, as I had wanted to believe. During those many, many nights and days in the hospital, I learned what it was to change and clean the bag; and I watched Denise as she had to succumb to dependence. When the bag needed changing and the nurses didn't show up despite repeated requests, well, then, you just have to let your sister of the heart put the gloves on and get right in there. For me, Denise allowing me to help her in this way shortened the ever strengthened tether between us; it was an intimacy that I was honored to accept. But I know that, although Denise was glad it was me there and not someone else, it had to be difficult to relinquish that control.

After the family care meeting with the doctors, collectively we all made the decision that it was time to turn off the ventilator. Her sedation was decreased so that she could regain consciousness in the hopes that she would then be able to say good-bye to her children. Unbelievably, as they gradually turned down the amount of breaths the ventilator was taking for her, Denise sustained breathing on her own. Each hour, each half day, each day...she grew stronger.

"Where's your dad?" I asked the kids, as I came into the hospital room after being gone for a few hours.

"He went somewhere to find a root beer float. They don't have them here."

"Your dad had a root beer float craving?" I asked, laughing.

"No, for Mom. They took out the ventilator tube."

I looked over at Denise, and sure enough, the ventilator was completely gone.

"Oh, my gosh! Oh...*wow!* That is so awesome! When did they take it out?" I was shocked that I hadn't noticed it the second I came in.

"A couple of hours ago," Kyle said. "And she wrote on Dad's palm that she wanted a root beer float, so he went to find one!"

I stared at Denise, who was sleeping, and at all three kids sitting there, and I just shook my head.

"That is just so, *so* your mom," I said. "Five minutes out of a coma and off the ventilator, and she's bossing your dad around!"

We all smiled.

This woman, they began saying at the hospital, is absolutely a cat with nine lives. No one could believe that she was actually getting stronger.

My worry was that I did not know exactly how many lives she had already used up.

* * * * *

"Buck, I think maybe we should talk to her about hospice." I looked at Buck as we stood by the coffee machine in the little lounge close to Denise's room. "She doesn't want to die here...and she can't go home..."

This was a difficult thing to bring up to someone's husband, but I knew from my experience with my dad that hospice was an incredible gift to families of people who were close to death. Usually they do not take patients unless they are what they call "imminent"—that is, close to the end with no hope for recovery—but in my dad's case, he ended up living in the hospice center for four months. In Denise's case, that did not seem to be an issue. Although she was stronger and breathing on her own, the reality was that Denise was dying. And I think at that point, we all knew it. Well, on some level we knew it. I am not sure you really believe a thing like that, even if you think you know it.

The next day Buck and I went together and looked at the nearby hospice center. It was so much nicer than the hospital...so much more relaxed and comfortable. It wasn't home, but clearly an effort had been put into designing the rooms so that they felt more like a home than a hospital. That night we talked to Denise about the idea of her moving over there.

It might have been difficult to use the hospice word with Buck, but for me it was far more painful to use it with Denise. Somehow saying it to Buck, I was able to keep the professional part of me up front and forward. Or at least, what used to be the professional part of me. But with Denise, talking about moving to the hospice center drove another layer of reality into the cocoon I used to keep myself functioning in one piece. I mean, everyone knows the reality that even if people are aware they are entering hospice, not many are aware of their exit.

On July 4, 2006, Buck rode in the ambulance with Denise. I drove my car, and with the rest of her family there to support her, Denise officially became a hospice patient.

But you know what they say: never underestimate a cat. What being there did for Denise was make her quite clear that she did not want to die there.

And so she didn't. Instead, she used the time to get strong enough to go home.

And that is *exactly* what made Denise so...*Denise*.

* * * * *

July 11, 2006 11:36 p.m. email:

My emotions run amok these days...one minute I am feeling such incredible happiness that Denise is still here and that we have this time together; the next I am weeping furiously, so distraught that time is running out. The pain of letting go, of saying good-bye...well, it is just bone/gut/soul deep and nearly impossible to fathom. Denise has been significant in and to my life for three and a half decades. To imagine her gone is nearly impossible for me to do. For any of us to do.

I treasure the 12-15 hour periods when it is only Denise and me in the quiet of the hospice room. There is a special kind of comfort between us, and I feel honored that she trusts me enough to let me care for her physically and share with her emotionally. It requires a near-constant vigilance to attend to her needs...which is a good thing. I would not want to have too much time just to sit here and think.

* * * * *

After entering hospice, Denise grew stronger on a daily basis. She was sitting up for a little bit of time each day (never mind that it required about a hundred pillows to keep her in an upright position), and she was even going for short jaunts in a wheelchair.

One night, a little after midnight, Denise looked at me and stated, "Slushy." Denise may have been getting stronger, but she was still weak enough to have to conserve her words.

"Slushy?"

"Uh huh. Slushy. Make me one." Denise looked at me earnestly.

"Okay, sure. They have an ice crushing machine down there...I suppose I could find some juice and use it."

"Cherry."

"You want a cherry slushy?" I asked, half-amused at her funny cravings and half-amused by the look on her face.

"Uh-huh."

She smiled this sweet and tender sort of smile that just about melted my heart. Sweet and tender were not adjectives I previously associated with Denise. Bold, yes. Dynamic, most certainly. But not sweet and tender.

I did not understand why the first time a caregiver was on duty they were still asking me if she was my mother. When I looked at her, I thought Denise looked beautiful. I mean, really, *really* beautiful. Of course, she was too thin and frail—only weighing maybe eighty or eighty-five pounds—but the lack of any body fat left her face with stunning angles. Her eyes, so blue, were huge, and high, defined cheekbones gave her face a striking elegance I had never observed in her before. I wanted to photograph her. I wanted to capture that beauty and those angles and the look on her face that I had so come to treasure. It was a look of utter trust in me. Of absolute faith in my ability to care for her physical needs and escort her emotionally on this journey without faltering. I had never seen or felt this gentle, fragile side of Denise, and the expression in her eyes as she entrusted the big and little things to me is a look I shall never forget.

And I thought she looked absolutely beautiful.

It wasn't until much later that I realized I wasn't seeing—and couldn't possibly see—Denise the way she really looked. I never did take any pictures, knowing without asking that she would not want me to. I am quite sure that throughout those days and weeks, what I was seeing was Denise's spirit. Her essence. I suspect were I to look at a picture now of how she looked then, I would be shocked. Probably horrified, actually. But at the time, I was absolutely stunned by a physical beauty that Denise had never displayed, even in her most vibrant of days.

"Make me a cherry slushy."

Well, at least she's feeling well enough to still boss me around, I thought, smiling.

"They don't have any cherry juice down there, Denise. How about apple?"

She shook her head no.

"Orange?"

Again, she shook her head no.

"Huh. Let me think about this a second." I was trying to figure out where I could go buy the right kind of cherry juice to make a slushy at 12:30 at night, when I remembered that when I moved to Utah, Denise had bought me a snow cone machine. It was one of those things I used a lot initially as I adjusted to the dry, desert heat, but then did not use much later on. I was almost positive I had some sugar-free cherry syrup left over from that summer, and since Denise was not able to digest sugar, this would be just perfect for her.

"You know what? I might have some cherry syrup at home. Are you sure you really, really want one? If you do, I'll run home and get it." I only lived two miles from the hospice center.

Denise, those blue eyes wide, shook her head yes, and I told her I would be back in twenty.

Of course, when I returned she was sleeping. But no matter. She knew I went to get her cherry syrup, and that was all that was really important.

* * * * *

July 18, 2006, 7:07 a.m. email to the principal of her school, Stratton Elementary:

Hi, Howard.

Denise and I had a most remarkable and gifted night Monday night, and we talked about so many, many things throughout a long and sleepless night. I asked her if she had a charity or organization she wanted people to donate to if they wanted to send money to something in her name, and she said, "Stratton."

So please know that this is what she wants and when the time comes, what we will tell people. Please let me know any specific information people will need such as whom to make the checks to, the address, etc.

Remarkable woman, isn't she?

* * * * *

July 28, 2006, 4:20 p.m. email:

I am writing this update from Denise's house, where I sit and watch her as she sleeps. Returning home from hospice was a wonderful thing, and the last ten days have been yet another gift to all of us. This has given Denise time to participate in many important things. Together, we have gone through all of her clothes, photos and jewelry, and we have talked of so many, many things.

Yesterday, I was lying on the bed beside her and Katie came into the room. She had been scrubbing the kitchen all morning (Katie HATES to clean, but Denise has always been a crazed *maniac* with the mop, broom and dusting cloth). I said to Denise, "You should see your kitchen! It's beautiful!!" And Katie said, "Mama! I am going to be your cleaning proxy. You are going to look down from heaven and say, *That's my daughter!* and you are going to be so proud!"

I thought I was going to lose it. I had to go into the bathroom and cry into a towel.

Emotional yes, but a good thing.

* * * * *

August 2, 2006, 11:12 p.m. journal entry:

Denise is weaker today. I played a song I chose for her memorial to see if she approved. It's Alabama's *"Angels Among Us."* She did.

I cried the rest of the day.

August 4, 2006 11:08 p.m. email:

Denise was in so much pain today. We started giving her full doses of pain medication every hour around 5:00 tonight. Up until now, she has preferred being less sedated and dealing with the pain so that she is alert enough to be with her children...but now it is just not an option. The pain is so intense and it literally feels like my own heart and guts are ripping apart a little bit, every time I look at her.

She still wants me to bathe her every day and I cannot tell you what that is like. It is this remarkable experience of feeling so tethered, bound by our sisterhood and at the same time, it is as if I am a mother...funny, I remember this same feeling giving my own mother sponge baths the last few days of her life...

Did I tell you I bought her a dress to wear to her funeral? That may have been the hardest thing I have ever done. Denise and I were talking about it, and I asked her what she wanted to wear. She looked at me with such...I don't know...such...*devotion* or something, and said, "What do you think I should wear?" and I told her it just depended on what she wanted to portray...elegant, a teacher-look, casual...what did she want? She thought about this for a minute and then said, "Well, what about that black skirt? The one I wore on the cruise. I love that skirt." I laughed and said, "Denise...that's a size eighteen! You aren't a size eighteen anymore; I don't even think you are a size three!" So, we decided that I would go to the mall and bring back several options and she could choose for herself.

She chose a dress that is so lovely...it's white and almost ethereal...she wanted me to show it to Buck and see what he thought, and I asked her if she was sure she wanted me to go get him. I said, "You know...he might think this is just too morbid or something. I mean, not many people shop for their own funeral dress." But you know Denise...she wanted him to see it, so I brought him upstairs and he gave his nod of approval. He was really good about it—I honestly don't know what he thought about the whole thing. I mean, I guess it *is* kind of morbid.

Anyway, we laughed together after he went downstairs, and it made me feel so happy in my heart...just to be laughing with her.

But I cried in the car all the way home.

This has been a remarkable, intimate journey—I feel like Dorothy in the Wizard of Oz—my life seems to be part nightmare, part magic, part friendship and love; and part filled with the pain of saying good-bye *(...I think I will miss you most of all, scarecrow?)*.

One thing I know for sure: in all things there are lessons, silver linings, and opportunities for growth. So I guess I am learning to value all three, even when life seems patently unfair and difficult to surmount. As Kyle said to me the other day, "You know what they say, Aunt Debra...even after the longest night, morning will come."

Wise words from such a young boy. Wise and true.

I so hope he remembers them a few months from now.

* * * * *

The next few days were filled with a quiet kind of winding down. I would lie on Denise and Buck's bed, which was pushed against the hospital bed that had been brought in for her, and sometimes we would talk a little, but mostly Denise would sleep. At one point, I held her hand and told her that her friendship had been a gift to me. And then I said I was going to miss her, and I started to cry. As weak as she was, she managed to touch my face, mouthing softly, "I know." I apologized for crying—I worked hard not to let my emotions get too near the surface while I was in their home. Denise just closed her eyes and smiled a little, and gave my hand the best squeeze she could manage.

I had been amazed by the things we had talked about over the last few months, but especially over the last three weeks. We had talked about little things and big things, and Denise was honoring me in the way she knew I would treasure most—by exposing hidden crevices of her being, and relying on me for help. She asked me to bathe her, reposition her, listen to her, talk to her, and read the Bible to her.

It was a time of nearly suffocating heartbreak wrapped inside an intimate cloak of love.

When the time came, it was when *Denise* was ready and not a moment sooner. She died on August 8, 2006 with her husband and children by her side, and me stuck in a traffic jam while driving over.

As it should be. Some things are reserved just for husbands and children, and even sisters of the heart must stand back a few feet.

This was how she wanted it; of that, I am sure.

Date with a Butterfly

Denise Kruse Lindsey

*The woman we loved, who loved God, family, children,
animals and especially the butterflies and dragonflies.*
Born October 9, 1954
Had a date with a butterfly
August 8, 2006

Friends: Following the graveside service on Tuesday, August 15, 2006 there will be a butterfly release in honor of our friend, mother, daughter, sister and teacher, Denise. We ask that you pick up a butterfly envelope prior to going to the graveside and when it is time, collectively release them to the sky

Why the butterfly? Because Denise loved them; and because we talked about this prior to her death, and she loved the idea of each of you releasing one in her honor and remembering the following:

Don't weep at my grave,
For I am not there,
I've a date with a butterfly
To dance in the air.
I'll be singing in the sunshine,
Wild and free,
Playing tag with the wind,
While I'm waiting for thee.

Despite my best intentions, all the emotions, trials, love, and heartbreak of the last few months seemed to converge and well up inside of me when I stood up in front of so many people to pay honor to Denise. The tears I had worked so hard at containing cut loose without any regard at all for my personal dignity, or for my need to share these words with other people who loved this friend of mine. Katie later told me she sat there silently urging me to regain control. I believe she told me she was uttering something along the lines of, *"Get it TOGETHER, Aunt Debra! You can DO this!"* Despite her silent encouragement, I never did quite seem to get it together that day.

So, for those who could not understand my words through the snot-filled nose and the choking, tear-filled voice, here they are for you to read; and for those who have shared my love for Denise through the story told in this book, here—in part—are the final words I offered in honor of my friend:

Denise's Eulogy: Sisters of the Heart

Hello... For those of you who don't know me...my name is Debra, and I am up here to tell you a little bit more about Denise; about the friendship that we shared. Ours was a friendship that began nearly thirty-five years ago and grew into something much more than ordinary friendship. Denise and I used to say we were "sisters of the heart"...the sister neither of us had, but had become by choice. Female soul mates.

All of you have said so many wonderful things about Denise...about her intelligence and intensity, her love of the Lord, her children, her husband...her commitment to and love of education. I also admired and loved those things in Denise. When I thought about the purpose of a eulogy...to share things about a person others may not know that they might find comforting, I decided I wanted to share with you a different side of Denise. A side that in spite of our years together, I really didn't know very well until this last year. I would like to share with you what I learned about a vulnerable Denise...the Denise that was not always in control.

...perhaps our biggest difference had always been in the way we functioned emotionally. I loved Denise's boldness: her take-charge, "I am in control," confident attitude. She made things seem easy and, as everyone here has already said, tackled the toughest of jobs and challenges with pure glee. In so many ways Denise was the personification of the phrase "strong, tough woman." I'm pretty sure that it was Denise who actually invented the phrase: "Life gave you lemons? Make lemonade." If not, there was no doubt that she was the one who added, "So suck it up, Missy, and get moving!"

I loved that about her. We all did.

...sharing is one of the things Denise did best. She always knew what people needed, whether it was organization, fund-raising, advice, an emotional boost, or just a perpetually cheery hello every day... and when she knew what they needed, that is what she shared with them of herself.

As young teenagers, Denise shared her friends with me. She was determined to keep me from being too much of an introvert. When my mother was going through her first bout of cancer and my parents were preoccupied with fourteen months of intense chemotherapy...Denise shared her family with me! I think I probably saw more of Norm and Betty in those days than I did my own parents. We were eighteen years old...the age that Ryan is now. Denise knew what I needed, and she shared it—and at that time, it happened to be friends and parents.

Later, oddly enough, we both discovered an inability to conceive or carry children, and this was very difficult for each of us. Then Denise and Buck were blessed with Katie, Kyle, and Ryan, and she had the children she so desperately always wanted, but I did not. So, to the very best of her ability, my sister of the heart shared her children with me. She let me be a godmother...take them on trips alone to faraway places. She told me kid story after kid story, and sent me pictures of everything so that even though I lived in Alaska—or was traipsing halfway around the world on a bicycle—I was able to somehow have a sense that I was part of someone's family.

Denise shared something else with me...something she knew I needed. My father died in 2000, and I was left with very little in the way of close family... I was going through a painful divorce at the time, and Denise shared the assurance that I was indeed her sister in soul if not in blood, and that no matter what, I would not die alone and I would not be sent to some pauper's grave. She assured me that I would be buried where she would be buried. I would share her spot in death...because she knew, she knew that for me, having no children, husband, or parents left me feeling a little nervous about those end-of-life details.

And so, at that time the consummate Planner and Organizer made me swear that I would put a Baggie in my freezer with a list in it titled, "In the event of my death," which had instructions to call her immediately. She was convinced that upon my demise, church ladies would miraculously appear in my life, immediately clean out the freezer and refrigerator, find the Baggie, and call her. Of course, neither one of us ever contemplated that she would go first. She was the organizer and the one in command central. That's the way it had always been, and it simply never occurred to either of us—despite her bouts with cancer—that that was not the way it would always be.

But, as we all know...it didn't turn out the way we planned. One bout turned into three; I wasn't the one to go first; and she wasn't the one in control of what was happening to her body...her life...her dreams.

And it was then that Denise shared the greatest gift of a lifetime with me. She shared her journey toward death, and she allowed me to become her escort...for as far as I could possibly go. The self-confident and bold woman who had always defined strength in terms of control and not showing vulnerable emotion allowed me to see her when she was scared and hurting, when she was full of tubes and stitches and bags and other things that were taking away the precious sense of control and command she had always maintained.

And she began, I believe, to redefine for herself what strength was, and what it wasn't.

To me, this was the ultimate gift that Denise honored me with. It has been, in fact, the most intimate gift I have had in my lifetime...and I am quite sure, the most intimate gift I will ever have in my lifetime. She trusted me to bathe her body day after day as it progressively weakened and withered; she allowed me to do for her what she could no longer do for herself. She trusted me to be her faithful escort on this most important journey; and most importantly, she allowed me to see her vulnerability.

...I sat in here hour after hour yesterday, listening and watching as one by one people came and were stunned into silence by what they saw in that coffin—were heartbroken by what they saw and what they perceived must have entailed tremendous suffering to reduce her to looking as she does now. But I want you to know that I believe with all my heart that Denise did not suffer over this last year. She hurt; she was in pain; and at times she was frightened...but she was not suffering.

To me, suffering implies being forced to endure something...but I believe that Denise willed herself to the fight in order to be able to share a piece of herself with those she loved, not because they needed something from her, but because she needed something from them...and she was, for the first time, okay with acknowledging her need. *I believe that Denise needed to share that part of herself she had kept pretty tightly bound...and she needed to see, and have others see, that this was not weakness on her part, but strength.*

And in so doing, I believe that at the end Denise was happiest with herself, not because she made the best lemonade out of lemons, but because she could cry openly and say that lemonade wasn't what she wanted.

In the end...I believe that Denise had redefined for herself what was strength and what was weakness. And in so doing, I believe she was able to see not just how much she loved us, but just how much we all loved her back. I believe, having watched her day after day, that the months and months of struggling, of illness and of pain were very, very worth it to her. If for no other reason than she could lie in bed with each one of her children, and with her husband, and love them even when she wasn't in control.

I do not think Denise would want you to leave here thinking she had suffered all these months. I believe that she would prefer you to think of her not as suffering, but as studying._Not as enduring, but as learning. I believe she would want you to leave here understanding that she was, as she had always been, an A+ student.

...thirty-four years is a long time, and her presence in my life has made me a much richer person. Letting her go has been difficult for me...as I said, we sort of depended on each other to share the qualities that we each needed to be a little more whole.

But I realize that Denise didn't leave me, or her children, or Earl, or any of us—taking with her those qualities we so needed from her. She left us with the knowledge and the example that just as she did, we have those qualities within ourselves. And so in the end, I think Denise did what Denise loved to do best: she taught. She taught us not only about the joy of living, but she taught us about the grace of dying.

I will miss her terribly.

Living with Gordian
Fall 2007

"You know what a Gordian knot is?" I asked Joyce in response to her question about how I was doing, as we were talking on the phone early one morning.

"Something that goes on forever?"

"Well, that's probably as good a definition as any. At least in terms of what I've been thinking. Legend has it—well, actually, I don't really know if it's legend or truth—but supposedly Alexander the Great is the only one who ever figured out the Gordian Knot. And he considered it to be his greatest accomplishment."

"Okay."

I suppose Joyce was hoping I would continue and at least give her some inkling as to the nature of this 8:00 a.m. history lesson.

"Well, I've been thinking about it. And, I've decided that this whole thing is like a giant Gordian Knot. Everything that happened in Blanding, at Carson...it's like this intractable problem that just can't be solved."

"Ever?"

"Probably. I mean, probably never solved. The thing is, as you know, I *hate* puzzles. I've always hated puzzles. I hated them before the accident, and I hate them even more now. *You're* the puzzle and Sudoku queen, not me."

Joyce was well-known for pulling out the Sudoku books when she was feeling under a lot of stress or down in the dumps. That had always so impressed me, considering the fact that just looking at a picture of one in the newspaper stressed me out. I always figured that in another few years, Joyce will have way less Alzheimer tendencies just because she is so diligent about working out her anxieties by spending hours and hours on puzzles.

Me? I'd been weaving potholders lately. It was pathetic. I bought a loom at the Dollar Store, and on bad days I'd been known to weave dozens of them. Of course, I didn't know how to tie them off, so I simply weaved and re-weaved them, using the same stretchy little pieces each time. At the end of the day, there was nothing to show for my time, but I felt a lot better.

"The problem for me, Joyce, is that even though I hate puzzles, I can't let them go. They plague me. I keep going back to them to see if I can figure them out, only I never do—they just torment me. I think I am going to have to resign myself to having to make Dollar Store potholders for the rest of my life. Now, *that's* a depressing thought," I said, only partially joking. "Of course, if I could learn how to tie them off, maybe I could sell them back to the Dollar Store for a penny apiece."

"You make me laugh! Well, you don't have to stick to potholders. You know, once you get the hang of the Sudoku's, they're not so hard to work out."

"Well, not so hard for you. For me, they would be impossible. Just like my Gordian Knot. Neither is ever going to be among the things I figure out."

"You don't think?"

"No," I said, and after pausing for a minute, added, "No, I don't, Joyce. I have nothing in common with Alexander the Great. I'm never going to really figure out what happened. I might start to unravel it—just as I've done over the past year. I figure out bits and pieces and think I understand it. Then I think about it some more, and I'm not sure I'm right. So, I start all over again, analyzing it, tearing it apart, trying to figure out how to untie the knot, only to realize that I can't."

I could tell by the silence on the other end of the line that Joyce was unsure if this was a good epiphany for me to have had, or not.

"But I think that's okay. I think I know what my piece is. I think I've figured out what part of it I own, where I have to assume responsibility—and I think I've reconciled what I've needed to understand in order to move on."

"Do you think you'll go back into a school?"

"No. No, I think I've accepted the fact that I can't perform or function within that setting anymore. But that's okay, Joyce. I mean, I'm still passionate about kids, about education...about teaching. But I can't use my voice like I once did. I lost that way I had that somehow let me fight for the right things to happen for kids. You know what I mean? I lost my ability to do that without creating havoc. And in the end, I didn't do the kids any good, Joyce. I didn't help them at all."

"That's not true, Debra."

"No, it is. I mean, not for the whole of my career...but in the end. In the end, I didn't help the kids I left behind in Utah—the ones I didn't stay and fight for—and I sure didn't help all those Carson kids. In fact, I probably hurt them, given how it all ended up. Just disappearing like that."

I had never quite reconciled what happened at Carson and how my career ended. Over the last year, there had been many times I looked back and wondered why I did not pursue litigation, either on behalf of myself or on behalf of the students. I had talked with lawyers, and it certainly appeared that there were sufficient grounds to pursue on behalf of both. But I guess it all coincided with what was happening with Denise, and I simply could not face both experiences at the same time. So, I let things drop with the school district, and I focused on the part of my life that was very separate from what had transpired there.

When the smoke cleared and I could see through the thick fog that had settled in my brain following Denise's funeral, I just did not have the energy or the confidence to pursue litigation against a school district. And for many, many months, the guilt of folding, of not staying true to what I believed was right in terms of students, immobilized me from doing much at all. It was then that I started to take it apart—to pick at it one fragment, one layer at a time—in order to figure out what piece of what happened I owned and needed to take responsibility for, and what piece or pieces I needed to let go.

"So, where does this leave you?" Joyce asked, clearly a little concerned with what I was saying. "I mean, where do you go from here? What's next?"

"Well, it still leaves me with a voice. And passion. I just have to find a way to use my voice that's effective." I was quiet for a minute before adding, "And I will, Joyce. I'll find a way to do that. I still have something to offer. I have to believe that I still have something to offer."

"You have a story to tell, Debra. You have a story people need to hear."

"Oh, yeah, Joyce. I can see it now: *Head-Injured Woman Tells All!* That'll go over big at the district offices."

Joyce laughed, and I could just picture that crooked, half-grin of hers as she said, "Hey, you're not popular now, Debra. Might as well tell the truth. One thing you can still do well is write. Just go for it."

Now it was my turn to laugh as I said, "Maybe I will, Joyce. Who knows?" I was smiling as I said to her, "You know what? You made me think of Denise when you said that. Something about the way you just said that really made me think of Denise."

And that, I thought, was a good sign.

A very good sign, indeed.

Epilogue

One day Alice came to a fork in the road and saw a Cheshire Cat in a tree. "Which road do I take?" she asked. "Where do you want to go?" was his response. "I don't know," Alice answered. "Then," said the cat, "it doesn't matter."

Alice and the Cat

Epilogue:
We Need To Do Better

As I say in my first chapter, I am partial to books—I love them. I have the greatest respect for any person who can invent a tale and tell it well, and/or who can research theirs or someone else's story and bring it alive in order to make it real for the rest of us. Some people seem born knowing they have the great American novel in them, and they spend their lives learning, working, studying, and writing in hopes of achieving that goal. Personally, I have always been quite content to read their words and stand in awe of their power to transport me into another's head, heart, and world. It was never my aspiration to be a great writer. It was my aspiration to be a great educational psychologist.

That said, writing has always been as natural to me as breathing, and for as long as I can remember, I have used writing as a way to sort through and sift through the thoughts, events, and confusions that have peppered every phase of my life. Confiding in my diary as a little girl and in my journals as I grew older provided a way for me to square off with myself. It was the one place I could strip myself of all defenses and look at my flaws and my mistakes—look at the behaviors I displayed that betrayed values I had hoped to uphold. It was the sanctuary where I could evaluate what moved me, impassioned me, drove me, and at times, had the potential to ruin me. It was the one place where I could be as awful, horrible, ridiculous, absurd, stupid, and inept as I felt and then work through it so that I could do better. So I could be better. So I could keep trying to be the person I wanted to be.

This is what I was doing when I started to write about the events that occurred in Utah and at Fort Carson. Although I had not been keeping a personal journal on a daily basis for several years, I was so confused, so devastated, so completely and totally bewildered and besieged by my confusion, my anger, my angst, and my fears, that I knew if I didn't open a book of blank pages and square off with myself, I would never move forward. Never forgive those whom I blamed and—perhaps most importantly—never forgive myself for failing the children and families I had come to care about so deeply. I did not know why or what explained all that had occurred—how I could go from being a successful and thriving professional to being the unemployed and isolated person I saw in the mirror—but I did know one thing. I knew that I owned a piece of what happened. My job in my private journal was to figure out what that piece was—what role I played in all that transpired. And then to do something in order to make sure I didn't do it again. To make sure I did not just *hope* to do better, but *would* do better.

Kara Swanson is the author of a book entitled, *I'll Carry the Fork* (Rising Star Press, 2003). It's a book about recovering a life after sustaining a brain injury, and the first line of her book may be the finest first line I have read in any book, fact or fiction. In *I'll Carry the Fork,* Kara's opening line is not only brilliant in that it manages to sum up the entire book in one sentence, but it also speaks a truth so real, so honest, and so poignant that every individual who has ever coped with the devastating effects of a head injury relates to it instantly. Kara Swanson begins her book by saying: "The curious thing about the auto accident that ended my life was that I lived through it."

My auto accident did not break bones, leave me in a coma, or cause me to have to relearn the steps to feed, dress, or care for myself as so many others with head injuries have had to do. Nevertheless, it did leave me having to relearn who I was, and it left me having to learn to like this new person as much as I had liked the person I had ceased to be.

One of the most difficult moments for me came when I moved to Colorado Springs and began the task of trying to find a new neurologist. The first individual I had an appointment with told me I was "being silly." That, "people don't have these kinds of symptoms from concussions." It took me months to find the confidence I needed to look for another doctor; and only when I was absolutely desperate for assistance did I find Dr. James Spadoni, the man who not only validated my symptoms as Dr. Willner had done, but who further helped me understand the effects of my injury.

Over the years of my life I had miscarried the children I hoped to parent; mismanaged the marriages I hoped were forever; and missed finding the financial stability I had hoped to find by age twenty-six, thirty-six, certainly by age forty-six. But never once had I misjudged my ability to do the right thing for children within the public education system. Never once had I misperceived my ability to empower those around me to step out of the comfort of their box and into the risky but important realm of doing things better for children.

Squaring off in the privacy and protection of my journal was not easy. On some absolute core level I had allowed the words of a neurologist who told me I was being silly to reinforce what I thought all along: I was simply not trying hard enough. Some part of me had always been sure that I was weak and pathetic for not finding a way to push through the fog, the fatigue, and the mental confusion— sure that I was "just fine"—merely psychosomatic. Ever the drama queen.

However, I was not being psychosomatic, and my symptoms were (and are) quite real. My disregard of the personality and cognitive challenges that remained after my accident and the continual pressure I placed on myself to "buck up" did not help anyone. Ignoring and denying the changes in both my skills and my personality did not help the administrators and teachers who had to deal with me. It certainly did not help the children I was there to serve, and it did not help me propel myself toward becoming the best new me that I could be.

Perhaps some of the fault indeed lies with me and my own lifelong drive toward being better than average, toward dispelling a deep-seated belief that I was never going to be smart enough or good enough. But in fairness to myself, after my accident no one told me that even concussions can result in long-term insult to the brain. Neither my training nor my personal experience had given me that critical piece of information.

There are estimates that as many as sixty percent of the soldiers returning from Iraq and Afghanistan are suffering from traumatic brain injuries (TBI). Traumatic brain injuries have been labeled the signature injury of these wars, and while soldiers' lives are being spared by the armor that protects their bodies, their brains—rattled inside their skulls by intense explosions—have not emerged so unscathed. Sometimes the head injuries are so severe the effects and changes in a person are obvious; but frequently, the injury—just as mine was—is labeled a concussion and left to become a hidden disability. The fatigue, impatience, irritability, mood swings, memory problems, sleep disorders, and the host of other behavioral changes demonstrated by the person with the head injury are often dismissed as postwar stress reactions, as depression, as something to be treated as a psychological disorder, or as something not treated at all. They are not symptoms treated as the very real medical insult to the brain that they are, and the rehabilitation needed to lessen the long-term effects and maximize recovery is often missed.

Bob Woodruff's unfortunate injury in Iraq has brought much needed attention to the issues surrounding traumatic brain injury and its impacts, not just on the person who sustains the injury, but on every person who is connected to them. The Woodruffs themselves are fabulous role models, as they have gone back to the business of being parent, coworker, friend, and spouse while reducing the stigma attached to the changes that can occur in a person with a traumatic brain injury.

But we need to do better.

According to the Centers for Disease Control and Prevention, of the 1.4 million people who sustain a TBI each year in the United States and seek medical treatment, 50,000 die, 235,000 are hospitalized, and—like me—1.1 million are treated and released from hospital emergency rooms. These numbers include people who have been involved in auto accidents, bicycle and skating accidents, sporting accidents, domestic violence disputes, or any other incident that causes a serious jolt or blow to the head. Many—just as I was—are diagnosed with a "mild concussion" and told to go home and rest. And just like me, they and their families, friends, and coworkers all have the expectation that things will be "just fine."

Doctors, emergency room personnel, teachers, social workers, and other mental health professionals must all do better in becoming educated about the changes that can affect not just cognitive abilities, but also a person's behavior and personality following a head injury. Whatever our politics—whether we support the wars in Iraq and Afghanistan or we do not; whether we support nontraditional marriages or we don't—the reality is that head injuries occur without regard to age, race, gender, culture, or religious orientation. People of all ages and ethnicities, people who are gay, lesbian, single, in cohabitating domestic partnerships and those in traditional partnerships—all sustain head injuries from falls, assaults, accidents, sports injuries, or domestic violence within the home.

We need to do better in getting the information to TBI survivors and their families that will help them with both recovery and acceptance, and we must do better in funding the research and the treatment that will help us understand the very complex and diverse damage that occurs to the brain.

A great deal has been written about both the positive and negative impacts of the *No Child Left Behind* legislation. But whatever our personal and professional feelings are about this legislation, the reality is that millions of children in our public and private schools struggle with the effects of both diagnosed and undiagnosed head injuries, auditory processing disorders, learning disabilities, emotional disturbances, and other disabling conditions (such as loss of hearing, poor vision, autism, and mental retardation, to name a few). We must do much better at the pre-service level in training all educators to understand not just the words of the laws, but the realities behind honoring those words. It is not enough to know that we are supposed to effectively teach these children; we must make sure we know *how* to effectively teach them.

Approximately thirteen percent of students in public education are diagnosed as having disabling conditions that adversely affect their abilities and are placed in special education. The number of children considered to be "at risk" is far, far greater. There are both programs and laws established to protect and serve these children, but we need to do better—much better—in how we implement these laws and regulations.

It is not good enough to identify that a student has learning disabilities, Asperger's syndrome, or any other condition adversely affecting a student's ability to be successful, and then not provide the educational environment needed in order for them to experience success. We must make sure that *all* educators (not just "special" educators) are comfortable with their skills and abilities to handle the specifics of educating *all* children. It is not good enough to say that the *i's* are dotted and the *t's* are crossed in the unrelenting amount of paperwork required of educators serving children with special needs—if, in reality, the programs identified in that paperwork are not carried out with integrity.

We must do better in training educational administrators to model what they advocate. We must do better in holding them accountable for demonstrating the kind of leadership that puts into practice what research has taught us about how the brain learns, and for upholding the laws that have been established to protect the rights of every child.

The research has already established that individuals do not learn or perform well in environments that are fraught with chronic stress. This is true for children, and it is true for adults. We cannot expect teachers to speak up and advocate for the children, much less effectively teach them, if they themselves do not feel secure and respected within their own professional communities. Academic *rigor* indeed becomes academic *rigor mortis* if we fail to use common sense and apply ethical standards to the applications of our research; or if we measure the worth of both students and educators solely on the basis of a yearly exam.

There will always be individuals in education, as in every other profession, who will rise to positions of power despite clear indication that they possess neither the leadership skill nor the commitment to ethical standards to perform effectively in those positions. But this does not mean they have to remain in those positions. We all must do better on behalf of our children in speaking up and advocating for the right things to happen in our schools and communities, and in making our individual and our collective voices heard.

I believed then, and I believe now, that there is too much mediocrity endorsed in public education. I believed then, and I believe now, that too much lip service is given to encouraging parents to be an active part of their children's educational planning, when in reality, what we communicate to them is that we want their participation only if they happen to agree with what we—the experts—believe needs to be done. I was much more effective at challenging this within the system prior to my accident.

Much more effective.

Warren Bennis, long considered a pioneer in the field of leadership studies, states that a leader must be able to "change an organization that is dreamless, soulless and visionless." He says that good leaders "...make people feel that they're at the very heart of things, not at the periphery." While I could not agree with this more, I have learned that an organization can *articulate* vision, but remain or become soulless if the individuals over whom leaders have control do not have the confidence or the skills to challenge the status quo. When leaders are not living up to the qualities that Bennis and others have identified as imperative if change is to occur, people must find the way to speak up. Hopefully they can do so with a little *panache*, so as to encourage and enable change rather than offend and alienate. But not everyone is so blessed. Still, people need to find a way to make their voices heard and not accept or endorse mediocrity through a veil of silence.

Life is complicated. Organizational systems are complicated. People are complicated. There are no quick fixes; however, we can each do better in striving toward excellence by rejecting the ease that accepting mediocrity brings.

As for me, my journey of reflection, hindsight, and at times painful introspection revealed many things that I certainly could have done differently—could have done better. *Would* have done both differently and better had I known then what I know now. And while I never set out to write a book, somewhere along the way I realized something. I realized that I do still have a voice. Just like Simon, though it might be just a whisper now, it is a voice with the potential to be strong. And if I no longer have the *panache* and the natural grace to use that voice within the daily workings of complex organizational systems, well, perhaps this is why paper was invented along with the words to place upon it.

I still have a voice. I can still continue to endorse and model excellence. I can continue to advocate for the right things to happen for children and for others who perhaps have not yet discovered the strength of their own voices. No doubt, I will continue to make mistakes along the way, but if I remain true to my beliefs, I will learn from those mistakes and continue to strive to both do better and *be* better.

The writing of this book was not easy, but it happened, and every person with a head injury should take heart in this fact. Things might not happen as quickly; they might not happen as easily, but they still can happen. That knowledge alone is worth any angst created during the process of getting this story from inside my heart and my head to the pages you have just read.

PostScript: "How could you write this book if you have a brain injury?"

Nearly twenty-five people test read this book in its various phases of completion. Some of these people knew me before the accident; some knew me only after the accident; and some had never met me at all. Both men and women were test readers, and they ranged in age from people in their mid-twenties to those in their mid-seventies. They came from all parts of the country, and they were equally disparate in their levels of education, socioeconomic status, background, and interests as they were in age. All of them offered valuable insights, suggestions, and reactions. And all of them at some point and in some way asked the question, "How did you do it? How could you write this book if you have the ongoing challenges with your brain that you say you have?"

It's an understandable question and one I imagine many readers will want to ask. Sometimes I even ask it of myself!

There are several things helpful to know if, as a reader, you found yourself curious about the "how" of this book's creation.

First of all, I had a great deal of help from various people who are referenced in this story. For example, I did not remember what happened between Denney and me. I had absolutely no memory of what it was that drove us apart or how it was that we ended our relationship. So, I tracked him down, and I asked him. That was difficult for each of us, and I am sure it was a bit stunning to Denney to hear me say, "I really do not know." But, as further testimony to the good man that he is, Denney opened the door that he, too, had painfully closed, and he wrote me his memories. The words in the confrontation between us—when he tells me that he doesn't know what is me and what is the head injury—came directly from his email recalling our story. Others who similarly sent me their specific memories contributed greatly to my being able to write this book.

Secondly, the literally hundreds and hundreds of emails and letters (both professional and personal) that still exist were an enormous tool for helping me recreate the events that transpired. Using them to piece the story together was very challenging for me. At times it was so overwhelming as to reduce me to tears, because my brain could not keep the information straight—and that was very painful for me to reconcile. I would spend hours and hours and hours sorting the emails by date so that I could make a timeline of events and conversations. I would sort them by individuals so that I could have that person's thoughts and words in one compilation, and/or at other times, I would sort them by topic matter. That was all fine and good; however, if I did not write that part of the story at the time that I completed the sorting, by the next day or the next week, I would have no recollection of even having them, much less of having read them. Many times, the act of sorting and organizing was all my brain would let me do on that day, and when I would sit down a day or two later to write, I would find myself facing the same confusions and blank spots that got me started with the sorting in the first place. So, I would start all over...and inevitably find myself saying in surprise: "Wow, I didn't even realize I *had* this documentation!" although I knew I must have known, because they were organized and highlighted.

It took some real mental cheerleading to push myself through the discouragement of knowing I had organized and read documents that seemed completely unfamiliar to me, in order to continue on with the task of writing. Fortunately, there were many who took up the pompoms when I tossed them down.

My reports and case notes helped a great deal in terms of accurately describing the children and in recreating the dialogue that took place between us. Similarly, my dozens of scraps of paper containing snatches and snippets of conversation were immensely helpful. As I went through the boxes, notebooks, calendars, and journals, I was always amazed to find these scraps of dialogue in existence—amazed and grateful, as I could not have recreated the portrayed events and conversations without them.

As to the conversations with Denise and Joyce, two things helped me with those. One is that after thirty years of friendship, the cadence and flow of conversation with each of them is simply a part of who I am. Emails would remind me or refresh me of the conversations we had during the stress of the Blanding and Carson months, and it wasn't difficult to recreate phone conversations that took place. Joyce, of course, could and did confirm my accuracy of those that transpired between us. I can only hope Denise would feel I did our conversations equal justice in terms of accuracy.

Three other things contributed to my being able to write this book.

One is that it is all I did for sixteen months. I could not, and did not, do much of anything else—with the exception of taking online writing classes in hopes of becoming more adept in the art and science of writing in the genre of creative nonfiction. I did not live up to my own expectations in terms of continuing to be a "good godmother" to Denise and Buck's children. I did not hold a paying job. I did not maintain friendships or relationships that deserved more time and energy than I had to give. Engaging in other, normal activities compromised my ability and/or took up all the energy and stamina I had for that day. I imagine it is much like what someone with a chronic fatigue disorder must contend with—if I went for a walk or a hike, it felt wonderful, and I felt emotionally and physically much better. But when I returned home, I would sleep. And sleep and sleep and sleep. And if a day or two went by in which I did not do much writing, I would have to re-read everything I had written from the beginning of the book. If I didn't, I could not remember what I had already included, and I would find myself unable to move forward with the story. I am probably the only person on the planet who has read their own memoir 403 times and still finds the information interesting and surprising.

So, as the weeks and months went by, I gained three pants sizes, Teek got chubby, Meka became undisciplined, and most of my friends suffered ongoing frustration with my lack of communication. But a book did get written, and quite likely chubbiness and loss of discipline can be corrected, and my friends will practice forgiveness. I have vowed to regain the skill of returning phone calls, and I have promised my dogs (and those who are subject to their bad behaviors) that we will all resume our quest for physical fitness and spiritual health.

Another thing that helped in the creation of this book is that although I am not a writer by training, I have used writing as a way to sort through my thoughts and keep track of my life since I was old enough to hold a pencil. The process of sitting and writing is comforting to me, and as "Dr. Freud" pointed out, my facility with words didn't take the hit in my brain that some other skills took. So, as frustrating as gathering, organizing, and holding on to the information was, the actual act of writing was very calming to me. Undoubtedly, this helped create a story that is readable and coherent.

And finally, our memory system is very complex, which I think is a good thing and contributed a great deal to my ability to tell this story. Our brains do not process all information in the same way, nor do we learn, store, or retrieve all information from just one location in our brain. Thankfully, we have multiple pathways in which we store and retrieve information. As is true for all of us, certain conversations and experiences seem to have taken root in my brain and others did not. In my case, it seems that experiences that were accompanied by the intense emotions of devastation, humiliation, and/or crushing despair (such as receiving Tony's letter, realizing I was not organizing and recalling visual information, and finding myself locked out of my classroom and forbidden to see my students) seem to have been stored and retrieved in such a way that I am able to recall them with little effort.

Finally, readers need remember that weaving a seamless story is one of the great tasks and challenges of any writer. What you are reading may seem like a very organized sequence of events, but realize, for every scene recounted in this book, there are undoubtedly hundreds of others that are not. I made the absolute commitment to myself that I would remain honest and true to the experiences and events communicated in the book; and I believe that to the absolute best of my ability, I was able to do that. I realize, of course, as I hope all readers do, that *Panache* is a memoir, and therefore the perspective is mine. I suspect every person noted in the book has a dozen conversations or interactions that they recall and I do not. Certainly there are dozens of conversations and events I *do* recall but for any number of reasons chose not to include in the story. I think that the art, the skill, and the satisfaction of writing a memoir has much to do with having the luxury, as well as the responsibility, of picking and choosing to present thoughts and events in such a way that they contribute to the flow of a story without ever compromising the truth or integrity of that information.

Now, all that said, let me quote from that marvelous book *Alice in*

Wonderland one more time and say—as did the March Hare—***Let's Change the Subject!***

I am oh-so-tired of talking about me, so now, let's talk about you!

Things you can do and places you can go for more information:

To find links to sites with information about head injuries, special education, advocacy, and other topics raised in this book, please go to my website: ***www.debrasanders.com*** and click on ***Resources.*** While there, relax and take a look around and please feel free to write me with questions or just to tell me about you. I always love to hear other people's thoughts and stories!

Acknowledgments

The following people deserve heartfelt thanks and appreciation for assistance, their friendship and their guidance. Without each and every one of them, there would be no book.

My deepest gratitude goes to the following individuals who kindly and patiently read various drafts of this manuscript and offered constructive criticism and insights. These same people have my eternal gratitude and friendship for their unwavering support of my efforts to tell this story, and for their unwillingness to let me stop at any point along the way: *Zev Chafets, John Drew, Judy Doolittle, Pat Huhn, Kiki Kristiansen, Joyce Slothower, John Tease, Holly Thomas, Harry Tucker, Kathryn Wenderski,* and *Helen Wyche*.

There are not words sufficient to thank *John Drew* for his cover design and the many, many hours of patient expertise he offered in the name of friendship to a woman he has never even met in person. John, you are one in a million!

A special, special thanks to *Doug Jones, Edward Keneski,* and *James Stuart* for their exceptionally detailed editing and feedback during the last year of this book's writing. For reasons I still can't quite fathom, each of you volunteered an uncountable number of hours to the development of this book. Your unrelenting patience, encouragement and assistance kept me afloat. To say I feel blessed doesn't even begin to convey how I feel about what you gifted me by sharing your time and your intelligence.

Elliot Holt, content editor extraordinaire, will forever remain in my heart for donating hours and hours (and hours) of reading and rereading, insightful comments and straightforward, dead-on-the-mark comments. This book is a clearer reflection of the events and truer portrayal of me for having had your guidance. That you offered all of your expertise and time as a gift of friendship despite our never having met, is the essence of what it means to bestow random acts of kindness in this world. I will do my best to *pay it forward* any time I can!

Thank you to *Deb Jones*, whose incessant lectures, ongoing editing, and unwavering cheer absolutely resulted in this book's completion. Thank you. Thank you. A million times over. I cannot even begin to express all the ways that I am not just a better writer, but a better person for being able to call you my friend.

And also to *Deb Jones*, it is impossible to convey my gratitude for your untold hours of unpaid work to get the website up and running. You are not only a good friend, you are brilliant and you are talented. You too exemplify the meaning of random acts of kindness, and I am so blessed that you have entered my life in such a significant way.

Helen Wyche, Kiki Kristiansen and Pat Huhn each deserve their own line of thanks for being the best neighbors and friends a person could hope to find. You checked on me, brought me groceries, shook the pom-poms and roasted endless marshmallows by my fire pit in an effort to shore me up and keep me going. I absolutely never would have made it to the end were it not for my "Spruce Street Ladies Under The Sun!"

To *Donna Hedden* and her lightning fingers, quick mind, and sharp eye—you commandeered the caboose in order to get me through a final leg of the journey toward publication. Jimmy Stewart couldn't claim a better eleventh-hour guardian angel!

To *Ana Marie Spagna, Jonathon Englert,* and *Kyle Minor*: each of you taught me a great deal, and this book is so much better for my having been one of your students. By trade, I am not a writer, and I thank each one of you and Gotham Writers' Workshops (GWW) for your availability and excellent instruction to help turn me into one. Special thanks to the amazing *Dana* and her patience with me!

Similar thanks to *Outskirts Press,* with special thanks to *Colleen Goulet,* Author Representative, for her infinite patience with my never-ending questions and confusions. To *Reba Hilbert,* all I can say is everyone should have you to copy edit their work. You are awesome! I will never use another comma or semi-colon without wishing you were there to place them correctly! And finally, I extend a special note of appreciation to **Jeanine Sampson**, Project Manager. Your commitment to excellence ensured the professional quality of this final edition.

Thank you to *PJP,* who set the bar in so many ways and who has always been the most gifted writer I've had the good fortune to know. Adhering to the truth, though not always easy, and attacking the writing and rewriting of a sentence or a word a thousand times until it expressed things just exactly right, are credited in large part to the fact that you are always perched on my shoulder, challenging me to see things through your eyes. The day I can pick up a pencil and use the fewest words to turn a phrase even half as powerful as one that would spill from your hand will be the day I know that I have become a true writer.

A heartfelt acknowledgement to *Denney Barrus*, who kept me sane for months and months and months after the accident and who took the only picture I have of Teek, Bo and me together. Thank you for your permission to use that photo in this book.

To all who shared and/or sent their memories, emails, and recollections—obviously, this book could not have been written without you. Thank you for helping to be my memory when my own brain could not provide adequately.

This story would not exist were it not for the **hundreds of children and adolescents** who have been my teachers over the past two and a half decades. There are not words to express the love and gratitude I feel toward each and every one of you, and toward your parents and guardians, each of whom I believe did the very best they could to love and protect you in the best way they knew how to do. You have all made me a kinder, gentler, more creative human being and I will continue to work hard to support your educational rights.

A special thanks to **C.S.J,** whose poetry will forever remain in both my heart and my soul; and to **her mother** just for being the woman that she is.

And to **S.S.** and his **wonderful parents**, you were all three with me every minute throughout the writing of this book. Know and trust in yourselves every step of the way. Your journey is worthy of its own book.

H.S., if you ever see this, know that you were as much my teacher as I was yours. I hope you have found a place where you are safe and at ease.

To my **Fort Carson "Fourteeners,"** I can only say thank you for being who you are. Each one of you is a unique and loving, brilliant and fascinating individual. I am sorry we never got to say goodbye and I hope your life travels take you (always) through kindly territory. Know and believe in your own strengths. Understand your weaknesses. Challenge them both.

Dr. Spadoni and Dr. Willner each deserve special acknowledgement for their professional, intelligent and caring treatment of me. I hope you both continue to practice medicine (forever!) in order to model compassionate and ethical treatment, and in order teach others about the wide range of impact caused by concussion to the brain.

To **Tony Done, Ila Starks, Jimmy Starks, Sandra Asbury,** and **Anne Howell**, I offer my heartfelt hope that you feel I have been fair in the telling of this story. None of you could possibly know the depth of my gratitude and love for all that you did, and tried to do for me, while I was in Blanding. Know that I hold every one of you close to my heart. I always will.

If these were the Oscars they would have cut me off long ago, but thankfully they are not, because this remaining acknowledgement is one that needs to be shouted loudly and read by all:

Last, but certainly not least, I must acknowledge **Merrilyne Lundahl**, who not only inspired and convinced me to write this story, but who patiently read every single word on a near daily basis. Your insights and intelligent guidance resulted

in improving me as a writer, and your memory, notes, and remarkable archives of emails allowed me to portray events, people, and conversations that would not have been recounted if I'd had to depend upon my own remembrances.
You are a blessing in my life, and as close to a daughter as I ever could have hoped to have been gifted.

Each one of you has been an angel on my shoulder.
Thank you.

CPSIA information can be obtained at www.ICGtesting.com
Printed in the USA
BVOW051846140512

290199BV00002B/9/P